ALSO BY CLIFFORD A. WRIGHT

ON COOKING

A Mediterranean Feast:
The Story of the Birth of the Celebrated Cuisines of the Mediterranean,
from the Merchants of Venice to the Barbary Corsairs,
with More than 500 Recipes

Italian Pure & Simple:
Robust and Rustic Home Cooking for Everyday

Grill Italian

Lasagna

Cucina Rapida:
Quick Italian-Style Home Cooking

Cucina Paradiso:
The Heavenly Food of Sicily

CONTRIBUTOR

"HAROLD L'AMÉRICAIN" IN *Saveur Cooks France*

On Politics and History

Facts and Fables: The Arab-Israeli Conflict

After the Palestine-Israel War: Limits to U.S. and Israeli Policy
WITH KHALIL NAKHLEH

CLIFFORD A. WRIGHT

THE HARVARD COMMON PRESS
BOSTON, MASSACHUSETTS

Mediterranean
VEGETABLES

Mediterranean VEGETABLES

A Cook's Compendium of All the Vegetables from the
World's Healthiest Cuisine, with More than 200 Recipes

The Harvard Common Press
535 Albany Street
Boston, Massachusetts 02118
www.harvardcommonpress.com

Printed in the United States of America
Printed on acid-free paper

Library of Congress Cataloging-in-Publication Data

Wright, Clifford A.
Mediterranean vegetables : a cook's compendium of all the vegetables from the world's
healthiest cuisine, with more than 200 recipes / Clifford A. Wright.
p. cm.
Includes bibliographical references and index.
ISBN 978-1-55832-775-7 (pbk.)
1. Cooking (Vegetables) 2. Cooking, Mediterranean. 3. Cookbooks. I. Title.
TX801.W75 2012
641.6'5—dc23
2011050223

Special bulk-order discounts are available on this and other Harvard
Common Press books. Companies and organizations may purchase books
for premiums or resale, or may arrange a custom edition, by contacting the
Marketing Director at the address above.

10 9 8 7 6 5 4 3 2 1

BOOK DESIGN BY DEBORAH KERNER
BOOK COMPOSITION BY JACINTA MONNIERE
COVER PHOTOGRAPHY AND PROP STYLING BY SABRA KROCK
FOOD STYLING BY MARIANA VELASQUEZ

www.cliffordawright.com

THIS BOOK IS DEDICATED
TO AN INTREPID TRAVELER,
A JOLLY GOOD FELLOW,
EATER OF MANY VEGETABLES,
THE LONG-SUFFERING BOYD "HEY, IS THAT CASSOULET I SMELL" GROVE,
WHO ACCOMPANIED ME OVER MANY A WINE DARK SEA

ACKNOWLEDGMENTS

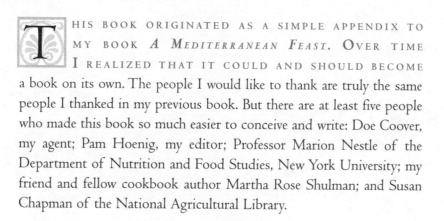

THIS BOOK ORIGINATED AS A SIMPLE APPENDIX TO MY BOOK *A MEDITERRANEAN FEAST*. OVER TIME I REALIZED THAT IT COULD AND SHOULD BECOME a book on its own. The people I would like to thank are truly the same people I thanked in my previous book. But there are at least five people who made this book so much easier to conceive and write: Doe Coover, my agent; Pam Hoenig, my editor; Professor Marion Nestle of the Department of Nutrition and Food Studies, New York University; my friend and fellow cookbook author Martha Rose Shulman; and Susan Chapman of the National Agricultural Library.

CONTENTS

INTRODUCTION

❧

RATATOUILLE, HUMMUS, AND GAZPACHO ARE NAMES OF MEDI-TERRANEAN VEGETABLE PREPARATIONS PROBABLY KNOWN BY MOST AMERICANS, ALTHOUGH IN BASTARDIZED FORMS THAT might not be recognized in the Mediterranean. But these three recipes (pages 132, 111, and 334), as good as they are, are like the mere glow of a firefly when one considers how truly dazzling the pantheon of Mediterranean vegetable preparations is.

The Mediterranean is alluring and, as a traveler, one encounters a fascinating range of cuisines that find vegetables at their center. Everyone has had a bland hummus, but a Mediterranean experience isn't complete until you've whipped together not only an authentic hummus (page 111), but an Egyptian *biṣāra*, a fava bean dip heavily flavored with fresh mint, fresh coriander, fresh dill, salt, pepper, and olive oil (page 156).

Did you know that ratatouille is only a single example of a class of vegetable relishes and stews that are found copiously throughout the Mediterranean? If a Lebanese cook prepared his or her "ratatouille" it might be called *ʿUlab Bādhinjān* (eggplant ragout) and would be a room-temperature dish of eggplant fried in olive oil with onions, ripe tomatoes, green bell peppers, a dozen garlic cloves sliced thinly, and a bunch of chopped fresh mint leaves (page 142). If our cook were Greek, we would also see a dish served at room temperature, *Dolmates Plaki,* made in a baking casserole (page 338). The bottom is layered with a kilo of garden-fresh tomatoes. On top are layers of very thinly sliced onions and finely chopped fresh parsley and dill. The dish is drizzled with olive oil; sprinkled with lemon juice, thyme, and a little sugar; and baked until it is a dense ragout. It's as memorable as any ratatouille found in Provence.

The fact that we Americans experiment so freely with what we eat is a testament to both the popularity of Mediterranean cuisine and the openness of American palates to new culinary flavors and ideas. High on everybody's list of foods they want to eat more of are vegetables. Strangely, we seem to have a hard time doing it. In the Mediterranean, a world of vegetable dishes exists all but unknown to Americans. They run the gamut from A to Z, and you will encounter more than two hundred of them here.

A Mediterranean vegetable preparation can be as simple as some bright green steamed broccoli, slightly crunchy and served with a drizzle of velvety olive oil and a spritz of lemon juice. But if that is the only way one knows how to prepare broccoli, boredom will quickly curtail the appetite, for variety is the spice of life. The variety of Mediterranean vegetable cookery goes well beyond olive oil; it encompasses an intriguing *Qara' bi'l-Ṭaḥina*, pureed pumpkin stirred with sesame seed paste, which the Lebanese enjoy as a kind of appetizer with warm flatbread (page 316); and a *Makbūba*, a potato and bell pepper frittata cooked in the style of the Tunisian Jews that is elegantly seasoned with garlic and spices (page 273); and a braised sorrel dish called *Acederas Rehogadas* in Spain that is deliciously creamy. If you've never had sorrel, this manner of preparing it is an excellent introduction (page 298).

But what are "Mediterranean vegetables"? Are they the vegetables that are native to the Mediterranean, or are they the vegetables used in Mediterranean cookery? For the purposes of this book, I embrace the latter definition, which means that the New World tomato as well as Old World spinach are Mediterranean vegetables. The inspiration for writing this book arose from a need I experienced over the decade I spent researching and writing my last book, *A Mediterranean Feast: The Story of the Birth of the Celebrated Cuisines of the Mediterranean, from the Merchants of Venice to the Barbary Corsairs.* What I wanted was a reference book for cooks rather than gardeners that would give me essential information about the vegetables used in Mediterranean cuisines: the name of each vegetable in various languages, its botanical Latin binomial, short paragraphs on its history and origin, as well as practical information on the essentials of how to grow, harvest, store, and cook it. I found countless gardening books, and they were indeed helpful, but there was no book for the cook who tended a vegetable garden and who was cooking Italian, French, and other Mediterranean foods. There were, of course, vegetable cookery books geared to particular countries and regions, nearly all French and Italian, but none that focused on the whole of the Mediterranean region.

The most exciting thing about Mediterranean vegetables is that the majority of the most popular vegetables in the Mediterranean are popular in the United States as well and easily found in an American market. This book is meant to be a comprehensive catalog and will introduce you to *all* of the vegetables in the Mediterranean, some of which you are unlikely to find not only in an American market, but also in the Mediterranean, unless you happen to be a Greek shepherd, Sicilian farmer, or Bedouin nomad. The reason is that many of these vegetables are not cultivated but rather gathered in the wild, an activity that fades with each passing year as Mediterranean peoples become ever more modernized.

The delight of Mediterranean vegetable cookery is found in the combination of ingredients that have given birth to a surprising treasure of delicious and thoroughly new tastes for Americans. I've crisscrossed the Mediterranean for over thirty years, uncovering culinary treasures in small isolated villages, in the kitchens of Italian *trattorie* and Greek tavernas, and in the home kitchens of my own extended Italian family, not to mention my ex-wife's extended Arab family. A Syrian dish called *Būrānī* sounds at first blush like another spinach dish, but it is a magically spiced dish with cool yogurt spread on top to complete a beautiful preparation (page 307). Fresh flat-leaf spinach is first wilted gently with steam, then drained and sautéed in olive oil with garlic. Next a freshly ground pungent spice mixture made of allspice, nutmeg, cardamom seeds, cloves, cinnamon, coriander seeds, salt, and black pepper is stirred in, and the spinach cooks for a bit. Meanwhile, a rich yogurt is whipped together with mashed garlic, then it is spooned over the spinach with a sprinkle of crushed walnuts.

Mediterranean vegetable cookery is suitable for every season. Toward the end of winter, the Tunisian cook will make one of my favorite vegetable stews, *Maraqat al-Khuḍra* (page 257). First, dried fava beans and chickpeas are soaked in water to make them softer for cooking. Onions, spinach, and parsley are cooked in extra virgin olive oil, and then diced turnips and carrots are added along with fresh artichokes. Finally the legumes that have been soaking are put into the pot. The mixture is left to cook for a while, then the famous *harīsa* of Tunisia, a paste made of hot chile peppers, caraway seeds, coriander seeds, salt, pepper, and olive oil, is added along with another spice mixture usually made of ground rose petals, coriander, and caraway, known as *tābil* (see the recipes on pages 263 and 106). The stew cooks for about 45 minutes while the flavors waft throughout the house, enticing everyone to the table.

In the summertime, we may go to the island of Sardinia off the Italian peninsula to sample *Stufato di Verdure*, or Vegetable Stew (page 246), an earthy summer vegetable stew with rich, aromatic flavors that derive from the secret garlic and parsley pesto used in the initial *soffritto*. In a skillet, extra virgin olive oil is heated and small white onions are cooked until golden. The pesto is deftly stirred in so it doesn't burn, and then the sauce is enriched with ripe tomatoes and fresh basil, whose large, fragrant leaves perfume the kitchen. After the mixture cooks for 30 minutes, new potatoes and fresh green beans are added and cooked until tender. It's a heavenly dish.

Supermarkets today carry a range of vegetables that were unthinkable to the last generation of home cooks. But the perennial problem for cooks is how to use and incorporate these vegetables into their cooking. How many times have we passed by a bin of leeks, or perhaps eggplants, because we don't know what to do with them? How many times have we looked at that gigantic vegetable that vaguely looked like a weird celery and passed it by? (It was a cardoon.) Or the vegetable whose bulbous root looked like Sputnik? (It was a kohlrabi.) These vegetables are in the supermarket and farmers' market because someone is cooking them. This book, I hope, will give you the information you need to decide to cook these vegetables in a wide range of recipes.

This book is a vegetable cookbook and not a vegetarian cookbook. Because I eat meat, I can't call myself a vegetarian, but I do call myself a vegeophile. A vegeophile is someone who simply loves the taste of vegetables and who, when his hand is on the skillet, thinks gastronomically rather than ethically. Although the vegetable cookery of the Mediterranean is renowned, and Mediterranean peoples eat a lot of vegetables, there are truly few vegetarians there. The reasons are related to history, economics, and the development of society. In the Mediterranean, many people use meat as a kind of condiment in the flavoring of vegetables. You will encounter meat in this book occasionally used in that way, although I have decided not to include too many recipes with that characteristic.

The popularity of vegetables has waxed and waned in all cultures over time. The Romans knew that plants received nitrogen from the air and not from the soil, and that by burying plants their nitrogen could be returned to the soil. The Romans called this process "green manuring." Green manuring was instrumental in enabling Roman farmers to successfully grow crop plants such as cabbage, along with a host of other vegetables. The writings of the classical Latin authors on the plant world are voluminous, and Pliny in particular concentrated on a wide variety of plants for food.

At the end of the first millennium A.D., Arab agriculturalists were responsible for what one scholar called the "medieval green revolution." As a result of scientific advances in irrigation, hydrology, and horticulture, Arab farmers introduced a wide range of new vegetables into the Mediterranean, such as taro, spinach, eggplant, and artichokes. The medieval Arab rulers established royal gardens, which began as purely decorative gardens and were transformed over time into kitchen gardens that provided the Arab chefs with the raw materials for their culinary inventions. These gardens were not the small household vegetable patches attached to a house that were common in Western Europe; they were more of a cross between an experimental horticultural station and a royal garden. The gardens were lush with vegetable crops, flowering bushes, and fruit trees; they were graced with water fountains and pavilions. The selecting out of particular vegetable cultivars must have happened early on in these gardens, for example, with cabbage, a member of the Brassica family. The glucosinolates that all the Brassicas contain are broken down by an enzyme when the plants grow in the wild, and the early varieties of cabbage leaves when chopped or crushed gave off a bitter taste and goitrogenic substances that led to the development of goiters, an enlargement of the thyroid gland. Arab botanists must have learned to select less bitter-tasting cabbages early in the domestication of the plant.

In medieval Spain, the Arab caliphs developed vast irrigation projects known as *huertas,* what we would today call truck farms, where a wide variety of vegetables were grown. These farms were not limited to Spain; in the lower Rhône, the Antipopes of Avignon grew romaine lettuce in their *huertas,* while in Languedoc the vegetable production of the garden was known as the *ortolagia.* Cabbage was the most common vegetable in these gardens.

In the Middle Ages vegetables were so popular among Arabs that they were sold by *bawāridiyyūn* (cold vegetable vendors) from street stalls. These vendors made and sold cooked green vegetables preserved in vinegar, a category of cold foods called *bawārid* that could also include meat, fowl, and fish. In the eastern Mediterranean, vegetables had long been popular in Arab lands. Vegetables were always associated with sweetness in the minds of Arab cooks. We see this mentality manifest in the Arabic expression *ārḍ ḥulāwa,* "sweet earth," used to describe land suitable for the production of beautiful vegetables. Arab farmers were usually responsible for the westward diffusion of new vegetables. For example, spinach, which is thought to have been native to Nepal and northwest India, slowly made its way from Persia to the Mediterranean by virtue of Arab agriculturalists. The Bedouin of the Levantine and Egyptian deserts, however, never liked fresh green vegetables, perhaps because they were unfamiliar with them.

The popular diet in medieval rural Italy consisted of more vegetables and greens grown in the kitchen garden than is popularly thought. The vegetables were eaten raw, in salads, boiled in water, fried in lard or olive oil, or mixed with small amounts of meat. Still-extant "menus" of fifteenth-century *trattorie* confirm the variety of uses for greens, which were served with bread and a glass of wine for daily meals.

Mazza, Mezze, or Meze

THROUGHOUT THE BOOK YOU WILL ENCOUNTER DISHES DESCRIBED AS *MAZZA* (ARABIC) AND *MEZZE* OR *MEZE* (GREEK AND Turkish). Most writers describe these dishes as appetizers because they are small amounts of food served on small plates and they look like they are meant to stimulate the appetite. In North Africa, *mazza* might be called *qimiyya* in Algeria and *ādū* in Tunisia. *Mazzāt* (plural) bear a resemblance to the antipasti of Italy, the hors d'oeuvres of France, and the tapas of Spain. In fact, there is nothing wrong in serving them as appetizers. But, for the record, it is incorrect to speak of the Middle Eastern *mazza* table as appetizers. To think of these small dishes as appetizers is to misunderstand the Arab culinary sensibility. For the Arab, the notion of a food needed to "open the appetite" is completely foreign. A *mazza* table can be the entire dinner, thus it is more appropriate to compare *mazza* to the Scandinavian smorgasbord, to which it is more philosophically related. This is what makes it different from tapas, which are eaten as one barhops before a later dinner. So, too, antipasti are meant to be eaten before the pasta course, and hors d'oeuvres are the original "appetite openers." In Italy, antipasti served in *trattorie* are usually displayed on an open buffet table called a *tavola calda*, where diners can choose which ones they want. This tradition exists in Sicily also, but there antipasti are called *grape ´u pitittu* and are actually closer in concept to the Middle Eastern *mazza* because they can sometimes constitute the whole of the meal.

The origin of the word *mazza* is unknown, but the most likely explanation is that *mazza* came from the Persian word for "taste, relish." This Persian *maza* was eaten in ancient Persia and consisted of fruit, nuts, and roasted meat to be eaten with wine. On the other hand, the Arabic word *mazza* derives from the root word "to suck," which also gives the word for "acidulous." One food writer offered the explanation that the word comes from the Italian *mezzano*, meaning "an intermediary course of foods," a term introduced by Genoese merchant-traders to the fourteenth-century Middle East to refer to certain foods. An Arab writer claims that *mazza* is a colloquial expression meaning "what" in the exclamation *mazza haza* (what is this?). Other Arabs have told me that that explanation is nonsense. Might the word have any connection with the Hebrew word for unleavened foods, *maẓẓot?*

In the rest of Europe, the situation was different. The European Mediterranean was not very much interested in vegetables in the medieval era. From the mid-fourteenth to the mid-fifteenth century, the European diet consisted mostly of meat. Then, from the late fifteenth to the early eighteenth century, the diet shifted to one of predominantly vegetables because the population recovered from the Black Death (1347–1350) and was able to bring more land under cultivation and to tend it. Also with the rise of Islamic civilization in the middle of the European Dark Ages, and with the emphasis on grains, legumes, and other vegetables in Muslim dietetic theory and culinary aesthetic, vegetables started to become more popular. In Arabic, vegetables are called *khadrawāt* (literally, "greens") and Arab cooks excelled in all kinds of vegetable preparations, far more than did their European counterparts. The Arabs were also big eaters of edible herbs, called *qaḍb,* and legumes, called *qiṭniyya,* which are still popular in Middle Eastern culinary cultures as we know by foods like tabbouleh, hummus, and falafel.

In preindustrial England, people were convinced that vegetables "ingender ylle humours and be oftetymes the cause of putrified fevers," melancholy, and flatulence. As a consequence of these ideas, there was a low demand for fruits and vegetables, and the population lived in a pre-scorbutic state.

Nutritionists and others have seemingly forever been trying to get people to eat more vegetables. That most famous of all vegetarians, Leonardo da Vinci was appalled by meat-eaters and cannibals. In the late fifteenth century he wrote in his notebook, "Does Nature not produce enough fruits and vegetables to satiate you? If you do not content yourself with fruits and vegetables can you not, by mixing them, create infinite combinations, as Platina wrote?" Baldassarre Pisanelli published his *Trattato della natura de' cibi et del bere (Tractate on the nature of food and drink)* in 1583 and gave nutritional recommendations concerning many fruits and vegetables, including information on the natural history of some vegetables. The style in which Pisanelli presented his information was also an inspiration for the layout that I chose in this book. In 1611 Giacomo Castelvetro was exiled from his home in Venice to Britain because of the Inquisition in Venice. He ended up teaching Italian at Cambridge University and was quite appalled at the amount of meat and sweets the English ate. Thus he wrote a book to promote the idea of eating more vegetables and to celebrate vegetable cookery—*Brieve racconto di tutte le radici, di tutte l'herbe et di tutti i frutti, che crudi o cotto in Italia si mangiano.* It was translated into English as *A Brief Account of the Fruit, Herbs and Vegetables of Italy.* Unfortunately, the text seems to have had no effect on the English.

THE VEGETABLE ENTRIES IN THIS BOOK RUN FROM A TO Z AND ARE ordered alphabetically by English common name or botanical name. Practically speaking, only about eighty to ninety of the over two hundred vegetables listed will be even remotely available to a typical American cook who has his or her own garden, living in a Mediterranean-type climate (namely, California) with access to quality farmers' markets. As mentioned earlier, many of the Mediterranean vegetables described here are gathered in the wild; others do not grow outside the Mediterranean region, and, in many cases, American supermarkets simply don't carry them.

Each entry begins with the *English name of the vegetable.* The vegetable is listed by its common name, if there is one. If there isn't an English name, then the vegetable is listed by its botanical Latin binomial (botanical name). On the next line is the Latin binomial and the botanical family to which the plant belongs. After that are any other English common names the vegetable is known by. Then I list the names of the vegetable in major Mediterranean languages, usually Arabic, French, Greek, Italian, Serbo-Croatian, Spanish, Turkish, and several dialects.

Next I describe the *plant's characteristics and varieties.* Here you can find which part of the plant is edible, as well as learn some general characteristics about the plant, including what varieties might be available. Not all cultivars (meaning cultivated varieties) of the plant are listed, though, because in some cases there are five hundred or more cultivars, and if I tried to list them all this book would become too unwieldy.

The edible part of a number of so-called vegetables is actually the fruit of the plant. Economic botanists generally consider the edible fruits to be cultivated vegetables. I have included most, but not all, of them in my catalog of vegetables. The fruits included as vegetables in this book are

- *angled loofah or Chinese okra (immature fruit)*
- *bell and chile peppers (mature fruit)*
- *bottle gourd or calabash gourd (immature fruit, leaves, and tender shoots)*
- *colocynth (fruit and seeds)*
- *cucumber (immature fruit)*
- *eggplant (ripe fruit)*
- *loofah or sponge gourd (immature fruit and leaves)*

- *mock tomato (fruit and leaves)*
- *muskmelon or Persian melon (ripe fruit)*
- *plantain (fruit)*
- *pumpkin (mature fruit and seeds)*
- *squash, winter and summer (young and mature fruit)*
- *tomato (ripe fruit)*

Fruits that can be treated as a vegetable but are not included as vegetables in this book are

- *canteloupe (fruit)*
- *cape gooseberry (fruit)*
- *casaba melon or honeydew melon (fruit)*
- *mango (fruit)*
- *watermelon (fruit and seeds)*

There are several plants that are not vegetables (or fruit) but that are very often treated as vegetables. For example, mushrooms, truffles, and galls are not considered vegetables. A gall (also called an oak apple) is a swelling of plant tissue usually owing to the presence of fungi or insect parasites. Gall is eaten by Bedouin tribes in North Africa and the Middle East and is called ʿafṣ in Arabic. The North Africans also eat palm core, what they call *qulb*, an edible tuber that grows at the upper end of the palm trunk. I have included mushrooms and truffles but not gall or palm core. There are also some plants that I have not been able to identify, and they, too, are not included. For instance, there is a wild plant that grows on the island of Ibiza in the Balearic Islands that the Ibizenco call simply *verdura* or "greens." It is boiled with Swiss chard and wild white peas and then drained and dressed with olive oil and seasoning in a preparation called *quinad,* not a Spanish word. I just can't find out what this plant is.

I also have not included the peanut, which is a legume, because in the Mediterranean it is usually used as a nut not a vegetable.

Some herbs are not included as vegetables, although they very well could be if they were more regularly eaten as vegetables. Technically, herbs are nonwoody plants with soft stems that die down at the end of the growing season, although this description doesn't apply to rosemary, sage, lavender, and some other herbs. In general usage, herbs are plants used for flavor and fragrance in cooking or in cosmetics or medicines. The only herbs that

I include in this ABC of vegetables are herbs used as vegetables in some Mediterranean cuisines. For instance, parsley, normally an herb, is treated as a vegetable in tabbouleh salads. I also have not included nuts in this catalogue of vegetables, although an argument could be made that they should be included. Likewise, I am not entirely satisfied that I am not including entries for the fruits of vegetables that are used for aromatizing foods, such as juniper (*Juniperus communis* L.), or vegetables or herbs used for flavoring sweets or liqueurs such as vanilla or licorice (*Glycyrrhiza glabra*), but I must exclude them to keep the book manageable.

The *plant's origin* is detailed next. The origins of agriculture and the places where particular plants originate are topics of great fascination and a good deal of complexity. The standard view is that agriculture is an invention. The two most important views were, first, that there were centers of diffusion or origin and, second (a view supported by archaeological, anthropological, botanical, and geographic evidence), that there were diffuse origins. Two of the greatest thinkers on the origin of agriculture were the Russian botanist Nicolay I. Vavilov, who proposed eight centers of origin, with a few subcenters, and the American botanist Carl O. Sauer, who argued that agriculture developed from a center in tropical Southeast Asia.* Another recent theory concerning the origin of agriculture claims that it

*The first scientist to systematically propose and study the notion of centers of diffusion and origin was Vavilov. But the major critique of Vavilov is that his methodology in measuring diversity was basically taxonomic. Although this approach did establish agroecological groups based on origin, disease reaction, adaptation, and other features and this information is a useful classification for plant breeding, it did not truly reflect genetic diversity. The advent of sophisticated computer modeling and programming meant that there was less reliance on subjective factors and that a much larger number of morphological characters could be integrated into the analysis. Modern studies have a much broader genetic analysis by isozyme, flavonoid, storage protein electrophoresis or chromatography, than was available to Vavilov. It's true that modern studies reveal greater diversity in some regions than others, but these nodes of concentration usually have no geographic affinity. The important study of a world rice collection by Professors J. Holcomb, D. M. Tolbert, and S. K. Jain in 1976 found the greatest diversity of rice in Indonesia and the least in Japan. If Vavilov's theory is correct, then Indonesia would seem likely to have been the center of the origin of rice, but we know that it was not. Professor S. K. Jain studied a world collection of durum wheats, and great diversity was found in Ethiopia as predicted by Vavilov, but diversity in Portugal was just as great, and that in Egypt was not much less.

In the mid-twentieth century, radiometric dating was developed and it became possible for botanists to determine the age of organic materials with some precision. But the dates given for many of the earliest crop plants are today being questioned because the 14-carbon determination of age are so-called contextual dates; that is, they are based on organic materials found along with crop remains but are not those crops themselves necessarily. The problem is that much of the material used for the identification of crop remains are seeds, and such small objects have a tendency to sift downward through older layers of earth, giving a false picture based on the carbon-14 dating of the strata they are located in. A new method of dating by atomic mass spectrometry allows the investigator to examine individual seeds; this method has produced different dates than the contextual dates.

was not an invention at all, but that people drifted or were forced into it. When one asks where is the origin of a particular food plant, one should remember that a particular vegetable of today may be very different from its ancestors. Recent studies have not been able to conclusively identify in a clear-cut way the geographical centers of diversity; therefore the entry in the category "plant origin" in this book should always be taken as provisional.

Then there is the "Plant History" section, where I concentrate on written history. For the most part, the sources I use are the classical Greek and Roman authors, the Bible, some ancient Egyptian writings, and a score of sources from late antiquity and the medieval period. Because so many of these writers' names are repeated throughout the book, they are identified once in the Biography section at the back of the book. As with the "Plant Origins" section, the full history of vegetables has not been written, so most of the information here will appear arbitrary, although I have written it to give the reader a sense of the role of the particular vegetable through historical time rather than to furnish a comprehensive history.

Horticultural information on *how to grow and harvest* these vegetables makes up the next section. Of all the sections, this section is the briefest in terms of depth. It will provide only the most basic information, and it may lead you to want to learn more about a particular vegetable. This text is not meant to replace gardening books, where cook-gardeners will find the most helpful and useful suggestions. Personally, I find that just plain experimenting is the best way to learn how to grow a plant, although books will help you consider the many factors that go into successful vegetable gardening such as the general climate, the soil, exposure to sun, the quality of seeds or seedlings, the geography, your location, exposure to wind, rainfall, and so forth.

Next is *how to buy, store, and prepare the vegetable for cooking*. This section is quite general and is meant to give you the most basic information about how to examine a vegetable for quality and freshness before you buy it. The storage of vegetables is pretty much straightforward: either cold storage or room-temperature storage. But in some cases the life or usability of a vegetable can be extended by taking certain precautions. The preparation of the vegetable for cooking is usually described in the recipes themselves, although some vegetables, such as artichokes, require a bit more information about preparation, and this is the section where you will find such information.

Finally there are the *recipes*. Not all entries will have recipes. As I mentioned before, although the cataloguing in this book is comprehensive, the availability of many of the vegetables is limited or nil, and therefore it is superfluous to provide a recipe for them. The recipes in the book are from every region of the Mediterranean and represent an authentic style of cooking that is typical in the home. My goal is to provide the reader with a culinary survey of how the vegetable is traditionally prepared throughout the Mediterranean.

Many readers might like to see nutritional and health information for each vegetable, but I have opted to provide a more general review of the relevant nutritional information in the next few pages. I want to avoid saying that one vegetable is nutritionally better than another, even if it is. When you are cooking, I encourage you to think gastronomically rather than medically or nutritionally. This preference is based on my personal philosophy that even though it is necessary to be nutritionally literate, in the kitchen you are first and foremost a cook. Cooks, to please themselves and others, must be guided primarily by taste. Generally, you probably already know that increasing the amount of vegetables you eat will fulfill your nutritional concerns and lead you away from what I believe to be the gastronomically destructive "food as fuel" concept.

VEGETABLES AND HEALTH

OF ALL THE FOODS IN THE WORLD, VEGETABLES—GROWN FOR THEIR flowers, seeds, fruits, shoots, leaves, roots, bulbs, rhizomes, corms, and tubers—offer the greatest diversity of form and nutrients. The nutritional importance of vegetables is well recognized, but the precise details of the connection between diet and health is not firmly established, although much is known. Some years ago the U.S. Department of Agriculture (USDA) provided the public a visual aid that demonstrated the federal government's latest dietary guidelines for Americans; it was called the Food Guide Pyramid. This pyramid replaced the "four food groups" concept that many people over forty years old remember having grown up with.

The USDA recommended that vegetables, along with fruit and grains, comprise the major part of a person's diet. In fact, the USDA recommended eating three to five servings of vegetables a day. A serving size was defined as I cup of raw leafy vegetables, ½ cup of other cooked or raw chopped vegetables, or ¾ cup vegetable juice.

Ongoing nutritional research continues to produce many contradictory results, which have also created confusion among the public, but, all in all, one thing is clear: a healthy diet is one that includes lots of vegetables, and the micronutrients in vegetables appear to help in preventing a variety of chronic diseases. Today there is a consensus among health experts that a diet rich in vegetables and fruits reduces the risk of certain cancers. Cruciferous vegetables, such as broccoli, cabbage, cauliflower, and so forth, appear to be particularly beneficial in reducing the risk for cancer, according to the latest research. There is evidence that the soluble fiber—part of the indigestible portion of a plant—of vegetables can reduce blood cholesterol, although the health benefits of fiber are far less modest than major food retailers' marketing hype would lead one to believe. Vegetables have also played a role in nutritional research concerning antioxidants, including beta-carotene and vitamins C and E. Studies have shown that these substances play a role in protecting one from cancer, heart disease, and other disorders.

The emphasis on the health benefits of vegetables also got a new impetus in the early 1990s when the Oldways Preservation and Exchange Trust, a Massachusetts-based nonprofit food think tank, organized an international conference focusing on the diets of the Mediterranean and seeking to preserve traditions and foster cultural exchange in the fields of food, cooking, and agriculture, along with the United Nations World Health Organization (WHO) European Regional Office and the World Health Organization/Food and Agriculture Organization Collaborating Center in Nutritional Epidemiology at the Harvard University School of Public Health. These three organizations developed and presented at this conference a Traditional Healthy Mediterranean Diet Pyramid. The Mediterranean Diet Pyramid offered substantive refinements on the USDA food pyramid; it was based on the dietary traditions of the Greek island of Crete, other areas of Greece, and parts of southern Italy circa 1960, and structured in light of current nutritional research. These areas were chosen because the rates of chronic diseases were the lowest in the world, and adult life expectancy was the highest among these populations, even though medical services were limited at that time. The availability of data describing the food consumption patterns of these areas at that time was good, and these dietary patterns converged with the current understanding of optimal nutrition based on epidemiological studies and clinical trials worldwide.

The Mediterranean food pyramid places a great emphasis on an abundance of food from plant sources, on seasonally fresh and locally produced foods, using olive oil as the principal cooking fat, and drastically reducing the typical American intake of food from animal sources, especially red meat. The pyramid also emphasized two other components of a healthy lifestyle: exercise and moderate consumption of wine, normally with meals, about two glasses a day. This last recommendation, although considered optional, created a vigorous debate among American health officials, but not among European health officials, because in Europe wine drinking has been part of the normal course of eating for thousands of years, whereas in America alcohol consumption is more closely associated not with dining but with partying and excess.

Insofar as the "Mediterranean diet" is defined as the diet consumed on Crete in 1960, it is a proven cultural model for healthy eating and has, in effect, stood the test of time. The USDA Food Pyramid is a theoretical construct that developed against the backdrop of a national dietary pattern that is known to be responsible for much of the heart disease, cancer, and other chronic diseases that persist at high rates in the United States. Although the U.S. model does have a valid research basis and is calculated to include all essential nutrients at Recommended Dietary Allowance (RDA) levels, it is not a proven cultural model, and, in fact, it does not represent how Americans actually eat but how they should eat. The USDA Food Pyramid represents a mix of well-supported findings, educated guesses, outdated approaches to grouping foods, and political compromises with powerful economic interests such as the dairy and meat industries. But it does, all in all, even if it doesn't do so directly, recommend a largely plant-based diet.

The basic message of the Mediterranean Diet Pyramid is to *eat a largely plant-based diet, low in saturated and trans fatty acids, such as butter and margarine.* The Mediterranean diet is an entire diet linked to certain lifestyles. Although it may be unlikely or impossible for an American at the beginning of the new millennium to eat and live like a Mediterranean person in 1960, you can keep the ratio of plant foods to animal food very high. You do not need to become a vegetarian, nor will certain vegetables provide the elixir to long life, but if you eat a lot of vegetables, you will be doing your body good.

Pots and Pans

THERE ARE NO SPECIAL POTS AND PANS YOU WILL NEED TO COOK THE RECIPES IN THIS BOOK. BUT FOR CLARITY, WHEN I CALL FOR something to be cooked in a casserole, ideally you will use a large, heavy, enamelled cast-iron vessel with two looped handles that can be used on the stovetop and is ovenproof, such as the ones made by Le Creuset. Of course, use whatever you have, but remember that the sides of a casserole should be at least four inches high.

The
VEGETABLES

ACANTHUS-LEAVED THISTLE

Carlina acanthifolia All. (Aspeniaceae)
ITALIAN: *carlino;* SPANISH: *carlina*

PLANT CHARACTERISTICS AND VARIETIES

Throughout the Mediterranean, the heart, or receptacle, of the thistle flower is sometimes used in the same way as one uses the heart of an artichoke. Another similar species is known as carline thistle *(C. vulgaris).*

ALBANIAN YAM

Dioscorea balcanica Kosanin
(Dioscoreaceae)
SERBO-CROATIAN: *krumpir*

PLANT CHARACTERISTICS AND VARIETIES

This is the only Mediterranean member of the yam family; it is native to Montenegro and Albania. It is usually boiled in stews.

ALEXANDERS

Smyrnium olusatrum L. (Umbelliferae)
Also called horse parsley, black lovage, black potherb; ITALIAN: *corinoli commune, smirnio;* SPANISH: *esmirnio, apio caballar*

PLANT CHARACTERISTICS AND VARIETIES

The edible parts are the young shoots and leaf stalks; the stems are used like celery, and the leaves like parsley. This vegetable, which was once a delicacy in Italy, tastes like celery when uncooked, but tastes better when blanched. In culinary terms, celery has replaced alexanders for the most part, although it is easier to grow. *Smyrnium perfoliatum* is a variety that is thought to taste better than *S. olusatrum.*

PLANT ORIGIN

Alexanders is probably native to Europe and parts of Asia.

PLANT HISTORY

Alexanders is mentioned by Theophrastus in 322 B.C. and by the first-century writer Dioscorides. The plant name is said to come from a corruption of Olusatrum, the name of a town located in Egypt. Columella and Pliny speak of the plant being under cultivation; Apicius gives a recipe for it in his cookery book; Charlemagne ordered that it be grown in his estate gardens; Matthioli, writing in 1558, refers to the plant's edible qualities. Castelvetro, writing in 1614, describes alexanders as a raw or cooked food, used especially in salads. In the spring, he adds, the roots are eaten.

HOW TO GROW AND HARVEST

The only way to find alexanders is to grow the plant yourself. Plant the seeds in the late fall, letting the plant stay in the ground through the winter to germinate the following spring.

AMARANTHUS

Amaranthus spp. *albus, caudatus, cruentus, dubius, gangeticus, hybridus, lividius, mangostanus, retroflexus, tricolor, viridis* L., and others (Amaranthaceae)

Also called tampala or Chinese spinach; ARABIC: *nabat urjuani, sawālif al-ᶜarus;* FRENCH: *amaranthe;* ITALIAN: *amaranto;* SPANISH: *amarantos, bledos blancos;* TURKISH: *pancar otu, kızıl sirken* (local names). It is also known by a great number of HINDI (TAGALOG: *kulitis*); JAPANESE (for example, *hiyu, inu-hime-shiro-biyu, senninkoku, ha-geitô*); CHINESE *(for example, yin tsoi, xian cai);* and MALAY names (for example, *bayam*)

PLANT CHARACTERISTICS AND VARIETIES

Amaranth is not that common in the Mediterranean. But it is eaten by Arabs, Spaniards, the French, and Italians. Amaranthus, or amaranth, is an annual whose tender shoots, leaves, and sprouted seeds are eaten either raw in a salad or cooked as a vegetable. The leaves are a very beautiful green and maroon color, are tender to eat, and taste vaguely like a cross between a nonbitter arugula and spinach. Only *A. gangeticus* (syn. A. *tricolor*), also called Joseph's coat, is found in the Mediterranean kitchen today. *Amaranthus lividus*—called purple amaranth, *vleeta*, or horsetooth amaranth—was cultivated by the ancient Greeks and Romans and eaten as a potherb.

PLANT ORIGIN

The cultivated species of amaranth are probably native to northwestern and central Mexico, southern Mexico, and the Argentine Andes. The wild species most closely related to the cultivated species are native to moister regions of eastern North America and the mild highlands of Central America. *Amaranthus gangeticus*, the species of amaranth used in the Mediterranean, is thought to have originated in an Indo-Chinese area, that is, eastern India, Assam, western China, or Burma.

PLANT HISTORY

Wild amaranth seeds were gathered by prehistoric American peoples. New World varieties of amaranth were introduced to Europe after the Spanish conquest. Another variety of amaranth is native to Asia, and it is this *A. blitum* that was described by Theophrastus and that Pliny may have been referring to in his *Natural History.* In 1575 Leonhard Rauwolf (or Leonhardus Rauwolffud) saw *A. gangeticus* growing in the gardens of Ottoman officials in Aleppo, Syria. *A. caudatus* was taken from the Andes to the Mediterranean sometime in the sixteenth century. The first illustration of this plant was in Carl Clusius's *Rariorum Plantarum Historia* published in 1601. The plant is also depicted in *Hortus Eystettensis*, originally published in 1613.

Amaranth is a tropical plant easily grown in full sun and in very fertile soil with lots of heat and moisture. Commercial growers feed the plant with liquid nitrogen during its growth. To harvest these large plants you can prune their leaves or plant rows a couple of weeks apart and pull the young plant as desired. It is not a frost-hardy plant.

HOW TO BUY, STORE, AND PREPARE FOR COOKING

Amaranth is usually found in farmers' markets, so look for fresh, crisp leaves presented under cool shade. Keep the leaves refrigerated in the crisper drawer for 2 or 3 days. Do not wash the leaves until you are ready to use them.

RECIPE

AMARANTH AND WATER SPINACH SALAD

Amaranth's colorful leaves make an inviting salad. Water spinach, also called *kangkong* or swamp morning glory, has long and slender leaves, like tarragon leaves, that taste more like a weedy salad green. This salad doesn't need much in the way of a dressing—just a drizzle of olive oil and a squirt of lemon juice. Orange beets taste the same as maroon-colored beets, but they seem as if they taste different because of their dramatic color. They are increasingly easier to find, but you may still be able to find them only in farmers' markets, so replace the orange beets in this recipe with any beets you find.

6 ounces amaranth leaves, rinsed and dried well
6 ounces water spinach, rinsed and dried well
1 orange beet, cooked until tender, peeled, and cut into 8 thin slices
Extra virgin olive oil for drizzling
Salt and freshly ground black pepper to taste
1 teaspoon fennel seeds, lightly bruised in a mortar
2 lemon halves, each tied in cheesecloth

Arrange a bed of the greens tossed together in 4 individual salad bowls or plates. Arrange 2 slices of beet on top of each salad and drizzle it with olive oil. Season the salad with salt and pepper and the fennel seeds. Serve, passing the lemon halves around.

Makes 4 servings

ANCHUSA

Anchusa azurea Miller (also *undulata* ssp. *hybrida*) (Boraginaceae)
TURKISH: *ballık, çoban çedenesi*

PLANT CHARACTERISTICS AND VARIETIES
Anchusa is a perennial plant with bristly hairs. The leaves and flowers are the edible parts. The flowers are bright blue and used in salads. In Turkey the fruit of the plant is eaten as a vegetable.

Anchusa is mentioned several times in Pliny's *Natural History*.

ANGELICA
Angelica archangelica L. (Umbelliferae)
ARABIC: *ḥashīsha al-malik*; FRENCH: *angélique*;
ITALIAN: *angelica, arcangelica*; SPANISH:
angélica

PLANT CHARACTERISTICS AND VARIETIES
The entire plant, a perennial with purplish stems and thick, corky, winged fruit, is used in a variety of ways. The leaf stalks are blanched and eaten like celery, while the leaves, which taste like licorice, are eaten in salads or cooked as a vegetable in some Arab countries, France, Italy, and Spain. Candied flower stems and leaf stalks are also used for confectionary and in the making of liqueurs such as vermouth and Benedictine. The young flower heads are used in omelettes in southern France, as an addition to pasta in northern Italy, or grilled and served with olive oil and vinegar in some regions of Italy.

PLANT ORIGIN
Angelica originated in Eurasia.

ARISARUM VULGARE TARG.-TOZZ. (AROIDEAE)

PLANT CHARACTERISTICS AND VARIETIES
In North Africa the roots of this plant are used in times of scarcity. The root is a little smaller than a walnut and contains an acid juice that is removed by repeated washings. The residue is nutritious and is boiled and mashed as a starch.

ARTICHOKE
Cynara scolymus L. (Asteraceae-Compositae)
ARABIC: *ḥarshuf, qināriyya, kankar, kharshūf, ḥarshaf, arḍī shawkī*; BERBER: *taga*; FRENCH: *artichaut*; GREEK: *ankinara*; ITALIAN: *carciofi*; SERBO-CROATIAN: *artičoka*; SPANISH: *alcachofa*; TURKISH: *kenger, enginar*

PLANT CHARACTERISTICS AND VARIETIES
The artichokes sold in the market are the unopened flower buds of a perennial thistle that belongs to the daisy family and can grow to 5 feet. The immature flower buds and inside flesh of the bracts are eaten cooked. The flesh at the bottom of the inside of the bracts, or phyllaries (they are not properly called leaves), is edible, as is the choke, the thickened receptacle also known as the foundation or heart. Cynarin, a substance that is present in artichokes, stimulates the taste buds responsible for detecting sweet flavors. The

type of artichoke you are most likely to find on the market is the globe artichoke, an Italian cultivar, which is sold in various sizes. A specialty greengrocer might carry the Tuscany violet artichokes, which taper off at the top into beautiful purple tips. There are about fifty other varieties grown around the world.

PLANT ORIGIN

The artichoke is not known in the wild and was developed from the cardoon or another thistle, *Cynara syriaca* Boiss., from the eastern Mediterranean by Arab or Berber horticulturists before the twelfth century.

PLANT HISTORY

The central question of interest to agricultural historians is, did the ancient Greeks and Romans know of the artichoke? Some mosaics in the Bardo Museum of Tunis in Tunisia are our iconographical evidence of what appears to be an artichoke. But this unidentified *Cynara* is, I believe, a cardoon and not an artichoke. In any case, the usual supplementary literary and historical evidence required by rigorous scholarship does not exist to support the notion that these mosaics depict an artichoke. The botanical description for distinguishing artichokes and cardoons in *Flora Europaea* (volume 4), *Plantaginaceae to Compositae (and Rubiaceae)* demonstrates the impossibility of conclusively identifying the images depicted in the mosaics at the Bardo.

Professor Andrew Watson, following the botanist Georges Gibault, claimed that the artichoke was developed from the cardoon; that only the cardoon was known in the Greco-Roman world, designated by names such as *kaktos, cynara, carduus, scolymus*, and *spondylium*; and that there is no reference in classical literature to a plant of this family with edible flesh on the bracts. Although J. André suggests that several Roman authors may have referred to the artichoke (or the cardoon) using the word *carduus*, two of the most important authors, Palladius and Pliny, say nothing that would make one think that the plant is not the cardoon. A recipe found in the Roman author Apicius's cookbook sounds as if it was meant for the soft stems of the cardoon rather than for the artichoke. Theophrastos says explicitly that the stem of the *kaktos* is eaten, so almost certainly he was referring to the cardoon. He goes on to mention another "thistle," the *pternix*, which has an edible receptacle but inedible bracts.

In Arabic the word for *artichoke* is, variously, *kharshūf, harshuf, qināriyya*, and *kankar*. The word *kankar* comes from the Persian *kangar*, which today means "cardoon" or "thistle." Abū Ḥanīfa al-Dīnawarī (d. 895) said he thought the Persian word *kankar* or *kangar* was used to designate the cardoon, a plant sometimes found cultivated in that time but more likely found growing wild, and that this plant was known by the Arabic word *harshuf*. The Arabic word *kankar* designated the acanthus, a cultivated plant resembling the wild cardoon. Abū al-Khayr (fl. eleventh century?) wrote of the cultivation of *qināriyya* in the gardens of

Seville, and this plant appears to be the wild cardoon. But Ibn al-ᶜAwwām, following Abū al-Khayr, said that there are two types of qināriyya, those of the fields and those of the garden, the latter appearing to be the artichoke. Ibn al-Bayṭār (1197–1228) said that kankar is the ḥarshuf of the garden. But Ibn al-Bayṭār later said that the plant in question has leaves longer and wider than those of lettuce and is the akanthos of Dioscorides. It could hardly have been the artichoke, Watson concludes. It is impossible to tell whether the kharshūf used in the thirteenth-century Hispano-Muslim cookery book the Kitāb al-ṭabīkh fī al-Maghrib wa'l-Āndalus was an artichoke or a cardoon. In any case, other early cookery manuscripts such as the fourteenth-century Le ménagier de Paris, the anonymous Italian Libro di cucina, and the Viandier of Taillevent conspicuously do not mention artichokes.

The nineteenth-century Italian botanist Targioni-Tozzetti describes the introduction of the artichoke to Tuscany around 1466, pointing out that Mattioli said it was brought to Naples from Sicily. As far as an early European distinction between the cardoon and the artichoke, the French historian Henri Bresc cites evidence of the artichoke being grown in the gardens of Palermo in the late fourteenth century; the documents distinguish the plant from the cardoon. Ermolao Barbaro, in his In Dioscoridem corollariorum libri quinque, finally published in 1530, writes that at the end of the fifteenth century artichokes were not always available in Italy; the implication may be that

they were not particularly esteemed at that time. The artichoke, he said, speaking of Venice, is found only in the foreign gardens in the Moorish quarter. The artichoke was brought to the New World by the French and Spanish colonizers in the sixteenth century. Today the Mediterranean and California are the major producers of artichokes.

HOW TO GROW AND HARVEST

Artichokes, a hardy perennial with a life of about four years, are difficult to grow from seed, so most kitchen gardeners start the plant from suckers, or offsets, from a well-established plant. Artichokes should stay in the same place for several years in a sunny location to develop into bushy plants. They need a long growing season and grow best in a warm, sheltered bed, in rich, fertile, and well-drained soil such as a sandy loam and in climates with mild winters, such as in California. Plant young plants or cuttings from side shoots in the spring about three feet apart and fertilize them with nitrogen once they are established. The roots of the artichokes should not be allowed to become dry. Artichokes planted in the spring can be harvested beginning in the fall through to midwinter. Harvest them by cutting the stem with a knife or pruning shears about 4 inches below the bud.

HOW TO BUY, STORE, AND PREPARE FOR COOKING

Artichokes can be found in the market year-round. Homegrown artichokes usually are

Artichokes

THE ARTICHOKE IS VERY POPULAR IN SOUTHERN ITALY AND THE MIDDLE EAST, WHERE COOKS LIKE TO STUFF THE HEARTS, AS you can see in the recipes that follow. There are so many other artichoke recipes that they could fill a book. There are the famous artichokes stuffed with mushrooms and ham from Provence called *artichauts à la barigoule,* the word *barigoule* derived from the Provençal word for "thyme," an herb that flavors this dish. The fact that artichokes lend themselves so well to stuffing is demonstrated in a Spanish recipe from Andalusia, *alcachofas rellanas,* in which the artichokes are stuffed with minced pork, breadcrumbs, and parsley; seasoned with nutmeg; and braised in a wine sauce. Cooking artichokes in wine is also a popular method on the Dalmatian Coast, where the hearts are baked with wine and butter and then drizzled with olive oil and vinegar in a dish called *artičoka s vinom,* artichokes and wine. The southern Italians are not the only ones who claim a love for artichokes. Certainly the Florentines delight in their *carciofi alla fiorentina,* a dish of cooked artichokes and spinach served with a lemon-flavored and Parmigiano-sprinkled béchamel sauce. The Greek contribution to artichoke cookery should not be overlooked. Although the Greeks like to cook artichokes in a manner very similar to that of the Turks, especially in lots of olive oil, they also have a wealth of recipes in which artichokes are cooked with other vegetables, such as in the dish *arakes me anginares,* in which the artichoke hearts are braised with peas, scallions, and olive oil, and seasoned with dill and lemon juice. Artichokes are also cooked with meat, such as in the artichoke and lamb dish called *arni me anginares avgolemono* from Crete, where the meat and hearts are cooked with a lemon-and-egg sauce and flavored with aniseed.

cropped in the spring and again in October. When shopping for artichokes, look for ones with the bracts tightly closed or only slightly open. The artichoke should feel heavy. Look at the stem for small holes that might indicate worm damage, and pass on that artichoke. Squeeze it—if it sounds squeaky, it's okay. Store artichokes dry in the refrigerator in a plastic bag for not more than 5 days.

A variety of artichoke products are sold. Marinated artichokes, sold in jars, the highest quality ones being found in Italian markets, are so-called baby artichokes. Fresh artichokes are preferred for all the recipes included here, but frozen or canned artichoke hearts are acceptable substitutes.

Preparing a raw artichoke heart for cooking requires a lot of work. Wash the artichoke and cut off the top half of the bracts with a large, sharp chef's knife. Remove the little bracts at the stem. Cut the stem off at the point near the bottom so the artichoke can stand up. Many people throw away the stem, but the flesh inside is edible, so slice off the skin and reserve the stem flesh (this is much easier to do if the artichoke has been boiled whole first). As you peel, slice, or break off the little pale green bracts near the choke, discard them and then, with a paring knife, slice off the woody parts surrounding the bottom stem. In a circular motion, cut out the hairy choke. Once the artichoke is cut, it will blacken, so you must always keep a cut half of a lemon nearby and immediately rub the artichoke heart when you reach it, or, as you fin-

ish each artichoke, put the heart into a bowl of water acidulated with lemon juice or vinegar to keep the vegetable from blackening while you prepare the rest of the artichokes.

Although all Mediterranean culinary cultures use artichokes, this vegetable is most popular in the Arab world and southern Italy.

RECIPES

Alcachofas en Escabeche
ARTICHOKE HEART SEVICHE

This is a magnificent preparation from the Spanish province of Valencia. The artichokes turn a golden brown and are delectable little morsels that beg to be eaten. It's an elegant preparation for a noble vegetable. I allow two artichokes per person, although you could easily eat the whole dish yourself. You will have enough marinated garlic sauce left over to prepare this dish a second time, and, believe me, you'll want to.

8 small to medium artichokes (about 3 pounds)
1 lemon, cut in half
1 cup extra virgin olive oil, and more for
   drizzling
1 bay leaf
3 large cloves garlic, peeled
½ teaspoon salt
1 tablespoon good-quality sherry vinegar, and
   more for drizzling
Salt and freshly ground black pepper to taste

1. Trim the artichokes and remove the hearts (see page 10), rubbing each one all over with the cut lemon half. Place the artichokes in a bowl of water acidulated with the juice from the other half of the lemon so the prepared artichokes don't discolor while you continue working.

2. In a large skillet, heat the olive oil over medium to medium-high heat until nearly smoking, preheating the skillet for about 10 minutes. Cook the artichoke hearts with the bay leaf in the hot oil until the artichoke hearts are golden brown all over and a skewer will glide into the center of the artichoke heart without too much resistance, 5 to 6 minutes. Remove the artichokes from the oil with a slotted ladle and transfer them to a shallow serving platter or bowl. Reserve the oil.

3. Meanwhile, pound the garlic with the salt in a mortar. Stir 3 tablespoons of the oil you cooked the artichokes in into the garlic, ½ teaspoon at a time. Then stir in the vinegar ½ teaspoon at a time until you have a creamy-looking sauce. Spoon small amounts of this mixture over the artichokes. Drizzle the artichokes with olive oil and a splash of vinegar and set aside for 1 hour before serving. Season with salt and pepper if necessary.

Makes 4 servings

Vellutata di Carciofi
ARTICHOKE VELOUTÉ

The Italian *vellutata*, meaning "velvety," comes from the French word *velouté*, with the same meaning. In this case, the *velouté* is the base for a creamy, smooth, and elegant artichoke soup that is typically served as a first course in northern Italy. Because this soup is rich, it is best followed by a simple second course such as grilled fish.

¾ cup (1½ sticks) unsalted butter, at room temperature, divided
¼ cup all-purpose unbleached flour
5 cups chicken broth (preferably homemade), divided
8 large cooked fresh artichoke hearts or 16 canned artichoke hearts (two 14-ounce cans, drained)
4 large egg yolks
1 cup heavy cream
Croutons (optional)

1. In a medium saucepan, melt ¼ cup (½ stick) of the butter over medium-high heat. Using a wire whisk, whisk in the flour, stirring and cooking until the flour becomes light brown and smells nutty, about 3 minutes. Slowly pour in 4 cups of the chicken broth, whisking all the time, until the mixture is smooth and creamy.

2. Place the artichoke hearts in a food processor and process them until they are the consistency of a fine puree, stopping the machine

and scraping down the sides when necessary before continuing. You should have about 2 cups artichoke puree. Beat the egg yolks and cream together in a medium bowl.

3. Remove the artichoke puree from the food processor and blend it into the broth mixture, stirring in the remaining 1 cup chicken broth. Return the artichoke broth to the food processor in batches and process until completely smooth and a little frothy, transferring the mixture to a medium pot as you process each batch.

4. Bring the soup to a boil. Remove it from the heat and vigorously and continuously whisk in the egg yolk-and-cream mixture. Return the soup to very low heat and whisk in the remaining ½ cup (1 stick) butter a tablespoon at a time until it is completely melted. Serve the soup immediately with croutons if desired.

Makes 4 to 6 servings

Carciofi con Mozzarella
ARTICHOKES STUFFED WITH MOZZARELLA

The artichokes in this preparation from the Campania region of southern Italy look rather majestic with their bracts pushed apart and stuffed with mozzarella. This dish is impressive served to guests as an antipasto. Although this recipe involves detailed preparation, you can make the work easier by parboiling the artichokes before you stuff them. This method makes stuffing the artichokes more manageable, but at the expense of a less pretty looking finished dish. Be careful not to use more cheese than I recommend, because you do not want to overwhelm the artichokes. The artichokes should be served communally, with each artichoke shared by the diners.

*2 large or 4 medium to large artichokes
    (about 2½ pounds in all)*
½ pound fresh mozzarella cheese, chopped
*2 tablespoons freshly grated Parmigiano-Reggiano
    cheese*
1 large egg, lightly beaten
¼ cup finely chopped fresh parsley leaves
Salt and freshly ground black pepper to taste
6 tablespoons dry breadcrumbs
4 salted anchovy fillets, rinsed and finely chopped
¼ cup extra virgin olive oil
1 lemon, cut into 6 wedges

1. Trim the stem and top third of the artichokes. Snip off the pointy tips of the bracts with kitchen scissors and boil the whole artichokes until there is still a slight resistance when you try to pierce the center of the artichokes with a skewer, about 40 minutes. Drain well and, when they are cool enough to handle, remove the central hairy choke and inner bracts using a paring knife and a teaspoon, going in from the top but being careful not to pull off too many bracts.

2. Preheat the oven to 375°F. In a medium bowl, mix together the mozzarella, Parmigiano-Reggiano, egg, and parsley. Season with salt and pepper. Spoon this stuffing into the

center of each artichoke and, with your fingers, spread the bracts apart and push some stuffing down between the individual bracts, too.

3. In a small bowl, mix the breadcrumbs with the anchovy and sprinkle this mixture over the stuffing in each artichoke. Drizzle all the artichokes with olive oil.

4. Arrange the artichokes in a baking pan and add a few cups of water to the pan. Cover the pan with aluminum foil and bake for 25 minutes. Remove the foil and continue to bake until the breadcrumbs are golden, about 20 minutes. Serve with a wedge of lemon.

Makes 6 servings

Carciofi "a l'Argintéra"
SILVERSMITH'S ARTICHOKES

The name of this dish refers to an old Sicilian way of preparing *caciocavallo* cheese, a hard Italian cow's milk cheese usually shaped like a gourd, tied off at the top to another gourd of cheese. The story, as reported by Mary Taylor Simeti, author of books on Sicilian cuisine, is that the dish was a famous preparation in Palermo that was originally made by an anonymous silversmith who was too poor to afford meat, so he disguised cheese so that it tasted like a tender young rabbit. In this preparation, the same concept is applied to artichokes. Some Sicilian cooks use *caciotta fresca*, a fresh cow, sheep, or goat's milk cheese with a delicate and buttery flavor similar to that of Bel Paese, but I make it with *caciocavallo* or imported provolone, both of which can be found in Italian markets.

8 medium artichoke hearts (page 10), sliced
2 tablespoons extra virgin olive oil
½ cup milk
Salt to taste
1 large garlic clove, finely chopped
¼ pound sliced caciocavallo or imported provolone
1 teaspoon dried oregano
1 to 2 teaspoons white wine vinegar, to your taste

1. Preheat the oven to 400°F. Toss the sliced artichoke hearts in a medium bowl with the olive oil and milk to coat, arrange in a small to medium baking casserole, and salt lightly. Bake until soft, about 35 minutes.

2. Sprinkle the artichokes with some garlic and lay the slices of cheese on top. Sprinkle with the oregano and vinegar, and return the casserole to the oven until the cheese has melted and is speckled black on top, 10 to 12 minutes.

Makes 4 servings

Carciofi con Mollica
ARTICHOKE HEARTS IN CITRUS SAUCE AND GOLDEN BREADCRUMBS

When artichokes are abundant, you will love making this tangy Sicilian recipe, which harks back to the days of the *monzù*, the French-influenced Sicilian chefs of the aristocracy who invented fabulous baroque recipes in the nineteenth century. This recipe requires the largest artichokes you can find—each should weigh about a pound. You can use smaller ones, but you will have to do a lot more work.

6 very large fresh artichoke hearts (from about 6 pounds of artichokes; page 10)
Freshly squeezed juice from 2 oranges
Freshly squeezed juice from 2 lemons
Salt and freshly ground black pepper to taste
3 tablespoons sugar
½ cup white wine vinegar
3 tablespoons extra virgin olive oil, and more for drizzling
1 cup fresh breadcrumbs
4 salted anchovy fillets, rinsed and chopped
1 tablespoon capers, rinsed if salted, chopped

1. Place the artichoke hearts in a large skillet with the orange and lemon juices. Season with salt and pepper. Bring to a gentle boil. Dissolve the sugar in the vinegar and add to the skillet. Reduce the heat to low and cook, stirring occasionally, until the liquid is nearly evaporated, the sauce is syrupy, and the artichokes are tender, about 1½ hours. Transfer the artichokes to a serving bowl or platter.
2. In a small skillet, heat the olive oil over medium-high heat and cook the breadcrumbs until golden, 2 to 3 minutes, stirring frequently. Remove them from the heat and mix with the anchovies and capers in a small bowl. Toss the breadcrumb mixture with the artichokes or spoon it over the artichokes

arranged on the serving platter. Drizzle with a little olive oil and serve at room temperature.

Makes 4 to 6 servings

Carciofi con le Uova
ARTICHOKES WITH SCRAMBLED EGGS

In 1614 Giacomo Castelvetro (1546–1616), author of *A Brief Account of the Fruit, Herbs and Vegetables of Italy*, suggested cooking very young artichokes that have not yet developed inedible bracts by boiling them first, then baking them in little tartlets with oysters and beef marrow seasoned with salt and pepper. That's an intriguing-sounding dish, and here's another one from the Calabrian region of southern Italy that has the semblance of a frittata, although I usually serve it as a *contorno*, vegetable side dish. This delicious preparation gives artichoke hearts their due.

5 to 6 medium artichokes (about 2 pounds in all)
Freshly squeezed juice from 1 lemon or 3 tablespoons white wine vinegar
3 tablespoons extra virgin olive oil
2 garlic cloves, peeled and crushed
¾ cup water, or as needed
Salt to taste
3 large eggs
¼ cup freshly grated Pecorino cheese
3 tablespoons finely chopped fresh parsley leaves
Freshly ground black pepper to taste

1. Trim the artichokes (see page 10) and remove all the hard bracts. As you reach the hearts, rub them with a cut half of a lemon. Slice the hearts into thin strips and leave them in a bowl of water acidulated with the lemon juice or vinegar so they won't discolor.

2. In a large skillet, heat the olive oil with the garlic over medium-high heat, cooking the garlic cloves until they begin to turn light brown, about 3½ minutes. Remove and discard the garlic. Add the drained artichokes and ¼ cup of the water, and season with salt. Reduce the heat to medium, cover the pan, and cook until there is still a slight resistance when you insert a skewer into the center of the artichoke hearts, 23 to 25 minutes, adding more water in ¼-cup increments when necessary so the skillet doesn't dry out.

3. When the artichokes are tender, let the last addition of water evaporate. Beat the eggs with the Pecorino cheese, parsley, and pepper. Pour this mixture over the artichokes, cover, and cook until the eggs set, 3 to 4 minutes. Serve immediately.

Makes 4 servings

Beignets d'Artichauts
ARTICHOKE FRITTERS

This recipe from Provence is really quite a delight. For many years I spent several weeks in Cannes every summer visiting my then wife, our very young children, her brothers and sister, and I would explore the neighboring region, going into the mountains to eat at a country restaurant. I was always surprised to find various vegetable *beignets* on the menu, and quite happy too, since I love them. These artichoke fritters are always a favorite with guests and perfect for a spring dinner.

5 very large artichokes or 20 small baby
  artichokes (about 5 pounds in all, or
  1½ pounds of hearts)
1 lemon, cut in half
4 tablespoons extra virgin olive oil, divided
3 tablespoons finely chopped fresh parsley leaves
3 garlic cloves, finely chopped, divided
Salt and freshly ground black pepper to taste
¾ cup all-purpose unbleached flour
2 large eggs, 1 whole and 1 separated and the
  white beaten to form peaks
½ cup beer (lager)
2 tablespoons heavy cream
1 tablespoon finely chopped fresh thyme, oregano,
  or tarragon leaves
6 cups olive oil, olive pomace oil, or vegetable oil
  for frying

1. Trim the artichokes (see page 10), rubbing each heart with one lemon half as you reach the heart, so it doesn't discolor. Cut the hearts into fifths and place them in a bowl of water acidulated with the juice from the other lemon half.

2. Drain the artichoke hearts, place them in a large saucepan, and cover them with cold water by several inches. Lightly season the water with salt and pepper. Bring the pot to a boil and cook the artichokes at a boil until

they are soft and can be pierced by a skewer easily, 20 to 25 minutes. Drain the artichoke hearts and place them in a large bowl. Toss them with 3 tablespoons of the olive oil, the parsley, and 2 of the chopped garlic cloves. Season with salt and pepper. Refrigerate for 3 hours, covered with plastic wrap.

3. In a medium bowl, make the batter by stirring together the flour, whole egg, egg yolk, beer, heavy cream, chopped herb of your choice, the remaining clove of chopped garlic, and the remaining 1 tablespoon olive oil. Season with salt and pepper. Stir until smooth, then fold in the beaten egg white. Refrigerate for 1 hour, covered with plastic wrap.

4. In a deep fryer or an 8-inch saucepan fitted with a basket insert, preheat the frying oil to 375°F. Preheat the oven to "warm," about 150°F.

5. Dip a handful of artichoke heart pieces in the batter and gently place them in the hot oil. Don't crowd the fryer. Fry the artichoke pieces until golden brown, turning if necessary, about 4 minutes. Remove them from the hot oil, drain well, transfer to a paper towel-lined baking pan, salt lightly, and keep warm in the oven while you continue to cook the remaining artichokes. Serve the artichokes hot. Once the frying oil has cooled, strain it and save it for future use.

Makes 6 servings

Zeytinyağlı Enginar Dolması
RICE-AND-PISTACHIO-STUFFED ARTICHOKES IN OLIVE OIL SAUCE

This recipe is a classic example of a more refined style of Turkish home cooking. You are likely to find this kind of recipe made in restaurants, too, but generally it is more often made for a special occasion at home. Although it does involve some preparation time, the culinary reward is certainly worth it: you will create an exceptional meal and probably impress your guests.

FOR THE ARTICHOKES:

8 medium to large artichokes (about 6 pounds in all), trimmed of bracts and stems (page 10)

1 tablespoon all-purpose unbleached flour

Freshly squeezed juice from 1 lemon

2 cups water

1 teaspoon salt

FOR THE STUFFING:

½ cup extra virgin olive oil

3 cups finely chopped onions

3 tablespoons shelled pistachios

¼ cup raw short-grain rice, soaked in tepid water for 30 minutes or rinsed under cold running water, and drained

1 teaspoon salt

1 teaspoon sugar

1 teaspoon freshly ground allspice berries

1 teaspoon freshly ground black pepper

½ cup water

Leaves from ½ bunch fresh parsley, finely chopped
Leaves from ½ bunch fresh dill, finely chopped
Leaves from ½ bunch fresh mint, finely chopped
5 ripe plum tomatoes, cut in quarters

1. Place the trimmed whole artichoke hearts in a bowl of acidulated water. Place the flour, lemon juice, 2 cups of water, and salt in a medium saucepan and bring to a boil. Add the artichokes and boil for 5 minutes. Remove the artichokes with a slotted ladle. Slice off a tiny portion of their bottom so they can sit upright. Arrange them on a baking tray. Save the cooking water and set it aside.

2. In a medium saucepan or skillet, heat the olive oil over medium-high heat and cook the onions and pistachios until the onions are translucent and light golden, about 10 minutes, stirring occasionally. Add the rice, salt, sugar, allspice, and black pepper and continue cooking for 4 to 5 minutes, stirring frequently. Add the water, place a paper towel over the skillet to absorb the steam, cover the saucepan with the lid, reduce the heat to low, and cook the rice mixture until the water is absorbed, 18 to 20 minutes, without taking off the lid to sneak a peek or stir the pot. Remove the skillet from the heat and stir in the parsley, dill, and mint until well blended.

3. Preheat the oven to 425°F. Stuff the artichokes with the rice mixture, then pour about two-thirds of the reserved artichoke cooking water over everything. Arrange the tomato pieces in between the stuffed artichokes. Place the pan in the oven and bake until the toma-toes are soft and the tops of the stuffed artichokes are dark, about 25 minutes. Remove the stuffed artichokes from the oven, let cool, then refrigerate for 2 hours before serving, but serve at room temperature.

Makes 8 servings

Kharshūf wa'l-Fūl
ARTICHOKES AND FAVA BEANS

In Syria there couldn't be two more favored vegetables than artichokes and fava beans, except maybe eggplant. This simple preparation is served at room temperature and is a favorite in Damascus in the spring when artichokes and fava beans come to market. Some of the fava beans that are available are so young that they do not need to be peeled. If your fava beans are older, you will want to peel them after boiling them for 5 minutes. Although peeling the beans creates more work, the bright green color makes the dish so appetizing, and, frankly, the peel is really too hard to digest if not cooked for a very long time.

9 medium artichokes (about 3 pounds)
1 lemon, cut in half
4 large garlic cloves, peeled
1 teaspoon salt
3 pounds fava bean pods, shelled (3 cups of beans)
½ cup extra virgin olive oil
1 tablespoon sugar
1 tablespoon finely chopped fresh parsley leaves

I. Prepare the artichokes according to the instructions on page 10, rubbing the hearts with one lemon half and placing them in a bowl of water acidulated with the juice from the other lemon half.

2. In a mortar, pound the garlic with the salt until mushy. Dice the artichokes and place them in a large skillet with the shelled fava beans, olive oil, pounded garlic, sugar, and ¾ cup of the acidulated water that the artichokes soaked in. Bring the mixture to a boil over medium-high heat and cook for about 6 minutes. Reduce the heat to low and simmer, covered, for 45 minutes.

3. Uncover the skillet, taste, and correct the seasoning, then simmer until the artichokes are soft and the sauce is syrupy, another 10 to 15 minutes. Transfer the artichokes to a serving dish, sprinkle with the parsley, and serve at room temperature.

Makes 4 to 6 servings

Yakhnit al-Arḍī shawkī
ARTICHOKE AND LAMB STEW

This is an authentic Syrian preparation that friends in Damascus made for me as I watched. What makes it authentic is demonstrated by the fact that it is considered a vegetable dish, the meat used sparingly, almost as a condiment, as is typical in Syrian cooking. Syrian cooks only use meat in abundance for special occasions such as religious feasts, weddings, or family reunions. For everyday cooking, vegetables hold sway.

8 large fresh artichoke hearts (from 7 to 8 pounds whole artichokes; page 10), cut in quarters

½ cup freshly squeezed lemon juice

6 tablespoons extra virgin olive oil

¾ pound boneless lamb, trimmed of fat and cut from the leg into ½-inch cubes

Salt and freshly ground black pepper to taste

1 large onion, grated

3 cups water

1 teaspoon salt

½ teaspoon freshly ground black pepper

2 tablespoons finely chopped fresh mint leaves

I. In a medium bowl, toss the artichoke hearts with the lemon juice and set them aside for 15 minutes. Drain the artichokes, reserving the juice.

2. Heat the olive oil in a casserole dish over medium-high heat and cook the artichokes until lightly browned, 2 to 4 minutes. Remove them with a slotted ladle and set aside.

3. Season the lamb with salt and pepper. In the same casserole dish, brown the lamb over medium-high heat on all sides, 3 to 5 minutes. Add the onion and cook, stirring, until translucent, about 4 minutes. Add the water, salt, and pepper, and bring to a boil. Reduce the heat to low, cover, and simmer until the meat is tender, 2 to 2½ hours.

4. Add the reserved artichokes and continue cooking until they are tender, about 30 minutes. Increase the heat to medium-low,

uncover the pot, and simmer until the water is reduced and the sauce is syrupy, about 20 minutes. Sprinkle the mint on top and serve.

Makes 4 servings

Arḍī shawkī Maqlī bi'l-Ṭaraṭūr
FRIED ARTICHOKES WITH ṬARAṬŪR SAUCE

In Syria, *taraṭūr* is made from tahini and parsley and used as a dipping sauce for these deep-fried artichoke hearts, which are usually served as part of an Arab *mazza* table, the smorgasbord of little appetizing dishes served in homes and restaurants. This dish works well as an appetizer, and the sauce is so delicious that you will find yourself using it for other foods, too.

FOR THE *ṬARAṬŪR* SAUCE:
8 garlic cloves, peeled
1 tablespoon salt
½ cup tahini
½ cup freshly squeezed lemon juice
4 tablespoons finely chopped fresh parsley leaves, divided

FOR THE ARTICHOKES:
8 medium to large artichokes (about 3 pounds)
6 cups olive oil for frying
½ cup all-purpose unbleached flour for dredging
Salt to taste

1. To make the sauce, in a mortar, pound the garlic with the salt to create a creamy mush. In a small bowl, beat the tahini paste and lemon juice together slowly. Stir the tahini and lemon juice mixture into the garlic and salt and beat well. Stir 3 tablespoons of the parsley into this mixture. Taste to check the consistency and correct the seasoning. If the sauce is too thick, add water, *never* more lemon juice. If you do need to adjust the taste, the preparation process must be repeated; in other words, mash some more garlic with salt or mix a tablespoon of tahini with a tablespoon of lemon juice.

2. In a large saucepan, steam or boil the artichokes until there is still a little resistance when you try to pierce them with a skewer at their base, 45 to 50 minutes. Drain and remove the artichokes from the pot. Trim the artichokes (see page 10). Scrape the inside of the bracts for the flesh and save that for another use. Cut the hearts in half or quarters.

3. Preheat the frying oil to 375°F in a deep fryer or an 8-inch saucepan fitting with a basket insert. Dredge the artichoke hearts in the flour, tapping off any excess through a strainer. Deep-fry the artichokes until golden, about 2 minutes. Cook them in batches if necessary so you don't crowd the fryer. Drain the fried artichokes on paper towels and season lightly with salt. Serve the artichokes with the sauce. Once the oil is cool, strain it and save it for future use.

Makes 4 servings

Arḍī shawkī bi'l-Ḥāmid
ARTICHOKES WITH POMEGRANATE SYRUP

Aleppo, in northern Syria, is considered one of the culinary capitals of the Middle East. After tasting these artichokes flavored with fresh coriander and pomegranate molasses, you will see why. Many Aleppine dishes are flavored in this manner. I find the sweet and tart taste of the syrupy pomegranate appealing with spring vegetables.

8 medium to large artichokes (about 3 pounds)

3 medium ripe tomatoes (about ¾ pound), peeled and seeded

8 large garlic cloves, peeled

2 teaspoons salt

3 tablespoons extra virgin olive oil, and more for drizzling

1 medium onion, chopped fine

¾ cup finely chopped fresh coriander leaves (1 to 2 bunches)

1 cup water

1 tablespoon freshly squeezed lemon juice

2 tablespoons pomegranate molasses (available in Middle Eastern markets)

1. In a large saucepan, steam or boil the artichokes until a skewer will glide easily into the base, 45 to 50 minutes. Drain and remove the artichokes from the saucepan. Scrape the flesh from the inside of the bracts and save for another use. Dice the artichoke hearts.

2. Place the tomatoes in a strainer over a small bowl and press the juice through with the back of a wooden spoon. You should have 1 cup of tomato juice. In a mortar, pound the garlic and salt together until mushy and set aside.

3. In a large skillet, heat the olive oil over medium-high heat and cook the onion until softened, 2 to 3 minutes, stirring. Add the mashed garlic and coriander and cook, stirring constantly, until fragrant, 1 to 2 minutes. Add the artichokes, tomato juice, and water and bring to a boil. Reduce the heat to low and cook until the liquid is somewhat reduced, 10 to 15 minutes, stirring frequently. Add the lemon juice and pomegranate molasses and continue cooking until the mixture becomes syrupy, about another 10 minutes, stirring. Transfer to a serving bowl and drizzle a small amount of olive oil over the artichokes before serving.

Makes 6 servings

Arḍī shawkī bi'l-Laḥm
STUFFED ARTICHOKES WITH LAMB

Stuffed artichokes is a classic Syrian dish, quite popular in the spring and summer. This recipe was given to me by my friend Mazen Halaby's aunt, Muheeba, while I was visiting Damascus. Artichokes are the perfect vessel for containing a stuffing, and in Damascus alone there seem to be innumerable ways of preparing this beloved dish. Today more and more Syrians use corn oil, but I prefer the traditional olive oil.

8 very large artichokes (6 to 7 pounds)

½ lemon

½ cup fresh lemon juice or white wine vinegar, divided

4 tablespoons extra virgin olive oil, divided

½ pound ground lamb

1 small onion, chopped fine

3 tablespoons pine nuts

Salt and freshly ground black pepper to taste

2 teaspoons bahārāt (see below)

1 cup water

½ cup cooked peas for garnish (optional)

½ cup diced cooked carrots for garnish (optional)

½ cup high-quality full-fat plain yogurt

1. Preheat the oven to 350°F. Remove the heavy bracts of the artichokes (page 10). Slice off the stem so the artichokes will stand upright on their base. With a sharp paring knife, remove all the bracts and create a well in the center by removing the hairy choke down to the heart. As you are trimming the artichokes, rub the hearts, when you reach them, with the cut lemon half to prevent them from discoloring. Place the cut artichokes in a bowl of water acidulated with ¼ cup of the lemon juice or the vinegar while you continue working.

2. In a large skillet, heat 3 tablespoons of the olive oil over medium-high heat and cook the lamb, onion, and pine nuts until browned, about 8 minutes, breaking up the lamb with a fork or wooden spoon. Season the mixture with salt and pepper and add the *bahārāt*. Mix well and set aside. Drain and dry the artichokes with a paper towel.

3. In another skillet, heat the remaining 1 tablespoon olive oil over medium-high heat and cook the artichokes on both sides until the cut edges turn slightly black and crispy, 2 to 3 minutes on each side. Remove with a slotted ladle and arrange in a baking dish. Fill each artichoke with about 2 teaspoons of the meat mixture, pressing down with your fingers. Add the water and the remaining ¼ cup lemon juice or vinegar to the baking dish so the artichoke heart bottoms rest in the liquid.

4. Bake the artichokes until they are tender, 30 to 35 minutes. The tops will be very dark and crispy. Transfer the artichokes to a serving platter and surround them with the garnish of cooked peas and carrots, if you wish. Place a 1-tablespoon dollop of yogurt on top of each artichoke and serve.

Makes 4 to 8 servings

Bahārāt

SPICE MIX FOR SYRIAN, LEBANESE, AND PALESTINIAN COOKING

Bahārāt is an all-purpose spice mix used in Lebanon, Syria, Jordan, and Palestine and found in many prepared savory dishes. The word *bahārāt* means "spice" in Arabic, derived from the word *bahar*, which means "pepper." So *bahārāt* is a mixed spice with black pepper.

This spice mix can be bought at Middle Eastern groceries and markets, but it is also quite easy to make your own fresh supply and keep it stored in a spice jar. There are many different variations, all based on the basic ingredients of black pepper and allspice. Some mixes might include paprika, coriander seeds, cassia bark, sumac, nutmeg, cumin seeds, or cardamom seeds. This recipe is basic; if you like, you can fiddle with it by adding some of the other spices mentioned.

¼ cup black peppercorns
¼ cup allspice berries
2 teaspoons ground cinnamon
1 teaspoon freshly grated nutmeg

Grind the peppercorns and allspice together and blend with the cinnamon and nutmeg. Store the spice mix in a jar in your spice rack, away from sunlight. It will lose pungency as time goes by, but, properly stored, it can be good for many months.

Makes about ½ cup

Ruzz bi'l-Arḍi shawkī
RICE PILAF WITH ARTICHOKES

Perhaps the fantasies of a long-forgotten chef of the Umayyad caliphs in the early days of Islam created this fluffy pilaf, which is so clearly influenced by Persian cuisine and is popular in Damascus. It's an extravagant preparation with artichokes, almonds, pistachios, and pine nuts that demands the most joyous of guests. The fragrance of the pilaf is enhanced by the use of cardamom, cinnamon, and nutmeg. By freshly grinding the spices yourself just before cooking, you will dramatically improve the taste and aroma of the finished dish. Before making the rice, read the sidebar on making pilaf on page 25.

2 large artichokes (about 1½ pounds)
3 tablespoons samna (clarified butter, page 23), divided
½ cup blanched whole almonds
2 tablespoons shelled pistachios
2 tablespoons pine nuts
½ pound ground lamb
½ teaspoon saffron threads, crumbled in a mortar with ½ teaspoon salt
1 teaspoon freshly ground cardamom seeds (from about 20 pods)
½ teaspoon ground cinnamon
¼ teaspoon freshly grated nutmeg
½ teaspoon paprika
3¼ cups water, divided
1½ cups long-grain rice, covered with water, soaked for 30 minutes, and drained, or rinsed well under running water
1 teaspoon salt
High-quality full-fat plain yogurt for garnish
Arabic flatbread

I. In a large saucepan, boil the whole artichokes in lightly salted water, uncovered, until there is still a little resistance when you try to pierce them with a skewer at the base, 45 to 50 minutes. Drain. When they are cool enough to handle, trim the artichokes (see page 10) and remove the hearts. Scrape off the flesh from the inside of the bracts and save for another use. Cut the hearts into ⅜-inch dice and set aside.

2. In a large skillet, melt 2 tablespoons of the *samna* over medium-high heat and cook the almonds until golden, about 3 minutes, shaking the pan frequently. Remove the almonds with a slotted ladle and set them aside. Add the pistachios to the skillet and cook them for 1 minute. Remove them with a slotted ladle and set them aside with the almonds. Add the pine nuts and cook them until golden, about 1 minute, stirring. Remove them with a slotted ladle and set them aside with the other nuts. Reduce the heat to medium.

3. In the same skillet in which you cooked the nuts, brown the lamb over medium heat until it loses its pinkness, about 2 minutes, breaking it up with a fork or a wooden spoon. Add the saffron and salt, cardamom, cinnamon, nutmeg, and paprika. Stir well and add ¼ cup of the water. Reduce the heat to low and simmer until the lamb is tender and fragrant, about 30 minutes. Add the chopped artichokes and cook them until they are tender too, about another 15 minutes.

4. Meanwhile, melt the remaining 1 tablespoon of *samna* over medium-high heat in a heavy casserole or saucepan with a heavy lid. Add the well-drained rice and cook it until it is coated, 1 to 2 minutes, stirring constantly. Add the remaining 3 cups water and the salt. Mix well, bring to a boil, and reduce the heat to very low. Cover the top of the pan with paper towels to absorb moisture, replace the lid, and simmer the rice until the water is absorbed, 15 to 18 minutes. Don't look under the lid for the first 12 minutes, and don't stir the rice. After the allotted time, turn the heat off then check to see if the rice is done. If it is still a little hard, add ¼ cup boiling water and cover the pot again with the paper towels and lid and leave off the heat for 10 to 15 minutes, until the extra water is absorbed.

5. Transfer the rice to a mixing bowl and fluff it. Drain the spiced lamb of any excess liquid and fat then mix the lamb into the rice. Arrange the pilaf on a large oval serving platter and mold it with your hands to form an even mound. Garnish the top and sides with the sautéed mixed nuts. Serve the yogurt on the side and pass the Arabic flatbread.

Makes 6 servings

Samna
CLARIFIED BUTTER

Samna is simply clarified butter, or butter from which the milk solids have been removed. Because the milk solids in butter burn easily and can go rancid, clarifying butter makes it suitable for cooking purposes and increases its shelf life. *Samna* is also known as *sman* (sometimes transliterated as *smen*) and by the Hindi word *ghee*. In the Middle East and North Africa, clarified butter is strained through salt into an earthenware container for storage, then aged, acquiring a unique taste. The Bedouin of the Sinai and Negev flavor their *samna* with the leaves of *nafal (Trigonella arabica)*, a kind of clover.

2 pounds (8 sticks) unsalted butter, cut in quarters

1. In a large, heavy saucepan, melt the butter over low heat until it is completely melted or until you detect the first signs of bubbling. At that point, turn the heat even lower or use a heat diffuser. Turn the heat off and let the butter cool but not solidify.

2. Tilt the saucepan and carefully gather all the foam to one side. Spoon it off and discard it. Carefully pour or spoon the liquid butter into the container you are using to store it, being careful not to let any of the milk solids on the bottom of the pan seep into the container. Alternatively, pour the butter through a damp cheesecloth-lined strainer into the container.

Makes 3 cups

VARIATION: I've made *samna* in a microwave, and it was the easiest method of all. Place the butter in a microwavable container, cover with plastic wrap, set the microwave on medium, and heat the butter until it is melted, about 1 to 2 minutes. Carefully pour the clarified butter into your container, making sure no milk solids seep in.

Makes 3 cups

Arḍī shawkī bi'l-Bayḍ
ARTICHOKE FRITTATA

This Syrian breakfast dish of fluffy scrambled eggs with artichoke hearts sautéed in butter is accompanied with warmed fresh Arabic flatbread and fried *jubna bayḍā'* (literally "white cheese"), a Syrian cheese now made in this country and sold (as "Syrian cheese") in Middle Eastern markets and some better supermarkets. If you find this cheese, cook it according to the method described in the Note below.

2 large artichokes (about 1½ pounds)
2 tablespoons unsalted butter
1 garlic clove, peeled and lightly crushed
6 large eggs, beaten with a wire whisk until frothy
Salt and freshly ground black pepper to taste
3 tablespoons finely chopped fresh parsley leaves

1. Place the artichokes in a pot filled with water, bring the water to a boil, and salt it lightly. Cook the artichokes until a skewer will glide into the base easily and the heavier bracts pull off easily, 45 to 50 minutes. Remove and, when cool enough to handle, trim the artichokes (see page 10) and chop the hearts somewhat fine. Scrape the flesh from the inside of the bracts and save it for another use.

2. In a large nonstick omelette pan, melt the butter with the garlic over medium-high heat. Remove and discard the garlic after 30 seconds. Add the chopped artichokes and cook them until heated through, about 1 minute. Remove the artichokes and set them aside, keeping them warm. Pour in the eggs and cook, stirring gently, until scrambled and set, but still a bit wet. Season with salt and pepper. Once the eggs are scrambled, transfer them to a bowl and toss them gently with the

Cooking Rice Pilaf

PILAF COOKERY REFERS TO THE METHOD OF MAKING RICE IN NORTH AFRICA, GREECE, TURKEY, ALL THE ARAB COUNTRIES, as well as Persia, Afghanistan, Pakistan, and India. *Pilaf* is originally a Persian word. It seems very likely that the Arabs and Turks both learned how to cook rice from the Persians. The best rices for pilaf are the long-grain Basmati and Patna rices, both named for places in India. Both types of rice are sold in supermarkets, Middle Eastern markets, Greek markets, and Indo-Pakistani markets throughout the United States. A long-grain American rice will also do fine, but not converted rice. The distinguishing characteristic of rice pilaf is that, once cooked, the grains of rice are tender and each is completely separate from the other without any stickiness. The rice should be fluffy and fragrant.

To achieve a perfect pilaf, first soak the raw rice in water for 30 minutes to an hour. Some cooks use hot water, others cold, and some add salt. Alternatively, if you are pressed for time, pour the rice into a fine-mesh strainer and let it sit under running water, rubbing the grains with your fingers for a minute. Rinsing or soaking removes the starch so that the grains will remain separate after cooking. Second, heat the fat—butter, clarified butter, vegetable oil, or olive oil—in a heavy saucepan with a heavy lid and sauté the rinsed and drained rice for about a minute or two, stirring all the time. Next add the liquid and salt to the pan. The rule of thumb for the ratio of liquid to rice is two parts liquid to one part rice, and 1 teaspoon salt for each cup of raw rice. Finally, and most important, bring the liquid to a boil, stir the rice once, reduce the heat to low, cover the pot with a heavy lid, and cook the rice until the liquid is absorbed, between 12 and 20 minutes. Once the rice is simmering in the pot, you must never stir or tamper with it. In fact, don't check the rice until 12 minutes have passed. The rice should always remain covered when cooking.

Sometimes, if I feel I might not be able to pay attention to the rice, I will turn the heat off once the liquid reaches a boil, cover the top with paper towels, replace the lid, and leave the rice undisturbed until all the liquid is absorbed, about 40 minutes.

artichokes. Serve the eggs and artichokes on individual plates or a serving platter. If you plan to make another batch, keep the first batch warm. Sprinkle the finished dish with parsley and serve with warm Arabic flatbread and the fried cheese on the side, if desired.

NOTE: Cut the cheese into ¼- to ½-inch-thick slices and cook it in hot butter, clarified butter, or olive oil in a medium skillet over medium-high heat until both sides are crispy brown, about 3 minutes in all, turning once. Turn the fried cheese with a spatula, scraping the bottom, and only add the cheese slices to the skillet after the melted butter has stopped bubbling.

Makes 2 to 4 servings

Salāṭat al-Qanāriyya
ARTICHOKE HEART SALAD

This Tunisian salad is a nice preparation that can be served as part of a *mazza* table. The artichokes are boiled first. The hearts are removed and sliced, and then served with a flavorful dressing made with *harīsa*, a hot chile pepper paste used ubiquitously in Tunisian cooking, and the water the artichokes were cooked in.

4 or 5 medium artichokes (2½ pounds)
1 lemon, cut in half
½ teaspoon harīsa (page 263)
12 imported black olives
1 tablespoon capers, rinsed if salted
2 large hard-boiled eggs, shelled and sliced
Salt to taste
Extra virgin olive oil to taste

1. Cover the artichokes with water in a large saucepan and boil them with the lemon half until a skewer will glide into the center easily, 50 to 60 minutes. Drain, saving 3 tablespoons of the water you cooked the artichokes in. Remove the hearts, slice them, and arrange them in a salad bowl or on a serving platter. Let them cool. Scrape off the flesh at the base of the bracts and add it to the salad bowl or platter or save it for another use.

2. Dissolve the *harīsa* in the reserved artichoke water. Arrange the olives in the salad bowl or on the serving platter. Sprinkle the salad with the capers and then with the dissolved *harīsa*. Arrange the slices of egg around the outside of the bowl or platter. Season the salad with salt, drizzle with olive oil, and serve at room temperature.

Makes 4 servings

ARUGULA
Eruca sativa Miller (syn. *E. vesicaria* subsp. *sativa*; *E. cappodocica* Reut.) (Cruciferae-Brassicaceae)
Also called rocket; ARABIC: *jirjīr* (*girgīr*,

EGYPTIAN ARABIC), *khūrrīdla*; FRENCH: *eruca, roquette*; ITALIAN: *eruca, rucola, ruca, ruchetta*; SPANISH: *roqueta, eruca*; TURKISH: *izgın* (local dialect)

PLANT CHARACTERISTICS AND VARIETIES

Arugula is a member of the mustard family. It is a sturdy leaf vegetable that resists cold well. The edible parts are the slightly bitter leaves, which are eaten raw in salads or cooked. Arugula is mostly used as a salad green and is most popular in France and Italy. In Egypt, *eruca sylvestris lutea*, called *girgīr* in Egyptian Arabic, is a variety of arugula that tastes like a cross between arugula and watercress. The greens are often eaten in Egypt as a salad with grilled meats or fish.

PLANT ORIGIN

The Russian botanist N. Vavilov suggested northwestern India, Tadzhikistan, Uzbekistan, western Tien Shan Province and southwestern Asia as the center of origin of arugula.

PLANT HISTORY

Arugula has a long history of cultivation in Europe and the Mediterranean as a salad vegetable and as a medicinal plant. The Arabic word for arugula, *jirjīr*, derives from the Hebrew. It is generally agreed that the vegetable mentioned in the Bible (2 Kings 4:39–40) as *oroth* is arugula. Both the Mishna and Talmud, Jewish holy writings that date from the first to fifth centuries A.D., mention arugula's uses as a food and medicine. The first-century Jewish historian Josephus mentioned arugula in his description of the hat of the high priest. The plant was cultivated by the Romans and thought by them to be an aphrodisiac. Both Galen and Dioscorides recommended eating arugula seeds to increase semen production. Ovid and Martial both referred to arugula in this context. Apicius used arugula in a sauce for boiled crane. Al-Qazwīnī in the thirteenth century also recommended eating the seeds with honey, saying that they would stimulate sexual desire. The early Roman Catholic Church knew of arugula's supposed erotic qualities and at one point banned its cultivation in monastic gardens. Albertus Magnus in the thirteenth century speaks of arugula being grown in gardens, as does Reullis in 1536, who calls it *roqueta*.

HOW TO GROW AND HARVEST

In the early spring and again in the late summer, sow arugula seeds densely in rows, and the plant will be ready to eat in about 40 days. It is not a good idea to plant arugula in the summer because the short nights force the plant to go to seed before enough vegetative growth occurs. The leaves are best picked when they are young. Harvest by shearing off the whole plants about 2 inches above the soil so that the central leaf buds can renew themselves.

HOW TO BUY, STORE, AND PREPARE FOR COOKING

Look for arugula with fresh, crisp leaves. Avoid any with wilted, yellowing, or blem-

Arugula

Even though the English word arugula comes from a Lombard dialect word for the plant, the leaves of arugula or rocket are used in Italy, and throughout the Mediterranean, in the same manner: exclusively for salads in traditional cuisine. Whether it appears in an Egyptian salad (page 313 of my book *A Mediterranean Feast*) served with some grilled fish, a *salade composée* from southern France, or a Spanish tapas, arugula is dressed simply with olive oil, vinegar, and maybe lemon juice. In the Arab world, Turkey, Greece, and North Africa, arugula is eaten much less frequently.

ished leaves. Store arugula in the refrigerator crisper drawer for up to 3 to 4 days.

RECIPE

Salad of Arugula, Chickpeas, and Miniature Tomatoes

This simple salad is inspired by the various *salades composées* that I have had throughout Languedoc and Provence. Not only is it pretty, but it is a very nice accompaniment to a rich-tasting meat, such as lamb. It also makes a light lunch salad.

1 bunch arugula, washed and dried well
1 cup cooked chickpeas, drained, rinsed, and
   drained again
1 cup ripe miniature tomatoes, stems removed
4 large fresh basil leaves, cut into thin strips
Kosher or sea salt and freshly ground black
   pepper to taste
Extra virgin olive oil to taste

Arrange the arugula on a serving platter or plate and scatter the chickpeas, tomatoes, and basil around. Season with salt and pepper and drizzle with olive oil.

Makes 2 servings

ARUM
Arum dioscoridis Sibth & Sm. (Aroideae)
FRENCH: *arum*; ITALIAN: *aro*; SPANISH: *aro, yaroi, sarillo*

PLANT CHARACTERISTICS AND VARIETIES
Arum is a tuberous perennial plant grown for its glossy, arrow-shaped leaves and showy spathe, a funnel-shaped bract surrounding the rodlike spadix that carries the tiny flowers. The bitter, burning taste of this plant's sap may have been responsible for its name, which derives from the Arabic word for "fire" (*ar*). The edible part is the root, which is eaten in the Levant, usually boiled.

PLANT HISTORY
Theophrastus mentioned that the roots and leaves of this plant were steeped in vinegar and eaten. One variety of arum, known as Italian arum (*A. italicum* Mill.), was mentioned by Dioscorides, who wrote that the roots of the plant were eaten raw or cooked. He also mentioned that in the Balearic Islands the root was mixed with honey and made into cakes.

ASPARAGUS
Asparagus officinalis L. (Liliaceae)
ARABIC: *ḥilyawn, sakkūm* (MAGHRIB); FRENCH: *asperge*; GREEK: *asparagkpho, sparaggia*; ITALIAN: *asparago*; SERBO-CROATIAN: *šparga*; SPANISH: *espárrago*; TURKISH: *kuşkonmaz*

PLANT CHARACTERISTICS AND VARIETIES
The edible part is the spear (or shoot), which is cooked. Asparagus is a perennial found growing in the wild in the Mediterranean, in sandy places, dry meadows, on volcanic hillsides, in woods, along riverbanks, and on limestone cliffs. As a cultivated vegetable, it takes up a lot of room in the garden. The young stalks or spears come up in the spring, and the tips are leaf buds that, if left unpicked, would grow into a fernlike plant. White asparagus is simply asparagus that has been blanched in the garden. In the Mediterranean a famous white asparagus is grown in Bassano in the northern Italian province of Veneto. In Sicily, the so-called *asparagi di giardino* (garden asparagus) is actually a kind of butcher's broom (*Ruscus hypoglossum*; see entry).

Asparagus is a large genus with about 300 species. *A. acutifolius* L. (wild asparagus) has a stronger flavor than garden-grown asparagus and is collected and eaten in Spain, southern Italy (called *sparie* in Bari), Sicily, and Turkey. The closely related genus *Smilax* also has edible young stems. *S. aspera* L. is eaten in Greece and Turkey. The young shoots of another variety, *A. verticillatus*, are eaten in the Peloponnesus region of Greece.

Chemicals in asparagus, S-methylmethionine and asparagusic acid, are converted in the body into several harmless compounds that contain sulfur, and these compounds seem to be responsible for producing a distinct ammonia-like odor that can be detected in the urine of nearly 40 percent of all asparagus eaters who have a gene that interacts with the sulfur compounds. The ability to detect this smell is genetic and possessed by an even smaller number of people, about 10 percent.

PLANT ORIGIN

Asparagus is found growing wild all over Europe; its native range or place of origin is not certain but is probably the Mediterranean.

PLANT HISTORY

The ancient Greeks ate asparagus, although some commentators have questioned whether they cultivated the plant or collected it in the wild. In any case, it seems that the plant in question was *A. acutifolius.* As for the Romans, we know that they both collected wild asparagus and cultivated it. Wild asparagus was called *corrudam, Libycum* (Libyan), or *orminum.* Pliny tells us in *Natural History* (Book XVI, 173 and Book XIX, 54, 145–150) that garden asparagus derives from wild asparagus, that the best plants were growing on the island of Nisita off the coast of Campania, and that cultivated asparagus was famous in the kitchen gardens (*hortorum*) of Ravenna. In the first century A.D., Pliny also mentions methods the Romans used for producing huge stems. Asparagus roots, he tells us, were used for making wine. Cato also describes asparagus, and the Roman poet Martial wrote about the quality of the asparagus from Ravenna as well. The Romans were well aware of the lifetime of an asparagus bed and how it needed to be replenished with soil nutrients. Columella mentions the cultivation of asparagus in the first century A.D., recommending that the young plants be transplanted from a seedbed. In the sixth century Anthimus wrote that both cultivated and wild asparagus were good to eat. In the Middle Ages asparagus seems to have receded in popularity in the Christian Mediterranean but not among the Arabs, who considered it an aphrodisiac, especially when covered with egg yolk. Later, asparagus was grown widely near Venice, where it was a profitable crop in the sixteenth century, and it is mentioned by the humanist philosopher Erasmus. By the seventeenth century its use was spreading. Through cultivation asparagus has come to have fleshier spears.

HOW TO GROW AND HARVEST

At least twelve asparagus plants are required to feed a family of four during the harvesting season. But there is a three-year gap between sowing and harvesting the crop, during which time the asparagus plants become established. Asparagus will be easy to grow in a well-made raised bed, about 6 inches above the surrounding soil, about 4 feet wide, and as long as you want. But it does not grow well in hot and humid climates. A planting bed can last twenty years, although the upkeep involves some work. The soil should be well drained, and there should be plenty of surface area above the plants to encourage thick, succulent spears. The soil should also be dug deeply with organic matter and phosphate added. Supplement the soil with some sand if it is not well drained. Sow the seeds in early spring, either indoors or in a seedbed outdoors, and watch the young plants carefully for the first year. Sandy, gritty soil should be spread on the surrounding soil. Apply a top dressing of fertilizer containing nitrogen and potash after planting. In the first year, it is desirable to build up a mat of heavy roots, which will support the growth of many thick spears during the following spring. If you want white asparagus, mound organic mulch over the asparagus beds. Harvest asparagus when the plants are 6 to 7 inches high (or 4 inches above ground and 3 inches below) and only an hour before they are needed for cooking so that they will taste their best.

HOW TO BUY, STORE, AND PREPARE FOR COOKING

Asparagus appears in the market year-round, since it is imported from South America in the winter months. It deteriorates quickly after it is picked, and needs to be kept cold. In supermarkets, asparagus should be sold refrigerated or standing upright in cold water. In farmer's markets, asparagus should be sold on ice or, at the very least, in shade away from sunlight. Look for asparagus spears that are firm with deep green shoots and slightly purple tips that are firmly closed and dense. Tips that appear to be separating are evidence of wilting from aging. Select asparagus spears that are firm over their entire length, not floppy or twisty or wrinkly. Asparagus with thick stalks are not any less good than thin-stalked asparagus, although most demanding cooks look for an ideal width of about half an inch at the thickest part of the stem.

Store asparagus that has been bought by untying it so the spears are relatively loose and can breathe. Then wrap the bottom portion of the spears in a wet paper towel and keep them in the crisper drawer of your refrigerator. Although asparagus spears will keep for up to a week, their taste diminishes with each passing day, so it is best to eat them the day you buy them.

Prepare asparagus for cooking by rinsing away any remaining sand or grit, then cut or snap off the tough bottom half inch of stalk and peel the skin off the bottom portion of the remaining stalk with a vegetable peeler. Prepare white asparagus in the same manner. Cook asparagus quickly until crisp-tender, not limp.

RECIPES

Spàresi con Vovo Sode
WHITE ASPARAGUS WITH HARD-BOILED EGG SAUCE

The famous tender white asparagus of Bassano in the Veneto province of Italy is used in a variety of preparations, although the recipes are all generally variations on the same theme. Asparagus is such a beloved

Asparagus

SOME OF MY FAVORITE ASPARAGUS RECIPES COME FROM ITALY, AS YOU CAN SEE IN THE RECIPES INCLUDED HERE. BUT ITALY IS not the only place where one can find excellent asparagus preparations. For some reason, one rarely finds asparagus eaten east of the Dalmatian coast (where people like to cook it and serve it with sour cream). Although it exists, and some people undoubtedly eat it, I don't recall ever seeing asparagus served in Greece, Turkey, and the Arab world, including North Africa. But in Spain, France, and Italy—that's another matter. In Spain, an Andalusian dish called *cazuela de esparragos a la Andaluza* is made with boiled asparagus dressed with a sauce made of breadcrumbs, garlic, saffron, and paprika. In the Haute-Provence of France, *tarte aux asperges*, a kind of quiche made with green or white asparagus and grated cheese and eggs, is very popular. In Italy, asparagus tips even find themselves atop pizza, usually along with the addition of anchovy fillets and Pecorino or Parmigiano cheese.

vegetable in Bassano that a proverb has been coined in its honor: *quando a Bassan vien primavera, se verze la cà e la sparesera* (when in Bassano arrives the springtime, if one opens the house it's '*spara*-time). The whiteness and thickness of this asparagus also figures in the obscene expression *sparagio*, referring to the virile member.

This preparation may be called *spàresi al butiro frito* (asparagus fried in butter), *spàresi lessi* (boiled asparagus), *spàresi con uova sode* (asparagus with hard-boiled eggs, see the next recipe), or simply *asparagi di Bassano.* Generally, the dish is boiled white asparagus

with some kind of egg sauce or scrambled eggs. I particularly like white asparagus with scrambled eggs. The key to this dish is fantastically fresh everything, including the eggs. Asparagus can also be cooked up with eggs cooked sunny-side up, in which case the dish is called *vovi l'ocio de bò*, or bull's-eye egg and asparagus.

The white asparagus of Bassano are thick stemmed and require longer cooking than the more common asparagus we're used to. The reason you cook asparagus in a tall and narrow pot is because the stems take longer to cook than the tips. Traditionally asparagus is eaten with the fingers or a special device used in Venetian restaurants for holding the spears. Knives and forks are not used. The dressing for a simple boiled asparagus is five parts olive oil to one part vinegar or lemon juice.

2 large fresh eggs, hard-boiled (see Note), or 4 beaten eggs, if you prefer to use scrambled eggs in this recipe

1 to 2 teaspoons freshly squeezed lemon juice, or to taste

2 tablespoons extra virgin olive oil, or to taste

2 salted anchovy fillets, rinsed and chopped

1 teaspoon chopped capers

Salt and freshly ground black pepper to taste

1 pound white asparagus, bottom halves scraped and tied together in a bunch to cook

1. Shell the hard-boiled eggs and divide them in half lengthwise. Remove the yolks and push them through a strainer. Chop the whites fine. In a small bowl, mix the yolks with the lemon juice, adding the lemon juice a teaspoon at a time. Begin adding the olive oil until the mixture is a little fluid. Mix the yolks and half the whites together with the anchovies and capers until they form a soft spreadable paste, and season with salt and pepper. Add more lemon juice if necessary.

2. Place the asparagus in lightly salted boiling water and cook until tender, about 8 minutes. Arrange the asparagus on a serving platter and cover with the sauce. Surround the platter with the remaining chopped egg white.

Makes 4 servings

VARIATIONS:

- *Fry the asparagus in butter.*
- *Sprinkle with vinegar and chopped fresh parsley and thyme leaves.*
- *Sprinkle with freshly grated Parmigiano-Reggiano cheese.*
- *Scramble the eggs in butter and place them on top of the asparagus.*

NOTE: To hard-boil eggs perfectly, slide room-temperature eggs into boiling water and remove them exactly 9 minutes later. Let them cool, then shell them.

Asparagi con Uova Soda
ASPARAGUS WITH HARD-BOILED EGGS

Even today the vegetable markets of Venice will remind you of a cityscape painting by Carpaccio. Thin asparagus grown in San Nicolò del Lido or the thick white asparagus of Bassano del Grappa can be found at the market and used in attractive preparations like this one. Whether you choose white or green asparagus depends on your mood and whom you are serving. This dish can be served hot or at room temperature. In this recipe the asparagus is boiled until soft, contrary to the instructions I have provided previously.

2 pounds thin asparagus
1 hard-boiled egg, shelled and chopped fine
1 tablespoon finely chopped fresh parsley leaves
Salt and freshly ground black pepper to taste
2 tablespoons unsalted butter, melted

1. Trim the lower third of the stem end or peel each asparagus. You should have about 1 pound of asparagus tips.

2. Place the asparagus tips in a large nonreactive skillet and cover with water. Turn the heat to high, bring the water to a boil, and cook the asparagus tips until they are soft, not crunchy, about 25 minutes. Drain and arrange them on an oval platter with all the tips pointing in one direction. Sprinkle the asparagus with the chopped egg and parsley and season with salt and pepper. Pour the butter over everything and serve immediately.

Makes 4 servings

VARIATION: Garnish with chopped salted anchovy fillets and whole capers if desired, along with the egg.

Insalata d'Asparagi alla Parmigiana
ASPARAGUS SALAD WITH PARMIGIANO CHEESE

In Italy one will often find this very pretty dish served as part of an antipasto. When composing the platter of vegetables, keep in mind that you want to present it artfully so that it looks as appetizing as possible. And make sure you use freshly grated

Parmigiano-Reggiano cheese and not grated cheese out of a can.

1½ pounds asparagus, bottoms trimmed and
stems peeled
4 cups ripped red leaf lettuce
1 cup yellow cherry tomatoes
3 tablespoons freshly grated Parmigiano-Reggiano
cheese
3 tablespoons extra virgin olive oil
Salt to taste

1. Place the asparagus in a large, wide nonreactive skillet, cover with water, and bring to a boil. Cook the asparagus until tender, 8 to 10 minutes. Remove from the heat, drain, and set aside.

2. Arrange the lettuce on an oval serving platter and, when the asparagus are cool, arrange them on top of the lettuce in the center of the platter with all the spears pointing in one direction. Scatter the tomatoes about, sprinkle the salad with the grated cheese, drizzle with the olive oil, and season with salt. Serve immediately.

Makes 4 servings

Asparagi con Lattuga alla Crema
ASPARAGUS AND LETTUCE IN CREAM SAUCE

In the spring, when asparagus spears push through the soil, Mediterranean cooks look forward to preparing a variety of recipes. This is an old-style one from northern Italy that I collected long ago and neglected to write down where it came from. It might seem a bit strange, but it's not. Save the stems of the romaine lettuce to make the Tunisian romaine lettuce salad on page 213.

2 pounds asparagus, bottoms trimmed

3 tablespoons unsalted butter

1 small onion, thinly sliced

½ cup chopped lean cooked ham

1 head romaine lettuce (about 2 pounds), stems, heart, and innermost leaves removed

¼ cup chicken broth

Salt and freshly ground black pepper to taste

Pinch of freshly grated nutmeg

¾ cup heavy cream

1. Preheat the oven to 400°F. Peel the bottoms of the remaining stem on the asparagus. Boil or steam the asparagus until crisp-tender, about 10 minutes. Drain and keep warm.

2. In a large skillet, melt the butter over medium-high heat and cook the onion until yellow, about 5 minutes, stirring occasionally. Add the ham and lettuce leaves, cover, and cook until the lettuce has wilted, about 4 minutes. Pour in the broth and cook, uncovered, until all the liquid is nearly evaporated, 8 to 9 minutes. Season with salt, pepper, and nutmeg. Remove the skillet from the heat and stir in the cream.

3. Arrange the asparagus in a baking dish with the spears pointing in one direction. Pour the lettuce sauce over the asparagus, spreading the pieces of ham and onion about evenly, and bake until bubbling, about 15 minutes. Serve immediately.

Makes 4 servings

Espárragos a la Parilla
GRILLED ASPARAGUS

Grilled asparagus is a favorite in the rural areas of Andalusia, where wild asparagus grows in the wheat fields. It makes sense, since you will have a grill going, to serve these asparagus with some simple grilled meat such as pork chops or lamb chops. The variation for this recipe is quite good and is adapted from Elisabeth Luard's *The Flavors of Andalucia.*

1 ½ pounds asparagus, bottoms trimmed and stems peeled

Extra virgin olive oil

Salt to taste

FOR THE GREEN SAUCE (OPTIONAL):

Leaves from 8 parsley sprigs

Leaves from 2 tarragon sprigs

3 scallions, finely chopped

2 garlic cloves, chopped

1 teaspoon Dijon mustard

½ teaspoon freshly ground black pepper

6 tablespoons extra virgin olive oil

1 tablespoon white wine vinegar

Prepare a hot charcoal fire or preheat a gas grill for 15 minutes on high. Brush the asparagus with olive oil and salt lightly. Place asparagus on the grill and cook until it blisters black on both sides, 8 to 10 minutes in all, turning with tongs. Remove to an oval serving dish and serve hot or at room temperature.

Makes 4 to 6 servings

VARIATION: To make a green herb sauce, place the ingredients listed in a blender and process until smooth, 2 to 3 minutes. Pour over the asparagus and serve.

ASPARAGUS BEAN

Vigna unguiculata L. Walp. *subsp. sesquipedalis* (L.) Fruw. (Fabaceae-Leguminosae)

Also known as yard-long bean, garter-bean, Chinese long bean, dow guak, snake bean, long horn bean; FRENCH: *haricot asperge, haricot kilomètre, dolique asperge;* ITALIAN: *fagiolini di Sant'Anna, fagiolo asparagio, fagiolo lungo un metro, fagiolino asparago, fagioletto americano;* SPANISH: *judía espárrago, judía chinas, dólico espárrago, poroto metro, chancha por metro*

PLANT CHARACTERISTICS AND VARIETIES

This plant is a relative of the southern cowpea. It is an annual climbing herbaceous plant that grows to 12 feet high and requires poles for support. The flowers are large violet blue. Although asparagus bean is mostly cultivated in southwest Asia where the pods can grow to 3 feet in length, it is associated with Mediterranean cooking. The edible parts are the seeds, eaten cooked in their immature pods.

PLANT ORIGIN

N. Vavilov identified the mountains of central and western China and adjacent areas as the place of origin of the asparagus bean.

PLANT HISTORY

The asparagus bean was first described in 1763 by Linnaeus, who identified it as a New World plant. This notion is no longer accepted. The name *asparagus bean* comes from the use of the very long green pods as a vegetable. In Naples the plant is sometimes called *faiolo e maccarone,* beans and macaroni, to convey the idea that the asparagus pod is long like uncut macaroni with the beans inside the pods.

HOW TO GROW AND HARVEST

If you want to try asparagus beans, you may have to grow your own. They require a long, hot growing season, with at least 75 days of warmth, and pole supports at least 8 feet high. Harvest the beans when they are about a foot long and eat them as you would snap beans. At the end of the season, any remaining pods can be dried or frozen for storage.

HOW TO BUY, STORE, AND PREPARE FOR COOKING

Asparagus beans are somewhat hard to find. I usually see them in farmers' markets or in supermarkets where the more unusual pro-

Asparagus Bean

THESE EXTREMELY LONG, PODDED BEANS ARE NOT VERY COMMON IN THE MEDITERRANEAN IN TERMS OF THEIR APPEARANCE IN cookbook recipes. Besides the recipe included here, I've never seen how other Mediterranean cuisines cook asparagus bean, but I imagine it is very similar to how they cook green beans.

duce is shelved. It seems that these beans are used in Chinese cooking more than in Mediterranean, so Chinese markets may have them, too.

Asparagus beans might look slightly wrinkled, but that is normal. Store these beans in the refrigerator for no more than a week.

RECIPE

Fagiolini di Sant'Anna
ASPARAGUS BEANS WITH TOMATOES

It is said that these long, thin string beans were first grown in Tuscany, the town of Pescia being well known for them. I don't make these beans too often, but when I do, I serve them as an antipasto. Because asparagus beans are so long and most people are unfamiliar with them, they become a topic of conversation.

2 tablespoons extra virgin olive oil
2 garlic cloves, peeled and lightly crushed
1½ pounds ripe tomatoes, peeled, seeded, and chopped
1 pound asparagus beans
1 cup vegetable broth or water
Salt and freshly ground black pepper to taste

Put all the ingredients in a large skillet. Cover, turn the heat to medium, and cook until the beans are bright green and malleable, about 8 minutes. Reduce the heat to low and cook until the beans are darker and have collapsed slightly and the tomatoes are saucy, about 15 minutes. Serve hot or at room temperature.

Makes 4 servings

ASPHODEL
Aspholedius ramosus L. *(Asphodeline lutea)*
(Liliaceae)
FRENCH: *asphodele;* GREEK: *asphuxia;* ITALIAN:
asfodelo; APULIAN DIALECT: *avuzze, aiu crestu,
cipuddazzu, laùzzu;* SPANISH: *asfodelo, gamón*

PLANT CHARACTERISTICS AND VARIETIES
Asphodel is a perennial herb in the lily family.
It is found covering large tracts of land in the
Apulia region of southern Italy; it was once
abundant in Sicily too, where it is a wild edible green. Asphodel is usually served in salads,
but it is also prepared in Greece as a *horta,*
boiled greens dressed with olive oil and lemon
juice.

PLANT ORIGIN
Asphodel is thought to originate in the
Mediterranean and Caucasus.

PLANT HISTORY
Asphodel was fabled to have grown in the
Elysian fields of the Greek paradise, and
therefore the ancients favored this herb as a
token to place on the tombs of friends.
Pythagoras mentions asphodel as a root that is
eaten. Pliny says the roots were roasted under
embers and eaten with salt and oil, and that
asphodel root was considered a delicacy when
mashed with figs.

ATHAMANTA MATTHIOLI WULF. (SYN. *A. TURBITH* (L.) BROT.) (UMBELLIFERAE)

PLANT CHARACTERISTICS AND VARIETIES
The roots of this carrot family plant are eaten
in Spain, while the seeds of a cousin, *A. cretenis,*
are used to flavor liqueurs. The plant also
ranges from northern Italy to Croatia.

ATHAMANTA SICULA L. (SYN. *TINGUARRA SICULA* BENTH. & HOOK.) (UMBELLIFERAE)

PLANT CHARACTERISTICS AND VARIETIES
This perennial with 3 to 4 pinnate leaves
grows to 3½ feet. The celery-like root is eaten
in Sicily.

PLANT ORIGIN
The plant is native to the Mediterranean,
probably Sicily or southern Italy.

BABY'S BREATH
Gypsophila paniculata L. (Caryophyllaceae)

PLANT CHARACTERISTICS AND VARIETIES
Baby's breath is an herbaceous plant of the
pink family with many small white or rose-
colored flowers. The edible part is the root,
which is used in Lebanon in preparing *natīf,* a
white vegetable foam that is sometimes used

as a dip for the Arab cookies called *mamūl.*
Two other plants can also be used to create
this "foam"—the dried bark of *Quillaja
saponaria,* a tree native to the Americas, and the
dried root of soapwort *(Saponaria officinalis).*

BARBARY-GUM

Acacia gummifera Willd. (Fabaceae-
Leguminosae)
FRENCH: *gomme arabique;* SPANISH: *guacia,
goma arábiga*

PLANT CHARACTERISTICS AND VARIETIES
Acacia is the name of various plants from
which gum arabic derives. Gum arabic is a
water-soluble gum used in manufacturing ink,
adhesives, pharmaceuticals, and confections.
As a food, gum Arabic from the barbary-gum
plant is mostly consumed in North Africa by
desert dwellers. There are a number of varieties of gum arabic, including babool-bark or
gum arabic tree *(A. arabica),* which is mixed
with sesame seeds and eaten in the desert
regions of the Maghrib. In Libya, *A. ehrenber-
giana* also yields a gum arabic eaten by Bedouin
tribes. *Acacia seyal* produces a gum arabic eaten
by the Arabs of Upper Egypt.

PLANT ORIGIN
Barbary-gum is native to Africa.

BARD VETCH

Vicia monantha Retz. (Fabaceae-
Leguminosae)
Also called Auvergne lentil, one-flowered
tare

PLANT CHARACTERISTICS AND VARIETIES
Bard vetch is a herbaceous plant with compound leaves and a variety of flower colors.
The edible parts are the thick and floury
seeds. The Bedouin of the Negev and Sinai
eat the plant in soups.

BEAN

Phaseolus vulgaris L. (Fabaceae-
Leguminosae)
Also called green bean, common bean,
snap bean, pole bean, French bean, string
bean, kidney bean, haricot bean, yellow
wax bean, and so forth; ARABIC: *lūbiyā,
lūbyā', lūbya, faṣūliyya;* FRENCH: *haricot vert,
haricot commun, phaséole;* GREEK: *fasolakia
freska, phasiolos, kuamos;* ITALIAN: *fagiolino,
fagiolo;* SERBO-CROATIAN: *mahune;* SPANISH:
judia vert, judia común, faséolo; TURKISH: *taze
fasulye*

PLANT CHARACTERISTICS AND VARIETIES
The bean plant is an erect bush or climbing
plant. The edible parts are the cooked immature pods and seeds. They are a popular food
in every country of the Mediterranean.

Phaseolus is a New World plant, and all Old World *phaseolus* are now classified to *vigna*. There are four major cultivated species: *P. vulgaris*, *P. coccineus* (scarlet runner bean, page 288), *P. lunatus* (lima or sieva bean, page 214), and *P. acutifolius* var. *latifolius* (tepary bean). A fifth species, *P. polyanthus*, is cultivated in the New World, but it is not found in Mediterranean cultivation. Today there are many cultivars of green beans, more than five hundred, with variations in pod, texture, or seed color, for example, yellow wax beans. Seed Savers Exchange, an international network of seed collections based in Iowa, has over four thousand varieties of beans in its collection, and the seed savers are still counting. The best-known dried, or horticultural, beans, such as kidney beans, pinto beans, black beans, and navy beans, are members of this species. So, too, are most of the familiar bean varieties such as great northern, flageolet, haricots verts, cannellini, borlotti, Jacob's Cattle, Kentucky Wonder, Blue Lake, and all the rest.

Horticultural beans are a class of beans grown specifically to be shelled when their seeds are mature. They usually have maroon-streaked pods, and their seeds are two-colored. Commercially, beans are either shell beans or pod beans. The pod beans are sold and eaten while still unripe and are called string beans, green beans, snap beans, or pole beans. String beans have, over the years, been cultivated so that they will be "stringless"; that is, so they do not have the fibrous inedible string along the pod seam. Shell beans are either low bushy plants that don't need support or climbing (pole) beans that do require support.

PLANT ORIGIN

The green bean originated in Central and South America. It was domesticated in ancient times, but researchers can't say exactly where, although seeds of cultivated forms were found in deposits from Callejon de Huaylas, Peru, with a radiocarbon dating of 7680 B.P. and from 7000 B.P. in Tehuacán, Mexico, although atomic mass spectrometry dating contests these dates by measuring the age as only 2,285 ± 60 B.P.

PLANT HISTORY

The green bean was introduced to the Mediterranean upon the return of Columbus from his second voyage to the New World in 1493. In Columbus's diary from November 4, 1492, he describes lands in Cuba planted with *faxones* and *fabas* "different from ours." Later he encountered *fexoes* and *habas* that were different from the ones he knew from Spain. *Faxones* was probably the cowpea (see entry) and *fabas* and *habas* was the fava bean (see entry). The beans Columbus found were undoubtedly what is now designated *P. vulgaris*. The earliest depiction of a New World bean in Europe is thought to be the woodcut in the herbal published by Leonhart Fuchs in 1543. The bean spread into the eastern Mediterranean, and by the seventeenth century it was cultivated everywhere in Italy, Greece, and Turkey. In a 1988 study of the phaseolin structure of the common bean, researchers traced the beans now grown in the western Mediterranean to ones originating in the Andes. The *phaselus* and *phaseolus* beans mentioned by the Roman authors Virgil and Columella are now believed to be another leguminous plant in the genus *Dolichus*, that is, the hyacinth bean (page 186).

HOW TO GROW AND HARVEST

Beans are quick-growing annuals. Since they were originally tropical plants, they enjoy warm soil in which to germinate. The seeds are usually sown in rows or in groups of 5 about 1½ feet apart. There are bush varieties and pole varieties, which require support; both plants can be harvested in 45 to 60 days. The plants produce heavy yields when picked regularly and when well watered. Plant seeds of the bush varieties of green beans about 2 inches apart in rows about 2 feet apart. Thin the seedlings to 3 inches apart after they start growing. Plant 3 seeds of the pole variety of beans around the pole and thin the seedlings to the strongest of the three. Twist the young runners around the pole. Harvest the beans when they are young and tender by picking them regularly, and the plant will continue to produce. Harvest shell beans once the pods are large but before the beans inside have dried.

HOW TO BUY, STORE, AND PREPARE FOR COOKING

Shell beans can be used both as fresh beans and as dried beans. For dried beans, it is best to let the beans dry on the plant rather than picking the beans and leaving them in the sun. Traditionally, cooks have soaked dried beans for anywhere from one hour to overnight, but soaking is not necessary.

Some green bean pods have a tough and inedible fiber or string along the suture of the pod. These strings must be removed before cooking, although the green beans bought in a supermarket, as I said before, usually will not have these strings. Buy green beans at the supermarket or farmers' market from bins of loose beans, choosing beans of equal size. The beans should feel crisp and be completely free of any blemishes. They should be relatively straight and about ¼ inch thick. They should snap when broken. Some varieties, such as haricots verts, will not snap so distinctly. Haricots verts, or filet beans, are green beans that are bred so the seeds develop more slowly than usual, giving the pods a better flavor and texture.

Store green beans in a plastic bag in the refrigerator for up to 5 days. Prepare green beans for cooking by snapping off both ends and pulling off the attached string, if there is any.

Most, if not all, dried shell beans bought by the consumer will be bought in the supermarket, sold in plastic bags or, occasionally, from bins in whole or natural food stores.

Beans

CAN THERE BE ANY ARGUMENT THAT THE TWO GREATEST VEGE-
TABLE INTRODUCTIONS TO THE MEDITERRANEAN FROM THE NEW
World were beans (*P. vulgarus*) and tomatoes? Well, maybe potatoes too. Beans are eaten
in every Mediterranean country. It was hard to choose the thirteen Mediterranean
recipes included here because, left to my own devices, I would offer another fifty delicious ways of preparing beans. In Andalusia, home cooks make *berza* (which means
"cabbage," but is also a word used by Andalusians to mean any green vegetable), a vegetable stew made with dry white beans, chickpeas, salt pork, potatoes, pumpkin, Swiss
chard, fresh green beans, chorizo, and blood sausage. In Provence, green beans are flavored with a unique lemon-flavored garlicky *aioli* (see page 44), and dry white beans
are the foundation in Languedoc for the famous cassoulet. In Greece, Turkey, and the
Arab world, fresh green beans are most often cooked in the manner described in the
fasolakia yiahni recipe in this section. The Turks might cook the beans in olive oil with
green peppers, while the Arabs might serve green beans with an olive oil and lemon
dressing or with yogurt. In North Africa, green beans often find their way into various vegetable ragouts served with meat or perhaps couscous.

Dried beans also appear in every Mediterranean cuisine. In North Africa, because
they store so well in the hot and arid climate, dried beans are usually featured in long-
simmering stews, although dried fava beans are probably more popular. In the eastern
Arab world, chickpeas and fava beans are more popular than white or red beans, but
the dried white or red beans do appear in dishes such as *yakhnat al-faṣ ūliyya*, a white
or red bean stew flavored with lots of fresh coriander, garlic, and olive oil. Dried beans
might also appear in salads dressed with olive oil and lemon juice and garnished with
black olives, hard-boiled eggs, and tomatoes. In Provence and Languedoc, dried beans
are usually white haricot, and very often these beans are found cooked with sausages
or duck. But in Corsica, dried red kidney beans are used not only in ragouts but in a
lasagne called *lasagne gratinées*, made with chopped beef cooked with onions, garlic, and
tomato, layered with béchamel sauce and tomato sauce, and baked with a delicious
cheese combination of *brocciu sec* (a kind of dried ricotta) and Gruyère. In Spain, dried
beans once again appear in stews for the most part, usually with meats, although the

recao de Binéfar from the province of Aragon is cooked with rice and potatoes and flavored with lots of garlic, bay leaves, onion, paprika (which gives the dish its red tinge), and olive oil. The province of Valencia also contributes a famous bean dish known as *Moros e Cristianos*, Moors and Christians, a dish of black beans (the swarthy Moors) and rice (the white Christians) that is cooked in a broth flavored with herbs, bacon, onions, and olive oil. Beans are popular in the Balkans. In Croatia one finds the obviously Italian-influenced *pašta i fažol*, pasta and beans, and the red kidney bean soup flavored with ham and paprika called *juha od crvenog graha*.

These beans usually have been picked over for stones and grit by the packager, but it is always wise to give them the once-over and rinse them before cooking.

RECIPES

Fresh Beans

Fagiolini alla Genovese
GENOESE-STYLE GREEN BEANS

This recipe from the great port city of Genoa in the region of Liguria seems so pedestrian given its provenance. Yet the green beans are cooked to an inviting green and tossed with an aromatizing mixture of parsley and anchovies, transforming a humble dish into a regal one. If you are able to find or grow a snap bean cultivar called Blue Lake, you will find the final preparation all the more enjoyable.

1 pound green beans, ends trimmed
3 tablespoons extra virgin olive oil
2 tablespoons unsalted butter
¼ cup finely chopped fresh parsley leaves
1 small garlic clove, chopped fine
4 salted anchovy fillets, rinsed
Salt and freshly ground black pepper to taste
Croutons fried in butter (optional)

1. Bring a pot of water to a rolling boil and blanch the green beans for 3 minutes. Drain and plunge them in ice water or place them under cold running water to stop them from cooking.

2. Bring another pot of water to a vigorous boil, add the green beans, and cook them at a boil until tender, 7 to 8 minutes. Drain well.

3. Heat the olive oil and butter with the parsley, garlic, and anchovies in a large skillet over medium-high heat, mashing the anchovies with a fork. Once the anchovies disintegrate, in 2 to 3 minutes, add the green beans, season with salt and pepper, and cook until the beans

are coated with the sauce and hot, about 3 minutes, tossing frequently.

4. Serve immediately garnished with the croutons, if you wish.

Makes 4 servings

Fagiolini alla Fiorentina
FLORENCE-STYLE GREEN BEANS

A Tuscan dish, and a very easy method of preparing green beans, *Fagiolini alla Fiorentina* has a complex flavor and tastes great even as leftovers the next day. The crushed fennel seeds provide an unexpected zing that makes these beans a fine accompaniment to roast chicken or braised rabbit.

2 tablespoons extra virgin olive oil
1 small onion, chopped
2 garlic cloves, sliced
1 pound ripe tomatoes, peeled, seeded, and chopped
¼ teaspoon fennel seeds
1 pound green beans, ends trimmed
½ cup water

Heat the olive oil over medium-high heat in a large skillet and cook the onion and garlic until the onion turns translucent, about 5 minutes, stirring so the garlic doesn't burn. Add the tomatoes and fennel seeds and cook until the tomatoes are thick and saucy, about 15 minutes, stirring occasionally. Add the green beans and water, stir, reduce the heat to

medium-low, and cook until the beans are tender, 20 to 30 minutes.

Makes 4 servings

Haricots Verts à "l'Eigressado"
GREEN BEANS IN AIOLI

A ioli is a popular garlicky mayonnaise from Valencia (where it is called *allioli*) to the French-Italian border. It is used with fish, salads, raw foods as well as in this recipe. Although serving green beans, and many other vegetables, crunchy and nearly raw is popular these days, traditionally vegetables should be cooked but not overcooked. This recipe calls for cooking the beans until the crunchiness is barely detectable. Serve at room temperature and use as much or as little of the aioli as you think necessary, although you might want to start off with the amount I recommend here. The yield for the aioli is far more than you will need for this recipe, but it is nice to have some aioli around as an all-purpose condiment for a variety of foods. The aioli should be prepared at least 2 hours before you cook the beans.

FOR THE AIOLI:
1 large egg and 1 large egg yolk
16 garlic cloves (1 head garlic), pounded until mushy in a mortar with 1½ teaspoons salt
2 cups extra virgin olive oil

½ teaspoon freshly ground white pepper
Freshly squeezed juice from 2 lemons
2 teaspoons water

2 pounds green beans, ends trimmed

1. Place the whole egg and egg yolk in a food processor along with the mashed garlic. Run the machine for 30 seconds, then drizzle in the olive oil in a slow, very thin stream. Add the white pepper, lemon juice, and water and continue to run the machine for a few more seconds. Transfer the aioli to a container or bowl and refrigerate it for 2 hours, covered with plastic wrap, before using.

2. When you are ready to eat, plunge the green beans in rapidly boiling lightly salted water to blanch them for 3 minutes. Drain and plunge the beans into ice water or cool them under cold running water to stop them from cooking. Bring another pot of lightly salted water to a boil and cook the green beans until they are soft but with a very slight crunch, 6 to 7 minutes. Drain well, leave at room temperature, then, when it is time to serve, toss them with ½ cup of the aioli.

Makes 6 servings

Fasolakia Yiahni
FRESH GREEN BEAN STEW

The Greeks, as well as the Turks, are quite fond of green vegetables cooked in lots of olive oil, a style of cooking called *ladera* in Greek. In this preparation I've cut down the amount of olive oil by about half of what would be typical. You wouldn't know it once you taste this excellent stew.

2 pounds green beans, ends trimmed, cut into
   2-inch lengths
⅔ cup extra virgin olive oil
10 scallions, chopped
2 garlic cloves, chopped
1 pound ripe tomatoes, peeled, seeded, and chopped
3 tablespoons finely chopped fresh parsley leaves
1 teaspoon sugar
Salt and freshly ground black pepper to taste

1. Bring a large saucepan of water to a rolling boil and blanch the green beans for 2 to 3 minutes. Drain the beans, reserving the water in the saucepan, and plunge the beans into ice water or pass them under cold running water to stop them from cooking. Return the saucepan of water to a boil, add the green beans, and cook them until they're soft, 8 to 10 minutes. Drain and set aside.

2. Heat the olive oil in a large skillet over medium-high heat and cook the scallions and garlic until wilted and soft, 3 to 5 minutes, stirring so the garlic doesn't burn. Add the tomatoes, parsley, and sugar, season with salt and pepper, and cook until the tomatoes melt into the sauce, 6 to 8 minutes. Add the green beans, cook until heated through, and turn the heat off. Let the green beans come to room temperature in the skillet. Transfer to a serving platter and serve.

Makes 4 servings

Fasolakia me Lathi
GREEN BEANS IN OLIVE OIL

If you have ever spent an extended amount of time in Greece, you will appreciate how people eat an enormous amount of vegetables and olive oil in delicious preparations. This recipe is another version of the previous one. It is also served in the same manner: at room temperature.

1 pound green beans, ends trimmed, sliced
   diagonally into 2-inch pieces
1 medium onion, chopped
⅓ cup extra virgin olive oil
1½ cups crushed or finely chopped tomatoes
1 to 2 cups water (use the greater amount if the
   green beans are older)
¼ cup finely chopped fresh parsley leaves
½ teaspoon dried summer savory
Salt and freshly ground black pepper to taste
⅛ teaspoon freshly ground cumin seeds

1. Bring a large saucepan of water to a boil and blanch the green beans for 4 minutes. Drain them and plunge them into ice water or pass them under cold running water to stop them from cooking. Drain and set aside.

2. In a casserole, preferably earthenware, spread the chopped onion over the bottom, then top with the green beans. Drizzle the olive oil over the beans, and turn the heat to medium. Once the onions and beans start to sizzle, cook them for 2 minutes, then add the tomatoes, water, parsley, and summer savory and season with salt and pepper. Cook the beans until they are tender, about 30 minutes for newer beans, 1 hour for older beans. Taste to check for doneness. The beans should not have any bite to them.

3. Stir in the cumin. When the water has evaporated and the sauce is thick, remove the casserole from the heat. Transfer the beans to a serving platter and let them come to room temperature before serving.

Makes 4 servings

Fasolakia Salata
GREEN BEAN SALAD

This Greek green bean salad flavored with fresh dill is typically served at room temperature. It is an excellent summer preparation and makes a nice accompaniment to grilled beef or veal or shrimp. You can also serve it as part of a *meze* table. Use a minimal amount of feta cheese.

1 pound green beans, ends trimmed
2 tablespoons extra virgin olive oil
2 tablespoons freshly squeezed lemon juice
1 garlic clove, chopped very fine
1 tablespoon chopped fresh dill
Salt and freshly ground black pepper to taste
Imported Greek or Bulgarian feta cheese
   (optional), crumbled

1. Bring a large saucepan of water to a boil and blanch the green beans for 5 minutes. Drain the beans and plunge them into ice water or place them under cold running water

to stop them from cooking. Bring another large saucepan of water to a boil, add the green beans, and cook them at a boil until tender, not crunchy, 12 to 15 minutes. Drain well.

2. Whisk the olive oil, lemon juice, garlic, dill, and salt and pepper together. Arrange the green beans on a serving platter and pour the dressing over them. Garnish the platter with feta cheese if desired.

Makes 4 servings

Lūbya bi'l-Rummān
GREEN BEANS WITH POMEGRANATE

This recipe is from Aleppo in Syria, where cooks use a lot of pomegranate molasses. I've adapted this dish from one described to me by Lubaba al-Daker, a young student from Damascus whose aunt lives in Aleppo and is quite a good cook. Typically the recipe can also be made with lamb, in which case, you would want to serve it with rice pilaf.

6 tablespoons extra virgin olive oil, divided
1 medium onion, chopped
1 tablespoon bahārāt *(page 21)*
1 teaspoon ground cinnamon
One 6-ounce can tomato paste
4 cups water
2 pounds fresh green beans, ends trimmed
Salt and freshly ground black pepper to taste
8 large garlic cloves, peeled
½ cup finely chopped fresh coriander leaves

2½ tablespoons pomegranate molasses
2 tablespoons freshly squeezed lemon juice

1. In a casserole, preferably earthenware, heat 3 tablespoons of the olive oil over medium-high heat and cook the onion, *bahārāt*, and cinnamon and cook until the onion is soft, 5 to 6 minutes, stirring occasionally. Dissolve the tomato paste in the water.

2. Reduce the heat to low, add the green beans and diluted tomato paste, and season with salt and pepper. Cover the casserole and cook the beans for 45 minutes. Uncover and cook until the green beans are tender (not crunchy), another 30 to 45 minutes, tasting a green bean to see if it is done.

3. Heat the remaining 3 tablespoons of olive oil in a small skillet over medium-high heat and cook the garlic and coriander together for 1 to 2 minutes, stirring constantly and paying close attention to any possible acrid smell that would indicate that the garlic is burning. Stir the garlic and coriander into the bean stew. Add the pomegranate molasses and lemon juice, stir to mix well, and cook for 10 minutes. Serve immediately.

Makes 4 servings

Mashurka me Vaj

YELLOW WAX BEANS WITH PAPRIKA

This pleasant and colorful recipe for yellow beans is from Albania. It's delicious served hot or at room temperature, perhaps with some veal or lamb.

¼ cup extra virgin olive oil
1 medium onion, chopped
1 tablespoon tomato paste
2 teaspoons paprika
1 pound yellow wax beans, ends trimmed
2 teaspoons finely chopped fresh mint leaves
2 teaspoons finely chopped fresh parsley leaves
Salt to taste
1 cup water

Heat the olive oil in a casserole over medium-high heat and cook the onion until translucent, about 5 minutes, stirring occasionally. Add the tomato paste, paprika, and wax beans. Stir and add the mint and parsley. Season with salt. Pour in the water and bring to a boil. Reduce the heat to low, cover, and simmer until tender, about 30 minutes. Serve hot or, preferably, at room temperature.

Makes 4 servings

Dried Beans

Fasoi Bogonadi

WHITE BEANS IN TOMATO SAUCE

Fasoi bogonadi is Piedmontese dialect meaning something like "reboiled beans." This dish is simple to make and a pleasing accompaniment to braised duck or roast chicken.

1 cup (about ½ pound) dried white beans, picked over and rinsed
2 tablespoons extra virgin olive oil
2 tablespoons tomato paste
½ cup water
6 tablespoons finely chopped fresh parsley leaves
1 garlic clove, finely chopped
Salt and freshly ground black pepper to taste

1. Place the beans in a medium saucepan with cold unsalted water to barely cover and bring to a boil. Cook until the beans are soft and tender but not falling apart, 1¼ to 1½ hours. Drain.

2. Heat the olive oil in a large skillet over medium-high heat and add the tomato paste, ½ cup water, parsley, and garlic. Once the pot begins to boil, add salt and pepper to taste. Add the drained beans, mix well, reduce the heat to very low, cover, and cook until the ingredients are well blended, about 10 minutes. Serve immediately.

Makes 4 servings

Fagioli Stufati
STEWED BEANS WITH CABBAGE STRIPS

This Sardinian recipe is pretty, smells great, and tastes even better. I think it is marvelous with grilled pork or lamb chops. It's also a very nice preparation to serve at room temperature. Cabbage was eaten frequently in Sardinia during the Middle Ages, and it is still a favorite vegetable among the islanders. Cannellini beans are found in Italian markets; use any dried white bean in its place.

1 cup (about ½ pound) dried white cannellini beans, picked over and rinsed
1 tablespoon extra virgin olive oil
1 large garlic clove, chopped fine
1 small onion, chopped fine
¼ pound pancetta, chopped
¼ cup finely chopped fresh parsley leaves
¾ pound Savoy cabbage leaves, sliced
¼ pound ripe tomatoes, peeled, seeded, and chopped
Salt and freshly ground black pepper to taste

1. Place the beans in a medium saucepan and cover them by several inches with cold water. Bring the water to a boil and cook the beans until they're still hard, but edible, about 25 minutes. Drain, saving the water.
2. In a large casserole, preferably earthenware, heat the olive oil over medium-high heat, add the garlic, onion, pancetta, and parsley and cook until the onion is translucent and the pancetta is somewhat crispy, about 10 minutes, stirring so the garlic doesn't burn.
3. Add the drained white beans, cabbage, and tomatoes. Pour in 1½ cups of the bean cooking water, season the beans with salt and pepper, and cook them over low heat until they are tender and the cabbage is soft, about 2 hours. If the pan is drying out, add a few more tablespoons of the remaining bean cooking water.

Makes 6 servings

La Brandade de Haricots
WHIPPED HARICOT BEAN PUREE

In southern France, the famous *brandade de morue*, salt cod whipped to a cream, that is usually associated with Nîmes is the inspiration for this "poor man's" *brandade* made with beans. In Marseilles, people like to sprinkle *poutarge*, that is *bottarga*, the Italian word, salted and pressed dried tuna roe, on top and eat the puree with toast points. *Bottarga* is still hard to find in this country, but an Italian market may carry small samples. In place of *bottarga* you can use some cut-up anchovy fillets, or leave both out entirely.

1 cup (about ½ pound) dried haricot beans,
    picked over and rinsed
6 tablespoons extra virgin olive oil
1 ¼ cups whole milk
2 tablespoons freshly squeezed lemon juice
1 ¼ teaspoons salt
¾ teaspoon finely ground white pepper
1 tablespoon freshly grated bottarga or 4 salted
    anchovy fillets, rinsed and chopped (optional)

1. Place the beans in a medium saucepan and cover with water by 4 inches. Turn the heat to high and cook at a boil until the beans are very tender, about 1 hour. Drain, saving ½ cup of the cooking liquid.

2. Place the drained beans in a food processor and process for 15 seconds. Slowly pour in the olive oil and milk in a slow, steady stream while the processor is running, as if you were making mayonnaise. Stir in the lemon juice. The consistency should be like that of hummus. Add the salt and white pepper. Check the consistency and add ¼ cup of the cooking liquid or more if necessary to make the mixture a little thinner than hummus. Correct the seasoning. Stir in most of the *bottarga* or chopped anchovies, reserving some for garnish. Transfer the mixture to a serving platter or shallow bowl and sprinkle the top with a little *bottarga*.

Makes 3 cups

Estouffat de Haricots Blancs
ÉTOUFFÉE OF WHITE BEANS FROM CARCASSONNE

Étouffée means "smothered," and this is a style of slow cooking in a tightly covered casserole with very little liquid or fat. In the southern French province of Languedoc, several foods seem so exalted that I forever think of them together—beans, duck, and garlic. These, of course, are some of the classic ingredients of cassoulet. In this preparation from Carcassonne, a medieval walled city between the capital of Languedoc, Toulouse, and the Mediterranean coast, small white beans are flavored with salt pork, duck fat, tomatoes, and garlic, creating a substantial and delicious dish that is very nice with roast sausages, duck, goose, or lamb.

½ pound salt pork, diced
2 cups (about 1 pound) small dried white beans,
    picked over and rinsed
2 teaspoons salt
¼ cup goose or duck fat
2 medium onions, sliced thin
1 pound ripe tomatoes, peeled, seeded, and
    chopped
2 large garlic cloves, peeled and crushed
Salt and freshly ground black pepper to taste

1. Bring a medium saucepan of water to a boil and blanch the salt pork for 5 minutes. Drain it and set it aside. Place the beans in a large saucepan, cover them with cold water by sev-

eral inches, add the salt, and bring the pot to a boil. Reduce the heat to medium-high and cook the beans until they are almost soft, about 45 minutes. Drain and set aside.

2. In a large casserole, preferably earthenware, cook the salt pork with the goose or duck fat over medium-high heat until brown and lightly crispy, about 5 minutes. Add the onions, tomatoes, and garlic and cook, stirring frequently, until the onions are soft and the tomatoes are saucy, about 10 minutes. Add the beans, season with salt and pepper, and cook, until the beans are tender, 5 to 10 minutes. Serve immediately.

Makes 8 servings

Zeytinyağlı Kuru Fasulye
WHITE BEANS IN OLIVE OIL

Although the amount of olive oil in this preparation may appear excessive, it is quite authentic and appropriate in this class of Turkish foods called *zeytinyağlı*, "olive oil foods." The oil makes the beans taste very heavenly. I would not reduce the amount. This dish is always eaten at room temperature. The green onions used in this recipe have small purple-streaked bulbs that are a little larger than scallion bulbs. They are slightly sweeter as well as a little more pungent.

1 cup extra virgin olive oil, divided
1 large onion, chopped
2½ cups water
1½ cups (about ¾ pound) dried small white
beans, picked over, soaked overnight in cold
water to cover, and drained
1 medium potato, peeled and diced
2 carrots, diced
2 celery stalks, chopped
3 large garlic cloves, chopped fine
3 large green onions or 6 scallions, chopped
1 teaspoon sugar
Salt and freshly ground black pepper to taste
Freshly squeezed juice from 1 lemon
¼ cup finely chopped fresh parsley leaves
4 slices French bread, toasted

1. In a large skillet or casserole, preferably earthenware, heat ½ cup of the olive oil over medium heat and cook the onion until it turns light brown, about 10 minutes, stirring occasionally. Pour in the water, bring to a boil, and add the drained beans, potato, carrots, celery, garlic, green onions, and sugar. Cover, reduce the heat to low, and cook until the beans are tender, about 1¼ to 1½ hours.

2. Add the remaining olive oil, season with salt and pepper, and cook, uncovered, until the water and olive oil look emulsified, about 10 minutes. Add the lemon juice, stir, and turn the heat off. Leave the beans in the casserole until they come to room temperature. Sprinkle with parsley and serve with the toasted French bread.

Makes 4 servings

BEET

Beta vulgaris L. Crassa group (syn. *B. vulgaris* subsp. *vulgaris*) (Chenopodiaceae) Also called beetroot, sugar beet; ARABIC: *shawandar, shūndar* (Syria), *banjar* (Egypt), *ārmalīta*; FRENCH: *betterave rouge, betterave potagé*; GREEK: *pantzari, patzari, teutlon, kokkinogouli*; ITALIAN: *bietola d'orta, barba bietola d'insalata*; SERBO-CROATIAN: *cikla*; SPANISH: *remolacha, remolacha hortelana, remolacha roja, remolacha de mesa*; TURKISH: *pancar*

PLANT CHARACTERISTICS AND VARIETIES

The edible parts are the leaves and roots, which are consumed either raw or cooked. The beet is closely related to Swiss chard and is the progenitor for nearly as many vegetables as is cabbage. The beet is a half-hardy biennial grown as an annual, and its root is usually round and a deep carmine red. Many other varieties, depending on how they are planted, can grow golf-ball-size roots while others grow long, cylindrical roots. The roots can also be different colors, such as orange (these are particularly good in flavor, although that might be my imagination at work), white, and multicolored with concentric rings of pink and white known as *barbietola di Chioggia*. Beets have the highest sugar content of any vegetable. Another beet variety is called *mangold*, mangel, or mangel-wurzels. It has a large white-fleshed root that is used for fodder or sugar. Beets contain betacyanin, pigments that give the root its maroon color. Some people do not metabolize this compound, so it passes through their system tinting their urine or feces red. This phenomenon is perfectly harmless but somewhat alarming, given the resemblance of betacyanin to blood.

In Turkey, the leaves of a related Chenopodiaceae, *B. macrorhiza* Steve., are eaten and called *kızıl pancar*, red beet.

PLANT ORIGIN

The cultivated beet developed from the wild beet (*B. vulgaris* subsp. *maritima* [L.] Arcangeli), a plant that commonly grows along the sea coasts of the Mediterranean. N. Vavilov suggests the Mediterranean as the center of origin for beets, with Asia Minor as a secondary location.

PLANT HISTORY

Beets probably date from prehistoric times when the leaves were used as potherbs. The beet was cultivated by the Greeks. Aristotle mentions red chard, and Theophrastus mentions light green and dark green chards used in the fourth century B.C. The Romans continued to cultivate the beet (Apicius has a recipe), using it as a food for both animals and people. In the late Middle Ages, it was still known as "Roman beet" in Germany, which may have been *B. vulgaris* subsp. *maritima*. The beet described by Horace and Cicero must have been very different from the one we know today. In Roman times the plant was appreciated for its leaves, not its roots, which probably were not the fleshy bulbous ones we know today. In any case, Pliny does mention a grilled beetroot eaten with garlic. Pliny describes cultivated beets, saying that the Greeks distinguished two kinds, the Sicilian beet, which is whitish, and the black beet. The Romans, on the other hand, distinguished two kinds of beets, based on their sowing season, autumn and spring. Romans ate beet leaves with lentils and beans in a salad. Pliny also describes the medicinal uses of cultivated beets and comments on the existence of a wild beet. There are written records referring to beets or chard (the word used is *beta*) in the ninth-century garden inventory of a royal estate at present-day Triel-sur-Seine near Versailles. In the thirteenth century, the great Hispano-Muslim agronomist Ibn al-ᶜAwwām described the growing of beetroots, which he called *ārmalīṭa*.

HOW TO GROW AND HARVEST

Beets require an open location and well-drained, slightly saline soil without too much manure worked into it. Beets do not grow well in hot, dry weather. They can be planted in the spring about 2 weeks before the average date of the last frost. The quickest-growing kinds will be ready to harvest in 2 months, so sowing the seeds in mid-June means the beets will be ready to harvest by the first of August. Plant the seeds about 3 inches apart in full sun and cover with ¼ to ½ inch of sand or fine, loose compost. You can sow a second crop in late summer if there is enough shade

to protect the germination process. Harvest beets by pulling up the whole plant with its roots when the root is about 1 inch in diameter. When you are thinning seedlings early in the season, the baby plant can be eaten as greens or baby beet roots. Old and large roots may be fibrous, so it is ideal to pull beets before the root grows beyond 3 inches in diameter.

HOW TO BUY, STORE, AND PREPARE FOR COOKING

Beets are available year-round, but their peak months are June to October. Always look for freshly harvested beets if you do not harvest your own. Choose beets of equal size so they will cook evenly. The most flavorful size is not larger than 2 inches in diameter. Baby beets, the small beets the farmer gathers when thinning the seedlings, are probably the best tasting of all. The larger the beet, the woodier and more unpalatable the root will be. It is best to buy beets with their leaves attached. The leaves deteriorate more quickly than the roots, so they should be cooked the day they are pulled or bought. The leaves should be crisp and green; if they are yellowed or limp, they have lost their nutritional value, although the roots themselves should be fine. When buying roots, look for ones that are round and smooth. Pass by beets that have wrinkled skin or soft spots.

Store beets by cutting off the leaves, leaving about an inch of the stem above the root to keep the roots from bleeding. The leaves

Beets

Beets are found in every Mediterranean cuisine and in a variety of interesting preparations beyond the recipes included here. Although beetroots are eaten everywhere, the leaves are favored mostly in southern Italy for some reason, perhaps because of southern Italians' love of that bitter taste mixed with vinegar, olive oil, and a little sugar. In Spain I had a salad that I loved called *remolachas con atún*, cooked baby beetroots served with an excellent Spanish canned tuna in olive oil flavored with garlic, red wine vinegar, and parsley. In Marseilles beetroots were once sold in the streets of the town, and the vendors would cry out about their cooked beets for sale. Today one might find these cooked beetroots pickled or diced and tossed in a salad of garlic, anchovy, and olive oil. In Egypt beetroot is always used in making *turshy*, a pickled turnip preparation, in order to turn the turnip slices pink (page 343). Beetroots served with horseradish also appear in salads in the Balkans, and in Greece cooked beetroots are served with the garlic and potato sauce called *skordalia*.

can be refrigerated for a day. The roots can be stored in a plastic bag in the crisper drawer of a refrigerator for up to 3 weeks.

Prepare the beet greens for cooking by rinsing them well. Rinse the beetroots but cook them with their stems attached and do not puncture them if you turn them while cooking, again, to prevent them from bleeding.

RECIPES

Beetroots

Barbabietole con Cipolle
BEETS WITH ROASTED ONIONS AND WALNUTS

In northern Italy a preparation like this one might be accompanied by roast pork, although it doesn't need to be as it makes an excellent salad or antipasto, too. This is a very attractive dish, especially once you dig into it and the beets begin to color the onions.

12 small beetroots (about 2¼ pounds)

Salt to taste

1 large onion, cut into ⅜-inch-thick slices

2 tablespoons extra virgin olive oil, and more to oil the baking pan

3 tablespoons finely ground walnuts

3 tablespoons finely chopped fresh parsley leaves

1 tablespoon freshly squeezed lemon juice

Salt and freshly ground black pepper to taste

1. Place the beets in a large saucepan and cover them with cold water. Bring the water to a boil with a little salt and cook the beets until a skewer will glide easily to the center of the beet, about 30 minutes. Drain, trim the remaining stems off, peel the beets, and cut them into ⅜-inch-thick slices. Set aside.

2. Meanwhile, preheat the oven to 425°F. Layer the onion slices in a lightly oiled baking pan and bake them until they are blackened at the edges, about 20 minutes.

3. Transfer the onions to a serving platter, arrange the sliced beets over the onions, and sprinkle with the walnuts and parsley. Whisk together the dressing of olive oil, lemon juice, salt, and pepper and drizzle it over the platter. Serve warm or at room temperature.

Makes 4 servings

Barbabietole alla Crema
ORANGE BEETS IN CREAM SAUCE

In this rich and beautiful preparation from northern Italy the cream sauce takes on the golden hue of the beets, making the dish quite appetizing to behold. Because of the heaviness of the cream sauce, it is best to accompany this dish with a simple meat such as poached chicken, pan-fried veal chops, or roast pork tenderloin. Save the beet leaves and make any of the preparations on pages 58–60.

12 to 14 small orange beetroots (about 1½ pounds)

1 teaspoon vegetable or olive oil

2 tablespoons unsalted butter

1 cup heavy cream

Salt and freshly ground black pepper to taste

1. Preheat the oven to 400°F. Place the beets in a lightly oiled baking pan and roast them until a skewer will glide easily to the center, about 50 minutes. Remove the beets from the oven and, once they are cool enough to handle, trim their stem ends, peel the beets, and cut them into ½-inch cubes.

2. In a large saucepan, melt the butter over medium heat, add the beets and stir until they are very hot, about 5 minutes. Remove the beets from the saucepan and keep them warm.

3. Add the cream to the saucepan and boil it until it is reduced by half. Season the cream with salt and pepper and pour it over the beets. Serve immediately.

Makes 4 servings

Pancar Salatası
BEET AND YOGURT SALAD

The Turks love the contrast between colors, between hot and cold, and between spicy and mild in their foods. One will often come across this culinary dichotomy in many dishes. For instance, in this dish the contrast between the red beets and the yogurt, which turns the edges pink, is very attractive and inviting. Ideally, the beets would be served hot with the cool yogurt on top. In any case, this preparation is suited to people who claim they hate beets. Remember to keep the beetroots whole when you boil them—try not to puncture them, and don't trim them until after they're cooked, when their skin will come off with a little rubbing. This recipe can easily be cut in half if you don't need to serve so many people. The Arabs also like this kind of preparation, as we will see in the recipe that follows this one.

7 medium-large beetroots (about 4 pounds), trimmed
Salt and freshly ground black pepper to taste
½ teaspoon caraway seeds
4 large garlic cloves, peeled
½ teaspoon salt
2 cups high-quality full-fat plain yogurt
Hot paprika for sprinkling

1. Put the beets in boiling water and cook them until a skewer will glide easily to their center, about 2 hours. Drain and, once they are cool enough to handle, peel the beets and slice them into ¼-inch-thick slices. Arrange the beet slices on a serving platter slightly overlapping and let them come to room temperature, if desired (you may also serve them while they're still warm). Season the beets with salt and pepper.

2. In a mortar, pound the caraway seeds until crushed, then add the garlic and salt and pound the garlic until it is mushy. Beat the yogurt and garlic mixture together in a medium bowl until smooth. Spread it over the beets. Sprinkle with paprika and serve.

Makes 6 servings

Shawandar bi'l-Laban
BEETS WITH YOGURT

When I first encountered this Lebanese preparation, I was quite taken with the appetizing color. Upon tasting it, I couldn't believe how good it was—how natural beets, yogurt, and mint seemed, even though I'm not sure the combination would have occurred to me. This dish can also be made with *shawandar*, that is, "white beets" (chard), but there is also another white beet cultivar known as Albinia Verecunda.

2 pounds small beetroots, with their leaves

Salt and freshly ground black pepper to taste

2 large garlic cloves, peeled

½ teaspoon salt

2 heaping tablespoons labna *(see below)*

1 ½ cups high-quality full-fat plain yogurt

2 tablespoons finely chopped fresh mint leaves

1. Cut the greens from the beetroots, leaving a bit of stem behind. Wash the leaves well, then steam or boil them in water over high heat in a large pot until they have wilted, about 10 minutes. Remove the greens from the water and drain. Steam the roots until a skewer glides easily to the center, about 30 minutes. Drain and let cool. Cut the greens into strips and arrange them on a serving plate. Peel the beets and cut them into ¼-inch-thick slices. Arrange the beetroot slices on top of the greens. Season with salt and pepper.

2. In a mortar, pound the garlic and salt together into a mush. Stir the garlic and *labna* into the yogurt and beat for 1 minute with a fork. Spread the yogurt over the beets, garnish with mint, and serve.

Makes 4 servings

Labna
STRAINED YOGURT

Labna is made all over the United States and called "yogurt cheese," "lebany," "lubny," and some other similar spellings. For some reason, supermarkets don't carry it, so you may want to go to a Middle Eastern or Greek market. But making it is so easy, too.

In the Middle East, strained yogurt is used as a breakfast spread for dipping pieces of Arabic bread sprinkled with dried mint or *za'tar* (a spice mixture of thyme, sesame seed, and sumac), served as a dip for hot foods, or eaten plain with some olive oil or honey.

Pour some high-quality full-fat plain yogurt into a linen towel or several layers of cheesecloth, tie off the top, and hang the "bag" from a kitchen sink faucet to drain overnight in a cool place. Refrigerate it. Alternatively, line a strainer with cheesecloth or a linen towel. Set it over a proper size bowl. Cover the bowl loosely with plastic wrap, and refrigerate overnight.

SALAD OF ORANGE BEETS AND GREEN BEANS

The inspiration for this recipe was all about color. It is a startling and radiant antipasto. The orange beets and the green beans must be very fresh, picked yesterday, so to speak (if not actually), and they will retain their natural flavors and sweetness. Save the beet leaves for the following side dish.

6 ounces green beans, ends trimmed
1½ pounds orange beets, leaves removed
Salt and freshly ground black pepper to taste
Extra virgin olive oil for drizzling

1. Bring a pot of water to a boil and blanch the green beans for 2 minutes. Remove them from the water with a slotted ladle or tongs and immediately plunge in ice water to stop their cooking. Place the beets in the water and boil until firm but tender, about 25 minutes. At the same time steam the green beans until slightly crunchy, about 6 minutes.

2. Remove the green beans and arrange around the perimeter of an oval platter. Drain the beets, peel, cut into small wedges or dice and arrange in the center of the platter. Season with salt and pepper and drizzle with olive oil.

Makes 2 to 3 servings

Beet Greens

Cime di Rapa all'Aceto
BEET GREENS WITH VINEGAR

The bitter taste of beet greens, as well as dandelion, chicory, turnip tops, and some other greens, is very popular in southern Italy. My grandfather, who was from a small village near Benevento in the region of Campania, loved to make this kind of dish, and he would keep leftovers in the refrigerator. This dish of slightly bitter greens is not very appealing to children, but for those with more sophisticated tastes, it can be served as an antipasto. It is also very nice alongside a steak. The roots can be used in the salad of orange beets and green beans.

Leaves from 1¼ pounds beetroots, washed well,
*   and heavy stems trimmed*
¼ cup water
2 tablespoons extra virgin olive oil
½ teaspoon sugar
1 garlic clove, chopped fine
1 tablespoon white wine vinegar
Salt and freshly ground black pepper to taste

Place the leaves in a large skillet with only the water adhering to them from their last rinsing. Turn the heat to medium-high and wilt the leaves, about 4 minutes. Add the water, olive oil, sugar, garlic, and vinegar and season with salt and pepper. Cook until the water has evaporated, 8 to 10 minutes. Transfer the greens to a serving dish and let them come to room temperature before serving.

Makes 2 to 3 servings

Cime di Rapa con Uve Sultanina e Pignoli
BEET GREENS WITH GOLDEN RAISINS AND PINE NUTS

This popular preparation from the region of Apulia in southern Italy is ideal during the hot summer months. I usually serve it with an assortment of other vegetable preparations, also at room temperature, or accompanied by a piece of grilled lamb. This dish can also be made with turnip or radish tops.

¾ pound beet greens, washed well, and heavy stems trimmed
1 tablespoon pine nuts
1 tablespoon golden raisins
6 to 8 imported black olives (such as Kalamata), to your taste, pitted and chopped
1 large garlic clove, chopped very fine
2 tablespoons extra virgin olive oil
Salt and freshly ground black pepper to taste
3 tablespoons water

I. Place the greens in a large skillet with only the water adhering to them from their last rinsing. Turn the heat to medium-high and remove the skillet from the heat as soon as the greens wilt but still remain bright green, 4 to 5 minutes, turning the greens a few times. Place the greens in a strainer and run cold water over them. Press out as much water as possible and cut the bunch of greens in half.

2. Return the greens to the skillet with the pine nuts, raisins, olives, garlic, and olive oil, and season with salt and pepper. Turn the heat to medium-high, add the water, and cook the greens, tossing frequently, until they are soft but still green, about 6 minutes. Remove the greens from the skillet, let them cool to room temperature, and serve.

Makes 4 small servings

Cime di Rapa all'Aglio e Olio
BEET GREENS WITH GARLIC AND OLIVE OIL

Turnip leaves, as well as beet greens and some other greens, can be confused in Italian because all of them can be referred to by the same term, *cime di rapa*, which literally means "turnip tops." In Apulia, the heel of the Italian boot, these greens are among the most popular vegetables. Usually the cook makes this preparation at the same time he or she is making another preparation using the turnip or beetroots. The leaves are slightly bitter, so they are cooked thoroughly in aromatics or vinegar and sugar to make them milder. In this preparation the greens are cooked simply and served at room temperature.

1½ pounds beet or turnip leaves or broccoli rapa

3 tablespoons extra virgin olive oil, plus more for drizzling, if desired

1 large garlic clove, chopped fine

1 tablespoon freshly squeezed lemon juice

Salt and freshly ground black pepper to taste

1 tablespoon water, if needed

1. Trim the heavy stems of the greens (there should be about 1 pound of leaves once the stems have been trimmed). Wash the greens well several times and place them in a stockpot with only the water adhering to them from their last rinsing. Turn the heat to high, cover, and cook the greens until they wilt but are still bright green, about 5 minutes, turning the greens occasionally.

2. Heat the olive oil with the garlic in a medium skillet over medium heat until the garlic begins to brown lightly, about 1 minute. Reduce the heat to medium-low, add the greens and lemon juice, season with salt and pepper, and cook until the greens are soft and dark, 8 to 10 minutes, stirring occasionally and adding the water if it looks like the greens are drying out. Serve the greens warm or at room temperature with extra olive oil if desired.

Makes 4 servings

BERULA ERECTA (HUDS.) COUVILLE (UMBELLIFERAE)

TURKISH: *kazayağı*

PLANT CHARACTERISTICS AND VARIETIES

In Turkey the leaves of this perennial plant (sometimes translated in Turkish-English dictionaries as pigweed or goosefoot but not related to those plants as described in this book), are edible wild greens that are served boiled or eaten raw in salads.

BIG MALLOW

Lavatera arborea L. (Malvaceae)

ITALIAN: *malvone* (Sicily-Linosa)

PLANT CHARACTERISTICS AND VARIETIES

This mallow family plant is used as a medicinal plant for treating domestic animals on the Sicilian island of Linosa. In southern Italy big mallow was once eaten as a vegetable, and the seeds were eaten raw in salads as a flavoring.

BLACK BRYONY

Tamus communis L. (Dioscoreaceae)

Also called tamoro; ITALIAN: *brionia*;
SPANISH: *brionia*

PLANT CHARACTERISTICS AND VARIETIES

Black bryony is a perennial vine with yellow flowers and poisonous berries and roots.

Although it is grown mostly as an ornamental, the young shoots are cooked and eaten as a vegetable in rural Spain and Italy.

PLANT ORIGIN

Black bryony is native to Europe.

PLANT HISTORY

In ancient Rome black bryony was preferred over asparagus and was popular in Tuscany into the medieval period. Today in the northern Italian region of Friuli black bryony is gathered in the spring and used in a dish called *pistic,* a vegetable dish composed of more than fifty wild greens. In Turkey, black bryony is used for stuffing *börek,* a fried stuffed pastry.

BLACK-EYED PEA

Vigna unguiculata (L.) Walp. subsp. *unguiculata* (L.) Walp. (syn. *V. sinensis* Endl.; *Dolichos lubia* Forsk. or *D. unguiculatus)* (Fabaceae-Leguminosae)
Also called cowpea, crowder, southern pea; ARABIC: *ḥummuṣ shamī, lūbya balādī, lūbya musalāṭ;* FRENCH: *haricot à oeil noir, haricot dolique, dolique chinois, niébé;* ITALIAN: *fagiolino dall'occhio, vecchia;* SPANISH: *caupi, judia de vaca, frijol de vaca, frijol de pinta negra, frijol de ombligo negro, caragilates*

The edible parts are the immature pods and seeds, which are cooked. There are five subspecies of *V. unguiculata,* two of which are wild. The black-eyed pea is one of the most important vegetables in Africa. The pods containing the seeds are about a foot long; they are eaten only when very young, usually boiled. As with other legumes, black-eyed peas have nitrogen-giving nodules on their roots, and for this reason the plant is often used as green manure or forage.

PLANT ORIGIN

One theory suggests that the black-eyed pea originated from *V. dekindtiana,* the wild ancestor found in the semiarid savannah of Africa. Another theory suggests that the Niger River basin of West Africa was a center of diversity but that the center of origin is Ethiopia. It is thought that black-eyed peas were first cultivated in Ethiopia from 4000 to 3000 B.C. Bianchini, Corbetta, and Pistoia claim the black-eyed pea is native to South America, but this contention is incorrect. Finally, there is a theory that the black-eyed pea is native to India and the Middle East.

PLANT HISTORY

In records from Sumer about 2350 B.C., a plant called *lu-ub-sar,* which appears to give the modern Arabic *lūbya* (bean), may have been the black-eyed pea. It appears that the ancient Egyptian bean known as *'iwryt,* described from the Old Kingdom (2686 to 2100 B.C.)

onward, was the black-eyed pea. Workmen at Deir al-Medina in ancient Egypt received beans as part of their wages. In pharaonic medicine black-eyed peas were used to treat constipation. The black-eyed pea arrived in the northern Mediterranean by about 300 B.C., and it was grown by the Romans. Pliny has a description of a plant called *dolichos,* but it is unclear if this is the black-eyed pea. The depiction of the plant called *fasilus* in the sixth-century codex drawing of Dioscorides's work appears to be the black-eyed pea. It is believed that the plant arrived in North America from the Mediterranean and in South America from West Africa as a result of the slave trade.

HOW TO GROW AND HARVEST

Black-eyed peas grow best in well-drained and somewhat acidic soil with a pH of 5.5 to 6.5. About 2 weeks after the average frost-free date for your area, prepare a raised bed (for better drainage) in a location that gets full sun. Plant the seeds 2 to 4 inches apart and one inch deep in rows that are 3 feet apart. Thin the seedlings to 6 inches apart. When the pods begin to turn color, harvest the peas by snapping them off, holding the stem in one hand and the pod in the other.

HOW TO BUY, STORE, AND PREPARE FOR COOKING

The unripe pods are bought, stored, and cooked in the same way that fresh green beans are. Fresh black-eyed peas are often available at farmers' markets and in many supermarkets, usually sold in plastic containers in the produce section. Dried black-eyed peas are cooked like any dried bean.

RECIPES

Lūbya Musalāṭ bi'l-Zayt
BLACK-EYED PEA SALAD

In Lebanon this appetizing dish is served as part of a *mazza*. I particularly like the way it looks—with the little black eyes of the peas glistening with olive oil, the whites of the beans speckled green with coriander—and let's not forget the aroma of garlic. If you don't serve this recipe as part of a *mazza* table, it's nice with grilled ground meat with spices.

2 cups fresh black-eyed peas (about ¾ pound)
3 tablespoons extra virgin olive oil
1 small onion, chopped fine
2 large garlic cloves, mashed in a mortar with 1 teaspoon salt
¼ teaspoon freshly ground allspice berries
¼ cup finely chopped fresh coriander leaves
Freshly ground black pepper to taste
Freshly squeezed lemon juice for drizzling

I. Place the black-eyed peas in a medium saucepan and cover them with a couple inches of water. Bring the water to a boil and cook the peas at a boil until they are tender but not falling apart, 15 to 20 minutes. Drain the peas, reserving several tablespoons of the cooking liquid.

2. Heat the olive oil in a small skillet over medium heat and cook the onion, stirring, until it is translucent, 2 to 3 minutes. Add the garlic and salt, allspice, and coriander, season with pepper, and continue cooking until the coriander and garlic are completely blended, about 2 minutes, stirring so the garlic doesn't burn.

3. Transfer the cooked peas to a serving bowl and toss gently with the onion mixture, being careful not to crush the peas. Sprinkle some lemon juice over the top and serve at room temperature.

Makes 4 servings

Silq bi'l-Lūbya
SWISS CHARD WITH BLACK-EYED PEAS

This Lebanese and Syrian dish is a wonderful way to serve fresh black-eyed peas, but dried will do just as well. The usually rough taste of Swiss chard is mellowed considerably by the onions and coriander in this preparation.

4 cups fresh black-eyed peas (about 1½ pounds) or 1½ cups dried black-eyed peas (about ¾ pound), picked over, soaked in water to cover overnight, and drained

2 pounds Swiss chard, washed well, and heavy stalks removed

5 tablespoons extra virgin olive oil

1 large onion, chopped fine

4 to 5 large garlic cloves, to your taste, mashed in a mortar with 2 teaspoons salt

½ cup finely chopped fresh coriander leaves

1 teaspoon freshly ground cumin seeds

1. Place the peas in a medium-size saucepan of cold water to cover and bring water to a boil. Cook the peas at a boil until they are tender, about 1 hour for dried peas and about 18 minutes for fresh. Drain the peas and set them aside.

2. Place the Swiss chard in a large pot with only the water adhering to the leaves from their last rinsing. Turn the heat to high, cover, and wilt the greens, 5 to 7 minutes, turning a few times with long tongs. Drain the greens and squeeze out excess liquid. Chop coarsely and set aside.

3. Heat the olive oil in a large skillet or casserole over medium-high heat and cook the onion, stirring, until translucent, about 8 minutes. Add the Swiss chard, mashed garlic, coriander, and cumin, reduce the heat to low, and cook until the mixture is fragrant and tender, about 30 minutes. Stir in the peas, cook until heated through, about 10 minutes, and serve.

Makes 6 servings

Borage

ALTHOUGH BORAGE MIGHT FIND ITS WAY INTO THE STEWS OF MORE RURAL COOKS IN TURKEY, SPAIN, AND SOUTHERN ITALY, its most intriguing use, I think, is in the traditional stuffing for *pansôti*, a Genoese-style ravioli served with walnut sauce. Throughout northern Italy, traditionalists use borage instead of spinach to make green spaghetti.

BLACK LOCUST

Robinia pseudoacacia L. (Leguminosae)
Also called false acacia; ITALIAN: *agaggio* (Tuscany)

PLANT CHARACTERISTICS AND VARIETIES
Black locust is a tree usually planted as an ornamental or for stabilizing the soil. In Tuscany the flowers of this plant are eaten as a vegetable, batter-fried or boiled.

BLOND PSYLLIUM

Plantago ovata Forsk. (Plantaginaceae)

PLANT CHARACTERISTICS AND VARIETIES
This perennial plant with one or a few rosettes of leaves grows in dry places. The edible part is the sprouted seed, used in salads, soups, and stews in parts of the Mediterranean, especially southeastern Spain, North Africa, and the Arabian Peninsula.

BORAGE

Borago officinalis L. (Boraginaceae)
ARABIC: *lisān al-thawr, kaḥīlā', lasīq (B. verrucosa)*; FRENCH: *bourrache*; ITALIAN: *borragine, borrana*; SPANISH: *borraja, borracha*; TURKISH: *lisanüssevr*

PLANT CHARACTERISTICS AND VARIETIES
The edible parts are the petiole and leaves, which are cooked. Borage is a hardy annual considered to be an herb. It is found in many parts of Italy growing by roadsides, in cultivated or untilled fields, and among ruins. The plant grows to about 3 feet and has large, fuzzy, and loose oblong and silvery leaves and clusters of bright starlike blue flowers. The flowers can be used as a culinary garnish. Borage flowers and leaves have a cool, cucumber-like aroma and taste. The leaves are used in salads or cooked as a vegetable. Borage is used mostly in the Mediterranean by the French, and in the Ligurian and central

regions of Italy, in omelettes, to stuff ravioli, and to make green spaghetti. Dried or fresh leaves are used to season stews and soups.

PLANT ORIGIN

Borage is believed to be native to the eastern Mediterranean.

PLANT HISTORY

Borage was used by the ancient Greeks, who called it *euphrosynon* because when it was put into a cup of wine it made those who drank it euphoric. In the seventeenth century Castelvetro suggested using borage in mixed salads.

HOW TO GROW AND HARVEST

Borage seeds should be sown once a month starting in the late spring. The plant grows well in full sun in temperate climates and with late afternoon shade in Mediterranean climates. Harvest the leaves or plant as needed.

HOW TO BUY, STORE, AND PREPARE FOR COOKING

Borage is sometimes found at farmers' markets, but mostly it is a home-grown herb. Store leaves in the refrigerator and use them within 2 days.

BOTTLE GOURD

Lagenaria siceria (Mol.) Standl. (syn. *L. leucantha* Rusby; *L. vulgaris* Ser.) (Cucurbitaceae)
Also called calabash gourd; Arabic: *ẓarf al-qara^c*; Catalan: *carbassa*; French: *calebasse, courge bouteille, calabassier, gourde*; Italian: *zucca da vino, zucca da nuoto, zucca bottiglia, cocozza, cocozelle*; Spanish: *calabaza de peregrinos, calabaza de San Roque, calabaza viñatera, calabaza viñadera, cojombro*; Turkish: *su kabağı*

PLANT CHARACTERISTICS AND VARIETIES

Bottle gourd is an annual plant that climbs to thirty feet or more. The edible part is the immature fruit. The fruits grow to many different shapes, from round to elongated. The flowers are large, white, and fragrant, and they open in the evening. The fruit, if allowed to mature, develops a hard shell that has been used as a container for liquids and foods throughout the Mediterranean in times past. Bottle gourd fruit is not eaten much anymore in the European Mediterranean.

PLANT ORIGIN

It has long been claimed that the bottle gourd is native to the tropical lowlands of Africa south of the equator, but N. Vavilov identified India, Burma, and Assam as the center of origin of the bottle gourd.

PLANT HISTORY

The bottle gourd is known to have been used by Egyptians between 3000 and 4000 B.C. There is evidence of its cultivation in South America from 7000 B.C., meaning that it appears possible that the gourd floated from Africa to South America. The plant that the Italians and Sicilians of the Middle Ages called *cucuzza* appears to have been the bottle gourd. There are recipes for bottle gourd in the fourteenth-century Catalan cookery book *Llibre de sent soví*, as well as in the Italian cookery works by Platina and Martino that were published in the late fifteenth century.

HOW TO GROW AND HARVEST

After the danger of frost has passed, plant seeds in groups of three at the base of a support such as a tall trellis or pole. Water the plants regularly. Harvest the fruits after they are about a week old and their skins are tender.

HOW TO BUY, STORE, AND PREPARE FOR COOKING

Scrape the skin off the fruit with a knife and cut off both ends. Cook as you would summer squash.

BROCCOLI

Brassica oleracea L. Italica (syn. Cymosa) group and Botryris group (syn. *B. oleracea* var. *italica, B. sylvestris* [L.]) (Cruciferae-Brassicaceae)

ARABIC: *qulībāt, brūklū*; FRENCH: *chou brocoli, brocoli*; GREEK: *brokoli, lachanou*; ITALIAN: *broccoli, cavolo broccoli*; SERB-CROATIAN: *prokulica*; SICILIAN: *sparaceddi*; SPANISH: *brocoli*

PLANT CHARACTERISTICS AND VARIETIES

The edible part is the immature flower stalk, which is eaten either raw or cooked. Broccoli is a biennial that is grown as an annual. Because of the complexity of this species, and its close relation to the cauliflower, there is some confusion among horticulturalists about its taxonomic divisions. Head broccoli is said to belong to the Botrytis group (a group that also includes cauliflower), but some writers have identified broccoli with the Cymosa group, which is also sometimes called the Italica group. Sprouting broccoli (also called asparagus broccoli) is another form of broccoli. It lacks a central head but has many tender shoots. Sprouting broccoli belongs to the Italica group. Broccoli rape is like a sprouting broccoli (the Ruvo group of *Brassica rapa*) but is actually a relation of the turnip (see entry). Broccolini (*B. oleracea* Acephala group) are the unopened flower clusters of kale, which taste like a cross between broccoli and asparagus.

For the most part, three types of broccoli are grown today: Calabrese, the type most common in the supermarket, which matures in the summer; Romanesco, which matures in late summer or autumn and is characterized by its conical groups of yellow green buds that are arranged in spirals; and sprouting broccoli,

Broccoli

EVEN THOUGH ITALY HAS HAD A MAJOR INFLUENCE ON OTHER REGIONS AROUND THE MEDITERRANEAN IN TERMS OF HISTORY and culture, apparently that influence does not extend to broccoli. It seems no one else eats it. For instance, I don't believe I've ever seen broccoli eaten by the French, and I also don't recall ever seeing broccoli in North Africa.

which is a winter broccoli that is ready to harvest in the spring.

PLANT ORIGIN

Broccoli, derived from a species of wild cabbage, is said to have come to Italy in the seventeenth century from the eastern Mediterranean, Crete, or Cyprus. It is also thought likely that broccoli, and other varieties of cultivated *B. oleracea,* may have evolved from other species besides just wild cabbage, for instance, *B. cretica, B. insularis,* and *B. rupestris.* These possibilities have led to some questions about taxonomy. Sprouting broccoli (*B. oleracea* Italica group) came from the Levant, Cyprus, or Crete to Italy, although it may have been developed about two thousand years ago from a form of wild cabbage.

PLANT HISTORY

Broccoli and cauliflower are closely related. Since both evolved from cabbage, it is difficult to separate their histories. The development of broccoli probably happened as follows: leafy cabbage→nonheading cauliflower or head cabbage→head cauliflower→sprouting broccoli→ head broccoli. Sprouting broccoli was once called Italian asparagus in eighteenth-century England. Some commentators believe that the *cyma* mentioned in Pliny's *Natural History* is broccoli. It is unlikely that the broccoli of the Middle Ages were the ones with the dense flowering head that are available in our markets today. They probably looked like what is today called sprouting broccoli or asparagus broccoli, with edible flower shoots but no head. Broccoli is not a popular vegetable in the Mediterranean even though it is native. The Arabs, Spanish, and French never eat it; only in Italy, the Dalmatian Coast, and Greece is this vegetable cooked with any frequency.

HOW TO GROW AND HARVEST

Broccoli grows best in places with a long, cool growing season. Broccoli is not as frost resistant as cabbage. If you are growing the plants from seeds, start them about ½ inch deep and tamp down the earth lightly. When the seedlings have 4 or 5 leaves, transplant them into 4-inch pots and, after they are hardy, transplant them back into the garden. Broccoli can be transplanted outdoors long after the last frost, usually in late summer for a fall or winter harvest. Plant the seedlings about 15 inches apart in rich, loamy soil that will retain moisture and is not too rich in nitrogen.

Sprouting broccoli should be planted in April or early May and transplanted in June or July in rows about 2 feet apart. Calabrese and Romanesco are planted about 8 inches apart in rows. The seedlings are then thinned out to a single plant that is grown as fast as possible with ample water.

Harvest broccoli by cutting the central stem about 2 inches below where it branches to form buds. Harvest sprouting broccoli when the individual sprouts are in the bud stage by cutting them off above where the skin gets tough.

HOW TO BUY, STORE, AND PREPARE FOR COOKING

The best-quality broccoli shows no signs of yellow flowers on the buds. Broccoli is available in the market year-round but is most abundant from October to May. Broccoli is best when picked young. If it is left to grow large, it converts its sugar to lignin, a type of fiber that will not become soft when cooked. Home-grown broccoli should be soaked in water with a teaspoon of baking soda for 30 minutes to force out any resident worms or bugs. Buy broccoli whose florets are tightly closed and green. Avoid broccoli that is limp, with the florets separating, loose, or yellowing. Color usually indicates nutritional quality; the darker green it is, the better.

Store broccoli in a plastic bag in the refrigerator crisper drawer. Broccoli should be cooked within 2 days of harvesting or buying, although it can be kept in the refrigerator for up to 4 days.

Broccoli, and all cruciferous vegetables, must not be overcooked; otherwise chemicals in the plant break down and release sulfurous compounds, such as ammonia and hydrogen sulfide, which interact with the chlorophyll in the plant, causing the broccoli to turn an unappetizing brownish gray color and to give off a very unpleasant smell. In fact, this smell is the reason that people who say they don't like broccoli probably don't like it. Broccoli should always be cooked in small amounts of water just until it is crisp-tender; it should never be cooked until limp. It should retain its bright green color.

RECIPES

Brokoli me Mezithra
BROCCOLI WITH BROWN BUTTER AND *MEZITHRA* CHEESE

Broccoli is not an altogether common vegetable in Greece, but this recipe is really quite nice in its simplicity. *Mezithra* (also *myzithra* and *mizithra*) cheese is a kind of Greek *ricotta salata*, a dried and salted ricotta cheese that is hard enough to be grated. It is usually found in Greek or Middle Eastern markets, but it can be replaced with *ricotta salata*, found in Italian markets and good cheese stores. This preparation can be served either as part of a Greek *meze*, very nicely accompanied by a glass of ouzo, or as a side dish with meat.

3 stalks broccoli (about 1½ pounds)
3 tablespoons unsalted butter
Salt and freshly ground black pepper to taste
2 to 3 tablespoons mezithra or ricotta salata
   cheese, to your taste

1. Separate the stems from the florets. Peel the stems and cut them into 1½-inch lengths. In a steamer pot, bring several cups of water to a boil and boil the stalks while you steam the florets in the steamer on top at the same time. Cook the broccoli until tender and bright green, about 8 minutes.

2. Meanwhile, melt the butter in a small skillet over medium heat until caramel colored, 3 to 4 minutes. Arrange the cooked broccoli on a serving platter, season with salt and pepper, drizzle the butter over the top, sprinkle with the cheese, and serve.

Makes 4 servings

Broccoli Lessati con Parmigiana e Burro
BOILED BROCCOLI WITH BROWN BUTTER AND PARMESAN CHEESE

This very simple recipe from southern Italy, which respects the natural taste of garden-fresh broccoli, is so similar to the previous Greek recipe that I wonder if there may be some historical connection.

1½ pounds broccoli
Salt and freshly ground black pepper to taste
3 tablespoons unsalted butter
¼ cup freshly grated Parmigiano-Reggiano cheese

1. In a large pot of lightly salted boiling water, blanch the broccoli whole until bright green, about 2 minutes. Immediately pull the broccoli from the water with tongs and plunge it into ice water to stop it from cooking.

2. Return the same water to a boil and cook the broccoli just until tender, about 6 minutes. Drain, separate the broccoli into florets and stems and arrange them on a serving platter. Season with salt and pepper.

3. Meanwhile, heat the butter in a butter warmer over medium heat until brown. Pour the butter over the broccoli and sprinkle with the Parmigiano. Serve immediately.

Makes 4 servings

Broccoli al Forno
OVEN-BAKED BROCCOLI "AU GRATIN"

This broccoli preparation from southern Italy's Calabria region makes a nice accompaniment to roast lamb. The broccoli should be boiled only briefly so that it is not only tender but remains bright green. The gratin topping bakes to a beautiful and glistening golden brown and is very appetizing.

1 large head broccoli (about 1¼ pounds), stems
  separated from the florets
3 tablespoons extra virgin olive oil
1 garlic clove, chopped very fine
2 tablespoons freshly grated Pecorino cheese
Freshly ground black pepper to taste
3 tablespoons dry breadcrumbs

1. Preheat the oven to 425°F. Bring a large saucepan of lightly salted water to a boil and cook the broccoli stems in one piece just until tender, 12 to 15 minutes. Remove with a slotted ladle and cut into 1½-inch pieces lengthwise. Cook the broccoli florets in the water just until tender, 7 to 8 minutes. Drain and separate the florets.
2. Lightly oil a medium baking casserole dish and arrange the broccoli in it. Sprinkle with the garlic and Pecorino cheese, season with pepper, and sprinkle the breadcrumbs on top. Drizzle with the remaining olive oil and bake until the top is golden brown, 10 to 15 minutes. Serve immediately.

Makes 4 servings

Prokulica Palačinka
BROCCOLI CRÊPES

Broccoli is a vegetable developed from the cabbage. Botanists believe its original home was in Crete, Cyprus, or Anatolia. It spread westward to Italy and Dalmatia. In the old medieval city of Dubrovnik this recipe sprung from the people's great love of broccoli and the fact that broccoli is grown in the market gardens in the countryside surrounding the city. Today these broccoli crêpes are favorites of the locals of Dubrovnik on the Dalmatian coast.

3 tablespoons unsalted butter
2 tablespoons pine nuts
2 cups chopped cooked broccoli florets
  (about ½ pound)

FOR THE CRÊPES:
1 large egg
½ cup all-purpose unbleached flour
¾ cup milk
⅛ teaspoon salt
¼ teaspoon baking powder

FOR THE BÉCHAMEL SAUCE:
3 tablespoons unsalted butter
3 tablespoons all-purpose unbleached flour
Salt and freshly ground black pepper to taste
Pinch of freshly grated nutmeg
2 cups milk
¾ cup freshly grated Gruyère cheese

1. In a nonstick omelette or crêpe pan, melt the butter over medium heat and brown the

pine nuts, 1 to 2 minutes, tossing frequently. Remove the pine nuts and set aside. Remove 1 tablespoon of the butter from the pan and toss with the cooked broccoli in a medium bowl.

2. In another medium bowl, beat the egg, then add the flour, milk, salt, and baking powder. Beat the ingredients together gently until the batter is smooth and thinner than pancake batter. Make 4 crêpes, one at a time. Slowly pour a quarter of the batter into the omelette or crêpe pan, tilting and turning the pan with the other hand so the batter just coats the surface of the pan. Use a spatula to scrape the batter so that it covers the bottom of the entire pan. The crêpe should be very thin. Cook the crêpe until it is brown on both sides, 1 to 2 minutes per side. Remove the cooked crêpes to a greased plate and set aside until needed. The crêpes can be made several hours or a day ahead of time and refrigerated.

3. Make the béchamel. Melt the butter in a medium saucepan over medium-high heat. Add the flour and cook the roux until it is nutty smelling, about 2 minutes, seasoning with salt, pepper, and nutmeg, and stirring constantly. Remove from the heat and pour in the milk in a slow, steady stream, whisking constantly. Return to the heat and, as it reaches a boil, reduce the heat to low and cook until thicker, about 15 minutes. Add the cooked broccoli and Gruyère and cook over low heat until quite dense, about 25 minutes.

4. Preheat the oven to 350°F. Arrange a crêpe in a baking dish and cover half of it with a quarter of the broccoli sauce. Fold the other half of the crêpe over. Continue filling the remaining crêpes, adding them to the baking dish slightly overlapping. Cover the baking dish with aluminum foil and heat in the oven until the crêpes are heated through, 10 to 15 minutes. Sprinkle the reserved pine nuts over the crêpes along with any butter remaining in the omelette pan. Serve.

Makes 4 servings

BROCCOLIFLOWER
See Cauliflower.

BROCCOLI RAPA
See Turnip.

BRUSSELS SPROUT
Brassica oleracea L. Gemmifera group (or var. *gemmifera* Zenk.) (syn. *B. gemmifera*) (Cruciferae-Brassicaceae)
FRENCH: *chou de Bruxelles*; GREEK: *lachanakia Bruxellou*; ITALIAN: *cavolo di Bruxelles*; SERBO-CROATIAN: *prokule*; SPANISH: *col de Bruselas, repollo de Bruselas*; TURKISH: *Brüksel lâhanası*

PLANT CHARACTERISTICS AND VARIETIES
The edible parts are the axillary buds, which are cooked. The Brussels sprout is a hardy biennial usually grown as an annual. The tall,

thick stem sprouts many tiny "cabbage" heads that are packed tightly between the bases of the leaf petioles, and these sprouts are usually removed when the plant is harvested for the market. Commercially grown Brussels sprouts are grown for the evenness of the sprout. There are several varieties, but their differences are minor.

PLANT ORIGIN

Brussels sprouts were originally cultivated from a form of wild cabbage around the fourteenth century in the area of Brussels, although some commentators have suggested that the *spruyten* mentioned in the Belgian official regulations for holding markets, which date from 1231 (or 1213), are Brussels sprouts. But K. F. Thompson argues that the earliest appearance of Brussels sprouts was 1750, and that the plant was initially grown for "sport." Thompson says that the earlier dating of Brussels sprouts from 1231 to 1472 in Belgium refers to *B. capitata polycephalos,* a plant with a large number of sprouts but no characteristic terminal head.

PLANT HISTORY

The first record of a cabbage similar to Brussels sprouts was illustrated in Jacques d'Alechamps's *Historia Generalis Plantarum* published in 1587. The first recorded Brussels sprouts were from Belgium in 1750, although some writers suggest an earlier date of 1623 (but see above). Some writers have mistaken the Latin *cauliculi* for Brussels sprouts, which it was not.

HOW TO GROW AND HARVEST

Brussels sprouts are grown in a manner similar to that of winter cabbage (page 80). All in all, Brussels sprouts are difficult to grow and may not be worth the effort. The seeds should be planted between February and April in pots or seedbeds and transplanted in May or June to rows about 2½ feet apart. Spacing the plants farther apart means you can harvest over a longer period. Add some compost or dried manure to the planting hole and mulch around the base of the plant to retain soil moisture. These plants need a very long growing season.

Harvest the sprouts, which mature from the bottom up, by pulling them off the axillary stem as they mature, that is, when they are firm and about 1 inch in diameter. If all of the sprouts mature together, you can remove the entire stem.

HOW TO BUY, STORE, AND PREPARE FOR COOKING

Brussels sprouts are sold year-round in supermarkets, but their peak growing season is from the fall through the early spring. Most Brussels sprouts are sold in pint-size plastic containers with a plastic covering. Remove the plastic covering and inspect the heads, then replace the covering. If you can buy the Brussels sprouts loose, choose small, even-sized ones so that they will cook evenly. Buy Brussels sprouts that are bright green with tightly packed heads. Examine the stem end: it should be clean and white. None of the leaves should be yellow or yellowing. Store Brussels sprouts in the refrigerator. For peak flavor, use Brussels sprouts within 5 days.

The ideal size for Brussels sprouts is 1¼ inches in diameter. Do not wash or trim the Brussels sprouts until you are ready to cook them. Do not remove the outer leaves, unless they are wilted, because these contain most of the nutrients of the plant. Trim only the smallest sliver of the stem; otherwise some of the attached leaves will fall off. With smaller Brussels sprouts it is not always necessary to trim the stem end. Do not overcook Brussels sprouts; cook them only until they are tender—when the tip of a skewer or knife glides to their center with only a hint of resistance.

RECIPE

Choux de Bruxelles
BRUSSELS SPROUTS

Brussels sprouts don't seem to be a very popular Mediterranean vegetable. I am not familiar with very many other recipes besides this one, which one may encounter in Provence. It is very important not to overcook Brussels sprouts. After cooking they should still be bright green with a little crunch when bitten into.

1 pound Brussels sprouts, split in half

1 or 2 large garlic cloves, to your taste, chopped very fine

3 tablespoons extra virgin olive oil, plus more for drizzling

1 cup water

Salt and freshly ground white pepper to taste

Place the Brussels sprouts in a medium nonreactive skillet with the garlic, olive oil, and water. Season with salt and pepper and turn the heat to high. Turn the heat off once the water has evaporated and the Brussels sprouts are ever so slightly crunchy to the bite, about 10 minutes. If the Brussels sprouts are not done to your taste, add a few more tablespoons of water and continue cooking to your taste. Transfer to a serving bowl, drizzle with olive oil if desired, and serve.

Makes 4 servings

BUCKSHORN PLANTAIN
Plantago coronopus L. var. *sativa* Fiori (syn. *Plantago major* L.) (Plantaginaceae)
Also called crowfoot plantain, buck's-born, capuchin's beard; ARABIC: *lisān al-hamal*; FRENCH: *corne de cerf*; ITALIAN: *còronopo, corno di cervo, tirafilo* (Tuscany), *orecchie d'asino* (Tuscany); SPANISH: *estrellamar, cuerno de ciervo*

PLANT CHARACTERISTICS AND VARIETIES
The edible part is the leaf, which is eaten cooked or raw. In the Arab world a variety of

plantain—this plantain having nothing to do with the fruit of the same name—is the species *Plantago major* L. In France the leaves are used in salads. The Italian raw salad known as *misticanze*, from the Marche region, is traditionally made with a mixture of wild and cultivated greens, including buckshorn plantain. In rural Tuscany the leaf is eaten in a vegetable soup, as is another variety of plantain, *P. lanceolata.*

PLANT ORIGIN

Buckshorn plantain is native to the Mediterranean and parts of central Europe.

PLANT HISTORY

Buckshorn plantain is mentioned in a medicinal context in the thirteenth-century Arabic pharmacological work by al-Samarqandī. This plant is mentioned in a German book of 1586 and by sixteenth- and seventeenth-century botanists.

HOW TO GROW AND HARVEST

Buckshorn plantain grows wild in sandy and saline soil along the coast and is often found in the spring. The plant must be picked when the leaves are very young, before the flowering stalk appears. It is nearly impossible to find this plant for sale, so if you want to find it you should grow it yourself or forage for it.

BUNCHING ONION

Allium fistulosum L. (Liliaceae)

Also called green onion, Japanese bunching onion, Welsh onion; ARABIC: *bassal al-mustatir, bassal al-ankūdy*; FRENCH: *ciboulette, cive, ail-ciboule, ciboule*; ITALIAN: *cipolla d'Inverno, cipoletta*; SPANISH: *cebolleta, cebolleta común, cebollino de verdeo común*

PLANT CHARACTERISTICS AND VARIETIES

This is a nonbulbing perennial onion with a number of shoots emanating from one seed. The bunching onion is unknown in the wild. The plant is grown for its edible tops and long leaf bases. In Greece a popular method for preparing these onions is to brush them with oil before grilling them.

PLANT ORIGIN

The bunching onion is said to originate in northern Mongolia and Siberia and/or central and western China.

PLANT HISTORY

The bunching onion arrived in the Mediterranean from the east or possibly from Germany. The name Welsh onion has nothing to do with Wales but is a corruption of the Old German word *walsch*, meaning "foreigner."

HOW TO GROW AND HARVEST

Sow the seeds 3 inches apart in the early spring in well-drained fertile soil in full sun.

Harvest established clumps by shearing off half the shoots at a time 2 inches above the soil.

BURNET

Sanguisorba minor Scop. (syn. *Poterium sanguisorba*) (Rosaceae)
Also called salad burnet; FRENCH: *pimprenelle;* ITALIAN: *sanguisorba;* SPANISH: *sanguisorba*

PLANT CHARACTERISTICS AND VARIETIES

Burnet is a hardy herbaceous perennial in the rose family. The leaves are edible and are used in salads or in the French herb mixture known as fines herbes. *Sanguisorba* species are not widely cultivated. The plant is found in the wild in grassy places, or among rocks, walls, and ruins. Its aromatic smell and cucumber-flavored leaves make it an excellent salad herb. The dried leaves are also used to make infusions.

PLANT ORIGIN

The plant may have originated in the northern temperate regions of Europe.

PLANT HISTORY

In the seventeenth century, Culpeper recommended burnet medicinally, and Castelvetro suggested that the tips could be used in salads. In 1693 Quintyne grew burnet in the royal vegetable garden in France.

HOW TO GROW AND HARVEST

Burnet is best grown from small plants bought at a garden shop and transplanted into a well-drained bed. Once the plants are established, harvest the tender leaves in the early spring after they push through the ground. You can harvest leaves again between late September until the end of December, depending on where you live.

BUTCHER'S BROOM

Ruscus aculeatus L. (syn. *R. ponticus* **Woronow**) (Liliaceae)
Also called Jew's myrtle; ITALIAN: *pungitopo, scaràsce* (Bari, Apulia); SPANISH: *brusco*

PLANT CHARACTERISTICS AND VARIETIES

Butcher's broom has flattened, leaflike branchlets with small flower clusters in the center or to the side of the branchlet. The fruit is a red berry. The plant's dried branches are used to make brooms (hence the name). The edible parts are the young, narrow, tapered shoots (or spears). Butcher's broom is sometimes used as a substitute for asparagus. The taste is pungent and rather bitter. In Sicily the so-called *asparagi di giardino* (garden asparagus) is *R. hypoglossum*, a relative of *R. aculeatus,* with very thin edible spears and tiny red berries as fruit.

PLANT HISTORY

Some scholars believe that the "pricking brier" mentioned in Ezekiel 28:24 is butcher's broom. Theophrastus describes how butcher's broom bears its fruit on its leaves, and Pliny mentions butcher's broom *(ruscum)* as a food and medicinal plant used to treat bladder stones in Italy.

HOW TO GROW AND HARVEST

Sow seeds in the fall in well-drained soil in sun or shade. Although the seeds may take 18 months to germinate, the young shoots are harvested in the spring.

BUTTERHEAD LETTUCE
See Lettuce.

BUTTERNUT SQUASH
See Squash.

CABBAGE

Brassica oleracea **Capitata group (syn.** *B. capitata, B. oleracea* **L. var.** *capitata* **L.) (Cruciferae-Brassicaceae)**
ARABIC: *krumb, kurunb* (colloquial), *malfūf* (Syria); FRENCH: *chou, chou cabus, chou blanc, chou pommé*; GREEK: *lachanon, lahanon, chrema*; ITALIAN: *cavolo, cavolo cappuccio*; SERBO-CROATIAN: *zelje, kupus*; SPANISH: *col, col roja, repollo morado*; TURKISH: *lahana*

PLANT CHARACTERISTICS AND VARIETIES

The edible part is the leaf, which is consumed either cooked or raw. Cabbage is a biennial grown as an annual. The plant has yellow flowers, although some species have white flowers. Today there are hundreds of varieties of cabbage that have been developed from the progenitor cabbage, called the wild cabbage; among the varieties are many forms of cabbage and further horticultural developments such as broccoli, cauliflower, Brussels sprouts, broccoliflower, and kohlrabi. Related species of the wild cabbage have produced the turnip, swede, Chinese cabbages, and rape or colza (*Brassica napus*). Several related species still grow around the Mediterranean, such as *B. montana* Pourret (syn. *B. oleracea* subsp. *robertiana* [Gay] Rouy and Foucaud) in Catalonia and northern Italy; *B. insularis* on the coasts of Corsica, Sardinia, and North Africa; *B. rupestris, B. incana, B. villosa,* and *B. macrocarpa* in southern Italy and Sicily; and *B. cretica* and *B. hilarionis* in the eastern Mediterranean.

Although *Brassica* taxonomy has changed often, contemporary botanical divisions are as follows for *B. oleracea*: Acephala group (kale, collard, colowort); Alboglabra group (Chinese broccoli, Chinese kale); Botrytis group (cauliflower, perennial broccoli); Capitata group (cabbage, Savoy cabbage, red cabbage); Gemmifera group (Brussels sprouts); Gongylodes group (kohlrabi); Italica group (Italian broccoli, asparagus broccoli, sprouting broccoli, purple cauliflower, cape

Broccoli); and Tronchuda group (tronchuda kale, Portuguese cabbage, seakale cabbage).

There are some 400 species of cabbage, and they can be divided into five groups. First are the familiar smooth-leafed cabbage that is green, red, or white, and the wrinkled-leafed varieties such as Savoy cabbage. Second are pointed cabbages such as Chinese cabbages. The third are cabbages with large budding stems like Brussels sprouts (see entry). Green curly, leafy cabbages such as kale (see entry) are a fourth group. The last group are flowering cabbages such as broccoli (see entry) and cauliflower (see entry). There are other suggested divisions too. For instance, some horticulturalists divide present-day cabbages into eight growing types: spring cabbage, summer cabbage, autumn cabbage, winter cabbage, Savoy cabbage, Savoy hybrids, January King, and red cabbage (details follow). Savoy cabbage, *B. oleracea* L. var. *sabauda* L. (syn. *B. oleracea* var. bullata, *B. bullata* var. *sabauda*)—known in French as *chou de savoie* or *chou de Milan*, in Italian as *verze* or *cavolo verzotto*, and in Spanish as *col de Milan*—is particularly popular in Provence and northern Italy. In the supermarket, one usually finds only three varieties of cabbage (*B. oleracea* L. var. *capitata* L.): green head cabbage, red head cabbage, and Savoy cabbage. Although Napa cabbage is a member of the larger family of cabbages, it is actually a "mustard" or "Oriental" green of the species *Brassica rapa*. The fact that broccoli, Brussels sprouts, kale, cauliflower, and kohlrabi are all

forms of cabbage complicates the discussion of the lineage of these plants.

PLANT ORIGIN

N. Vavilov wrote that the cabbage originated in the Mediterranean and Asia Minor, although K. F. Thompson maintains that wild cabbage is native to the coasts of northwestern Europe as well as the Mediterranean. It is doubtful whether the many cultivated varieties of *B. oleracea* evolved solely from the wild cabbage (*Brassica oleracea* L. subsp. *oleracea*) because there are other wild diploid relatives of the cabbage that may have contributed to the evolution of the cultivated varieties.

PLANT HISTORY

Cabbage was one of the most common foods on the Mediterranean table for more than a millennium. The earliest record of cultivated cabbages in the Mediterranean dates from about 600 B.C., a mention of kale in early Greek literature. Because that source describes the eating of the stems of this plant, it is thought that the plant is a precursor to a primitive cauliflower or broccoli. Theophrastus wrote of three kinds of cabbage, the curly-leafed, smooth-leafed, and the wild cabbage. He noted the medicinal value of the latter. There are many descriptions of kale and cabbage, related plants, in the writings of the Roman authors. Thompson claims a heading cabbage was known by the Romans, but this view is not generally accepted. There are some obscure references by Pliny and Columella to what has been taken by some to be head cabbage. These writings refer to the head of the plant being a foot in diameter, but it is not at all clear whether the writers are referring to the compact headed cabbage that we know today or whether they are simply referring to the above-ground portion of the plant. Cato's description of various cabbages, which are referred to by Pliny, does not mention head cabbage but three other kinds: one with leaves wide open, one with a crinkly leaf (perhaps Savoy cabbage), and a third with very small stalks. Pliny also described an open heading cabbage he called *tritianon,* but some botanists don't consider this a true "head" cabbage and are disposed to wait until a real hearting cabbage, *B. oleracea* var. *capitata,* makes its appearance by 1150 in Germany. Pliny has several very long sections on the cabbage in his *Natural History,* describing the vegetable both in culinary terms and medicinally. In the period after Cato, the wealthy citizens of Rome thought of cabbage as poor people's food as we know from Juvenal's satire in which he described the difference between the food that the patron ate, namely olives to garnish an excellent fish, and the food of the client, who finds cabbage in his "nauseous dish."

The original Mediterranean cabbage resembled today's rapa or kale; it was a wild field cabbage found growing along the coast and did not have the head we associate with cabbage today. The original cabbage contained a large amount of mustard oil, which had an unpleasant taste. Over centuries this wild coastal cabbage evolved through cultivation in manor gardens until it lost its mustard oil and developed into a plant with tender and copious leaves. The cabbage continued to develop under cultivation by the peasant farmer and was bred for fleshier leaves that started to curl in on themselves to form a head. This development may have happened earlier than the twelfth century because we know that the famous conservative theologian St. Hildegard of Bingen (d. 1179) was familiar with both white and red head cabbages. Albertus Magnus, who lived in the twelfth century, refers to a plant called *caputium,* which may be a head cabbage, although he gives no description. The botanist Joannes Ruellis, in *De natura stirpium libri tres,* published in Paris in 1536, provides what some people consider the first clear reference to head cabbage, which he calls *capucos coles* ("head-stem") or *cabutos.* The ancients, on the other hand, never knew the head cabbage.

In classical Greece, this leafy cabbage was cooked with plenty of coriander and rue, then sprinkled with honey vinegar and a little silphium (*Silphium perfoliatum*), according to Mnesitheus (fourth century B.C.) who is quoted in Oribasius (fourth century A.D.).

The Romans grew cabbage, along with a host of other vegetables. They had a love of cabbage because of its supposed medicinal value. Pliny (*Natural History,* XX, xxxiii, 78) said it would be a long task to make a list of all the praises of cabbage. It was believed that

Cabbage

As my selection of recipes shows, cabbage has continued to be a popular vegetable in the Mediterranean, its ubiquitousness having carried over from the Middle Ages. The French, among Mediterranean cooks today, are the least likely to cook and eat cabbage. But there is no denying that one of the most fabulous of cabbage recipes, *sou fassum*, comes from Provence. In this dish, cabbage leaves are stuffed with a mixture of rice, peas, tomatoes, Toulouse sausage, and pork tenderloin and steamed and braised in beef broth flavored with lamb shoulder. Cabbage is also found in North Africa, stuffed, too, but often as an ingredient in the ragout for couscous.

eating cabbage could ward off a hangover, as well as act as a laxative. The Romans ate cabbage raw dipped in vinegar or boiled and served with lots of oil, a little salt, cumin, and fine barley flour, which was thought to be a cure for colic. The Roman writer Cato (in *On Agriculture*, CLVI–CLVII, 10–11), who said the medicinal value of cabbage surpassed that of all other vegetables, recommended that women bathe in the urine saved from a person who habitually ate cabbage. By washing her private parts with this solution she would never be diseased. In the thirteenth- and fourteenth-century gardens of Palermo the largest quarter of the garden was given over to growing cabbages, leading the contemporary French historian Henri Bresc to call the vegetable the "inevitable cabbage." Contracts from taverns and inns in Palermo two cen-

turies later show the *ortolani*, the growers, grew only cabbage and onions and ate only cabbage minestrone reinforced with fava and chickpeas, and eaten with stale bread.

Cabbage was the most common vegetable in the Spanish garden, the medieval *huerta*, and was also eaten nearly every day in medieval Languedoc and Provence, which we know because students at the Papal school in Tret (in Provence) ate cabbage soup 125 days out of the year. Cabbage was known by three names: white cabbage, green cabbage, and *choux cabus* (large-headed cabbage). The *Ménagier de Paris*, a household reminder book written in late-fourteenth-century France, says a lot about cabbage—that the best cabbages are those picked before the frost, and that they should be cooked in the morning and served with olive oil.

In fifteenth-century Italy, cabbage and bread were the main elements of the diet. Three kinds of Savoy cabbage were described in a German herbal from 1543, and it is thought from the name of this cabbage that it was first cultivated in the Savoy region of France in the Middle Ages.

K. F. Thompson writes that marrow-stem kale, *Brassica oleracea* L. Acephala group, was recorded with certainty for the first time only in the Vendée region of France in the nineteenth century and that its origin is not known. Leafy, unbranched kales and branching, thin-stemmed kales were the earliest cultivated Brassicas.

HOW TO GROW AND HARVEST

Spring cabbages, "greens," or "hearting" cabbage, are planted in late September and are harvested in April or May. When they are to be eaten as greens they are grown for their loose, leafy heads; when they are grown to be eaten as hearts, they are grown as "hearting" cabbages.

The various cultivars of summer cabbages are hearting cabbages; they are planted in April or May and harvested from June to August. Autumn cabbages, which are hearting, are planted in June and harvested in September and October.

Winter cabbages are large cabbages grown for winter storage. They are planted in June and harvested in the late fall. Savoy cabbages are very hardy; they are planted in early July and

harvested throughout the winter. Their leaves are crinkly. Savoy hybrids are also very hardy, a cross between Savoy and white cabbages.

January King is a cultivar planted in early June and harvested in the late fall. It has slightly crinkly leaves and a very good flavor.

Red cabbages are harvested in October or November and usually stored through the winter.

Cabbages grow well in well-drained soil and full sunlight. The seeds can be started in pots or a seedbed and the seedlings transplanted to their final garden spot when they are 1 or 2 months old. The soil should be firm without much fertilizer at first. Once established, cabbages should be watered well until maturity.

Harvest spring cabbage when the head is hard and before hot weather causes the head to split. Harvest fall cabbage before the head freezes in the winter. Cut the head from the stalk an inch above ground level, which will encourage new grow around the stem.

HOW TO BUY, STORE, AND PREPARE FOR COOKING

When shopping for head cabbage, look for a solid, heavy head with tight, crisp outer leaves that are not peeling away from the head. Buy whole cabbage of the size you'll need rather than cut-up cellophane-wrapped pieces, because once the leaves are cut, the cabbage begins to lose vitamin C. By the same token, do not wash or chop cabbage until you are ready to cook it; otherwise the cabbage will lose vitamin C. A two-pound head of cabbage will serve six people as a side dish.

Cabbage keeps well in the crisper drawer of your refrigerator. Although it is not necessary, storing cabbage in a perforated plastic bag is ideal—the cabbage will keep for 2 weeks. Once the cabbage has been cut, use it within 2 days for optimal taste.

To core a cabbage, cut around the core with a paring knife angled inward so the core comes out as a cone. Remove the outermost leaves if they are peeling or damaged.

When using cabbage leaves to wrap other foods, gently boil the whole head for ten minutes, then peel off each leaf. Cabbage juice reacts to carbon steel, so use a stainless steel knife when cutting and a nonreactive cooking vessel when cooking, not an aluminum or cast-iron pot.

RECIPES

Coles con Castañas
CABBAGE WITH CHESTNUTS

In Andalusia, where this recipe comes from, cabbage finds its way into many preparations, especially thick, flavorful stews. The combination of cabbage and chestnuts is particularly enticing. Although it sounds elegant today, this was poor people's food in the Middle Ages. There may be some very old Alsatian influence here,

because there is an identical dish in Alsace. This hearty cabbage dish goes very well with a braised pork chop.

One 1-pound head cabbage, damaged outer leaves
*   removed, cored, and cut into thin strips*
1 cup milk
¼ pound shelled and chopped roasted chestnuts
*   (about ¾ cup)*
2 tablespoons pork lard
2 tablespoons all-purpose unbleached flour
¾ teaspoon salt

I. Bring salted water to a boil in a large nonreactive pot and cook the cabbage strips until they are completely wilted, about 10 minutes. Drain and return the cabbage to the pot, along with the milk and chestnuts. Bring the pot to just under a boil, reduce the heat to low, cover, and cook until the cabbage is completely soft, 1 to 2 hours (keep checking on it).

2. Mix the lard, flour, and salt together, stir into the cabbage, and cook until the cabbage almost resembles soft mashed potatoes, about 10 minutes. Serve hot.

Makes 4 servings

Verza Ripiene alla Napoletana
NEAPOLITAN-STYLE STUFFED CABBAGE

In Campania, stuffed vegetables are common. In this recipe, cabbage leaves are stuffed with *scamorza* and mozzarella cheese and baked with a tomato sauce. *Scamorza* is a soft mozzarella-type cheese originally made in the Abruzzi and Molise provinces of Italy with water buffalo milk. Today this cheese is made with cow's milk and is found mostly in Italian markets, as is the smoked version used in this recipe. If you can't find *scamorza*, replace it with regular or smoked imported provolone cheese.

One 2-pound head Savoy cabbage, damaged outer leaves removed
¼ pound smoked scamorza cheese, cut into 18 small wedges
¼ pound fresh mozzarella cheese, cut into 18 small wedges
2½ cups tomato sauce (page 337)
Salt and freshly ground black pepper to taste
3 tablespoons freshly grated Parmigiano-Reggiano cheese

1. Steam or boil the head of cabbage until a skewer will glide into the center of the core with a little resistance, but the cabbage is still firm, about 35 minutes. Let it cool, then core the cabbage and remove the leaves carefully so they don't rip. You should have 18 leaves.

2. Preheat the oven to 350°F. Arrange a cabbage leaf in front of you with the central stem rib closest to you. Place a piece of *scamorza* and a piece of mozzarella in the center of each leaf and roll it up, tucking the sides in as you do, creating a nice, neat little package. Continue rolling the leaves until you have about 18 rolls. Pour half the tomato sauce over the bottom of a large nonreactive casserole or baking dish and lay the rolled-up cabbage leaves in the dish in two layers. Season each layer with salt and pepper. Cover the cabbage rolls with the remaining tomato sauce and sprinkle the Parmigiano on top. Bake until the top is dappled black and the sauce is bubbling, 12 to 15 minutes. Serve immediately.

Makes 4 to 6 servings

Pirjati Zelje
BRAISED CABBAGE

Cabbage is a very popular vegetable in the Balkans. It is served raw, in the form of sauerkraut, and cooked in a variety of ways. In the northern part of the former Yugoslavia, cabbage may be cooked with sour cream or tossed with noodles and smoked bacon. In Bosnia or Montenegro, to the south and closer to Greece, cabbage is cooked with tomatoes. This recipe for braised cabbage from Slovenia (in the north near Hungary) is typically served as a bed for a roast duckling.

¼ cup extra virgin olive oil
2 bay leaves
2 tablespoons tomato paste
1 cup dry white wine
One 2-pound head green cabbage, cored and sliced as thin as vermicelli
15 black peppercorns
8 juniper berries, lightly crushed
1 teaspoon dried thyme
1 tablespoon freshly squeezed lemon juice
Salt and freshly ground black pepper to taste

1. Heat the olive oil in a large skillet over medium-high heat. Add the bay leaves, and cook them until they begin to sizzle. Reduce the heat to medium and very carefully add the tomato paste and wine, which will spurt and splatter rather dramatically. Cook for a minute, then add the cabbage, peppercorns, juniper berries, and thyme. Mix the cabbage so it is covered with sauce.

2. Add the lemon juice and continue to braise the cabbage over medium heat until it softens, 6 to 8 minutes. Reduce the heat to low, season with salt and pepper, and cook until the cabbage is completely soft, about 45 minutes. Correct the seasoning and serve hot.

Makes 4 servings

Kestaneli Lahana Dolması
CABBAGE LEAVES STUFFED WITH CHESTNUTS AND SPICES

When I first came across this recipe in Turkey, I was intrigued, because I had already collected another cabbage recipe with chestnuts (page 81) in Andalusia, on the opposite end of the Mediterranean. But the differences are profound. The Spanish recipe is simple and peasantlike, while this recipe must be the invention of a restaurant chef. Turkish cooks are masters of the stuffed vegetable. In this preparation, the stuffing is made with chestnuts and rice and spiced with cinnamon and allspice. The stuffed cabbage leaves can be eaten hot, but it is also common to serve them at room temperature. I believe the latter serving method allows the flavors to mellow better. This recipe is from Bursa and is adapted from one found in Ghillie Başan's *Classic Turkish Cooking*.

One 1½-pound head green cabbage
3 tablespoons extra virgin olive oil, divided
1 small onion, chopped fine
4 large garlic cloves, chopped fine
1 teaspoon sugar
⅓ cup raw short-grain rice, soaked in cold water to cover for 30 minutes or rinsed under cold running water until it runs clear, drained
1 teaspoon freshly ground allspice berries
1 teaspoon ground cinnamon
½ teaspoon salt
⅔ cup water
1½ cups shelled and chopped roasted chestnuts
1 small bunch fresh dill, thick stems discarded, chopped
6 tablespoons finely chopped fresh parsley leaves
Salt and freshly ground black pepper to taste
Freshly squeezed juice from 1 lemon
Lemon wedges

1. Steam or boil the cabbage until a skewer will glide to the center with a little resistance but the cabbage is still firm, about 20 minutes. Drain the head of cabbage and place it under cold running water to stop it from cooking. In a circular motion, remove the hard central core with a knife, carefully pull apart the leaves without ripping them, and stack them.

2. Heat 1 tablespoon of the olive oil in a small skillet over medium-high heat. Cook the onion, garlic, and sugar until the onion is translucent, about 5 minutes, stirring frequently so the garlic and sugar don't burn. Add the rice, allspice, cinnamon, and salt, and barely cover with ⅔ cup water. Bring the pot to a boil, reduce the heat to low, cover, and simmer until all the liquid is absorbed, 15 to 20 minutes.

3. In a large bowl, toss together the chestnuts, rice mixture, dill, and parsley. Season the mixture lightly with salt and pepper. Arrange a cabbage leaf in front of you with the central stem rib closest to you. Put a heaping tablespoon of stuffing mixture on the portion of the cabbage closest to you and roll the leaf over once. Tuck in the sides and continue rolling until the leaf forms a nice, neat little package. Continue to stuff and roll the cabbage leaves in this manner, packing the rolled-up cabbage leaves snugly in a large nonreactive skillet or casserole.

4. Mix the remaining 2 tablespoons olive oil with the lemon juice and pour over the cabbage rolls. Invert a heavy plate over the cabbage rolls then cover the skillet or casserole with its lid. Bring the liquid in the skillet to bubbling, reduce the heat to low, and cook until the cabbage leaves look translucent, about 25 minutes. Allow the cabbage leaves to come to room temperature in the skillet. Transfer to a serving platter and serve with wedges of lemon.

Makes 6 to 8 servings

Lahano Salata
CABBAGE SALAD

The Greeks are quite fond of vegetable salads. In this recipe, cabbage, green pepper, and onions are flavored with a dressing of yogurt, mayonnaise, and dill. It's a perfectly fine accompaniment to meat grilled outdoors during the hot summer months. Serve this Greek cabbage salad with grilled lamb chops marinated in olive oil, lemon juice, garlic, and oregano.

*4 cups finely shredded cabbage (about one
 1¼-pound head cabbage, cored)*
2 large garlic cloves, chopped very fine
*2 large green bell peppers, 1 cut in half width-
 wise, seeded, and thinly sliced; 1 seeded and
 cut into rings*
3 tablespoons grated onion
1 teaspoon sugar
¼ cup white wine vinegar
Salt and freshly ground black pepper to taste
1 cup plain yogurt
½ cup mayonnaise (preferably homemade)
*1 small bunch fresh dill, heavy stems discarded,
 chopped*

1. In a large bowl, toss together the cabbage, garlic, finely sliced green pepper, and onion. Add the sugar and vinegar and season with salt and pepper. Toss again and let stand until serving time.

2. When ready to serve, toss the salad with the yogurt, mayonnaise, and dill, transfer to a

serving platter or bowl, and garnish with the green pepper rings. Serve.

Makes 4 servings

CABBAGE THISTLE

Cirsium oleraceum (L.) Scop. (Asteraceae-Compositae)
Also called meadow thistle; ITALIAN: *stioppone, stramontano*; TUSCAN DIALECT: *perticone (C. arvense)*

PLANT CHARACTERISTICS AND VARIETIES
The edible parts of this thistle, which is similar in appearance to an artichoke, are the young shoots. The heads have pale yellow flowers with yellowish green bractlike and nearly spineless leaves. The young leaves of Canada thistle *(C. arvense)* are used in rural Tuscany in vegetable soups and stews.

PLANT ORIGIN
Cabbage thistle is native to the European Mediterranean.

PLANT HISTORY
The *cirsion* described by Pliny as a tender little sprout surrounded by prickly leaves with small purple heads on top might be cabbage thistle. He says it is used as an amulet to relieve the pain of varicose veins.

HOW TO GROW AND HARVEST
This plant is largely no longer cultivated. It is sometimes harvested from the wild.

CALAVANCE

Dolichos barbadensis and *D. sinensis* etc. (Leguminosae)
GREEK: *phaseloi*

PLANT CHARACTERISTICS AND VARIETIES
Calavance is the name given to several varieties of pulse in the *Dolichos* genus, a genus that also includes the hyacinth bean. It is not known how the word *calavance* entered the English language. Athenaeus relates that the Spartans would serve green calavances, beans, and dried figs at *kopides*, feasts given for strangers. Today this vegetable is eaten by Bedouin and Berber tribes in North Africa.

CAMELINA HISPIDA BOISS. VAR. *GRANDIFLORA* (BOISS.)(CRUCIFERAE-BRASSICACEAE)

TURKISH: *bozot*

PLANT CHARACTERISTICS AND VARIETIES
In Turkey, the ear-shaped leaves of this annual or biennial plant are gathered in the wild and used in salads.

CAMPION

Silene inflata Sm. (Caryophyllaceae)
Also called catchfly; ARABIC: *ḥubāḥib*;
FRENCH: *silène enflée, crousilloun* (Provence-
Roya Valley); ITALIAN: *licnide, carletti*
(Veneto), *orecchiella* (Tuscany), *boccon di
pecora* (Tuscany); SPANISH: *colleja*; TURKISH:
tavşan ekmeği

PLANT CHARACTERISTICS AND VARIETIES
Campion is a member of the pink family, a
genus of ornamental plants. The leaves are
eaten in salads. White campion *(S. alba)*, red
campion *(S. dioica)*, and bladder campion *(S.
vulgare* or *vulgaris)* are all used in the Veneto and
the Val Colvera areas of the western Friuli
region of northern Italy in a preparation
called *pistic*, a spring stew made with more
than fifty other wild greens. Bladder campion
is also a wild edible green that is used for food
in the Aksaray Province of Turkey. In rural
Tuscany the young leaves are used in vegetable
soups.

PLANT ORIGIN
Campion is native to temperate zones in
Europe.

CARDAMINOPSIS HALLERI (L.) (CRUCIFERAE-BRASSICACEAE)

PLANT CHARACTERISTICS AND VARIETIES
This plant produces many stolons and has
numerous flowers. The leaves are the edible
part. The plant is used in the Friuli region of
northern Italy in a ritual spring stew dish
called *pistic* that contains up to fifty different
wild greens.

CARDOON

Cynara cardunculus L. (Asteraceae-
Compositae)
ARABIC: *kharshūf, kharshaf, kankar*; FRENCH:
cardon; ITALIAN: *cardo, cardone*; SPANISH: *cardo
comestible, cardo de huerta*; TURKISH: *kenger*

PLANT CHARACTERISTICS AND VARIETIES
The cardoon is a perennial usually grown as
an annual. It is grown for its fleshy celery-
looking leaf bases, which are formed by the
basal rosette of huge leaves. The leaf bases are
tied up and blanched. The dried flowers can
be used as a substitute for rennet in cheese
making. There is some controversy among
botanists about the cardoon. One group
believes that both the cardoon and the artichoke derive from a wild perennial herb,
Cynara cardunculus var. *silvestris*, that grows in
the Mediterranean. The second group holds
that there are two distinct species, the cardoon

(*C. cardunculus*) and the artichoke (*C. scolymus*). The third group argues that the artichoke is a cultivated form of the cardoon. The cultivated cardoon (*C. cardunculus* var. *altilis*) is quite different from the wild cardoon. It is nearly twice as tall, about 7 feet, with fleshier leaves and fewer thorns.

As far as the cardoon's presence in North Africa is concerned, the "wild artichoke" mentioned by cookbook author Paula Wolfert and called *coques* (properly, *quq*) is not the artichoke, but is *C. humilis,* the name deriving from the ball-like capitulum, and also known generally as *kharshaf,* or cardoon. The *tesekăra* of the Berbers, which is eaten by animals, is *Carduus sphærocephalus.*

PLANT ORIGIN

The cardoon is probably native to the Mediterranean and perhaps into central Asia.

PLANT HISTORY

Cardoons are found growing wild in the Mediterranean from Crete to Sicily and west to Spain and Portugal and in North Africa, where they are a popular food. The cardoon was known to the Greco-Roman world by names such as *cynara, carduus, scolymus, cactos,* and *spondylium.* The *cynara* or *kinara* mentioned in Athenaeus has been mistranslated in English editions as "artichoke." This is incorrect; the plant Athenaeus was referring to was the cardoon. He also describes a plant called *kakton* (cactus) growing in Sicily, as well as a plant called *pternix*; both are thistles. The Latin *carduus* was used as a generic name for all thistles. Pliny says that the cardoon was much desired in Rome and yielded a higher price at market than any other garden vegetable. In particular, he mentions the cardoons from Carthage. In the sixteenth century, Ruellius speaks of the cardoon as a food that was appreciated as asparagus is today. Castelvetro described cardoons as a vegetable to be enjoyed throughout the winter. The Italians, he said, ate the stems, not the flowering heads.

HOW TO GROW AND HARVEST

Cardoons are perennials grown as annuals. They are raised from seeds that are started indoors in sandy soil in the early spring. The seedlings are transplanted outside after the last frost and set about 3 feet apart in full sun. They can be grown in the same type of soil as the artichoke, although they are sturdier and easier to grow. Cardoons should be well watered. Once the leaves are large, they should be tied together when they are very dry and wrapped in black polyethylene to blanch, which takes 2 or 3 weeks. Harvest the plant by severing the root and cutting off the leaves where the green blades begin, as well as discarding the head.

HOW TO BUY, STORE, AND PREPARE FOR COOKING

Cardoons usually appear in markets in December. They look like oversize celery bunches and are a whitish, dull green color. Choose cardoon bunches with firm stalks.

Strore cardoons in the refrigerator unless you intend to cook them within 2 days. The cardoon is a bitter, vaguely artichoke-tasting vegetable that requires long cooking in salted and acidulated water because of the toughness and bitterness; vinegar or lemon juice is used to prevent the cardoon from discoloring. Remove all the leaves if they have not already been removed. With a vegetable peeler, peel the tough, stringy part from the outside edge. If you have a nonreactive pot big enough, tie the loose stalks and head together with string and steam the cardoon whole, or break off individual stalks to cook. Alternatively, an easier approach is to cut the stalks into 2-, 3-, or 4-inch lengths and boil them in salted water acidulated (with the juice from 1 lemon or ½ cup vinegar) until tender, about 3 hours. Drain and dry the stalks a bit, and you can then freeze them for later use.

RECIPE

Cardi alla Parmigiana
PARMA-STYLE CARDOONS

Cardoons are well loved by Italians; my grandfather was so wild about the scrambled eggs and cardoons that he used to prepare for himself that, when on drives in the country, he would sneak into strangers' yards and cut down the wild plants. All the while his children, cringing with embarrassment, would try to coax him off the prop-

erty. This recipe from Parma is a simple one using the local Parmigiano cheese.

1 cardoon (about 2 pounds)
Freshly squeezed juice from 1 lemon
Salt
6 tablespoons (¾ stick) unsalted butter, melted
½ cup freshly grated Parmigiano-Reggiano cheese

1. Trim the cardoon of its leaves and peel the ribs on the outside of the stalks with a vegetable peeler. You don't have to do this very thoroughly, just enough to get the major strings off. Slice the leaves into 4-inch lengths. Bring a large pot of water (with the lemon juice and some salt) to a boil and cook the cardoon until tender, about 3 hours. Drain.
2. Preheat the oven to 350°F. Butter a 12 x 9-inch ceramic or glass baking pan with 1 tablespoon of the melted butter. Arrange a layer of cardoon leaves on the bottom of the baking pan. Sprinkle half the cheese over the cardoon, salt lightly, and drizzle half the remaining butter over the leaves. Add another layer of cardoon leaves, finishing with a layer of the remaining cheese and melted butter. Bake until the cheese is completely melted and the butter is sizzling on the edges, 20 to 30 minutes. Serve very hot.

Makes 4 to 6 servings

CARROT

Daucus carota L. subsp. *sativus* (Hoffm.)
Arcang. (Umbelliferae)

ARABIC: *jizar, jazar, zurūdiya* (Algeria);
FRENCH: *carotte*; GREEK: *daukion, koroto,
karoto (caroto)*; ITALIAN: *carota*; SERBO-
CROATIAN: *mrkva*; SPANISH: *zanahoria*;
TURKISH: *havuç*

PLANT CHARACTERISTICS AND VARIETIES

The carrot is a cool-weather herbaceous biennial that produces usually orange roots in the
first year and flowers the following spring,
although the plant is often cultivated as an
annual. The roots and leaves are eaten either
raw or cooked. Wild carrots have white roots,
but cultivated carrots have been developed for
orange, red, yellow, and other colored roots.
Carrots are members of the Umbelliferae
family, which includes parsnip, celery, parsley,
and some poisonous parsleylike plants.
Several varieties of wild carrot are found in
the Mediterranean, usually growing on coastal
cliffs or dunes. Wild carrots are popular in
North African cooking, and the ones with red
or purple roots are still found in Afghanistan
today. By the end of the eighteenth century,
four varieties were recognized, and all modern
varieties derive from these four: Long Orange,
Late Half Long, Early Half Long, and Early
Scarlet Horn.

PLANT ORIGIN

The carotene carrot, with its familiar orange
roots, is derived from the anthocyanin carrot,
with its purple roots, whose center of diversity is Afghanistan, and therefore that area is
thought to be its center of origin. Whether
carrots were first cultivated there is not
known, but early cultivars must have been
selected for fleshier, less forked varieties that
were conical in shape and ranging in color
from purple to light black. N. Vavilov proposed what he called the inner-Asiatic center
of origin for cultivated plants, an area consisting of the Indian Punjab, Kashmir, and
northwestern border republics, Afghanistan,
Tadzhikistan, Uzbekistan, and the western
portion of the Chinese province of Tien Shan.

In the *Wellness Encyclopaedia of Food and
Nutrition* Sheldon Margen suggests that the
carrot may have been domesticated from the
wildflower known as Queen Anne's lace *(Ammi
majus)*, but that is not a generally accepted
view. Philips and Rix suggest that if carrots
did not originate in Afghanistan, they were
first cultivated in the eastern Mediterranean.
Taylor's Guide to Vegetables and Herbs suggests the
Mediterranean or possibly Persia as a place of
origin.

PLANT HISTORY

Some commentators argue that the carrot was
brought east from Central Asia by the Arabs
in about the tenth century, because the carrot
appears in Anatolia at that time. We know,
however, that carrot seeds have been found at

Carrot

✺ IN THE MEDITERRANEAN, CARROTS USUALLY FIND THEIR WAY INTO BROTHS, STEWS, *SOFFRITTI*, AND RAGOUTS AND ARE NOT eaten often as a side dish. When they are, they are prepared more simply than in the recipes that follow, perhaps boiled and dressed with vinegar and olive oil, or made into carrot soup in the Balkans, or cooked with monkfish in Spain. Carrots are also pickled. In Algeria one often finds a whole cooked carrot arranged attractively on top of a mound of couscous.

Neolithic sites in Switzerland. It appears in Islamic Spain in the twelfth century as we know from descriptions by Ibn al-ᶜAwwām. Philips and Rix claim that the Romans grew carrots. We do know from written sources that the cultivated anthocyanin carrot spread westward and eastward and that the plant can be traced to Asia Minor in the tenth century and to Arab-occupied Spain in the twelfth century. Bianchini, Corbetta, and Pistoia claim that the Greeks and Romans knew the carrot only as a wild plant that grew in scattered locations. Galen seems to imply that the carrot was cultivated when he wrote that the root of the wild carrot was less fit to be eaten than was the domestic one. The word used to denote carrots by the Roman authors, *dauca*, was a generic term for a variety of plants, including parsnips. Pliny discusses the four kinds of *dauca* that had been enumerated by Petronius Diodotus. The best grew on Crete; the next best grew in Greece (Achaia), resembled fennel, and had a root with a pleasant taste and smell. It seems likely that the Romans may have known the wild carrot. On the other hand, Albertus Magnus, writing in the thirteenth century, talks of the *pastinaca*, which appears to be the parsnip, although it might be the carrot. The Latin poet Virgil and the fifteenth-century Italian scholar Ermolao Barbaro describe the carrot under the name *pastinaca*. Apicius, the Roman cookbook writer of the first century, gives directions for preparing *carota seu pastinaca*, which must be the carrot we know. Leonhardus Rauwolffud reports that carrots were growing in the gardens of sixteenth-century Aleppo, Syria.

The familiar orange carrot does not show up until it was cultivated in seventeenth-century Holland.

Carrots grow best in sandy soil that is chalky or well limed. The soil should be manured the autumn before planting because, as with other umbellifers, if manure is applied when the seeds are in the ground, the roots will fork. The soil should be loose and friable with equal parts sand; peat moss; and sifted, limed, and fertilized compost. Sow the seeds thinly in rows about 1 inch deep 1 or 2 weeks before the last frost. The size of the carrot will depend on how densely the area is sown; the denser the planting, the smaller the carrot. The young carrots that are pulled out in the thinning process can be eaten. To distinguish carrot seedlings from weeds, make sure the rows are planted straight and about 12 inches apart. The carrot plant is particularly susceptible to damage by the carrot root fly (root maggot flies). Harvest carrots as you need them, leaving the rest in the ground. Mulch the plants if heavy frosts seem imminent.

HOW TO BUY, STORE, AND PREPARE FOR COOKING

Carrots can be left in the ground through the winter as long as they are mulched or there is snow cover. They can also be stored in a root cellar in a box of moistened sand or sawdust. Carrots bought at the supermarket or farmers' market can be kept refrigerated in a plastic bag in the crisper drawer of the refrigerator for 2 weeks. Limp carrots can be used in stocks. Do not store carrots with fruits that produces ethylene gas as they ripen, such as apples or pears, as the carrots will deteriorate more quickly.

Cooking carrots until they are just tender but still crisp makes their nutrients more accessible. Overcooking carrots can significantly decrease their beta-carotene level.

RECIPES

Carota al Marsala
CARROTS WITH MARSALA WINE

This Sicilian recipe is very simple to make, but it is so good that you will find yourself making it often as an accompaniment to a wide range of dishes, such as grilled veal, braised duck, beef stew, or baked swordfish. If you can manage to find baby carrots, not only will you not need to peel them—just brush them off well—but the dish will be much more delicious.

2 tablespoons extra virgin olive oil
2 pounds baby carrots (about ½ inch in diameter), trimmed and peeled, if desired
1 cup water
4 teaspoons sugar
Salt to taste
1 cup sweet Marsala wine

1. Heat the olive oil in a large skillet over medium-high heat and cook the carrots for 1 to 2 minutes before pouring in the water. When the water has nearly evaporated, sprin-

kle the carrots with the sugar and salt and let the sauce caramelize for 1 to 2 minutes.

2. Add the Marsala wine and continue cooking until it is nearly evaporated and the carrots are glazed. Serve immediately.

Makes 4 to 6 servings

Carottes Nouvelles aux Petits Pois

NEW CARROTS AND NEW PEAS

Springtime in Provence is such a beautiful time of year. The tourists are not yet out in full force, and in the small villages along the Durance Valley, farmers' markets sell the freshest new carrots and peas. I love to serve this delicate recipe with succulent pan-fried or grilled veal chops.

¾ pound new baby carrots, each about the size of a very large garlic clove
¾ pound baby peas, fresh (preferably) or frozen
2 tablespoons unsalted butter, cut into pieces
Salt and freshly ground black pepper to taste
Pinch of freshly grated nutmeg
½ cup chicken broth (preferably homemade)
2 large egg yolks
1 tablespoon heavy cream

1. Bring a pot of water to a boil and blanch the carrots for 5 minutes. Drain them and plunge them in ice water to stop them from cooking or place them under cold running water. Set aside.

2. In a medium casserole, toss together the carrots, peas, and butter and season with salt, pep-

per, and nutmeg. Turn the heat to medium-high, cover, and cook until the peas are crunchy, 7 to 8 minutes. Add the chicken broth, reduce the heat to low, cover, and cook until the liquid is nearly evaporated, about 12 minutes.

3. Beat the egg yolks and cream together and turn into the casserole with the peas and carrots. Stir and remove from the heat. Serve hot.

Makes 4 servings

Korotes Plaki

CARROTS AND SCALLIONS

In Greece I was always fascinated by the inventiveness of mixed vegetable dishes presented to me. Here's an example of a very nice dish with bright and fresh baby carrots, just pulled from the ground. This is perfect to accompany some grilled lamb chops that have been marinated in lemon and olive oil.

2 pounds young carrots, peeled and sliced on the diagonal
3 tablespoons extra virgin olive oil
2 garlic cloves, chopped fine
8 scallions, sliced on the diagonal
½ to 1 teaspoon dried oregano, to your taste
Salt to taste
½ teaspoon finely chopped fresh dill
1 to 2 tablespoons freshly squeezed lemon juice, to your taste

1. Bring a large saucepan of lightly salted water to a boil, add the carrots, and cook them at a boil until they are halfway tender, about 5 minutes. Drain.

2. In a medium saucepan or skillet, heat the olive oil over high heat and cook the carrots, garlic, scallions, oregano, and salt until sizzling vigorously, 1 to 2 minutes. Reduce the heat to low and cook until the carrots are tender, about 15 minutes. Sprinkle with the dill and lemon juice and serve.

Makes 4 servings

Havuç Kızartması
BATTER-FRIED CARROTS WITH YOGURT SAUCE

The Turks do wonderful things with root vegetables, as do the Greeks. I'm a great fan of this recipe, and when my kids were preteens they loved it too—it's a great way to prepare carrots. This dish is best served with rice pilaf and a roast chicken. You will need to slice the carrots by hand, since a mandoline or food processor will probably slice them too thin. What makes this dish so interesting is that the carrots are sliced lengthwise.

1½ cups beer (lager)
1½ cups all-purpose unbleached flour
1 tablespoon tomato juice (tomato paste mixed with water, or juice squeezed from a ripe tomato)
Salt to taste
6 cups vegetable oil for frying

6 large carrots (about 3 pounds), peeled and cut into ¹⁄₁₆-inch-thick slices lengthwise
2 cups high-quality full-fat plain yogurt
2 garlic cloves, mashed with a little salt

1. In a large bowl, stir together the beer, flour, tomato juice, and salt until it forms a smooth crêpe-like batter. Preheat the oil to 375°F in a deep fryer or an 8-inch saucepan fitted with a basket insert. Preheat the oven to "warm," about 150°F.

2. Dip the carrot slices in the batter and let the excess drip off. Without overcrowding the pot, deep-fry the carrots in batches until golden brown and crusty, about 4 minutes. Salt the carrots immediately and transfer them to a baking tray lined with paper towels. Keep warm in the oven.

3. Stir the yogurt and mashed garlic together. Transfer the carrots to a serving platter and serve with the yogurt on top or on the side. Once the frying oil has cooled, strain it and save it for future use.

Makes 4 servings

Yoğurtlu Havuç
CARROT SLAW IN YOGURT SAUCE

This Turkish carrot slaw was very popular with my kids, although they had to be coaxed to try it because they were unable to imagine that it would taste good. It does. The dish is traditionally served at room temperature. It can also be served either as part of a *meze* or as a side dish.

¼ cup extra virgin olive oil
1 pound carrots, peeled and grated
½ teaspoon salt, divided
4 garlic cloves, peeled
2 cups high-quality full-fat plain yogurt

1. Heat the olive oil in a skillet over medium-high heat. Add the carrots and ¼ teaspoon of the salt and cook, stirring occasionally, until the carrots are soft, 5 to 6 minutes.
2. Transfer the carrots to a serving bowl. Pound the garlic with the remaining ¼ teaspoon salt in a mortar until mushy. Stir the garlic into the yogurt and whisk vigorously. Once the carrots are cool, stir in the yogurt and serve at room temperature.

Makes 6 meze servings

Maᶜqūda bi'l-Jazar
TUNISIAN-STYLE CARROT FRITTATA

A *maᶜqūda* (pronounced maKOODA) is a dish of beaten eggs that set in the oven. The name of this dish is derived from the Arabic word meaning "to congeal," or to "set like a pudding." *Maᶜqūda* is a Tunisian version of what the Italians call *frittata* and the Spanish a *tortilla*. Usually these eggs are made in a frying pan. Another kind of Tunisian frittata, the *ṭājin* (*orṭājīn*), is usually made in an earthenware pan in the oven. The Tunisian *ṭājin* should not be confused with the Moroccan *ṭājin*, which is an entirely different preparation—namely, a kind of dry stew that the French call *étouffée*. A *maᶜqūda* can be eaten hot, but it is most popular served at room temperature so that the flavors have a chance to permeate the spongy texture of the cooked eggs. You can hard-boil the eggs needed for this recipe at the same time that you cook the carrots.

1 pound carrots, peeled and sliced
2 tablespoons freshly ground caraway seeds
1 tablespoon harīsa (page 263)
¼ cup finely chopped fresh parsley leaves
6 large garlic cloves, finely chopped
1½ teaspoons salt
½ teaspoon freshly ground black pepper
2 hard-boiled eggs, shelled and chopped fine
8 large eggs, beaten
3 tablespoons extra virgin olive oil

1. In a large saucepan, boil the carrots in salted water until tender, about 25 minutes. Meanwhile, boil the two eggs if you haven't already. Drain the carrots and mash them with a fork with the caraway, *harīsa*, parsley, garlic, salt, and pepper. Stir in the chopped eggs and the beaten eggs.

2. Heat the olive oil in an 8- to 9½ -inch skillet over high heat. When the oil begins to smoke, add the carrot-and-egg mixture, cover, and cook it until the oil is bubbling up around the sides and the edges are browned, about 2 minutes. Reduce the heat to low and cook, covered, until the center is cooked through, 18 to 20 minutes. Gently loosen the sides with a spatula and invert the *ma'qūda* onto a round serving platter. Serve at room temperature or warm.

Makes 6 servings

CARUM FERULIFOLIUM (DESF.) BOISS. (UMBELLIFERAE)

PLANT CHARACTERISTICS AND VARIETIES
This plant, related to parsley and caraway, is a perennial herb with small edible tubers. It is found on the Balkan Peninsula and in the Aegean region.

PLANT HISTORY
Dioscorides said that this plant's white and bitter roots could be eaten raw or cooked. It is still eaten today in Cyprus as a boiled food.

CASSAVA

Manihot esculenta Crantz. (syn. *M. utilissima*) (Euphorbiaceae)
Also called manioc, yuca, tapioca;

FRENCH: *manioc, cassave;* GREEK: *peponiou;* ITALIAN: *cassàve, manioca, iucca;* SPANISH: *yuca, mandioca, guacamote;* TURKISH: *manyok, tapyoka*

PLANT CHARACTERISTICS AND VARIETIES
Cassava is a perennial shrub that grows to 12 feet. The edible parts are the tubers and leaves, which are cooked. The refined starch of cassava is called tapioca. Cassava is a staple in the diets of many peasants in South America, Africa, parts of Asia, and the tropical islands of Asia and the Pacific. In the Mediterranean, it is only eaten by some Saharan oasis dwellers and in parts of Egypt. In West Africa it is made into a porridge called *foo-foo*.

PLANT ORIGIN
Cassava is native to equatorial South America and Florida. The word *cassava* comes from the Arawak word *kasabi,* while the word *yuca* is the name the Caribs used for the plant. *Manioc* comes from *maniot* in the Tupī language of coastal Brazil.

PLANT HISTORY
Some writers have suggested that cassava was the first food plant used by humankind when our common ancestors migrated south into Central and South America. There is evidence that cassava flour was used in South America in the third millennium B.C. The earliest European description of cassava comes from 1494, referred to by Columbus's chronicler Peter Martyr as a "venomous root" that was used to

prepare bread. Cassava is a New World plant introduced to the Mediterranean by way of the Gulf of Benin in West Africa at the end of the sixteenth century by the Portuguese.

HOW TO GROW AND HARVEST

Cassava needs a tropical climate to grow and is propagated vegetatively by cuttings.

CATNIP

Nepeta cataria L. (Labiatae-Lamiaceae)
FRENCH: *cataire*; GREEK: *edousmou*; SPANISH: *calamento, calaminta*

PLANT CHARACTERISTICS AND VARIETIES

Catnip grows to about 3½ feet and has spike-like flower stems. The edible parts are the leaves and young shoots, which are used in France and the Piedmont region of northern Italy in salads, stews, and for seasoning sauces. It has a substance attractive to cats and was once smoked to produce a light euphoria.

CAUCALIS LATIFOLA L. (SYN. TURGENIA LATIFOLIA [L.] HOFFM.) (UMBELLIFERAE)

ARABIC: *jazar al-shaytān*; ITALIAN: *lappola maggiore* (also a name used for burdock)

PLANT CHARACTERISTICS AND VARIETIES

This plant is a member of the parsley family and is used similarly to parsley. Two other species are *C. anthriscus*, known as hedge pars-ley, and *C. daucides*, known as hen's foot. The leaves are used in the rural cooking of Albania, Crete, Greece, Lebanon, and Italy.

PLANT HISTORY

Caucalis anthriscus and *C. daucides* were both mentioned by Pliny. The plant was known by the ancient Egyptians and called a potherb by Dioscorides and Pliny. Galen said it is pickled for use in salads in the wintertime.

CAULIFLOWER

Brassica oleracea Botrytis group (syn. *B. botrytis, B. oleracea* L. var. *botrytis* L.) (Cruciferae-Brassicaceae)
ARABIC: *qunnabīṭ, qarnabīṭ, zahra* (Lebanon, colloquial); FRENCH: *chou fleur*; GREEK: *kounou, kounoupithi*; ITALIAN: *cavolfiore*; SERBO-CROATIAN: *cvjetača, karfiol*; SICILIAN: *vrocculu, brocculu*; SPANISH: *coliflor*; TURKISH: *karnabahar, karnabit*.

PLANT CHARACTERISTICS AND VARIETIES

Cauliflower is a biennial plant usually grown as a half-hardy annual. It is a cabbagelike plant that forms a large central cluster of flower buds. The edible part is the immature flower stalk, which is consumed either cooked or raw. There are cauliflower varieties that mature quickly, in about 50 days during the summer, and varieties that grow throughout the winter, taking about a year to mature. Cauliflower is white because growers blanch the heads by tying the outer leaves of the plant around them, shading the heads from the sun. Cauliflower florets would otherwise have ugly brown splotches. Purple varieties are sometimes referred to as Cape broccoli and are very popular in Sicily, where they are called *vrucculu*, a word also used to refer to broccoliflower (see entry).

Cauliflower, a cultivar of wild cabbage, is believed to have its center of evolution in Cyprus, Crete, or somewhere in the eastern Mediterranean.

PLANT HISTORY
Cauliflower, in its present form, was unknown before the early Middle Ages, contrary to the claim that it was introduced or reintroduced by the Arabs after the fall of the Roman Empire, although the Arabs may have been responsible for its diffusion at a much later date. Three different forms of "Syrian cabbage," a possible description of cauliflower, were described in the twelfth century in a work by an Arab botanist in Spain, but it is not known if the cauliflower was grown in Spain at that time. The cauliflower is thought to have been introduced to Italy by the Genoese in 1490 from the Levant or Cyprus, although some claim that a similar vegetable was grown by the Romans. The first clear reference is in a German herbal of 1576.

HOW TO GROW AND HARVEST
Cauliflower needs a long, cool growing season. The soil should retain moisture, not be too high in nitrogen, and have a pH higher than that required for most cruciferous plants. Cauliflower plants need to be well watered; otherwise their heads will be very small or deformed. Seeds are usually sown in October, and the seedlings are kept protected or indoors until March, when they are transplanted into rows spaced about 1½ feet apart. Summer and fall cauliflower are planted from March to May. Winter cauliflower is a very hardy plant and survives the winter without much nitrogen. The large outer leaves are wrapped around the head and tied off. Before harvesting the cauliflower, unwrap it and check it: when the head is smooth and compact, cut the stem just below the head.

HOW TO BUY, STORE, AND PREPARE FOR COOKING
Buy cauliflower that has a firm, creamy white compact head, of any size, and crisp-looking green leaves. Avoid cauliflower that has brown splotches or bruises or open florets. Cauliflower can be stored in the crisper drawer of the refrigerator for up to 5 days. If you buy ready-cut cauliflower florets, use them the day you buy them. Although not all recipes call for it, the best way to cook cauliflower is by steaming it. Do not cook cauliflower in an aluminum or iron saucepan, since the inside of the pot will discolor owing to chemical reactions.

Cavolfiore Soffocato
SAFFRON-"SMOTHERED" CAULIFLOWER

This Sardinian recipe for "smothered" cauliflower demonstrates a popular style of vegetable cookery found in the Italian islands of Sicily and Sardinia. The smothering comes about from sealing in the flavors so the vegetable "sweats"; that is, the vegetable releases its own moisture from the heat without the addition of water. I love to prepare this dish as an accompaniment to lamb, and I think it's delightful the next day served at room temperature as an antipasto and drizzled with a little olive oil.

One 2-pound head cauliflower, trimmed and cut into 6 wedges
¼ cup extra virgin olive oil
Pinch of saffron threads crumbled in a mortar with ½ teaspoon salt
10 imported green olives, pitted

1. Preheat the oven to 350°F. Toss the cauliflower pieces with the olive oil in a large bowl. Toss again with the saffron.
2. Place the cut-up cauliflower in a large baking pan in a single layer. Sprinkle the olives around in the spaces in between. Cover the pan tightly with aluminum foil so the steam can't escape, and bake until the cauliflower is tender, about 1 hour. Serve hot or at room temperature.

Makes 6 servings

Psito Kounoupithi
CAULIFLOWER GRATIN

This delicious cauliflower preparation from Greece is also called *kounoupithi o graten*. It is made with *krema mi tyri*, béchamel sauce with cheese. *Krema*, which means "cream" sauce, is a very popular embellishment in the Levant. Syrians love to put *krema* on French fries, although the *krema* there is made of yogurt and mashed garlic. *Kasseri* or *kefalotyri* cheese is easily found in Greek markets and many Middle Eastern markets, and now even in some supermarkets. If you can't find either *kasseri* or *kefalotyri*, use a mild white cheddar cheese or provolone.

¼ cup (½ stick) unsalted butter
¼ cup all-purpose unbleached flour
1½ cups whole milk
½ cup heavy cream
Salt and freshly ground black pepper to taste
1 cup freshly grated kasseri or kefalotyri cheese
One 2-pound head cauliflower, trimmed of leaves but left whole
4 large eggs
¼ cup to ½ cup dry breadcrumbs, to your taste

1. Preheat the oven to 475°F. Prepare a white sauce. Melt the butter in a medium saucepan over medium-high heat. Once it has melted, stir in the flour and cook, stirring constantly, until the flour has taken on a very slight light brown tinge. Remove the saucepan from the heat and pour in the milk and cream in a slow

stream, whisking constantly. Season with salt and pepper. Reduce the heat to medium, return the saucepan to the heat, and cook the sauce until thick, about 15 minutes, stirring frequently. Stir in the cheese and continue stirring until it has melted and blended in with the sauce.

2. Meanwhile, bring a large nonreactive pot full of water to a boil and cook the cauliflower until tender, 12 to 15 minutes. Drain the cauliflower, cut it into florets, including a portion of the stem, and place the florets in a medium bowl. Lightly butter a medium baking pan.

3. With an electric mixer, beat the eggs in a medium bowl until nearly white and frothy but not forming peaks, about 5 minutes of beating at high speed. Stir the eggs into the pan of white sauce off the heat. Correct the seasoning. Stir half the white sauce into the bowl of cauliflower and toss well. Transfer the cauliflower to the baking pan and pour the remaining white sauce over it. Sprinkle the breadcrumbs over the cauliflower and bake until golden brown, 12 to 15 minutes. Serve hot.

Makes 6 servings

Ma*ᶜqūda bi'l-Brūklū*
CAULIFLOWER FRITTATA

This cauliflower *maᶜqūda* (frittata) is a favorite dish in Tunisia, eaten the same way an Italian frittata or Spanish tortilla would be eaten. (Remember that a Spanish tortilla is a frittata, not a flatbread, as in Mexico). For this recipe I usually hard-boil the eggs in the same saucepan I use to cook the cauliflower. Most Tunisians would eat this frittata at room temperature as part of a *mazza*, or as a light dinner.

One 2-pound head cauliflower, trimmed of leaves, with the heavier part of the stem removed
1 small onion, chopped fine
6 tablespoons very finely chopped fresh parsley leaves
2 tablespoons freshly grated Parmigiano-Reggiano cheese
4 hard-boiled large eggs, shelled and chopped
6½ tablespoons extra virgin olive oil, divided
2½ tablespoons unsalted butter, divided
½ teaspoon harīsa (page 263) dissolved in 1 teaspoon water
4 large eggs, beaten
Salt and freshly ground black pepper to taste

1. Place the cauliflower in a large nonreactive pot full of cold water and bring to a boil. Cook until the head is very soft in the center when pierced by a skewer, about 30 minutes. Drain the cauliflower and mash it with a fork. Let it cool while you continue with the preparation.

2. Preheat the oven to 350°F. Transfer the mashed cauliflower to a large bowl and stir in the onion, parsley, cheese, hard-boiled eggs, 6 tablespoons of the olive oil, 2 tablespoons of the butter, the harīsa, and the uncooked eggs. Season with salt and pepper and mix well.

Grease an earthenware casserole with the remaining ½ tablespoon olive oil and ½ tablespoon butter. Transfer the cauliflower and eggs to the casserole and bake until the eggs set, 25 to 30 minutes, or until the tip of a knife inserted into the center of the casserole comes out clean.

Makes 4 to 6 servings

Vrocculu c'Anciova
BROCCOLIFLOWER WITH ANCHOVIES

Broccoliflower is a modern cross between cauliflower and broccoli. It is a popular vegetable in Sicily. The ideal pot for this preparation is a heavy enameled cast-iron casserole with a heavy lid. You want to trap all the flavors and steam while you cook the raw broccoliflower, and a heavy pot works very well. This dish is ideal served with roast chicken. The so-called eating pecorino in the ingredients list is an approximately six-month-old pecorino that can be eaten at the table; it is softer than the pecorino used for grating. In an Italian deli, ask for pecorino Crotonese or describe the cheese as I have here.

2 tablespoons extra virgin olive oil, divided
1 medium onion, sliced very thin
8 salted anchovy fillets, rinsed and chopped
2 ounces caciocavallo, provolone, or eating pecorino cheese, grated
1 cup imported black olives, pitted
1 broccoliflower (1½ to 2 pounds), trimmed of leaves and cut into thin slices
Salt to taste
¾ cup dry red wine
¼ cup dry white wine
4 slices toasted Italian bread (crostini)

Coat the bottom of a small enameled cast-iron casserole with 1 tablespoon of the olive oil and layer the onion, anchovies, cheese, and olives, in that order. Add the broccoliflower, pressing it down to make it compact. Sprinkle with the remaining 1 tablespoon olive oil and season with salt. Pour both wines over everything, cover the pot with a heavy lid, and cook over low heat, without tossing or turning, until the broccoliflower is tender, about 40 minutes. Serve immediately with *crostini* if desired.

Makes 4 servings

CELERIAC
Apium graveolens L. var. *rapaceum* (Mill.) Gaud. (syn. *A. rapaceum*) (Umbelliferae)
Also called celery root; ARABIC: *sharafis*; FRENCH: *céleri tubéreux, céleri rave*; ITALIAN: *sedano-rape*; SPANISH: *apio nabo, apirrábano*; TURKISH: *kereviz*

PLANT CHARACTERISTICS AND VARIETIES

The edible parts are the corm and leaves, which are eaten both cooked and raw. Celeriac is a hardy biennial that is grown as an annual. In this form of celery the lowest part of the stem, or corm, has been developed by growers over time into a swollen state; it is not the root. The cultivation of the plant for the corm is a recent development, within the past century. Celeriac tastes like a strong celery. In Mediterranean cuisine, it is most favored by Turkish cooks and is popular as a vegetable used for making broths and stocks. The French and Italians also use celeriac in stocks and in various salads cut in julienne form.

PLANT ORIGIN

See Celery.

PLANT HISTORY

Today's celeriac or celery root is not the celery root of the Middle Ages. In those days celery root was actually the root of the celery plant while today's celery root is the swollen corm. Celery root was a popular vegetable in Egypt in the Middle Ages and was introduced to England in the mid-eighteenth century from Alexandria, Egypt. A traveler to Aleppo, Syria, in 1536 reports that celery root was eaten as a delicacy with salt and pepper. In 1575 Rauwolffud tells us that it is a delicacy among the Arabs.

HOW TO GROW AND HARVEST

Growing celeriac into a large corm is difficult. Commercial growers achieve good results by giving the plant a long growing season, planting it in rich soil with lots of organic matter, and providing sufficient water so that the plant never becomes dry in the summer. Seeds are usually sown indoors in the early spring. The outer leaves are removed in midsummer, and the plant is then mulched so it will retain water. Celeriac is grown in raised beds dressed with manure or compost and drip irrigated. At harvest time the entire plant is pulled from the ground.

HOW TO BUY, STORE, AND PREPARE FOR COOKING

The best celeriac is of medium size, without secondary corms, but with a modest clump of leaves. Store celeriac in the refrigerator, where it should have a relatively long life. Peel the celeriac before using it.

Terbiyeli Kereviz
CELERIAC WITH LEMON
AND EGG SAUCE

Whether you like celeriac, or have never tried it, this Turkish recipe is perfect for you. The Turks as well as the Greeks love to serve this lemon-and-egg mixture, known as *avgolemono*, on many kinds of foods, and here it works quite well with celeriac.

2 pounds celeriac (about 1 or 2) corms, peeled, washed, and cut into 2-inch pieces

3 cups water

2 tablespoons all-purpose unbleached flour

1 lemon, cut into quarters, juice squeezed out and saved

1 medium onion, cut into quarters

2 tablespoons extra virgin olive oil

Salt to taste

2 large eggs

2 tablespoons freshly squeezed lemon juice

1. Place the celeriac in a large bowl with the 3 cups water, flour, and lemon juice and lemon quarters to prevent the root from discoloring as you work.

2. Discard the lemon pieces and transfer the celeriac, water, and flour to a large nonreactive saucepan. Add the onion and olive oil and season with salt. Turn the heat to high and, as the water begins to shimmer, reduce the heat to low. Partially cover the pot and cook the celery

root until it is tender, about 1 hour. Remove and discard the onion. There should be about 2 cups of liquid left. If there is more than that, remove the excess liquid with a ladle.

3. Mix the eggs and lemon juice together in a medium bowl, add 1 cup celeriac cooking liquid from the saucepan, and stir. Pour this mixture over the hot celery roots, bring the mixture to a boil, and serve immediately.

Makes 6 servings

CELERY (also see Celeriac)
Apium graveolens L. (Umbelliferae)
ARABIC: *karafs, baṭrasāliyūn* (wild celery);
FRENCH: *céleri, ache* (smallage); GREEK:
selino, selinon; ITALIAN: *sedano;* SERBO-
CROATIAN: *celer;* SPANISH: *apio blanco;*
TURKISH: *sap kerevizi, kereviz*

PLANT CHARACTERISTICS AND VARIETIES
The petioles and leaves of celery are eaten either raw or cooked. Celery is a biennial grown as an annual. The plant has many stems and sessile umbels of white flowers. The fleshy leaf stalks of celery have been developed by growers over time. Celery comes in three forms today. The first, *A. graveolens* var. *dulce,* is the common form we find in the supermarket, known as Pascal celery. The second is *A. graveolens* var. *rapaceum,* or celeriac, the swollen corm (see page 100). The third is *A. graveolens* var. *secalinum,* a leafy celery, formerly known as smallage, which is used especially in

soups and is similar to Chinese white-stalked celery. Wild celery grows in marshes and in the mud on the edges of tidal rivers in saline conditions; it is also called water parsley. In North Africa, wild celery was traditionally used in making *jashīsh* (or *dashīsh*), a preparation consisting of pan-griddled crushed wheat boiled with a little butter and smallage. *Apium nodiflorum,* called *crescione* in Tuscany, is collected in the wild and used in salads and vegetable soups and boiled or steamed as a vegetable.

PLANT ORIGIN

Wild celery is native to the Mediterranean region and parts of Asia.

PLANT HISTORY

Celery was probably first used medicinally and as a flavoring agent. The plant was grown in Egyptian gardens of the New Kingdom (about 1000 B.C.). Classical Greek authors mention celery in both a gastronomic and a medicinal sense, and as a symbol of life and fertility the plant was used to crown the heads of athletes. The great Sicilian city of Magna Graecia, founded in 628 B.C., was called Selinunte, named after the wild celery (*A. graveolens* var. *petroselinum*) that grew abundantly there. Parsley is sometimes confused with celery in ancient writings because parsley was known as mountain celery. Cooks in ancient Greece used celery to counteract the tang of vinegary dishes and put celery in bags and immersed them in wine to rid it of odors.

Celery also figures in Homer's *Odyssey.* Dioscorides mentions celery, too. In the sixteenth century, Cyprus exported a white *apium,* a sort of water celery crystallized in sugar. The nineteenth-century Italian botanist Targioni-Tozzetti wrote that celery was grown as food for the Tuscan table by the sixteenth century, although there is no mention of celery in the classical herbals and botanical works of the time. Sturtevant says that celery was ignored as a food plant until the sixteenth century. In the Middle Ages, celery became more common as a table vegetable and was cultivated on a wider scale. Celery stalks were probably first grown in sixteenth-century Italy, although the first mention of celery as a food plant is by the French agronomist Olivier de Serres, who describes its cultivation in 1623.

HOW TO GROW AND HARVEST

Growing celery demands a lot of attention from the gardener. Growing your own celery from seed without a greenhouse is difficult because the plants will go to seed if subjected to a week of temperatures in the low forties. Celery enjoys rich soil high in nitrogen with a pH factor above 6.6. The soil should be moist and, ideally, in low-lying alkaline, peaty areas. Celery needs lots of water, about 4½ gallons per square yard per week. If the plants don't get this much water, the stalks will be narrow, stringy, and tough. Sow seeds about 1 foot apart in late March or April as long as the temperature does not go below 50°F for more than 12 hours; otherwise the plants will bolt before they mature. Celery can be fertilized with sodium nitrate applied as a top dressing. Harvest the celery by pulling the plant or cutting off individual stalks as needed.

The best celery is light green in color. Darker green celery stalks will carry a bit more nutrients but will also be stringier. A bunch of fresh celery should have firm stalks and fresh-looking leaves. The stalks should not bend at all. Celery will keep for up to 2 weeks in a plastic bag refrigerated in the crisper drawer. But make sure you keep celery away from the coldest part of the crisper drawer; otherwise it might freeze and be damaged. Celery can be kept fresh by misting it with water. Old celery that has gone somewhat limp can be used in making stock.

RECIPES

Apio a la Andaluza
CELERY IN THE STYLE OF SEVILLE

This is a surprising dish from Andalusia. It's surprising because we Americans don't cook celery as a stand-alone dish, usually preferring to eat it raw or to use it in small amounts in sauces or stocks, stews, soups, or salads. This is a wonderful preparation that goes very nicely with roast veal or turkey.

4 cups water plus more for adjusting consistency of sauce
3 tablespoons all-purpose unbleached flour, divided
1 bunch celery, trimmed and cut into 2-inch lengths
4 tablespoons extra virgin olive oil, divided
1 medium onion, chopped fine
Salt and freshly ground white pepper to taste
⅛ teaspoon freshly grated nutmeg
2 large garlic cloves, chopped
1 tablespoon freshly ground cumin seeds
¾ cup cooked chickpeas, drained
1 large ripe tomato, peeled, seeded, and cut into large pieces
2 tablespoons finely chopped fresh parsley leaves
2 tablespoons finely chopped fresh mint leaves

1. Bring the water to a boil with 2 tablespoons of the flour. Reduce the heat so the liquid is gently bubbling. Add the celery and cook until tender but firm, about 15 minutes.

2. Meanwhile, heat 2 tablespoons of the olive oil in a large skillet over medium-high heat and cook the onion with the remaining 1 tablespoon flour until it changes color, about 4 minutes, stirring, and adding 2 to 4 tablespoons of water so the sauce doesn't become too thick. Season with salt, pepper, and the nutmeg. Keep warm or turn the heat off until the celery is cooked.

3. When the celery is done, drain it, reserving ½ cup of the cooking water. Place the garlic, cumin, cooked chickpeas, and tomato in a food processor and blend well until smooth.

Slowly drizzle in the remaining 2 tablespoons of olive oil and then ¼ cup of the celery cooking water. Transfer to the skillet with the onion and mix well.

4. Transfer the celery to the skillet, mix well, and bring to a boil, adding more of the celery cooking water only if the sauce is too thick. It should be the consistency of a smooth gravy that is not too thick. Sprinkle with the parsley and mint and serve immediately.

Makes 4 servings

CELERY AND POTATO SALAD WITH *HARĪSA* SAUCE

This Tunisian-inspired salad is spicy and an excellent accompaniment to grilled chicken in the summer. There are three very typical Tunisian ingredients in this recipe, and although you can't buy them readily (unless you are in Tunisia as you read this) all of them are easy to make if you follow the recipes I provide elsewhere. *Harīsa* is a Tunisian condiment made by pounding chile peppers, garlic, caraway seeds, coriander seeds, and olive oil into a paste. *Tābil* is the name of a Tunisian spice mix; you can't buy it, but making it is easy. Preserved lemons add a delightful tang to foods.

6 cups olive oil for frying
1 bunch celery, trimmed of its root end, leaves, and innermost stalks, each stalk split in half lengthwise, then cut in half widthwise, and dried well

1 ½ pounds new Yukon Gold potatoes
1 tablespoon harīsa *(page 263)*
2 teaspoons tābil *(page 106)*
3 garlic cloves, mashed in a mortar with 1 teaspoon salt
2 tablespoons chopped preserved lemon (see Note)
5 tablespoons extra virgin olive oil
1 tablespoon white wine vinegar
Freshly ground black pepper to taste
16 imported green olives

1. Preheat the oil to 375°F in a deep fryer or an 8-inch saucepan fitted with a basket insert. Fry the celery in batches without crowding until the stalks are soft and slightly golden on the edges, about 3 minutes. Remove with a slotted spoon, drain on paper towels, and transfer to a large bowl.

2. Meanwhile, put the potatoes in a medium pot and fill it with water. Bring the pot to a boil, and boil the potatoes until tender but firm, about 15 minutes. Drain, let cool, and cut into quarters. Transfer to the bowl with the fried celery.

3. Whisk together the *harīsa*, *tābil*, garlic and salt, preserved lemons, olive oil, and vinegar. Season with pepper. Pour the sauce over the vegetables, toss to coat evenly, and taste. Correct the seasoning. Transfer the salad to a serving platter, sprinkle with green olives, and serve. Let the frying oil cool, strain it, and save it for another use.

Makes 4 servings

NOTE: To make preserved lemons, just scrub 2 thin-skinned lemons, preferably Meyer, dry them, and cut each one into 8 wedges. Toss the lemon wedges with ⅓ cup salt and place in a ½-pint jar with a glass or plastic lid. Cover the lemons with ½ cup freshly squeezed lemon juice and screw on the lid. Leave the jar at room temperature for 7 days, shaking it occasionally. After a week, pour in olive oil to cover and use the lemons for up to 6 months, storing them in the refrigerator.

Tābil
TUNISIAN SPICE MIX

In earlier times, the word *tābil*, which means "seasoning" in Tunisian Arabic, was used to denote "coriander." Paula Wolfert makes the plausible claim that *tābil* is one of the spice mixes brought to Tunisia by Muslim-Andalusi (Spanish Muslims from Andalusia) in 1492. I agree with her, and it does seem possible that *tābil* may have originated in their community of Testour.

Today *tābil* is closely associated with the spice mix used in Tunisia in cooking beef or veal and that features coriander seeds. This spice blend is pounded in a mortar and then dried in the sun. My recipe uses all dried spices except the garlic, which you should air-dry a bit; otherwise replace it with dried powdered garlic, per recipe.

2 large garlic cloves, peeled, or 2 teaspoons
   powdered garlic
¼ cup coriander seeds
1 tablespoon caraway seeds
2 teaspoons cayenne pepper

In a mortar, pound the garlic with the coriander, caraway, and cayenne until homogeneous. Dry in the open air for 2 days or freeze. Store in the refrigerator or freezer. *Tābil* will keep indefinitely but will lose pungency over time.

Makes about ¼ cup

CENTAUREA CHAMAER-HAPONTICUM (ASTERACEAE-COMPOSITAE)

PLANT CHARACTERISTICS AND VARIETIES
This annual herb has violet inner florets and dark blue outer ones. The edible part is the root, which is still eaten in Algeria. *Centaurea depressa* Bieb., called *gökçebaş* in the mountain villages around the Aksaray Province in central Anatolia, is eaten on an irregular basis by portions of the population.

PLANT ORIGIN
The plant is native to Mediterranean coasts.

Chickpea

THE CHICKPEA APPEARS AROUND THE MEDITERRANEAN IN EVERY CUISINE. I HAVEN'T PROVIDED ANY RECIPES FROM ITALY, but there are a number of delightful Italian chickpea preparations such as (and this is a small sampling) the Ligurian *ceci in zimino* (chickpeas cooked with beets and tomatoes with a little celery, onion, and olive oil), or the famous Sicilian *pannelle* (chickpea flour fritters, which are identical to the Provençal *panisse*, a fritter derived from the pan-fried chickpea-polenta-pancake dish famous in Nice called *socca*). In the rural countryside outside Naples, and in Basilicata, too, *ceci con pasta* (short macaroni with cooked chickpeas and olive oil and some garlic) is a real favorite.

CHARLOCK

Sinapsis arvensis L. (*Brassica sinapistrum* Boiss.) (Cruciferae-Brassicaceae)
Also called field mustard; GREEK: *vrouva*; ITALIAN: *senape selvatica*; SPANISH: *mostaza silvestre*; TURKISH: *hardal otu*

PLANT CHARACTERISTICS AND VARIETIES
This annual herb has rough, bristly leaves. The leaves, seeds, sprouting seeds, and flowering buds are edible and used as a piquant flavoring in salads, omelettes, and sandwiches. In Greece the unopened buds are boiled and eaten at room temperature with a dressing of olive oil and lemon juice. In the Aksaray Province of Turkey, charlock is gathered in the wild and eaten as a green.

CHICKPEA

Cicer arietinum L. (Leguminosae)
Also called garbanzo; ARABIC: *ḥummuṣ*; FRENCH: *pois-chiche*; GREEK: *revithia*; ITALIAN: *ceci*; SPANISH: *garbanzo*; TURKISH: *nohut*

PLANT CHARACTERISTICS AND VARIETIES
The chickpea is an annual plant that grows into a 2-foot-high bush. The leaves are compound, formed of about 15 leaflets, and the pods are short. Each pod carries one or two large round seeds. The edible part is the seed, which is cooked. Chickpeas are grown in hot, dry climates such as in the Mediterranean. The chickpea is not known as a wild plant, although one wild species, *C. echinospermum* P. H. Davis, has been found growing in rocky areas of southeastern Turkey.

PLANT ORIGIN

The chickpea, in all probability, originates in a very small area of southeastern Turkey, where it was first domesticated. N. Vavilov has identified the area of India, Burma, and Assam as the center of origin of the chickpea. Others suggest Southeast Asia. The contemporary Dutch botanist Professor L. J. G. van der Maesen claimed that the center of diversity of the chickpea was probably the Caucasus and/or Asia Minor.

PLANT HISTORY

The chickpea is one of the earliest of the neolithic crops in the Near East. The oldest archaeological record of the chickpea is from the aceramic (7500 B.C.–6800 B.C.) level of Çayönü, near Diyabakir, Turkey, and Tell Abu Hureya in Syria of about 7000 B.C. A third center of diversity is Ethiopia, which may have received the crop from the Mediterranean as early as the first millennium B.C. The chickpea was not present in western Europe in the prehistoric period. Carbonized seeds of chickpeas dating to the third millennium B.C. have been retrieved from several sites in southern France. Although chickpeas have only occasionally been found on prehistoric sites in the Mediterranean, they are more abundantly evident in early Bronze Age deposits at Jericho and other sites in Palestine and Iraq. They have also been found in sixth-century B.C. funeral pyres at Salamis on Cyprus.

The Jews, Greeks, and Egyptians all cultivated the chickpea in ancient times. The chickpea was known early on in Egypt and was known in Greece in Homer's time. The ancient Greeks preferred to eat their chickpeas either roasted or boiled. Theophrastus describes in detail the growing of chickpeas, calling some varieties "rams." Athenaeus relates a scene in which he was lying on a soft couch in front of a fire during the winter, sipping sweet wine and munching chickpeas. He tells us that the use of chickpeas was revealed by the god Poseidon. The Roman authors Columella and Pliny also mention the chickpea. Different colors of chickpeas (red, white, and black) were mentioned by Albertus Magnus in the thirteenth century and by herbalists in later centuries.

HOW TO GROW AND HARVEST

Chickpeas are cultivated in sandy soil in warm climates. In the Mediterranean the seeds are sown in February about 6 inches apart. They should be well watered and grow to bushy plants. At least 2 dozen plants need to be planted to make the effort worthwhile. Once several pods have dried on a plant, harvest the pods or the entire plant and dry the pods in the sun.

HOW TO BUY, STORE, AND PREPARE FOR COOKING

Fresh chickpeas are sometimes found at farmers' markets. Nearly all Mediterranean recipes call for dried chickpeas. If you don't want to cook dried chickpeas, the chickpeas sold in cans are a perfectly fine replacement.

Potaje de Vigilia
FASTING SOUP

This recipe from Huelva in Andalusia makes a hearty soup with lots of flavor, and no meat—hence the name "fasting" soup. Yet it is a substantial soup, very nicely spiced with paprika, saffron, and black pepper.

6 tablespoons extra virgin olive oil, divided

4 slices French bread

3 tablespoons sherry vinegar

1 medium onion, chopped

2 medium ripe tomatoes, peeled, seeded, and chopped

2 teaspoons paprika

2 cups cooked chickpeas, with their liquid

1 pound spinach, trimmed of stems, washed well, and ripped into smaller pieces

3 potatoes (about 1 pound), peeled and cut into small pieces

½ cup dry white wine

2 teaspoons salt

1 teaspoon freshly ground black pepper

4 cups water

3 large garlic cloves, chopped fine

3 tablespoons pine nuts

¼ cup finely chopped fresh parsley leaves

Pinch of saffron threads

1 large hard-boiled egg, shelled and chopped

1. In a soup pot or casserole, heat 4 tablespoons of the olive oil over medium heat and fry the French bread until golden brown and crispy on both sides, 4 to 5 minutes. Remove the bread, rip it into smaller pieces, put in a small bowl, and douse it with the vinegar.

2. In the same pot or casserole, pour the remaining 2 tablespoons olive oil and cook the onion and tomatoes with the paprika until they form a thick sauce, 10 to 12 minutes.

3. Add the chickpeas, spinach, potatoes, wine, salt, pepper, and water. Turn the heat to high and, once the spinach wilts and the broth begins to boil, reduce the heat to low and cook until the potatoes are very nearly tender, about 45 minutes.

4. Add the garlic, pine nuts, parsley, fried bread, saffron, and hard-boiled egg. Turn the heat off, let the soup rest for 10 minutes, then serve.

Makes 6 servings

Pois Chiches en Salade
CHICKPEA SALAD

This salad, found in Languedoc and Provence in the south of France, is almost always served with tuna that is mashed fine, although some cooks also use shavings of *poutargue*, dried, pressed, salted tuna roe. (If you use tuna, buy a good-quality brand packed in olive oil.) The salad can be served in a variety of ways, first, as a salad, of course, but also as an appetizer or as an accompaniment to other foods. I like to serve this dish with grilled fish, and when I do I leave out the canned tuna, as in this recipe that I have adapted from Michel Barberousse's *Cuisine Provençale*. Try to serve the salad warm, at room temperature, if you can.

1 teaspoon Dijon mustard
Salt and freshly ground black pepper to taste
½ teaspoon dried herbes de Provence
1½ tablespoons white wine vinegar
1 small onion, chopped very fine
1 garlic clove, chopped very fine
3 tablespoons imported canned tuna in olive oil, mashed
6 tablespoons extra virgin olive oil
6 cups cooked chickpeas (two 28-ounce cans), drained and rinsed if necessary
1 yellow bell pepper, seeded and sliced into thin strips
1 tablespoon finely chopped fresh tarragon leaves
1 tablespoon finely chopped fresh parsley leaves

1. In a small bowl, whisk together the mustard, salt, black pepper, *herbes de Provence*, vinegar, onion, garlic, and tuna, if you are using it. Slowly beat in the olive oil to make an emulsion. Check the seasoning.

2. Toss the chickpeas and bell pepper together in a large bowl. Toss again with the dressing until evenly coated. Transfer to a serving bowl or platter and sprinkle with the tarragon and parsley. Toss again and serve at room temperature.

Makes 6 servings

Revithia Yahni
BRAISED CHICKPEAS

This lemony chickpea preparation from Greece is ideally served at room temperature. Although you can serve chickpeas as part of a *meze*, I have also served this recipe as an accompaniment to a braised lemony rabbit.

¼ cup extra virgin olive oil
½ cup chopped onions
3 cups cooked chickpeas (two 15-ounce cans), drained
1 cup water
Salt and freshly ground black pepper to taste
Freshly squeezed juice from 1 lemon
1 tablespoon all-purpose unbleached flour

1. Heat the olive oil in a medium skillet over high heat and cook the onion until some pieces are turning brown, 4 to 5 minutes, stirring occasionally. Add the drained chickpeas and water, season with salt and pepper, and cook for 5 minutes.

2. Meanwhile, in a small bowl, whisk together the lemon juice and flour until well blended and smooth. Whisk several tablespoons of the hot liquid from the chickpeas into the lemon-flour mixture until well blended. Pour this mixture back into the chickpeas, reduce the heat to low, and simmer until the water is nearly evaporated and the sauce has thickened, 1 to 1¼ hours. Turn the heat off and let the chickpeas cool in the skillet. Serve at room temperature or warm.

Makes 4 servings

HUMMUS

On every Arab *mazza* table you will find hummus with tahini, called *ḥummuṣ bi'l-ṭaḥīna* in Arabic. The word *ḥummuṣ* means "chickpea" in Arabic. Today hummus can be found in every supermarket, but this recipe will yield a hummus that tastes far better than anything you can buy in a store. Tahini is the sesame seed paste that one stirs into the mashed chickpeas. It is easily found today in supermarkets, natural food stores, or Middle Eastern markets. Sumac is a spice made from the dried red berries of the sumac bush *(Rhus coriaria)*, which grows wild throughout the Middle East. Sumac is sold in ground form in Middle Eastern markets.

No matter how you make hummus, it is important to peel and discard the thin white skins of the chickpeas. This recipe calls for the use of dried chickpeas, but there is no reason that you shouldn't feel comfortable using canned chickpeas instead.

3 cups dried chickpeas (about 1½ pounds), picked over and soaked overnight in cold water mixed with 1 teaspoon baking soda to cover, or four 15-ounce cans chickpeas with their liquid

12 tablespoons extra virgin olive oil, divided

8 large garlic cloves, peeled

1 tablespoon salt

½ cup tahini

½ cup freshly squeezed lemon juice

Freshly ground black pepper to taste

¼ cup pine nuts

⅓ cup finely chopped fresh mint leaves, and fresh whole mint leaves for garnish

½ teaspoon ground sumac for garnish

1. If you are using dried chickpeas, drain the presoaked beans and place them in a pot of lightly salted water to cover by 2 inches. Bring the water to a boil over high heat until it foams, 5 to 10 minutes. Remove the foam with a skimmer and continue to boil the chickpeas, partially covered, until tender, about 3 hours. Keep checking on them, and add boiling water to the pot to keep the chickpeas covered. When the chickpeas are done, drain them, saving 1½ cups of the cooking water. Return the cooked chickpeas to the same pot filled with some cold water. Rub the skins off the chickpeas with your fingers (many of them will rise to the surface). Drain the chickpeas again, discarding the skins. If you are using canned chickpeas, heat them in their liquid for 10 minutes over medium heat and save 1 cup of their liquid.

2. In a food processor, blend the chickpeas with ½ cup of the olive oil and I cup of the reserved chickpea cooking water until creamy.

3. In a mortar, pound the garlic with I tablespoon salt until the mixture resembles a creamy mush. Beat the tahini and lemon juice together slowly in a small bowl. If the consistency is too thick, add water—*never* more lemon juice. Stir the tahini-and-lemon-juice mixture into the garlic and salt. Stir this mixture into the chickpea puree, adjust the salt, and season with pepper. Run the processor again to mix. Check the consistency; if the hummus is too thick, like an oatmeal, add some of the remaining reserved chickpea cooking water until the hummus is smoother, like Cream of Wheat. Check the taste and adjust the seasoning if necessary. If you need to adjust the taste, the process must be repeated. In other words, mash some more garlic with salt or mix a tablespoon of tahini with a tablespoon of lemon juice.

4. In a small skillet, cook the pine nuts in I tablespoon of the olive oil over medium heat, stirring, until light brown, about 4 minutes. Remove from the skillet and set aside.

5. Spoon the hummus onto a large round serving platter, not into a bowl. Warm the remaining 3 tablespoons extra virgin olive oil. Make spiral or fan-shaped furrows in the hummus and fill them with the warm olive oil. Sprinkle the reserved pine nuts around. Garnish the edges with mint leaves and sprinkle the chopped mint on top. Sprinkle the sumac over the top. Serve with warm Arabic flatbread or pita bread.

Makes 6 servings

N O T E : Other garnishes that are used are whole cooked chickpeas, black olives, pomegranate seeds, cayenne pepper, red Aleppo pepper, paprika, and ground cumin.

Makes 6 servings

Murshān

CHICKPEA AND SWISS CHARD RAGOUT

Tunisian vegetable stews are usually quite saucy because of the technique of long simmering and the use of olive oil and the ubiquitous red chile pepper paste called *harīsa*, which is mixed with a little water. This recipe is from Chef Abdel Haouari Abderrazak of Djerba, who told me that *Murshān* is a typical dish of the Sahel and the island of Djerba in southeastern Tunisia. Other similarly named recipes are from the Sousse region further north and may feature turnip tops and Swiss chard.

*1¼ cups dried chickpeas, picked over, soaked in
    water to cover overnight, and drained*

*1 small onion, cut into quarters and separated
    into layers*

1 ripe plum tomato, chopped

Salt to taste

3 tablespoons extra virgin olive oil

1 small onion, chopped

2 large garlic cloves, chopped fine

2 tablespoons tomato paste

1 tablespoon harīsa (page 263)

¾ cup water

2 teaspoons freshly ground coriander seeds

*1¼ pounds Swiss chard, the heavy part of white
    stalks removed, washed well, and chopped*

Freshly ground black pepper to taste

1. Place the drained chickpeas in a large saucepan with the onion pieces and tomato. Bring to a boil, season with salt, and cook until tender, about 3 hours, replenishing the pot with boiling water occasionally to keep the chickpeas well covered with water. Drain and set the chickpeas aside, discarding the onion pieces.

2. In a large skillet, heat the olive oil over medium heat and cook the chopped onion and garlic until translucent, 4 to 5 minutes, stirring frequently so the garlic doesn't burn. Dissolve the tomato paste and harīsa in the water and add to the skillet along with the coriander and Swiss chard. Season with salt and pepper, stir, cover, and cook over very low heat, using a heat diffuser if necessary, until the liquid is much reduced, about 1½ hours.

Uncover and continue to cook until the liquid remaining looks like a sauce, the chickpeas are completely tender, and the Swiss chard looks as if it could melt, another 25 to 30 minutes. Serve immediately.

Makes 4 servings

Ḥummuṣ bi'l-Kammūn
CHICKPEA SOUP WITH CUMIN

In the Middle Ages the chickpea was so popular from Spain all the way to Morocco and the North African coast to Egypt that upon receiving large shipments of barley and wheat, the Spanish commander of the La Goletta presidio in Tunisia, Alonso de Pimentel, wrote in 1570, "What a misfortune that we have been sent no chickpeas!" This simple soup, a favorite today of Algerian dockworkers, is healthy, filling, and has a nice spicy flavor.

4 cups cooked chickpeas, drained

1 quart vegetable or chicken broth, divided

1 garlic clove, peeled and crushed

¼ cup extra virgin olive oil

1 teaspoon freshly ground cumin seeds

1 teaspoon paprika

1 teaspoon harīsa (page 263)

1 tablespoon tomato paste

1 teaspoon salt, plus more as needed

*1 teaspoon freshly ground black pepper, plus more
    as needed*

FOR GARNISH:

½ *green bell pepper, seeded and chopped fine*

¼ *cup finely chopped onions*

1 *small ripe tomato, peeled, seeded, and chopped fine*

1 *hard-boiled egg, shelled and chopped fine*

3 *tablespoons finely chopped fresh coriander leaves*

3 *tablespoons drained capers, chopped*

2 *tablespoons* harīsa

Extra virgin olive oil

I. In a medium saucepan, simmer the chickpeas in water to cover for I hour over medium-low heat until tender. Drain, reserving the cooking liquid, and remove as much of the chickpeas' white skins as possible. Put the chickpeas in a food processor or blender and puree while adding I cup of the broth in a drizzle.

2. Put the garlic, olive oil, cumin, paprika, harīsa, tomato paste, salt, and black pepper in a soup pot. Turn the heat to medium and simmer for 5 minutes, stirring occasionally. Pour in the chickpea-and-broth mixture and the remaining 3 cups broth and bring to a boil. Cook at a gentle boil until bubbling and smooth, about I0 minutes, correct the salt and pepper, and serve with small amounts of the garnishes on the side.

Makes 4 servings

CHICKWEED

Stellaria media (L.) Vill. (Caryophyllaceae)
Also called stitchwort; ARABIC: *baqlī*;
FRENCH: *mouron, mouron des oiseaux, morgeline*; SPANISH: *morgelina, pamplina*;
TURKISH: *haval otu*

PLANT CHARACTERISTICS AND VARIETIES

Chickweed is the name of either of two species of small-leaved weeds of the pink family.

The plant grows to about I½ feet and remains low growing. It has very small, delicate white flowers. Chickweed is a wild green typically used in the Lebanese-Syrian-Palestinian bread salad called *fattūsh*. As a wild edible green it is also used in salads in the Aksaray Province of Anatolia.

PLANT ORIGIN

Chickweed is native to Europe. The plant's seeds often appear in samples of prehistoric seeds found in, for example, the stomachs of Tollund and Grauballe man, two Iron Age men found in amazingly well-preserved states in Denmark and at a site at Peschiera in northern Italy.

CHICORY

Cichorium intybus L. (Asteraceae-Compositae)

ARABIC: *shikūriyā* (or *shikūriyya*), *hindab, hindibā, sarīs, ṭiblīdaj, murra, qishnīza, luᶜāᶜ;* FRENCH: *chicorée sauvage;* GREEK: *kichorion, radiki;* ITALIAN: *cicoria comune, cicoria da taglio;* SERBO-CROATIAN: *cikorija;* SPANISH: *achicoria silvestre, achicoria de raíz, achicoria de hojas verdes, amargón, almirón;* TURKISH: *hindiba, güneğik, çıtlık* (Aksaray Province)

PLANT CHARACTERISTICS AND VARIETIES

Chicory is a wild herbaceous biennial or perennial that is found growing all over the Mediterranean. Its leaves, which are eaten raw, have a basal rosette of runcinate leaves; that is, the lobes are deeply incised and recurved at the tip. The heads are large, with loose, dark green leaves that taste bitter. The flowering stalk grows out of this rosette up to a height of 3 feet or more in some cases. The flowers are blue and, rarely, pink or white.

There are many varieties of chicory, some of which I will review here. Although chicory is eaten throughout the Mediterranean, Italians appear to be the true connoisseurs of this herb. Belgian endive, also called Witloof chicory, is a chicory that was brought to the Veneto region of northern Italy by a Belgian in the nineteenth century. *Barbe di Capuchin* is close to Belgian endive and may be identical to wild chicory. It is raised in France by forcing the plant to grow in darkness; this form of chicory is highly prized by connoisseurs. *Pan di zucchero, bianca di Milano,* and *dolce bianca* are all know as sugarloaf chicories *(zuccherina).* The *catalogna* variety of chicory looks like a gigantic dandelion plant; its younger leaves are used in salads, and the older leaves are cooked. Varieties include *radichetta* or *catalogna, San Pasquale, dentarella,* and *foglia verde frastagliata,* with narrow leaves that are quite bitter. Asparagus chicory is in this group. In late winter or early spring it sends up succulent flower stalks that vaguely resemble asparagus. Some varieties have stalks that twist or curl, called *galatina, Pugliese,* and *puntarelle.* Another major, and familiar, variety is red radicchio, such as *radicchio di Chiogga,* the radicchio that most Americans know, which looks like a little round red cabbage. *Radicchio di Verona* has slightly longer leaves, and *radicchio di Treviso,* a forced and blanched plant, has the longest leaves and is prized by connoisseurs. *Radicchio di Treviso* is an older variety from the sixteenth century, while *radicchio di Verona* is a cultivated variety from the eighteenth century. *Radicchio di Castelfranco* looks like Boston head lettuce. Among the *grumolo* or *ceriolo* chicories are *grumolo verde scuro* and *grumolo verde,* both of which feature dark green, compact, 8-inch-wide rosettes of leaves. These bitter-tasting chicories are popular in the Lombardy region of northern Italy. *Spadona* (or *lingua di cane*) has paler, narrower leaves. It is vigorous and winter hardy and best when harvested young, about 4 to 6 inches tall. *Biondissima Trieste,* popular in northern Italy, has smooth, rounded green leaves.

PLANT ORIGIN

N. Vavilov suggests the Mediterranean as chicory's center of origin.

PLANT HISTORY

Also see Endive. Wild chicory has been used in salads from time immemorial. It is not known if the ancients cultivated chicory. Theophrastus may be talking about chicory in his description of *kichorion*. When Pliny discusses *cichorium* he is referring to endive, not chicory. Chicory is not mentioned in Albertus Magnus's list of garden vegetables used in the thirteenth century. In 1535 Ruellis mentions two kinds of chicory but does not say whether they were cultivated. Other botanical writers of that century also don't mention its cultivation. Castelvetro in the seventeenth century describes the wild plant being dressed with oil, vinegar, and salt and served in a salad bowl rubbed with garlic.

HOW TO GROW AND HARVEST

Chicory grows best in cool weather and in rich and slightly acid soil with a pH factor of 6.0. When fully grown, the plants resemble large romaine lettuce. Sow seeds in spring about 8 inches apart and cut them when 4 to 6 inches tall. Seeds may be sown again in mid-summer for a winter crop, which can survive temperatures as low as 20°F.

Radicchio di Treviso and *radicchio di Verona* take 4 to 9 months to grow and are very hard to grow. They fail about half the time even with expert gardeners. The following newer vari-eties are easier to grow: *Giulio* has a tennis-ball-size deep burgundy head with white veins. *Augusto* is slightly larger and tolerates heat and cold better. Early *Treviso* looks like a bright burgundy Belgian endive. Belgian endive has to be harvested, plant and roots, before the winter frost.

Chicory that is planted in the spring should be harvested just before the fall frost. Late summer chicory is ready by late winter or early spring.

HOW TO BUY, STORE, AND PREPARE FOR COOKING

Radicchio is a chicory that looks like a small head of red cabbage. Look for heads that feel slightly heavy and whose leaves are tight to the head, although there are some varieties of radicchio with fleshier, longer and looser leaves. Store chicory in the refrigerator for not more than 3 days.

Chicorée a la Crème
CHICORY IN CREAM SAUCE

The bitter taste of chicory is subdued by the butter and cream in this classic preparation from Provence. The sugar should not be noticeable; just a little will do the trick. This is an old-fashioned recipe—people generally don't cook like this anymore, using cream and sugar with salad greens. Chicory in Cream Sauce is perfect accompanied by roast chicken, pork, or veal.

1 large bunch chicory, washed well
2 tablespoons unsalted butter
Salt and freshly ground black pepper to taste
Pinch of freshly grated nutmeg
½ cup heavy cream
1 teaspoon confectioners' sugar

1. Place the chicory in a large saucepan with only the water adhering to it from its last rinsing. Turn the heat to high and cook until it wilts, about 3 minutes. Remove, drain, and chop fine. Once it's cool enough to handle, pick the chicory up with your hands and squeeze out any remaining liquid.
2. Place the chicory in a small saucepan greased with the butter. Season with salt, pepper, and nutmeg and cook the chicory over low heat until it is soft and bright green, about 20 minutes. Add the cream and cook until thick, about 10 minutes. Sprinkle on the confectioners' sugar, stir to mix well, cook 1 more minute, and serve hot.

Makes 4 servings

Hindab bi'l-Zayt
CHICORY LEAVES IN OLIVE OIL

Chicory is a bitter-tasting green, but it is very popular in the Mediterranean. All kinds of ingenious Mediterranean recipes take advantage of this bitterness and turn it to useful advantage, as in this dish from Lebanon that is sometimes served as part of a *mazza* table. Here the chicory is garnished with crispy brown onions that make a pleasing contrast to the soft green leaves.

1½ pounds chicory, washed well and shredded
*   very fine*
1 cup olive oil
1 large onion, cut into ¹⁄₁₆-inch-thick slices and
*   pulled apart into rings*
1 tablespoon salt
3 large garlic cloves, chopped fine
2 to 3 tablespoons freshly squeezed lemon juice,
*   to your taste*

1. Bring a large saucepan full of water to a boil. Boil the chicory for 2 minutes. Drain, squeeze dry, and set aside.
2. Heat the olive oil in a large skillet over medium-high heat. Add the onion rings and coat with the oil. Continue cooking and turning the onion rings as they change from white to yellow to brown. Once they turn brown, 10

Chive

 CHIVES ARE USUALLY USED IN MEDITERRANEAN COOKING AS A GARNISH OR AS AN HERB FLAVORING. BUT IN FRANCE SOME cooks like to make a chive soup, using chicken or vegetable broth as the base, and sometimes adding heavy cream.

to 20 minutes, continue to cook until some turn dark brown, another 2 minutes. Remove the skillet from the burner and quickly transfer the onion rings to a platter lined with a paper towel to cool and drain. Once they are cool, they will become crispy. Save the oil in the skillet.

3. Transfer the chicory along with the garlic to the same skillet in which you cooked the onions, using the same oil. Sprinkle the chicory with the salt. Cook over medium heat until the chicory is very hot and flavorful, 15 minutes. Pour the lemon juice over the chicory, stir, and let cool. Arrange the chicory on a platter. Garnish with the onion rings and serve at room temperature.

Makes 4 servings

CHIVE

Allium schoenoprasum L. *(syn. A. sibiricum)* (Liliaceae)
ARABIC: *bassal al-shify*; FRENCH: *ciboulette, fines herbes*; GREEK: *krammous*; ITALIAN: *cipollina*; SERBO-CROATIAN: *luk, vlasac*; SPANISH: *cebollino*.

PLANT CHARACTERISTICS AND VARIETIES

A member of the onion family, chive is a hardy perennial with bluish green hollow leaves. The edible part is the leaf. Chives are used as an herb or for salads. They are also used in a chive soup. Chive is a widespread species, ranging from the Arctic to the mountains of North America, Europe, and Asia.

PLANT ORIGIN

Chives are said to originate in the Mediterranean, but there is evidence that they are the only one of the allium species native to the Old and New Worlds.

There is no record of chives in the Mediterranean before the sixteenth century when the English botanist John Gerard included chives in his herbal published in 1597.

HOW TO GROW AND HARVEST

Chives grow best in a cool place with moist, well-drained soil, and especially in pots. Harvest the leaves when the first flower buds appear by snipping off leaves from the plant as needed.

HOW TO BUY, STORE, AND PREPARE FOR COOKING

Look for straight green stalks that are crisp and smell nice. The flavor of chives is quite subtle, so it is best to use the leaves as an uncooked garnish with omelettes, mashed potatoes, dips, spaghetti, or other simple foods. Dried chives lose their flavor, so it is better to freeze fresh chives.

CHONDRILLA JUNCEA L. VAR. JUNCEA (ASTERACEAE-COMPOSITAE)

TURKISH: *karaavlık*

PLANT CHARACTERISTICS AND VARIETIES

This plant is a grayish green biennial or perennial with many ascending branches with smooth leaves and raceme inflorescences. In the Melendez River basin of the Aksaray Province of central Anatolia, the leaves and roots of this plant are commonly collected in the wild and eaten raw or cooked.

CHUFA

Cyperus esculentus L. var. *sativus* Boeckeler (Cyperaceae)
Also called tiger nut, earth almond, rush nut; ARABIC: ḥabb al-samar, ḥabb ʿazīz, sād; FRENCH: *amande de terre, chufa, souchet comestibile*; SPANISH: *chufa*

PLANT CHARACTERISTICS AND VARIETIES

Chufa is an annual or perennial plant, but the cultivated chufa has elongated tubers with conspicuous bands and it rarely flowers. The edible part of the plant is the tuber, which is very sweet. Chufa is most popular in two places in the Mediterranean, Spain and Egypt (especially around Damietta). In Spain, especially in the region of Valencia, chufa is used to make a drink called *horchata*. The tubers are soaked for about 3 days in water and then pounded. The liquid that is produced is saved, strained, and drunk chilled with ice.

PLANT ORIGIN

N. Vavilov suggests the Mediterranean as the chufa's center of origin.

PLANT HISTORY

Evidence of the chufa has been found in the tomb of Rekhmire, the vizier of King Tuthmosis III in the fifteenth century B.C.

What was found were remnants of bread loaves made from chufa flour. The chufa was mixed with honey to form a dough, cooked over a fire with some fat, and then cooled and formed into conical loaves. Pliny briefly mentions chufa as a plant eaten by Egyptians.

The chufa was introduced to Europe by the Arabs. There are written records from the thirteenth century indicating that a drink was made near Valencia in Spain from the chufa, a descendant of the present-day *horchata.*

In the seventeenth century, John Gerarde's herbal mentioned the use of chufa in Italy, especially in Verona. The chufa was known in eighteenth-century Venice as *bagigi,* a corruption of the Arabic word *ḥabb ʿazīz,* which, literally translated, means "pleasing," or "dear seed."

HOW TO GROW AND HARVEST

Chufa is an easy-to-grow perennial with 2-foot-long grasslike leaves. The tubers should be planted about 6 inches apart, and the clumps need to be divided now and then over the next few years.

CLEMATIS

Clematis vitalba L. (Ranunculaceae)
Also called traveler's joy, virgin's bower, or old-man's-beard; FRENCH: *clématite;*
ITALIAN: *clematide, vitalbe, vezzadro*
(Tuscany), *vitarva* (Apulia); GREEK:
klmatitis; SERBO-CROATIAN: *pavit, bijela loza;*
SPANISH: *clemátide*

PLANT CHARACTERISTICS AND VARIETIES

Clematis is a genus of perennial climbing shrubs in the buttercup family. The leaves of the species that is popular among Italians for eating is called traveler's joy or old-man's-beard *(C. vitalba).* It is this variety that is used in the region of Friuli in northern Italy in a spring preparation known as *pistic,* which is made up of more than fifty wild greens. In a recipe called *vitarva e ovi* (clematis and eggs), from the Apulia region in southern Italy, the clematis is boiled first, then fried in olive oil with eggs and salt. In rural Tuscany, clematis is used in *frittate.*

Another variety of clematis is called virgin's bower *(C. flammula).* The boiled young shoots of this plant are eaten in many Mediterranean regions, such as the Balearic Islands, Crete, Spain, and the European part of Turkey.

PLANT ORIGIN

Clematis seems to be native to the Mediterranean.

PLANT HISTORY

Pliny described clematis as being used medicinally and as a food. He tells us that, eaten with vinegar, clematis works as an aphrodisiac. The leaves were usually eaten as a salad with oil and salt.

COLOCYNTH

Citrullis colocynthis (L.) O. Kuntze
(Cucurbitaceae)
**Also called bitter gourd, wild
watermelon;** ARABIC: *habd, ḥanzal;* FRENCH:
coloquinte; GREEK: *kolokynthe;* SPANISH:
coloquíntida

PLANT CHARACTERISTICS AND VARIETIES
The edible part of this herbaceous vine,
which is related to the watermelon, is its
spongy fruit. Before it can be eaten, the fruit
must be boiled repeatedly to remove its bitterness, which can have a purging effect. The
fruit is then made into preserves. The seeds
are eaten roasted or ground into flour. In
southern Africa the colocynth sometimes
served as the only source of water for humans
and animals over extended dry seasons. The
Arabic word *māṣ* refers to a preparation of
colocynth made with honey while *nahīda* is a
kind of food made with flour and the seeds.

PLANT ORIGIN
Colocynth is native to North Africa, although
it also grows on some islands of the Aegean.
Harlan suggests the plant's origins as the dry
savanna of southern and eastern Africa.

PLANT HISTORY
Colocynth has been used as a purgative since
antiquity and is grown commercially today for
medicinal purposes. In the Old and New
Testaments, colocynth is referred to as *gall.*

The "wild gourds" mentioned in the Book of
Kings in the Bible are colocynths. One popular legend has the prophet Elisha cursing all
gourdlike fruit because of his bad experience
with colocynth.

CONRINGIA ORIENTALIS
(BRASSICACEAE)
TURKISH: *yabani tütün*

PLANT CHARACTERISTICS AND VARIETIES
This plant is an annual that grows to about 2
feet and has oval and heart-shaped leaves and
yellowish flowers. In Turkey the ¼-inch-long
seeds of *Conringia orientalis* are ground and used
as a vegetable or condiment.

CORNFLOWER

Centaurea cyanus L. (Compositae)
Also called bachelor's button; ITALIAN:
centaurea; GREEK: *araxositoagron, anthoston;*
SPANISH: *centaura*

PLANT CHARACTERISTICS AND VARIETIES
This annual, which grows to 3½ feet, is native
in Spain and Sicily and has been naturalized
in cornfields elsewhere in the Mediterranean
and Europe. In the Mediterranean the flowers
are eaten as a cooked vegetable or used as a
garnish for salads. The plant also yields a blue
dye used for coloring sugar or jelly. Some taxonomists categorize this plant as an
Aspleniaceae.

CORN ROCKET

Bunias erucago L. (Cruciferae-Brassicaceae)
Also see shepherd's purse; ITALIAN: *barland*
(colloquial), *sportavecchia* (Tuscany)

PLANT CHARACTERISTICS AND VARIETIES
Corn rocket is a bristly annual or biennial that
grows to 3 feet and features yellow petals. The
edible part is the tender young leaf, which is
mostly used in soups or as a side dish. *Ris e
barland* is a delightful rice preparation from
Lombardy that includes corn rocket.
Although mostly a wild green herb, corn rocket has been cultivated in some places.

COSTMARY

Balsamita major Desf. (syn. *Chrysanthemum
balsamita* [L.] Baillon; *Pyrethrum majus*
[Desf.] Tzelev) (Asteraceae-Compositae)
Also called bible-leaf, alecost; ITALIAN:
erba di Santa Maria (Tuscany)

PLANT CHARACTERISTICS AND VARIETIES
Costmary, a leafy perennial herb, is used
mostly as an ornamental. But in rural Tuscany
people use the leaves as a vegetable, combining
it with other vegetables in *frittate*.

COTTON THISTLE

Onopordum acanthium L. (Asteraceae-
Compositae)
Also called Scotch thistle

PLANT CHARACTERISTICS AND VARIETIES
The edible part is the large flower receptacle,
or heart, which can be eaten like an artichoke.
Cotton thistle is eaten mostly in North
Africa.

COW PARSNIP

Heraculeum sphondylium subsp. *monatanum*
Scheicher ex. Gaudin *(syn. H. cordatum)*
(Umbelliferae)

PLANT CHARACTERISTICS AND VARIETIES
This bristly biennial grows to 8 feet. The
sweet-scented black roots are eaten in Sicily as
a cooked dish. In Turkey the petioles and
fleshy shoots of *H. persicum* are boiled and
eaten for breakfast. The young shoots of *H.
pubescens* are eaten raw in Turkey. In France one
subspecies of *H. sphondylium* is used to flavor
liqueurs.

CUCUMBER

Cucumis sativus L. (Cucurbitaceae)
ARABIC: *khiyār, qiṭṭaᶜ, quṭṭaᶜ, bajūr* (Syria, obsolete); FRENCH: *concombre*; GREEK: *angouri*; ITALIAN: *cetriolo, cetriolino*; SERBO-CROATIAN: *krastavac*; SPANISH: *pepino, cohombro*; TURKISH: *hıyar, salatık*

PLANT CHARACTERISTICS AND VARIETIES

The cucumber is a climbing or trailing annual herbaceous plant that can be trained on stakes or vertical wires. The fruit—the cucumber—is actually a large berry that forms a hard epicarp when mature. But the edible part is harvested as an immature fruit, which is eaten cooked, raw, or preserved. When picked very small, cucumbers are called gherkins, as are a variety known as West Indian gherkin, *C. anguria*. There are two main varieties of cucumber: those meant to be eaten fresh and pickling cucumbers.

Snake cucumber, or Armenian cucumber (*C. sativus* L. var. *flexuosus*), is popular in Egypt, where it is called *faqqūs* (the word also refers to muskmelon, *Cucumis melo* L. Reticulatus group, syn. *C. melo* var. *reticulatus*) and is usually eaten plain as a snack or after dinner. Squirting cucumber (*Ecballium elaterium*) is from another genus, but it too is eaten in the same way in Egypt, where it is called *qiththāᶜ*, an Arabic word for a long cucumber that also means "penis." In the Arab world there is a kind of cucumber, known as *jurb*, that has a white skin.

PLANT ORIGIN

The cucumber appears to be native to northern India. The evidence is circumstantial because a wild cucumber has never been found there or anywhere else. Although some writers make the flat-out claim that the small, bitter, spiny plant known as *C. hardwickii*, which grows wild in the foothills of the Himalayas, is this wild ancestor, and it certainly appears so, there is not yet any conclusive evidence. N. Vavilov identified the mountains of central and western China and the adjacent areas as the cucumber's place of origin. Other species of *Cucumis* are mostly African in origin.

PLANT HISTORY

The nineteenth-century botanist Alphonse de Candolle thought the cucumber had been cultivated in India for 3,000 years. There is controversy as to whether the cucumber was known by the ancient Egyptians. Some botanists claim that it was already known by the time of the Twelfth Dynasty. The cucumber is mentioned in the Bible, and it is believed that the Jews imported it from Egypt to Palestine, where it became a very popular food. The Greeks knew of cucumber, and it was cultivated by the Romans. Theophrastus says there are three kinds of cucumber, Laconian, club-shaped, and Boeotian, and that cucumbers are more succulent if the seeds are soaked in milk or honey-syrup before they are sowed. Athenaeus related a Greek proverb about the cucumber: "Munch a cucumber, woman, and keep on weaving your cloak."

The Roman emperor Tiberius is said to have been fond of cucumbers, and Columella describes their cultivation in his *De re rustica.* Pliny mentions the cultivation of cucumbers as well. It has long been argued that the horticultural ordinances called *Capitulare de Villis* were drawn up in A.D. 812 by Charlemagne for his domains. Some believe that they were in fact drawn up in A.D. 795 by Louis the Pious, the son of Charlemagne, for his estates in Aquitaine. By the ninth century A.D., Charlemagne ordered cucumbers planted for his estate. Egyptian Copts used cucumbers for medicinal purposes, mixing the leaves of the plant with salt and placing them on women's breasts to encourage milk production. The first record of the cultivation of cucumbers in France is from the ninth century according to Sturtevant. In his medical treatise, the eleventh-century Egyptian physician Ibn Riḍwān recommended eating cucumbers, snake cucumbers, and squirting cucumbers during hot weather and to relieve heartburn and upset stomachs. The famed nineteenth-century British traveler Richard Burton notes that the Arabs made a salad oil from cucumber seeds.

HOW TO GROW AND HARVEST

Cucumbers need to be grown in full sun in a very rich soil with lots of manure and compost. They also need to be well watered. The seeds are usually sown in late fall and then transplanted to raised beds in rows at least a foot apart in January where they need a minimum temperature of 60°F to grow. Where that temperature is not possible, the planting is delayed to May. The apical shoot can be pinched to encourage side growth. In the warmer Mediterranean climates, which enjoy a warm growing season of five or more months, a second crop is planted after midsummer and harvested before the first frost. As soon as a cucumber reaches an edible size, which is less than full size, it should be picked to encourage further fruit production.

HOW TO BUY, STORE, AND PREPARE FOR COOKING

When shopping for cucumbers in a supermarket, make sure they are displayed cool, preferably under refrigeration. At farmers' markets, make sure cucumbers are sold under shade and not placed directly in the hot sun. Cucumbers should feel firm over their entire lengths and should have firm, rounded tips. Thicker cucumbers will have more seeds than slimmer ones. Cucumbers should be kept cool; otherwise they can wilt. But if they are frozen or overcooled their insides will turn mushy. Store cucumbers in the refrigerator crisper drawer. Because many of the cucumbers sold in supermarkets are waxed, it is best to peel them. I also prefer to scoop out the seeds before using cucumbers.

Cucumber

THROUGHOUT THE MEDITERRANEAN, CUCUMBERS ARE ALMOST EXCLUSIVELY PICKLED OR USED IN SALADS. THE VARIETY OF preparations is limited only by the imagination of the cook. In Italy one might find cucumber in a salad with sardines, or with rolled and stuffed turkey fillets, or in eggplant ragout, or in a large salad made with cooked and cooled potatoes, green beans, zucchini, and onions dressed with mustard, olive oil, and egg yolk.

RECIPES

Horiatiki Salata
GREEK COUNTRY SALAD

Here is the familiar salad we all know as Greek salad, a salad the Greeks call a country salad (or sometimes a village salad). A proper Greek salad should not be boring, but a delightful mix of very fresh vegetables with briny, creamy feta cheese and a *ladolemono* dressing made of two parts extra virgin olive oil, one part lemon juice, seasoned with dried oregano, chopped fresh parsley, dill, or thyme, and with salt and pepper. Don't make the salad until the last minute.

FOR THE SALAD:

2 pounds ripe tomatoes, sliced into wedges
2 cucumbers, peeled, sliced lengthwise, seeded, and cut into chunks
2 green bell peppers, seeded and cut into strips
1 large red onion, sliced and pulled apart into rings
16 imported black Kalamata olives, pitted, if desired
¼ pound imported feta cheese, in 4 large chunks
4 salted anchovy fillets, rinsed (optional)

FOR THE DRESSING:

¼ cup extra virgin olive oil
2 tablespoons freshly squeezed lemon juice
1 teaspoon dried oregano
1 tablespoon finely chopped fresh parsley leaves
1 garlic clove, chopped fine
Salt and freshly ground black pepper to taste

1. Arrange all the vegetables in a serving platter. Top with the olives and feta cheese, and anchovies, if you are using them.
2. Whisk together the dressing ingredients and pour over the salad right before serving.

Makes 4 servings

Tzatziki

GREEK CUCUMBER AND YOGURT SALAD

In Greece one will find *tzatziki* served with just about anything. It is a cool accompaniment to grilled foods, delightful on top of rice, and quite nice as a *meze* to be scooped up with pieces of flatbread. People enjoy *tzatziki* as much in Turkey, where they call it *cacık* (pronounced *jajuk*), and they eat it the same way. If the yogurt you are using is not thick, use the lesser amount of oil.

2 cups high-quality full-fat plain cow's milk
    yogurt
¼ to ½ cup extra virgin olive oil, to your taste
1 small cucumber, peeled, seeded, and grated, with
    its water squeezed out
3 to 5 garlic cloves, to your taste, peeled and
    mashed with ½ teaspoon salt
2 tablespoons finely chopped fresh dill

I. Put the yogurt in a medium bowl and beat the olive oil into it. Add the remaining ingredients and blend well. Refrigerate before using and serve cold.

Makes 2 cups

Tarator

CUCUMBER AND YOGURT SOUP

Tarator is a Macedonian and Bulgarian cucumber and yogurt soup made with garlic and walnuts and served cold. The word *tarator* is Turkish, but in Turkey it refers to a walnut and garlic sauce. Here the walnuts and garlic flavor a cold soup that is ideal for a hot summer day. To achieve the right consistency, the walnuts and garlic should be pounded in a mortar, not crushed in a food processor.

FOR THE SOUP:

5 large garlic cloves, peeled
3 ounces shelled walnuts (about 1 cup walnut
    halves)
1 ounce day-old French or Italian bread (1 thick
    slice), crusts removed
2 tablespoons walnut oil
2 cups high-quality full-fat plain cow's milk
    yogurt
1 large cucumber, peeled, seeded, and cut into tiny
    dice
⅔ cup cold spring water
1 tablespoon freshly squeezed lemon juice
12 ice cubes

FOR THE GARNISH:

6 tablespoons crushed walnuts (about 1 ounce
    shelled)
2 tablespoons walnut oil
2 tablespoons finely chopped fresh dill
2 lemons, cut in quarters

I. In a large mortar, pound the garlic until mushy. Add the walnuts a little at a time and pound them too until they are mushy. Soak the bread in some water and then squeeze out the water. Add the bread to the mortar and pound it with the other ingredients until creamy. Once the ingredients have formed a smooth paste, drizzle in the walnut oil a little at a time, pounding to incorporate it. Transfer the mixture to a medium bowl and beat in the yogurt until smooth. (At this point you could put the soup into a food processor if you like and run the machine for 30 seconds to make the soup smooth.)

2. Add the cucumber to the soup and stir in the cold water and lemon juice. Serve the soup in bowls with 2 ice cubes per person, and the crushed walnuts, walnut oil, and dill sprinkled over the top. Pass the lemon quarters at the table.

Makes 6 servings

Salāṭat Banadūra wa Khiyār
TOMATO AND CUCUMBER SALAD

Among the Palestinians, and the Lebanese and Syrians, too, there is a great love of vegetable salads made with very fresh vegetables and especially very ripe tomatoes. In fact, the Syrians sometimes like these vegetable salads to become soupy from their liquid, which sounds like the philosophical predecessor to a gazpacho (page 334), thought to be originally an Arab contribution. But in this fine Palestinian salad, from a recipe given to me by my ex-wife, Najwa al-Qattan, the salad must be prepared close to the time you intend on serving it; otherwise it will become very liquidy.

2 pounds ripe tomatoes
4 cucumbers, peeled and seeded
1 large red onion, peeled
¼ cup extra virgin olive oil
3 tablespoons freshly squeezed lemon juice
Salt and freshly ground pepper to taste
½ cup finely chopped fresh mint leaves

Dice the tomatoes, cucumbers, and red onion and transfer to a large salad bowl. Add all the rest of the ingredients and toss together. Serve within 15 minutes.

Makes 6 servings

DANDELION
Taraxacum officinale (L.) Wiggers (Asteraceae-Compositae)
ARABIC: *salāṭa murra*; FRENCH: *dent de lion, pissenlit, pissenlit commune*; GREEK: *padiki*; ITALIAN: *dente de leone*; SERBO-CROATIAN: *maslačak*; SPANISH: *diente de léon, taraxacón*; TURKISH: *karahindiba*

PLANT CHARACTERISTICS AND VARIETIES
Dandelion is a hardy perennial that is cultivated as an annual. There are some 1,200 microspecies of dandelion. Most dandelions are wild, although some are cultivated for large leaves. The edible parts are the leaves and roots, which are consumed either raw or cooked. One of the French names for the plant, *pissenlit*, refers to the sticky substance that oozes from the stem when the plant is picked; this name is also a reference to the

plant's diuretic properties, translating literally as "piss-in-bed." Dandelion has a bitter taste. In the Mediterranean the dandelion is most popular in Italy and Greece.

PLANT ORIGIN

Wild dandelions are found throughout the world.

PLANT HISTORY

The name *dandelion* derives from the medieval Latin *dens leonis* through the French *dent de lion,* lion's teeth, referring to the shape of the leaf. I'm not absolutely certain, but I believe the first mention of dandelion as a medicinal plant is in the works of the Arab physicians of the tenth and eleventh centuries.

HOW TO GROW AND HARVEST

Wild dandelions are found in every garden and most every lawn. If no pesticides have ever been used on your lawn, you can pick and eat your own dandelions. For the least bitter-tasting leaves, pick the plant, roots and all, before it flowers. Cultivated dandelion is seed-sown indoors in peat pots in early spring and transplanted to rich and well-watered soil in full sun about 6 inches apart. Harvest dandelion before the plant flowers, taking roots and all.

HOW TO BUY, STORE, AND PREPARE FOR COOKING

Store dandelion greens in the refrigerator in a plastic bag for a few days before using them,

because the bitterness will fade and their flavor will improve.

RECIPE

Verdure Miste alla Parmigiana
MIXED BOILED VEGETABLES WITH PARMESAN CHEESE

This recipe, from my grandfather's homeland in the Campania region in southern Italy, is the type of preparation he loved. The Greeks also like to eat these kinds of foods in a preparation they call *horta.* This dish can also be eaten at room temperature.

1 pound dandelion leaves, trimmed of heavy stems, washed well
20 to 22 ounces spinach, trimmed of heavy stems, washed well
1½ pounds zucchini, sliced
1 tablespoon sugar
3 tablespoons red wine vinegar
3 tablespoons extra virgin olive oil, plus more for drizzling
2 large garlic cloves, peeled and lightly crushed
Salt and freshly ground black pepper to taste
3 tablespoons freshly grated Parmigiano-Reggiano cheese

I. Place the dandelion and spinach in a large pot with only the water adhering to the leaves from their last rinsing. Wilt the leaves over high heat, covered, 5 to 7 minutes, turning a few times. Remove and drain well in a colander. Cut the leaves into smaller pieces.

2. Bring a medium saucepan of lightly salted water to a boil and cook the zucchini until they are soft, with only a slight bite to them, about 5 minutes. Drain well. Dissolve the sugar in the vinegar.

3. Heat the olive oil in a large skillet over medium-high heat and add the garlic, zucchini, dandelion, and spinach. Cook for 1 minute. Pour in the vinegar and sugar mixture, season with salt and pepper, and cook until the liquid has evaporated, 6 to 8 minutes, stirring gently occasionally.

4. Arrange the greens on a serving platter and let them come to room temperature. Drizzle the top with olive oil and sprinkle Parmigiano over it all. Serve immediately.

Makes 6 servings

DESERT CANDLE
Eremurus caucasicus Steven (syn. *E. spectablis*) (Liliaceae)

PLANT CHARACTERISTICS AND VARIETIES
This perennial herb has long stems and sharp three-angled leaves. The edible parts are the young leaves and shoots, which are eaten as a vegetable in Turkey. The leaves are also added to herbal cheeses made in Turkey. The taste is said to be similar to that of spinach and purslane.

DWARF FAN-PALM
Chamaerops humilis L. (Palmae)
Also called palmetto; ITALIAN: *cafaglion;* ARABIC: *dum;* BERBER: *dum*

PLANT CHARACTERISTICS AND VARIETIES
This palm grows to about 6 feet with yellow or brown oval fruit that can be up to a foot in diameter. The young shoots or suckers from the bottom portion of the plant are cooked and eaten by southern Italians. Along the North African coast, Arabs and Berbers eat the plants, shoots, and roots cooked. The Tibu, a nomadic tribe of the Sahara, use the dried and ground fruit to make bread.

PLANT ORIGIN
This plant is found in the western Mediterranean.

EARTH CHESTNUT
Lathyrus tuberosus L. (Leguminosae)
Also called groundnut; FRENCH: *gesse tubéreuse, anette, châtaigne de terre;* ITALIAN: *cicerbia tuberosa, ghianda di terra, tartufo di Prato;* SPANISH: *arveja tuberoso, guija, cicértula tuberosa*

PLANT CHARACTERISTICS AND VARIETIES
This perennial legume has a stem that grows to 4 feet. The edible part is the tuber, which is cooked. The name *earth chestnut* is also used to

denote *Conopodium majus* Gouan (*C. denudatum* Koch.), an umbellifer whose tuberous roots are roasted or boiled in Corsica, Spain, and Sicily.

ECHIUM ITALICUM L. (BORAGINACEAE)

ITALIAN: *echio*; TURKISH: *kurt kuyruğu*

PLANT CHARACTERISTICS AND VARIETIES

The leaves of this biennial plant, which is related to borage, are used in vegetable soups, for pickling, and as the stuffing for *tortelli* in rural Tuscany. In Turkey the plant is used by apiarists to make a uniquely flavored honey.

EGGPLANT

Solanum melongena L. (Solanaceae)
Also called aubergine; ARABIC: *bādhinjān, kahkam, ānab* (colloquial), *ḥīṣal, qahqab, maghad*; FRENCH: *aubergine*; GREEK: *melitzana*; ITALIAN: *melanzane, petronciano*; SERBO-CROATIAN: *patlidžan, melacana*; SPANISH: *berenjena*; TURKISH: *patlıcan*

PLANT CHARACTERISTICS AND VARIETIES

The eggplant is a tender perennial that is grown as an annual. Modern cultivars are bushy plants that grow to about 3 feet in height. The flowers are purple and the fruit is deep purple, violet, striped violet, or white. The edible part is the ripe fruit, which is eaten cooked. The modern eggplant found in the supermarket is a hybrid grown for its large dark-skinned fruit. In Turkey a species of eggplant called *S. integrifolium* grows to 4 feet and bears miniature eggplant that are orange-red in color, round, and weigh 2 to 3 ounces. Several varieties of eggplant are now available on the market, including the familiar globe eggplant. There are also long, thin eggplant of purple, light purple, or white color called Japanese or Chinese eggplant. A white eggplant is available that looks like a large egg, and there is a round, ribbed eggplant called Italian Rosa Bianco.

PLANT ORIGIN

Although most botanists believe that southeastern India is the place of origin of the eggplant, and some botanists make a case for China, as well as the Malay Peninsula, the place of origin is still unknown. N. Vavilov identified the area including the mountains of central and western China and the adjacent areas as well as India as a center of origin. It seems clear, though, that India is, at least, a secondary area of origin. The cultivated eggplant appears to be an improved form of either *S. insanum* or *S. incanum,* both of which are native to India.

PLANT HISTORY

The history of the eggplant in the Mediterranean begins when Arab agriculturists brought the vegetable from Persia and perhaps from the Arabian Peninsula in the ninth or tenth centuries. Arabs seem to have discovered the eggplant already growing in Persia shortly after their conquest of that country in A.D. 642 yet several ancient Arabic names for the eggplant seem to come directly from other Indian names, indicating that the plant may have arrived in the Arabian Peninsula in pre-Islamic times.

Arabs have long been fond of the eggplant, and medieval Arabic cookery manuscripts include lots of recipes. The eggplant was treated with suspicion at first, but soon it became a favorite vegetable. In fact, the medieval Arab toxicologist Ibn Waḥshīya (writing circa A.D. 904) said it would be fatal if eaten raw. Sicily was one of the first places in Europe where eggplant was grown after being introduced by Arab farmers. The plant was grown in Spain by the tenth century, as we know from a brief mention in the anonymous Cordovan Calendar, although the first clear reference to the eggplant in Sicily is from 1309. In Sicily the plant was called *melingiana* and was grown in a garden along with cucumbers and a kind of gourd (squash). Although the eggplant was once called "mad apple" (*mala insana*) because it was thought to produce insanity, this expression is not the etymological root of the Italian and Sicilian words for eggplant, *melanzane* and *mulinciana*, respectively. These words derive from the Arabic word for the plant, *bādhinjān*, with the addition of the initial *m*. There are numerous recipes for eggplant from thirteenth-century Spain, which is notable because eggplant was relatively new to Europe at the time, so it is

remarkable that the plant was in common use. *Tortilla de berenjenas*, an eggplant puree *tortilla* from Seville, is a recipe from the thirteenth-century Arab-Andalusi (the Spanish Arabs of Andalusia) cookbook of Ibn Razīn al-Tujībī, the *Kitāb faḍālat al-khiwān fī ṭayyibāt al-ṭaᶜam wa'l-alwān*.

HOW TO GROW AND HARVEST

Eggplant requires much the same growing conditions as does the tomato. Eggplant seeds need warm soil, above 75°F. Three weeks after the average frost-free date, set out the plants outdoors, spaced 2 feet apart. The air temperature should be above 60°F, and the soil needs to be well-manured and -drained with a high potash content to encourage root growth. Each plant should produce about five large fruits. Once the fruits begin to swell, fertilizer can be applied. When the eggplant is about 1½ feet tall, the top of the plant can be pinched to encourage more leaf growth. Harvest eggplant when the fruit are half grown and the skin is shiny. To harvest, cut off the fruit at the stem.

HOW TO BUY, STORE, AND PREPARE FOR COOKING

Eggplant should be uniformly smooth and colored, without bruises. Squeeze the eggplant gently with a finger and then let go: If it is fresh, the eggplant will reform smoothly again. The eggplant should feel heavy. Store eggplant in the refrigerator, where it will keep for 2 weeks.

Eggplant

Eggplant is found in every Mediterranean cuisine, although I believe it is most popular in a swath that starts in Jerusalem, arcs through Turkey, Greece, and southern Italy, and ends in Sicily. But the Provençal also love eggplant and stuff them, too. We have as proof their dish *aubergines farcies aux anchois*, eggplant stuffed with fresh breadcrumbs and anchovies, which one could easily imagine encountering in a restaurant in Nice. In Spain, eggplant appears in dishes such as the Andalusian *alboronía*, a medley of summer vegetables cooked as a ragout, known as *pisto* in La Mancha. In Catalonia, cooks stuff eggplant in a dish called *berenjenas rellanas a la Catalana*. The stuffing features ground meat seasoned with onion, cinnamon, and white wine and blended with a nutmeg-flavored béchamel sauce made with eggs, and the dish is given an au gratin finish in the oven. And there is the famous eggplant-and-cheese dish, *berenjenas con queso*, which is four centuries old and is made with cheese and flavored with mint, onion, nutmeg, and cloves.

Many recipes call for salting eggplant slices before cooking them in order to leach out the bitter juices. Not all eggplants are bitter, so this step is not absolutely necessary. I salt eggplant out of habit, no matter what I read, and I will continue to do so.

RECIPES

RATATOUILLE

Many Americans think of ratatouille as the quintessential dish of Provence. It also has many cousins throughout the Mediterranean. Nevertheless, ratatouille is probably an invention of the twentieth century. It doesn't even appear in J. B. Reboul's classic Provençal cookbook, *La cuisinière Provençale*, from the late nineteenth century.

There are many ways of cooking ratatouille. This recipe is one of the easier ones, but you will get even better results if you have the time to cook the vegetables separately and then mix them together at the end. Ratatouille is almost always eaten at room temperature. In this recipe the eggplant is peeled to make it uniform in color and easier to digest.

2 medium eggplants (about 2½ pounds),
  trimmed, peeled, and cubed

Salt

½ cup extra virgin olive oil

2 medium onions, chopped or sliced

3 ripe but firm tomatoes (about 1 pound),
  seeded, peeled, and cut in quarters

2 medium zucchini, peeled and sliced thin

3 green bell peppers, seeded and cut into thin
  strips

1 garlic clove, peeled and crushed

2 tablespoons dried herbes de Provence,
  wrapped in cheesecloth

Freshly ground black pepper to taste

1. Lay the eggplant cubes on some paper towels and sprinkle them with salt. Leave them to drain of their bitter juices for 30 minutes. Pat them dry with paper towels.

2. Heat the olive oil in a large skillet or casserole over medium heat and cook the onions, stirring occasionally, until they are translucent, about 6 minutes. Add the eggplant, tomatoes, zucchini, peppers, and garlic and shake or stir gently. Add the *herbes de Provence,* season with salt and pepper, and stir to mix. Cover and simmer over medium-low heat until much of the liquid has evaporated and the vegetables are tender, 45 minutes to 1 hour, stirring occasionally to prevent sticking. Strain away any remaining liquid and serve at room temperature with bread.

Makes 6 servings

VARIATION: In step 2, cook each vegetable separately, one after the other, until tender, adding more olive oil when required, and mix all the vegetables together once they are cooked.

Parmigiana di Melanzane
EGGPLANT PARMESAN

The classic eggplant Parmesan is said to come from Parma in Emilia-Romagna, or Campania, or Sicily, although it is also found in Calabria. The first mention of something resembling an eggplant Parmesan is from *Il saporetto* by Simone Prudenzani (1387–1440); the recipe refers to Parmigiano cheese. In his book *Il cuoco galante*, published in 1786, the eighteenth-century Neapolitan chef Vincenzo Corrado mentions that eggplant can be cooked *alla Parmegiana,* meaning that the eggplant was seasoned with butter, herbs, cinnamon and other spices, and grated Parmigiano cheese. It was then covered with a cream sauce made with egg yolks and baked in the oven.

There are several theories about the origin of eggplant Parmesan. The most obvious is that the name derives from the use of Parmigiano cheese, the predominant cheese used in the dish. Many food writers suspect this explanation because the dish is thought to originate in Campania or Sicily, where Parmigiano is not native. I've never been persuaded by that line of thinking, because from at least the fourteenth century on,

Parmigiano was a widely traded cheese and could be found throughout Italy. In any case, the Sicilian authority Pino Correnti suggests that the word *Parmigiana* actually comes from *damigiana*, a sleeve made of wicker into which you put a wine bottle, or, in this case, the hot casserole. Cookbook authors Mary Taylor Simeti, Vincent Schiavelli, and several others have another explanation. They theorize that the name derives from the Sicilian word *palmigiana*, meaning "shutters," because the layered eggplant slices are meant to resemble the louvered panes of shutters or palm-thatched roofs. Simeti suggests that since the Sicilians have a "probrem" pronouncing the letter l, the word became *parmigiana*. Another Sicilian food writer, Franca Colonna Romano Apostolo, suggests that the name is not *parmigiano*, since this cheese is not important to the original dish; the word is *parmiciana*, the equivalent in the Sicilian dialect to "Persian."

In Sicily, eggplant Parmesan is popular in Palermo, as well as in other parts of the island, and is sometimes made with potato slices. The Sicilian version does not emphasize Parmigiano cheese, as does the Campanian version, and it may include raisins and pine nuts, too.

4 large eggplants (about 4 pounds), sliced ¼ inch thick
Salt
4 pounds ripe tomatoes, peeled, seeded, and chopped
3 cups olive oil for frying
All-purpose unbleached flour for dredging
¼ cup extra virgin olive oil
1 medium onion, chopped
Leaves from 1 bunch fresh basil, chopped, divided
Freshly ground black pepper to taste
1 pound fresh mozzarella cheese, sliced very thin or chopped
¼ pound Parmigiano-Reggiano cheese, freshly grated
4 large hard-boiled eggs, shelled and sliced, or 4 large eggs, beaten one at a time as needed

1. Lay the eggplant pieces on some paper towels and sprinkle them with salt. Leave them to release their bitter juices for 30 minutes. Pat them dry with paper towels. Meanwhile, place the chopped tomatoes in a colander or strainer and drain them for 1 hour.

2. Preheat the oil to 375°F in a 12-inch skillet, about 10 minutes of preheating over medium-high heat. Dredge the eggplant slices in the flour, patting off any excess, and fry the slices in batches until golden brown, about 4 minutes per side. Don't overcrowd the skillet. Drain the fried eggplant on paper towels. Change the paper towels at least once; this way you will remove a good deal of residual olive oil.

Making Eggplant Parmesan

THE EGGPLANT IS CUT INTO SLICES AS THIN AS PAPER OR AS THICK AS ½ INCH, ALTHOUGH I FIND THE BEST WIDTH TO BE about ¼ inch thick. Different cooks leach the eggplant of its bitter juices for varying amounts of time, ranging from 30 minutes to 2 hours. Thirty minutes is sufficient.

Next the eggplant is fried—and here recipes diverge. Eggplant Parmesan is made a bit differently by Italian-Americans, many of whom bread the eggplant before frying it. Some cooks dip the eggplant slices in batter or egg before frying, some just fry it, and many flour it first, then fry it. Others who are more concerned with making the dish light will bake or grill the eggplant slices. If you are frying the eggplant, flouring the slices first is a good idea because the flour will reduce the amount of oil the eggplant absorbs. Alternatively, some cooks don't bother to fry the eggplant at all, creating a much lighter, but less authentic, preparation.

The tomato sauce is a typical, simple sauce, but you must pay attention to get it right. The onion is fried in olive oil and then the tomato is cooked with basil, salt, and pepper until quite dense. The sauce is passed through a food mill to make it smooth. At this point, the eggplant is layered with the sauce and other ingredients. On the bottom of the baking casserole goes a little tomato sauce, then the eggplant, the mozzarella or *fiordilatte* cheese, some basil, Parmigiano cheese, egg slices (sometimes), and then tomato sauce. One continues in this manner, finishing with a layer of tomato sauce sprinkled with Parmigiano cheese, sliced eggs, mozzarella cheese, and more Parmigiano. Then the dish is baked.

The traditional Eggplant Parmesan is a heavy dish because the eggplant absorbs an enormous amount of oil even after it has been blotted and drained. For this reason, one normally does not serve huge portions, but rather smaller ones, which are very filling.

3. In a large skillet or casserole, heat ¼ cup of the olive oil over medium-high heat and cook the onion until translucent, about 5 minutes, stirring frequently. Add the drained tomatoes and 2 tablespoons of the chopped basil, reduce the heat to low, and simmer, stirring occasionally, until the sauce is quite dense, about 30 minutes. Pass the tomato sauce through a food mill and return to a medium saucepan. Season with salt and pepper and cook over medium heat until the remaining liquid is nearly gone, 8 to 10 minutes.

4. Preheat the oven to 400°F. Cover the bottom of a large baking dish with a few tablespoons of the tomato sauce and place a layer of eggplant slices on top, overlapping slightly. Sprinkle on some mozzarella, Parmigiano, basil, and a few egg slices or a beaten egg, season with salt and pepper, and begin again with the tomato sauce. Continue to layer the ingredients in this order until the eggplant is used up, finishing the last layer with a sprinkling of Parmigiano cheese. Bake until the sauce is bubbling and the Parmigiano on top is beginning to brown slightly, about 20 minutes. Serve hot or at room temperature.

Makes 8 servings

Melanzane alla Cariatese
BAKED STUFFED EGGPLANT

This is a preparation from the fishing port of Cariati Marina, a small tourist area in the province of Calabria in southern Italy. The combination of anchovies, olives, and capers is quite enriching and makes this stuffed eggplant a delight. This dish is not always served as a side dish and is excellent as an antipasto. The amount of anchovies may look excessive, but you'll have to trust me that it is not—but make sure you use salted anchovies and not the fillets packed in oil and sold in little cans.

2 eggplants (about 2½ pounds), cut in half
Salt
20 salted anchovy fillets, rinsed and chopped
14 imported black Kalamata or Gaeta olives,
  pitted and chopped
¼ cup capers, rinsed and chopped
3 garlic cloves, chopped fine
6 tablespoons extra virgin olive oil, divided
6 tablespoons dry breadcrumbs

1. Hollow out the eggplant halves using a spoon and lay them on some paper towels, cut side down, along with the eggplant flesh and sprinkle with salt. Leave them to release their bitter juices for 30 minutes. Pat them dry with paper towels.

2. Preheat the oven to 350°F. Chop the eggplant pulp. In a medium bowl, mix the eggplant pulp with the anchovies, olives, capers, garlic, and 2 tablespoons of the olive oil. Stuff

the eggplants with this mixture and sprinkle the breadcrumbs and the remaining 4 tablespoons olive oil on top. Place the stuffed eggplants in a baking dish.

3. Bake until the stuffing on top of the eggplants is a dark mushroom color, about 1½ hours. Serve hot.

Makes 6 servings

Melanzane Piccanti sulla Graticola

SPICY GRILLED EGGPLANT "SANDWICHES"

This spicy grilled eggplant "sandwich" is a popular antipasto in the Apulia region of southern Italy. It is a wonderful thing to make when you have a grill going for other foods. Once the little sandwiches are cooked, arrange them nicely on a platter. They will look very inviting.

2 pounds eggplant (1 large eggplant), trimmed and cut into ¼-inch-thick slices
Salt
2 large garlic cloves, chopped fine
½ teaspoon freshly ground black pepper
1 dried red chile pepper, seeded and crumbled or chopped fine
1 tablespoon dried oregano
¾ cup freshly grated Pecorino cheese
¼ cup extra virgin olive oil
3 tablespoons pork lard, melted

1. Keep the slices of eggplant in order by size so you can match them later to make "sandwiches." Lay the slices on some paper towels and sprinkle them with salt. Leave them to drain of their bitter juices for 30 minutes. Pat them dry with paper towels.

2. In a small bowl, mix together the garlic, black pepper, red pepper, oregano, and Pecorino cheese.

3. Prepare a hot charcoal fire or preheat a gas grill for 15 minutes on high.

4. Arrange half the eggplant slices on a work surface, matching each slice with a top half, to be added shortly. Sprinkle each bottom slice with the cheese mixture and drizzle with a little olive oil. Place the top slice on top and gently squeeze down with the palm of your hand. Brush the top with melted lard and move the eggplant sandwich to the grill, with the top side down. Grill. Brush the other side of the sandwich with the lard before turning the sandwich over with tongs or a spatula and continuing the grilling. Cook the sandwich until golden brown on both sides, about 8 minutes, basting with more melted lard if desired. Serve immediately.

Makes 4 servings

Melanzane al Forno
OVEN-BAKED EGGPLANT WITH MOZZARELLA AND FRESH HERBS

In Sardinia, eggplant is as popular as in the rest of Italy. This is a nice eggplant preparation that is not as heavy as recipes that call for frying. First you grill the eggplant slices. Then you bake them in an aromatic tomato sauce heavily laced with herbs.

3 eggplants (about 3½ pounds), trimmed and cut into ⅜-inch-thick slices
Salt
½ cup extra virgin olive oil
1 small onion, chopped fine
2 garlic cloves, chopped fine
2 pounds ripe tomatoes, peeled, seeded, and chopped
2 tablespoons fresh thyme leaves
3 tablespoons finely chopped fresh mint leaves
Freshly ground black pepper to taste
½ cup loosely packed fresh basil leaves, coarsely chopped
¾ pound fresh mozzarella cheese, sliced

1. Lay the eggplant slices on some paper towels and sprinkle them with salt. Leave them to release their bitter juices for 30 minutes. Pat them dry with paper towels.
2. Prepare a charcoal fire, preheat a gas grill for 20 minutes on high, or heat a ridged cast-iron skillet over high heat for 10 minutes. Brush each slice of eggplant with olive oil, reserving 3 tablespoons of the oil for later. Place the slices on the grill or skillet and cook until even black grid marks appear, about 4 minutes per side. Remove the cooked slices to a baking tray and continue cooking the rest.
3. In a large skillet or saucepan, heat the remaining 3 tablespoons olive oil over medium-low heat and cook the onion and garlic until the onion is translucent, about 8 minutes, stirring so the garlic doesn't burn. Add the tomatoes, thyme, and mint and season with salt and pepper. Cook until the sauce is thick, about 35 minutes, stirring occasionally.
4. Preheat the oven to 400°F. Arrange a layer of eggplant in a lightly oiled baking dish, cover with a few ladlefuls of sauce, and sprinkle with basil. Continue layering like this until the eggplant is used up. Lay the mozzarella slices on top of the last layer of eggplant and cover with the remaining sauce. Bake until the cheese starts to bubble, about 35 minutes. Serve hot.

Makes 6 servings

Makaronada me Melitzanes
MACARONI WITH EGGPLANT

In Greece, pasta is usually eaten as a main course, and not as a first course as in Italy. The Greeks also like their pasta well cooked and not al dente in the style of the Italians. I enjoy this kind of cookery, because the emphasis is on vegetables and olive oil. In this recipe, which I think of as a kind of taverna meal, the pasta is cooked until soft and then tossed with *kefalotyri* cheese, a Greek cheese that can be found readily in Middle Eastern and Greek markets. You can substitute *kashkaval* cheese, which is also found in the same kinds of stores. The pasta used in this recipe is what the Italians call *ziti lunghe, regine,* or *mezzani ziti,* and what the Greeks call *makaronia tirpita,* macaroni with a hole in it. It is a long pasta that is wider than the Italian *perciatelli (bucatini)*. In Greece *macaroni* refers to all dry pasta except spaghetti.

The eggplant in this recipe is cooked in an aromatic sauce of tomatoes and wine, flavored with allspice and cinnamon. It is then layered on top of the cheesed pasta and baked a bit. Many Greek cooks prepare this dish with ground beef and onions cooked in olive oil with some parsley, which you can do too in step 2 below.

1 ½ pounds eggplant, peeled and cut into small cubes
Salt
½ cup extra virgin olive oil, divided
1 ½ pounds ripe tomatoes, peeled, seeded, and chopped
3 large garlic cloves, chopped fine
1 cinnamon stick
¼ teaspoon freshly ground allspice berries
½ cup full-bodied dry red wine
3 tablespoons tomato paste
Freshly ground black pepper to taste
½ pound ziti lunghe, regine, mezzani ziti, or makaronia tirpita
1 cup freshly grated kefalotyri cheese, divided
2 tablespoons unsalted butter

I. Lay the eggplant cubes on some paper towels and sprinkle them with salt. Leave them to drain of their bitter juices for 30 minutes or longer. Pat them dry with paper towels.

2. Heat ¼ cup of the olive oil in a casserole or large skillet over medium-high heat and cook the eggplant, tomatoes, and garlic, stirring occasionally, until they are bubbling and the eggplant looks soft, about 10 minutes. Add the cinnamon stick, allspice, wine, and tomato paste and season with salt and pepper. Stir, reduce the heat to low, and simmer until thick and dense, about 30 minutes. Remove and discard the cinnamon stick.

3. Meanwhile, bring a large pot of water to a rolling boil, salt abundantly, and add the pasta. Cook the pasta until it is almost soft, then drain it and toss it with ½ cup of the cheese.

4. Preheat the oven to 350°F. Pour the remaining ¼ cup olive oil into a large casserole or baking dish and cover with the macaroni. Spread the eggplant and tomato mixture over the pasta and sprinkle the remaining ½ cup cheese over the top. Dot with the butter and bake until bubbling, about 30 minutes. Serve hot.

Makes 4 servings

Zeytinağlı Patlıcan Dolması
STUFFED EGGPLANT IN OLIVE OIL

In Turkey a whole class of foods is called *zeytinağlı*, meaning "olive oil foods." The delicious stuffed eggplants in this recipe are served at room temperature either as a vegetable side dish or as a *meze*. Seasoning with allspice and including currants and pine nuts in prepared dishes is typical of Turkish cuisine. The best way to serve these stuffed eggplants is sliced with a sprig of mint or parsley.

3 large eggplants (about 3½ pounds)
¾ cup extra virgin olive oil, divided
2 medium onions, coarsely chopped
1 teaspoon salt, divided
½ cup uncooked medium-grain rice, soaked in
     tepid water for 30 minutes and drained or
     rinsed well
1 tablespoon pine nuts
1¾ cups water, divided
½ cup ripe tomatoes, peeled, seeded, and chopped
     fine or canned crushed tomatoes
1 tablespoon dried currants
½ teaspoon freshly ground black pepper
½ teaspoon freshly ground allspice berries
1 tablespoon finely chopped fresh mint leaves
¼ cup chopped fresh dill
½ teaspoon sugar

1. Cut off the stem end of the eggplant and save this as a "lid." Hollow out the eggplant by removing the seeds and flesh, being careful not to puncture the skin. Reserve the eggplant pulp to make another dish such as eggplant fritters. Place the hollowed-out eggplants in a bowl or stew pot filled with salted water and let them leach their bitter juices for 30 minutes. Drain and pat dry inside and out with paper towels.

2. Heat ¼ cup of the olive oil in a skillet over medium heat and cook the onions with ½ teaspoon of the salt, stirring, until the onions are translucent, about 8 minutes. Add the drained rice and pine nuts and cook, stirring frequently, until the rice is well coated with oil, about 2 minutes. Add ¾ cup of the water, the chopped tomato, currants, pepper, allspice, mint, and dill. Stir, reduce the heat to low, cover the skillet, and cook until the rice has absorbed the liquid but is still a little hard, about 15 minutes. Sprinkle with the sugar.

3. Stuff the eggplants with the rice, not too tightly, not too loosely. Replace the "lid" of the eggplant, and arrange the stuffed eggplants in a deep casserole, side by side. Divide the remaining 1 cup water, ½ cup olive oil, and ½ teaspoon salt among the 3 stuffed eggplants, cover, and cook until the eggplants are soft but still maintain their shape, about 1¼ hours. Let the eggplants cool in the casserole. Serve sliced at room temperature.

Makes 6 servings

Bādhinjān Maqlī ma Laban
FRIED EGGPLANT WITH YOGURT

In this Lebanese preparation, often served as part of a *mazza*, the eggplant slices are fried then arranged on a platter and covered with a pungent garlic-flavored yogurt sauce that features lots of fresh coriander. Both Turks and Arabs delight in dishes that are hot and cool at the same time. This dish is also excellent with grilled lamb.

2 eggplants (about 2½ pounds), halved
*   lengthwise and cut into ¼-inch-thick rounds*
6 cups olive or olive pomace oil for frying
6 large garlic cloves, peeled
1 teaspoon salt
4 cups high-quality full-fat plain yogurt
Leaves from 1 bunch fresh coriander, chopped fine

1. Lay the eggplant slices on some paper towels and sprinkle them with salt. Leave them to drain of their bitter juices for 30 minutes. Pat them dry with paper towels.
2. Preheat the oil to 375°F. Fry the eggplant slices in batches until golden brown, about 3 to 4 minutes per side. Try not to crowd them. Remove the slices from the oil with tongs and let them drain and cool on a tray lined with paper towels.
3. Mash the garlic with the salt in a mortar until mushy. Stir the mashed garlic into the yogurt along with the coriander. Transfer the eggplant slices to a serving platter and cover with the yogurt. Serve at room temperature.

Let the frying oil cool completely before straining it and saving it for a future use.

Makes 4 servings

Bādhinjān bi'l-Zayt
EGGPLANT IN OLIVE OIL

This eggplant dish is also served as part of a *mazza*, not only in Lebanon, but throughout the Levantine Arab world. The variety of eggplant preparations is considerable, and this one, with its mixture of eggplant, onion, and ripe tomatoes, is one of the more delectable ones.

¾ cup pure or virgin olive oil
8 small, long eggplants (about 2 pounds),
*   alternately peeled in strips lengthwise to create*
*   stripes, trimmed, and cut in half lengthwise*
1 large onion (about ¾ pound), sliced thin and
*   pulled apart into rings*
4 ripe tomatoes (about 1½ pounds), sliced
4 large garlic cloves, crushed in a mortar with
*   1 teaspoon salt*
Freshly ground black pepper to taste
½ cup water
Salt to taste

1. Heat the olive oil in a large skillet over high heat until it begins to smoke slightly, about 10 minutes. Add the eggplant halves, flesh side down, and cook them in batches until golden brown, 3 to 4 minutes. Remove the cooked eggplant from the skillet and set aside.
2. In the same skillet, in the same oil, cook the onion, stirring, until half the rings are light

brown, 5 to 6 minutes. Turn the heat off. Arrange the onion rings on the bottom of a stovetop casserole, preferably earthenware. Arrange the tomatoes on top of the onion rings and the fried eggplant, flesh side down, on top of the tomatoes.

3. Put the mashed garlic in the same skillet that you used to cook the eggplant and onion. Cook the garlic until very light brown, about 1 minute, stirring. Sprinkle the garlic over the vegetables and season them with pepper. Pour the water over the top and cook the mixture over medium heat until the liquid begins to bubble, about 10 minutes. Reduce the heat to very low (use a heat diffuser if you need to), cover, and cook until the vegetables are very tender, about 2 hours.

4. Remove the eggplant pieces to a serving platter with a slotted spatula, inverting them so the flesh side of the eggplant is on top. Cover the eggplant with the tomatoes and onion. Season with salt and allow the dish to come to room temperature before serving.

Makes 4 to 6 servings

ᶜUlab Bādhinjān

PRESERVED EGGPLANT AND VEGETABLE RELISH

The variety of eggplant preparations in the Levantine Arab world is truly remarkable. There is a saying in the Middle East that a young girl should know a hundred ways to prepare eggplant. Among the hundred this recipe counts as one of the best. Typically it would be served as part of a *mazza*. There are some obvious similarities to ratatouille.

3 pounds eggplant, sliced ⅜ inch thick
Salt
2 cups olive oil
4 large ripe tomatoes, peeled, seeded, and sliced
2 green bell peppers, seeded and sliced thin
12 garlic cloves, sliced thin
2 medium onions, sliced thin
Leaves from 1 bunch fresh mint, chopped
Freshly ground black pepper to taste
½ cup freshly squeezed tomato juice

1. Lay the eggplant slices on some paper towels and sprinkle with salt. Leave them to drain of their bitter juices for 30 minutes. Pat them dry with paper towels.

2. Heat the olive oil in a large skillet over medium-high heat for 8 minutes. Add the eggplant slices and cook them until they are light brown on both sides, about 8 minutes in all. Remove with tongs and drain on paper towels.

3. In a heavy, deep stove-top casserole or skillet layer half the tomatoes, green peppers, garlic, and onions. Place half the eggplant slices on top. Sprinkle with half the mint leaves and season with salt and pepper. Repeat this layering, pour the tomato juice over the whole, and bring to a boil. Reduce the heat to low and simmer without stirring until the liquid is reduced by more than half, about 45 minutes. Serve at room temperature.

Makes 4 to 6 servings

Bādhinjān Misharmla
Griddled Eggplants with Caraway Marinade and Green Peppercorns

This Algerian recipe is usually served as a side dish, but it is excellent as an accompaniment to grilled lamb chops. A number of Algerian cookbooks have been published in French (there are no Algerian cookbooks published in English), and it is commonplace for Algerian authors to describe some dishes as "grilled," when the ingredients are actually griddled on an oiled cast-iron or steel plate. There is a Provençal recipe that this Algerian one vaguely reminds me of. In the French recipe a room-temperature dish of tomatoes, green peppercorns, and *crème fraîche* is described. The Algerian version is one that should be eaten the next day, once the flavors have had some time to work their magic.

15 long, thin eggplants (about 3 pounds), trimmed

Salt

3 tablespoons white wine vinegar

9 tablespoons extra virgin olive oil

1 tablespoon coarsely ground caraway seeds

6 large garlic cloves, sliced thin or slivered

3 tablespoons preserved green peppercorns

3 cups fresh or canned crushed tomatoes or tomato sauce (page 337)

5 ounces imported black Gaeta or Kalamata olives (about 3 dozen), pitted

1. Slice the eggplants lengthwise ¼ inch thick without peeling. Sprinkle the sliced eggplants with salt and leave on paper towels for 30 minutes to leech their bitter juices. Pat them dry with paper towels.

2. In a small bowl, mix together the vinegar, olive oil, caraway, and salt to taste. Sprinkle these ingredients over the eggplant slices, along with the garlic, and let the eggplant marinate for 30 minutes.

3. Meanwhile, lightly oil a cast-iron griddle, place it over two burners, if rectangular, and heat over medium-high heat until smoking. Scrape away any excess marinade from the eggplant slices and cook them in batches until golden brown on both sides, about 10 minutes, turning a few times and rearranging them over the burners with long tongs so all of them cook evenly.

4. Return the cooked eggplant to the marinade mixture, add the green peppercorns and tomatoes, season with salt, and leave at room temperature for 1 hour before serving. Stir in the black olives and serve.

Makes 6 servings

Shakhshūkha
Algerian "Ratatouille" with Eggs

Shakhshūkha is a kind of ratatouille from North Africa made with vegetables as well as eggs. In fact, in Algeria and Tunisia especially there are countless ways of making *shakhshūkha*. But one always finds them made with many eggs. Although many food writers consider *shakhshūkha* to be a quintessential North African vegetable dish, the word *shakhshūkha* is not an Arabic word but a Turkish one. The dish appears to derive from the nearly identical Turkish dish called *menemen* or *şakşuka*. It probably found its way from Turkey to the western Mediterranean either during the Ottoman era or perhaps through traveling merchants.

2 green bell peppers (about 1 pound)
1 pound ripe plum tomatoes
1 fresh green chile pepper
2 small eggplants (14 to 16 ounces in all),
    peeled and sliced into ½-inch-thick rounds
1 cup extra virgin olive oil
2 medium zucchini (8 to 9 ounces in all), peeled
    and sliced into ½-inch-thick rounds
10 large garlic cloves, chopped fine
¼ cup finely chopped fresh parsley leaves
½ teaspoon cayenne pepper
Salt and freshly ground black pepper to taste
4 large eggs, beaten

1. Prepare a hot charcoal fire, preheat a gas grill, or preheat the oven to 425°F. Place the bell peppers, tomatoes, and chile pepper on the grilling grate or on a baking tray and grill or bake until the skins blister black all over the peppers and the skins are coming off the tomatoes, about 40 minutes. Once cool enough to handle, peel the peppers and tomatoes and remove the seeds. Cut the peppers into strips and the tomatoes into rounds.

2. Lay the eggplant slices on some paper towels and sprinkle them with salt. Leave them to drain of their bitter juices for 30 minutes. Pat them dry with paper towels. Cut all the eggplant slices in half.

3. Heat the olive oil in a large casserole over medium-high heat and add the eggplant in batches without crowding. Cook the eggplant slices until they are light golden, about 8 minutes altogether, turning only once. Remove the eggplant slices with a slotted ladle to a platter covered with paper towels. Let the oil cool significantly, about 20 minutes with the heat turned off.

4. Using the same casserole, turn the heat to low, add the zucchini, peppers, tomatoes, garlic, and parsley, season with salt, black pepper, and cayenne pepper, cover, and simmer until most of the liquid is evaporated, about 30 minutes. Add the eggplants to the casserole.

5. Season the eggs with a little salt and pepper and a few tablespoons of the broth from the casserole. Raise the heat to high for a minute, stir the eggs into the casserole, and cook them until they set, about 6 minutes, folding, not stirring, them as they cook. Serve hot.

Makes 6 servings

EGYPTIAN RUE
Ruta chalenpensis L. (Rutaceae)
Arabic: *fujl* (Tunisia); Italian: *ruta*
(Tuscany)

PLANT CHARACTERISTICS AND VARIETIES
This perennial herb grows to 2 feet high. The
above-ground parts of the plant are used in
rural Tuscany to make a distilled liquor.
North African Jews traditionally used
Egyptian rue as a condiment in cooking. It is
also used in the making of *mirqaz* (also
transliterated as *merguez*), a spicy, thin Tunisian
lamb, veal, or mutton sausage, as well as the
Tunisian egg dishes known as *ʿujja,* a generic
term for eggs cooked in several ways.

ELEPHANT GARLIC
Allium scorodoprasum L. (Liliaceae)

PLANT CHARACTERISTICS AND VARIETIES
Elephant garlic is actually a kind of leek. The
bulbs grow very large, up to a pound, and contain about four cloves, which have a mild garlicky taste.

PLANT ORIGIN
Elephant garlic is probably native to the Near
East and Mediterranean.

PLANT HISTORY
Although we don't know for sure, perhaps the
large garlic called *ulpicum* by Pliny in his
Natural History (Book XIX, 112) is the elephant garlic.

HOW TO GROW AND HARVEST
Elephant garlic grows best in areas with mild
winters. Plant cloves 4 to 6 inches deep in the
soil. Remove the flower stalk to encourage the
growth of larger bulbs.

HOW TO BUY, STORE, AND PREPARE
FOR COOKING
Look for firm heads. The cloves can can be
stored in the refrigerator or in a dark cabinet.
Do not use elephant garlic as a replacement for
garlic because you think it's easier to peel; elephant garlic and garlic are two different plants.
Elephant garlic does not have the pungency
needed for many recipes calling for garlic.

ENDIVE
Cichorium endivia L. (Asteraceae-
Compositae)
Also called escarole; Arabic: *hindab;*
French: *chicorée endive* (chicory), *scarole*
(broad-leaved Batavian endive), *chicorée
frisée* (endive); Greek: *pikrosalata, antidia;*
Italian: *endivia, scarola;* Serbo-Croatian:
endivija; Spanish: *endivia, escarola;* Turkish:
hindiba

PLANT CHARACTERISTICS AND VARIETIES
Endive is an annual or biennial plant that is
closely related to chicory, which is a perenni-

al; this is the main difference between the two. Endive leaves are eaten raw and sometimes cooked. Endive and escarole are the same vegetable, but endive has leaves that are cut and curled, while escarole has smooth, broad leaves. Both endive and escarole have a slightly bitter taste. There are three varieties of marketable endive: *chicorée frisée*, a flat, frizzy-leaved type, such as *riccia Pancalieri*; the flattened and broad-leaved type called *scarole, chicorée scarole*, or Batavian endive, such as the *géante maraichere* type, which has a superior taste; and the upright type called *cornet d'Anjou, cornet de Bordeaux*, or *cartocciate d'ingegnoli. Ricciutissima d'ingegnoli*, an upright type, has a buttery yellow heart with a delicious flavor. In Europe, Belgian endive is known as Witloof chicory. Endives are more heat tolerant than chicories and lettuce, so they are perfect in midsummer for salads. The varieties known as *crispa* have curly leaves. Endive is eaten by nearly everyone in the Mediterranean, usually in salads.

PLANT ORIGIN

The origin of endive is not known, although some believe it is native to India or northern China. Another theory posits that the plant originated in the eastern Mediterranean as a hybrid between chicory and a wild species, *C. pumilum* Jacq., which is native to Turkey (*çıtlık* in Turkish) and western Syria. N. Vavilov suggests that the Mediterranean is a center of origin of the endive. Finally, endive is thought to be a cultivated subspecies of *C. pumilum*, which was then renamed *C. endivia* subsp. *divar-*

icatum (Schousboe) P. D. Sell, the subspecies *endivia* being the cultivated endive.

PLANT HISTORY

Endive was cultivated by the ancient Egyptians and grown by the Greeks and Romans to be used in salads. Pliny's discussion of chicory is not about true chicory but about endive. He considered endive to be both a medicinal plant and a food to be eaten with oil in salads. Some commentators argue that the "bitter herbs" that are referred to in the Book of Numbers and that are eaten as part of the Passover ceremony were endives or chicory. Endive and chicory are mentioned by Aristophanes in his play *The Frogs*, and in Horace and Pliny. Ovid mentions endive in his tale *Philemon and Baucis*. There are two botanical forms of endive, curly-leaved and broad-leaved. The first does not seem to have been known by the ancients, although Dioscorides and Pliny name two kinds. In the sixth century, Anthimus wrote that endives were good for both sick and healthy people. In the late fifteenth century, the Veneto region of northern Italy became a center for the growing of varieties of endive. By the sixteenth century the various kinds of endives are mentioned frequently in the literature. These plants were considered medicinal before the fourteenth century, after which time they became more common as food.

Endive

Endive (escarole) is used almost exclusively for salads in the Mediterranean. Besides the recipe that follows, one is unlikely to find escarole cooked, except occasionally in Greece, Turkey, or the Arab world, where the cooked greens may be dressed simply with a lemon and oil dressing.

HOW TO GROW AND HARVEST

There are many varieties of endive and escarole, and they are grown in different ways. Endive and escarole do well in areas where the summers are cool. Endive should be planted in deep chalky or sandy soil in late May or early June and kept well watered so that the plant does not flower the first year. The plants are grown in darkness (by partially covering them), which means their leaves are much less pigmented, making them crisper and more tender. Harvest the entire plant. A fall crop can be planted in late June in temperate climates and late August in Mediterranean climates, and harvested before the first heavy frost.

HOW TO BUY, STORE, AND PREPARE FOR COOKING

Belgian endive is light sensitive, so it discolors and tastes bitter if it gets too much light. Buy small pale heads of endive with yellow leaf tips. Store Belgian endive in a refrigerator crisper drawer for up to 3 to 4 days. If you are buying an endive or escarole with loose leaves, look for leaves that are crisp and fresh looking, not wilted. Store all these salad greens in the refrigerator crisper drawer for not more than 3 days. The inner leaves of escarole are used for salads, and the outer leaves can be cooked with other greens.

RECIPE

Scarola Imbottita
STUFFED ESCAROLE

Stuffed escarole (curly endive) is a very impressive dish. The stuffing of vegetables is as popular in Sicily as it is in the Near East. Some culinary historians believe that the popularity of stuffed vegetables in Sicily is the result of an Arab influence. This recipe is unique in that the individual leaves of the vegetable are not used for stuffing, as you might expect; instead the whole head of escarole is flattened and stuffed, then closed up, tied off, and cooked whole. At first glance, it would appear that this is not possible to accomplish. It is possible, although you do need a bit of dexterity to pull the splayed leaves all together to encase the stuffing. The stuffing of ground meat, pine nuts, olives, raisins, and anchovy is typically Sicilian. This dish is usually served as either a first course or a main course, and hardly ever as a side dish.

8 tablespoons extra virgin olive oil, divided
Salt and freshly ground black pepper to taste
½ pound very lean ground beef (only 7% fat)
1 tablespoon pine nuts
1 tablespoon dark or golden raisins
5 imported black olives, pitted and chopped
½ cup fresh breadcrumbs
4 salted anchovy fillets, rinsed and chopped
1 tablespoon finely chopped fresh parsley leaves
1 garlic clove, chopped fine
2 medium to large heads escarole (curly endive)

1. Heat 2 tablespoons of the olive oil in a medium skillet over medium-high heat. Add the lightly salted and peppered ground beef and brown it, about 4 minutes, breaking up the clumps of meat. Remove the skillet from the burner and stir in the pine nuts, raisins, olives, breadcrumbs, anchovies, parsley, and garlic, mixing well.

2. If the outer leaves of either escarole are damaged or broken, remove them. Gently set each whole escarole upright on its stem and pull the leaves out from the center, flattening them outward without breaking them off. Place half the mixture in the center of each escarole. Pull up all the leaves so they enclose the stuffing. Tie off each head with twine in one or two places so the stuffing can't escape.

3. Place both heads of escarole on their sides in a large casserole, preferably earthenware, and pour the remaining olive oil over them. Cover tightly and cook over low heat until the escarole is tender and fragrant, about 40 minutes, turning the escarole once or twice. Serve immediately.

*Makes 6 first-course or
4 main-course servings*

ENGLISH DAISY
Bellis perennis L. (Asteraceae-Compositae)
Italian: *margheritina* (Tuscany)

PLANT CHARACTERISTICS AND VARIETIES
In rural Italy the leaves of this plant are used in vegetable soups. The flower buds are preserved in vinegar and used as a substitute for capers.

ENGLISH PRIMROSE
Primula vulgaris Hudson (Primulaceae)
ITALIAN: *primola, fior di primavera*
(Tuscany)

PLANT CHARACTERISTICS AND VARIETIES
In rural Tuscany the leaves of the English primrose are eaten in vegetable soups. English primrose is also used as a stuffing for meat and poultry and as a cooked vegetable. The flowers are used in salads.

ERODIUM CICUTARIUM (L.) L'HERIT. SUBSP. *JACQUINI-ANUM* (GERANIACEAE)
TURKISH: *innelik*

PLANT CHARACTERISTICS AND VARIETIES
The edible part of this robust annual herb is the tubercle, which is boiled and eaten by Egyptians. In Turkey the leaves of *E. cicutarium* (L.) L'Herit. subsp. *cicutarium*, a plant in the geranium family, are gathered in the wild in the Aksaray Province of Anatolia and eaten.

ERYNGO
Eryngium creticum Lam. (Umbelliferae)

PLANT CHARACTERISTICS AND VARIETIES
Eryngium creticum is a perennial herb thistle with an erect stem and bluish flowers. The young shoots of one variety of *Eryngium*, snakeroot *(E. campestre)*, are used as a substitute for asparagus in France. Also see Sea Holly (page 291).

PLANT HISTORY
Eryngium creticum is a thistle thought to be one of the bitter herbs mentioned in the Book of Numbers. The Jews ate the thistle for Passover, calling it *ḥarḥavina*.

EUROPEAN BROOKLINE
Veronica beccabunga L. (Scrophulariaceae)
ITALIAN: *crescione* (Tuscany)

PLANT CHARACTERISTICS AND VARIETIES
In rural Tuscany the leaves of this plant are eaten in salads and torte.

EUROPEAN ELDER
Sambucus nigra L. (Caprifoliaceae)
Also called black elder

PLANT CHARACTERISTICS AND VARIETIES
This small tree has a corky bark. The black fruits are used in Europe, generally, for making wines, jams, preserves, and juices. In rural Tuscany the infloresence is fried and eaten as an antipasto or snack.

EVENING PRIMROSE
Oenothera biennis L. (syn. *O. erythrosepala* Borbas) (Onagraceae)
ARABIC: *duwayk al-jabal*; FRENCH: *onagre bisannuelle, herbe aux ânes*; ITALIAN: *enàgre comune*; SPANISH: *onagra, hierba del asno, enotera*

PLANT CHARACTERISTICS AND VARIETIES
This herb grows in open habitats. The edible part is the root, which is cooked, and the seeds, which are used for their oil. The roots are similar to those of salsify. In the mountains of Lebanon peasants use the leaves of the primrose for stuffing, usually the same stuffing as they use for grape leaves, with the addition of walnuts. The stuffed primrose is cooked with pomegranate molasses, lemon juice, and red chile pepper.

PLANT ORIGIN
Evening primrose is a native of North America.

HOW TO GROW AND HARVEST
The plant will grow in any soil, but it will produce better if it is planted deep in a fine soil without stones. The plants are hardy and can grow in deserts and sand dunes by the sea. Sow seeds in early spring, and later thin the plants to 10 inches apart. The plant is harvested in October.

HOW TO BUY, STORE, AND PREPARE FOR COOKING
Prepare evening primrose in the same manner as you would salsify (page 286).

FAVA BEAN
Vicia faba L. (syn. *Faba vulgaris*) (Leguminosae-Fabaceae)
Also called broad bean, Windsor bean, horse bean; ARABIC: *fūl*; FRENCH: *fève*; GREEK: *koukia*; ITALIAN: *fava*; SERBO-CROATIAN: *bob*; SPANISH: *haba*; TURKISH: *bakla, ful*

PLANT CHARACTERISTICS AND VARIETIES
The fava bean is a half-hardy annual that is a member of the vetch group of the Fabaceae-Leguminosae. Fava beans are grown in 4 variety groupings (the nomenclature of which is not recognized by all taxonomists): the most common is the *V. faba* and its varieties, which are used throughout the Mediterranean; *V. equina*, which is grown as fodder; *V. minor*, the tic bean, which is grown in the United States; and *V. paucijuga*, which is grown in Central Asia. The edible part is the immature seed, which is cooked. When very young, the pods can be eaten, too. When mature, the pods can grow to a foot long. The fava bean is particularly popular in the Arab Mediterranean, in Egypt in particular, where the dish known as *fūl* uses the smaller, rounder fava beans called

fūl hammān (bath fava). The other kinds of fava beans used by Egyptian cooks are *fūl rumī*, the large kidney-shaped fava beans you may be more familiar with; and the *fūl balādī*, country beans of middling size. *Fūl nabit* (or *nabid*) are fava beans sprouts, *fūl akhḍar* are fresh fava beans, and *fūl madshūsh* are crushed fava beans.

PLANT ORIGIN

The cultivation of fava beans originated in the eastern Mediterranean in late Neolithic times, but the wild ancestor is not known. G. Ladizinsky, a contemporary Israeli researcher, investigated the genetic relationship between the fava bean and its wild relatives and concluded that the accepted ideas that fava beans are related to the wild species *V. narbonensis* (which is found in the Mediterranean but differs from *V. faba* in the number of chromosomes), and that the pods of *V. narbonensis* do not have the fuzziness associated with *V. faba* are not true. He believes that the place of origin of the fava beans is not the Middle East and suggests Afghanistan. The French botanist L. Trabut claims that the original species of fava bean may have been *Faba pliniana*, which he discovered growing near some Algerian villages in the interior. Another theory is that fava beans developed under cultivation from white sweet clover (*Melilotus alba medicus*) or a similar subspecies that the fava resembles in many characteristics. The earliest evidence of the cultivation of fava beans in the Mediterranean comes from a pre-pottery

Neolithic B level at Jericho in Palestine, although there are other very early sites on the Iberian Peninsula. Evidence suggests both an eastern and a western Mediterranean origin. Fava beans have been found among Bronze Age dwellings, too. N. Vavilov suggests northwestern India, Tadzhikistan, Uzbekistan, and western Tien Shan as the centers of origin of the fava bean. Others suggest southwest Asia and North Africa.

PLANT HISTORY

No prehistoric remains of the fava bean have been found east of a line running close to the coast in Israel north and east to Turkey and Greece. It is thought that the fava bean came to Europe late, not with the primary crops of wheat, barley, lentils, and peas. The plant may have traveled along the Mediterranean coast to the Iberian Peninsula with early metal prospectors. Fava beans have been found in Egypt from 2400 to 1800 B.C., and the Greeks and Romans wrote about the fava bean. Although well associated with Egypt today, the fava bean was not popular in ancient Egypt, where, Herodotus tells us, priests had such an aversion to the fava bean that the seeds were not sown in their gardens, although the common people apparently ate fava beans. Hippocrates believed that eating fava beans injured one's vision. Pythagoras believed that after people died their soul entered the plant and that they were made of the same matter as man. Another reason for this aversion to fava beans may be a result of the knowledge of a disease called favism, which we know is a genetically determined red blood cell deficiency that afflicts Mediterranean men in particular, resulting in hemolytic anemia, fever, and jaundice. Dioscorides wrote about the fava bean, and a codex from the sixth century A.D., a few hundred years after his death, has a depiction of the plant. Pliny said that the highest place of honor belongs to the fava bean because of its excellence as a food, and he devotes some attention to describing the growing of the plant. The Roman cookbook of Apicius describes several methods of cooking fava beans. In the Middle Ages, the fava bean was a staple food throughout the Mediterranean.

HOW TO GROW AND HARVEST

The fava bean can be sown in the autumn and will survive the winter for early summer harvesting. The beans require about 70 days of cool, frost-free weather for optimal production of abundantly filled pods. Seeds can also be planted in the early spring about 1 inch deep and 8 inches apart in rows about 4 feet apart. The best soil for this plant is heavy, well-drained, and well-manured soil. If you want to eat the pod and the bean, like a snap bean, harvest fava beans when the pods are 2 inches long. If you are only interested in the beans, harvest favas when the pod is about 8 inches long and filled with plump beans.

HOW TO BUY, STORE, AND PREPARE FOR COOKING

Most of the fresh fava beans you will find at the market will be large, about 8 inches long. Choose pods that are full and unblemished. They should look like they are full of beans from the outside. Store fresh favas in the refrigerator crisper drawer for up to a week.

Prepare the beans for cooking first by pulling off the "string" of the pod to help separate the pod; the string almost acts like a zipper. Then remove the beans inside. Bring a pot of water to a boil and cook the beans for about 4 minutes so their skin will loosen. Once the beans are cool, pinch them where the little black seam is and pull off their skins. Dried fava beans also need to be skinned, so you can follow the same method for them as for fresh beans.

Crushed dried fava beans, *fūl madshūsh,* can be found in Middle Eastern markets. The recipes here call for either fresh or dried fava beans. Fresh beans are in season from May to July, and dried favas are available in Middle Eastern markets and whole food stores. Whole dried fava beans, yellow favas, and crushed fava beans are usually well stocked in Middle Eastern markets more so than in supermarkets.

Fava Bean

THE FAVA BEAN IS AN OLD WORLD BEAN, AND, AS A RESULT, IT IS POPULAR ALL OVER THE MEDITERRANEAN, ESPECIALLY IN THE eastern Mediterranean. When spring arrives the fava arrives and everyone in the Mediterranean can dream up a way of cooking it. In Spain, fava beans go into a spring vegetable stew called *menestra de primavera*, along with the two other famous spring vegetables, peas and artichokes. In Provence, housewives give their name to their *fèves à la ménagère*, a dish of fava beans braised with onions in olive oil and accompanied by some beaten eggs at the end of the cooking. The Sicilians make their beloved *frittedda*, a dish of peas, fava beans, artichokes, spring onions, mint, lemon juice, and olive oil. Today this preparation is frequently served as a kind of antipasto. The Greeks and Turks also have a wealth of fava bean recipes, such as the Greek soup called *fassoulada*, made with onions, carrots, tomatoes, and fava beans, and flavored with mint or thyme. There is also the Turkish dip made with cooked fava beans pureed with onions, olive oil, lemon juice, and dill and served with warm flatbread.

RECIPES

Purea di Fave con Cime di Rapa

FAVA BEAN PUREE WITH BROCCOLI RAPA

This recipe is adapted only slightly from Marcella Hazan's *Marcella's Italian Kitchen*. Her suggestion of how this dish should be eaten will lead everyone, as it led me, to try it. She said, "Reverently is how I eat it, as slowly and as wordlessly as I can manage." I believe you will agree. In my recipe I use the already peeled, dried fava sold in Middle Eastern markets as yellow fava.

¼ cup milk

1 thick slice Italian or French bread, trimmed of
  its crust and torn into pieces

¾ pound dried, skinned, and crushed yellow fava
  beans

Salt

8 tablespoons extra virgin olive oil, divided

¾ pound broccoli rapa, trimmed of heaviest stems

2 garlic cloves, peeled and crushed

1. In a small saucepan, warm the milk and soak the bread in it. Turn the heat off and leave the mixture until it is needed.

2. Place the fava beans in a large saucepan with some salt and cover them by several inches with cold water. Bring the pot to a boil, reduce the heat to medium-high, and cook the beans until they are completely tender, 45 to 60 minutes. Keep checking on them and adding hot water to the saucepan to keep the beans covered.

3. Pass the beans through a food mill or puree them in a food processor with the milk-soaked bread and ¼ cup of the olive oil. Blend the mixture until it is smooth and the consistency of mashed potatoes.

4. Bring 1 quart salted water to a boil in a large saucepan and cook the broccoli rapa until it is wilted and soft, about 7 minutes. Drain well. Place the pureed fava bean mixture in the top part of a double boiler and heat the water in the bottom part to heat the fava beans gently, stirring them frequently.

5. Heat 2 tablespoons of the olive oil in a skillet over medium heat and cook the garlic until it begins to turn light brown. Remove and discard the garlic. Add the broccoli rapa and cook it until it is hot and softer, 5 to 6 minutes.

6. Spread the fava bean puree on the bottom of a serving platter and distribute the broccoli rapa on top. Drizzle with the remaining 2 tablespoons olive oil and serve hot.

Makes 4 servings

Tubettini con Fava Fresche
TUBETTINI WITH FRESH FAVA BEANS

This rustic dish from the region of Apulia in southern Italy is typically made with the young fava beans that local cooks say you don't need to peel. With the beans peeled, the dish takes on a brilliant and inviting green color. *Tubettini* are a very short macaroni, "little tubes," that are easily found nowadays in supermarkets. Apulian cooks will add some onion peel to whatever they are cooking for a more intense onion flavor, and I do that in this recipe.

5 pounds fresh fava beans in their pods, beans
  and peels removed (about 1½ pounds unpeeled
  individual beans and ¾ pound peeled beans)

¼ cup extra virgin olive oil

1 medium onion, chopped, peel saved

Salt and freshly ground black pepper to taste

1¼ cups tubettini

Freshly grated Parmigiano-Reggiano cheese

1. Bring a large saucepan of lightly salted water to a boil and cook the fava beans until the skins come off with a little pinch, 3 to 5 minutes. Drain the beans and remove their skins.

2. Heat the olive oil in a stove-top casserole or skillet over medium heat and cook the onion with some of the onion peel until the chopped onion is soft and translucent, about 10 minutes, stirring occasionally. Add the fava beans, season with salt and pepper, and cook until the beans are soft but not breaking apart, about 35 minutes, adding water in ¼-cup increments so the skillet doesn't dry out, and stirring gently occasionally. Discard the onion peel.

3. Meanwhile, bring a large pot of abundantly salted water to a vigorous boil and add the pasta. Cook until al dente and drain well. Transfer the tubettini to the pot with the fava beans, stir to mix, cook for 1 minute, and serve hot with Parmigiano cheese.

Makes 4 servings

Fūl Mudammas

This is a famous Lebanese breakfast dish, although it is prepared throughout the Levant. This version is very different from the Egyptian one, which is also famous (see page 304 in my *A Mediterranean Feast*). The Egyptian version is the country's national dish; it is more like a soupy stew. Although *fūl mudammas* is most commonly eaten for breakfast, Arabs will eat it at any time.

There are different kinds of fava beans with different cooking times, depending on their size based on when they were harvested, so make sure you use the right kind here. The best fava beans for making *fūl* are the smaller, rounder ones called *fūl ḥammām* (bath beans) by the Egyptians. These beans should be cooked until they are soft; there should be no "bite" to them. I regularly find 27-ounce cans of cooked *fūl ḥammām* beans in Middle Eastern markets, where cans of them are sold under the name *foul medammas*.

Two 27-ounce cans "foul medammas" (fava beans)
2 large garlic cloves, mashed in a mortar with 1 teaspoon salt until mushy
¼ cup extra virgin olive oil, plus more for drizzling
2 tablespoons freshly squeezed lemon juice
Finely chopped fresh parsley leaves for garnish (optional)
Scallions, both whites and greens, cut into ½-inch lengths for garnish (optional)

Place the beans with their liquid in a large saucepan and turn the heat to medium. Bring the beans to a simmer, and once they have been bubbling gently for 5 minutes (after about 25 minutes in all), drain the beans, mash one-third of them, and stir all the beans together with the mashed garlic, olive oil, and lemon juice. Spread the beans on a serving platter and garnish with parsley and scallions, if desired. Drizzle some more olive oil on top, if desired (and I do recommend all these garnishes). Serve at room temperature with Arabic flatbread cut into triangles.

Makes 6 mazza *servings*

Fūl Mūaᶜlla
FRIED FAVA WITH SCALLIONS AND DILL

This recipe from Syria was one my hosts were quite ecstatic about, and their enthusiasm infected my culinary thinking as well. *Fūl mūaᶜlla* are very young, fresh fava beans that can be eaten with their skin on. The taste is "explosive," according to Tariq Salahiya, who lives in Damascus and is a connoisseur of these young fava beans. We both enjoyed this dish prepared by our friend Nadia Koudmani. Unfortunately, unless you grow your own favas, you will be forced to use the more mature fava beans whose skins must be removed. But you still will not be disappointed in the result.

3 pounds fresh fava beans in their pods (about 1 pound unpeeled individual beans and 10 ounces peeled beans)
3 tablespoons extra virgin olive oil
3 scallions, sliced thin
2 tablespoons finely chopped fresh parsley leaves
½ teaspoon sugar
½ teaspoon salt
½ cup water
1 to 2 tablespoons coarsely chopped fresh dill, to your taste

I. Bring a medium saucepan of lightly salted water to a boil and cook the fava beans at a boil until their skins can be pinched off, 3 to 5 minutes. Drain.

2. Place the peeled fava beans, olive oil, scallions, parsley, sugar, and salt in a medium skillet. Turn the heat to medium-high and cook until everything has been sizzling for I minute. Add the water, cover, and cook until the liquid is very nearly evaporated, about 5 minutes. Check the seasoning and correct it if necessary. Toss the beans with the dill while the fava are still hot, and serve them hot or at room temperature.

Makes 4 servings

Bişāra
EGYPTIAN FAVA BEAN PUREE

Bişāra is an Egyptian fava bean puree made and eaten in the same manner as Lebanese and Palestinians would eat hummus, as part of a *mazza* with Arabic flatbread—although this puree is prepared and flavored differently. *Bişāra* has lots of fresh mint, coriander, and dill. The kind of fava bean used here is a skinless dried fava that has been crushed, called *fūl madshūsh*. The best dried fava beans for this preparation are the ones called yellow fava, which can be found in Middle Eastern markets in this country, sold whole or crushed.

¾ pound dried, skinned, and crushed yellow fava
  beans

4 medium onions, 2 chopped and 2 sliced thin

10 large garlic cloves, chopped

Leaves from 1 bunch fresh dill, chopped

Leaves from 1 bunch fresh coriander, chopped

Leaves from 1 bunch fresh parsley, chopped

Leaves from 1 bunch fresh mint, chopped

1 teaspoon freshly ground cumin seeds

2 tablespoons fresh mulūkhiyya (page 191;
  optional)

1 teaspoon freshly ground coriander seeds

¼ teaspoon cayenne pepper

2 teaspoons salt, or to taste

¼ teaspoon freshly ground black pepper

5 tablespoons samna (clarified butter; page 23)
  or extra virgin olive oil

Extra virgin olive oil for drizzling

8 lime or lemon wedges

Arabic flatbread

1. Place the fava beans in a large stockpot with the 2 chopped onions and the garlic, dill, coriander, parsley, and mint and cover by 6 inches with water. Bring the pot to a boil and cook the beans at a gentle boil until they are tender, 1½ to 2 hours, skimming the surface of foam as it appears and replenishing with hot water if the beans are still hard after the allotted cooking time. Drain the beans and herbs, saving at least 1 cup of the cooking water.

2. Place the drained beans and herbs in a food processor or blender and process them until they are almost completely smooth, about 1 minute. Spoon the puree into a large saucepan and heat over medium heat with the cumin, mulūkhiyya (if you are using it), coriander, cayenne, salt, and pepper until the puree tastes well blended and flavorful, 7 to 8 minutes, adding the reserved cooking water if necessary to keep the mixture from drying out and to make the biṣāra of the same consistency as hummus.

3. Meanwhile melt the samna or heat the olive oil in a large skillet over medium-high heat. Add the 2 remaining sliced onions and coat them with the samna or oil. Continue turning the onions as they turn from white to yellow to brown, from 10 to 20 minutes. Once they turn brown, continue to cook them until some of the slices turn dark brown, another 2 minutes. Remove the skillet from the burner and quickly transfer the onions to a platter lined with paper towel and let them cool and drain. Once they are cool, they will become crispy.

4. Transfer the biṣāra to a shallow serving platter, drizzle it with olive oil, and garnish it with the fried onions. Serve at room temperature with lime or lemon wedges and Arabic flatbread.

Makes 8 servings

FENNEL

Foeniculum vulgare var. *vulgare* (syn. *dulce*)
Fiori (var. *azoricum* [Miller] Thell.)
(Umbelliferae)
Also called Florence fennel; ARABIC:
bisbās, rāziyānaj, rāznaj, sūbr, shumr; FRENCH:
fenouil; GREEK: *marathon;* ITALIAN: *finocchio;*
SERBO-CROATIAN: *komorač, anis;* SPANISH:
hinojo; TURKISH: *rezene*

PLANT CHARACTERISTICS AND VARIETIES

Fennel is a biennial that forms a bulb in the
first year and flowers the following summer.
There are two subspecies that are not completely distinct. The first is *F. vulgare* var. *vulgare
(dulce),* which is sweet tasting. Its seeds and
leaves are used for flavoring. The second is *F.
vulgare* var. *azoricum,* which forms swollen bulbs
that are eaten raw or cooked. A third subspecies is *F. vulgare* var. *piperitum* (Ucria)
Coutinho, called *carosella;* it is a perennial
whose seeds are used to flavor liqueurs. The
fleshy leaf stalk of fennel has been developed
by growers over time. Fennel is essentially
composed of water, cellulose, and anethole, a
volatile oil that makes the plant very fragrant.

PLANT ORIGIN

Foeniculum vulgare is native to the Mediterranean, according to N. Vavilov. Philip
Miller believes that *Foeniculum vulgare* var.
azoricum originated in the Azores. *F. vulgare* var.
piperitum (Ucria) Coutinho is native to the
Mediterranean also.

PLANT HISTORY

No ancient names for fennel have been found,
but the plant is believed to have been known
in ancient times. The earliest inscriptions that
refer to fennel are Coptic, describing its use
for treating eye ailments. In Greek mythology
knowledge came to man from Olympus in the
form of a fiery coal contained in a fennel
stalk. The Greeks grew fennel, as did the
Romans, and the bulb variety was probably
developed in Italy. Pliny described fennel as a
garden plant that could be dried and used to
season dishes. He also described its medicinal
uses. In Pliny's time it was believed that snakes
ate fennel in order to shed their skins, and that
fennel juice improved eyesight. The growing
of fennel became more common in Europe
after Charlemagne enjoined its growing on
imperial farms in the ninth century. The
anonymous Hispano-Muslim agricultural
work known as the Cordovan Calender, written in 961, mentions the growing of fennel.
Florence fennel was very popular among
Italians of the Middle Ages. In fact, during
the Italian Middle Ages agrarian cults of
benandanti, or good witches, claimed that they
fought nocturnal battles with evil witches,
who were armed with stalks of sorghum,
while *benandanti* were armed with bundles of
fennel.

Fennel

FENNEL IS A FAVORITE OF ITALIANS. IN THE REST OF THE MEDITERRANEAN, ONE SEES FENNEL OCCASIONALLY, IN THE cuisines of Provence, for instance, *fenouil braisé à la Niçoise,* a simple dish with several fennel bulbs braised in tomato and olive oil; or in Spain, near Málaga, where one may find striped bass cooked in a fennel and wine sauce; or in the town of Almería, where home chefs make *olla de trigo con hinojo,* a stew with wheatberries, white beans, pork, fennel bulb, and sausages. In North Africa fennel is likely to turn up, refreshingly, in *salāṭat al-bisbās,* a salad from the island of Djerba made with *harīsa* (page 263), black and green olives, anchovy fillets, and hard-boiled eggs with a dressing of oil and vinegar. From Tunisia comes fennel couscous, *kisskiss bi'l-bisbās,* made with a ragout of tomatoes, garlic, paprika, scallions, *harīsa,* fresh coriander, potatoes, and long green peppers. Also in Tunisia one may find a chicken, as well as a mutton, ragout cooked with fennel, white beans, eggs, lemon, saffron, and olive oil called *maraqat al-bisbās bi'l dājaj* (chicken) or simply *maraqat al-bisbās* (with mutton).

HOW TO GROW AND HARVEST

Fennel grows well in light soil with plenty of water. The plant needs warmth in its early stages but a cool growing season. Sow seeds from April onward, planting about 10 seeds per foot in rows spaced 18 inches apart. Seeds can be sown in early August for a winter harvest. Fennel should be well watered as it grows. Cut off seed stalks as they form. Harvest fennel in late summer by pulling the entire plant when the bulbs are the size of an egg or larger.

HOW TO BUY, STORE, AND PREPARE FOR COOKING

The fennel bulb should be firm and free of brown blemishes. The stalks should be straight and firm. Fennel can be stored in the refrigerator crisper draw for up to 3 to 4 days. Trim the stems about ½ inch from the bulb. The heavier stems can be cooked with the bulb, and the leaves can be used for garnish or flavoring in a bouquet garni.

Finocchi e "Castraùre" de Carciofini in Tegame
BRAISED FENNEL AND YOUNG ARTICHOKES

In the region surrounding Venice both fennel and artichokes are favorite vegetables. In markets the fennel is sometimes so fragrant that you can smell it even before you reach the vendor.

The best artichokes in Venice are sold as *nostrano*, meaning local, but also implying the best quality. One variety much liked by connoisseurs is the *castraùre*, the so-called castrated young artichoke plucked from the stem. This recipe is perfect from late spring throughout the summer.

2 ounces salami or pancetta
3 tablespoons extra virgin olive oil
1 medium onion, chopped
2 large garlic cloves, chopped fine
12 small artichokes (20 to 22 ounces in all), trimmed, inedible bracts removed, and split in half lengthwise
1 pound fennel bulb, cut up
1½ cups vegetable or chicken broth (preferably homemade)
Salt and freshly ground black pepper to taste

1. Pound the salami or pancetta in a mortar until flaky. In an oven-proof skillet (make sure it does not have wooden or rubber handles), heat the olive oil over medium-high heat and cook the onion, salami or pancetta, and garlic until the onion is very translucent, about 8 minutes, stirring frequently so the garlic doesn't burn. Add the artichokes and fennel and cook until the fennel is a little soft, about 12 minutes. Reduce the heat to low and pour in the broth. Season with salt and pepper and cook until tender, about 1 hour.
2. Preheat the broiler. Place the skillet of vegetables under the broiler until the vegetables are slightly crispy on top, 5 to 10 minutes. You may need to keep the oven door ajar while you do this because the skillet and its handle might not fit in the oven. Serve immediately.

Makes 4 servings

Finocchio con Besciamella
BAKED FENNEL WITH BÉCHAMEL SAUCE

My family, the DeIeso's, both in Italy and America, make this old Neapolitan favorite. It is quite luscious, and if you are a fan of fennel, as I am, this is probably one of the best fennel recipes you'll come across. I can't prove it, but I believe that the use of béchamel sauce in the Naples area is a result of the influence of the famous *monzù*, the French-influenced Italian chefs of the Neapolitan aristocracy of the nineteenth century.

2½ pounds fennel bulbs (without stalks or
    leaves), cut into quarters
4 tablespoons (½ stick) unsalted butter, divided
Salt and freshly ground white pepper to taste
Freshly grated nutmeg to taste
¾ cup freshly grated imported provolone cheese

3 tablespoons unsalted butter
3 tablespoons all-purpose unbleached flour
Salt and freshly ground white pepper to taste
Freshly grated nutmeg to taste
2 cups milk
2 heaping tablespoons dry breadcrumbs

1. Bring a large pot of lightly salted water to
a boil and cook the fennel at a boil until soft,
about 20 minutes. Drain, toss with 3 tablespoons of the butter in a baking dish, and season with salt, pepper, and nutmeg. Cover the
top evenly with the provolone.

2. Preheat the oven to 400°F. Meanwhile, prepare the béchamel sauce. Melt the butter in a
medium saucepan over medium-high heat and
stir in the the flour until a roux is formed.
Season with salt, pepper, and nutmeg and
cook the roux until it has been sizzling for
about 1 minute, stirring. Take the saucepan
off the heat and slowly pour in the milk,
whisking so the milk is well blended. Return
the pot to low heat and cook until the sauce is
thick, 15 to 20 minutes.

3. Pour the béchamel sauce over the fennel
and sprinkle the breadcrumbs on top. Dot the
top with the remaining 1 tablespoon butter
sliced very thin. Bake the dish until it is gold-
en on top, about 20 minutes. Turn the oven
up to the broil setting and crisp the top until
it turns brownish in spots, about 5 minutes.
Serve hot.

Makes 6 servings

FENUGREEK

Trigonella foenun-graecum L. (Fabaceae-
Leguminosae)

ARABIC: *ḫulba;* CATALAN: *senigrec;* FRENCH:
trigonelle, foin grec, fenugrec; ITALIAN: *fieno
grec;* SPANISH: *alholva, fenogreco, heno griego;*
TURKISH: *çemen otu*

PLANT CHARACTERISTICS AND VARIETIES

Fenugreek is a slender annual herb that grows
to about 3 feet and features light green trifo-
liate leaves and small white flowers. The edible
parts are the leaves and the tender shoots,
which are used in salads and soups. The dried
seeds are used as a spice and ground into flour
for bread. In North Africa, fenugreek is also
grown as a fodder plant. The seeds are borne
in long and slender, curved pods that are up to
6 inches long. The Turkish name for fenugreek, *çemen otu,* is also the name of the spice
mix used to rub into the beef fillet used for
the making of *pastırma,* a dried beef fillet seasoned with a rubbing of cumin, garlic, paprika, and other spices.

PLANT ORIGIN

One theory suggests that fenugreek is native
to southern Europe and the Mediterranean

region. N. Vavilov identified the area of India, Burma, and Assam as the center of origin of fenugreek.

PLANT HISTORY

Fenugreek has been known in Egypt and Palestine since time immemorial. Pliny spoke of using fenugreek medicinally. In 1600 a traveler named William Biddulph was traveling from Aleppo to Jerusalem and saw many poor people gathering mallow and a "three-leaved grass." He asked the people what they did with it, and they told him it was the only food they had, and they ate it.

RECIPE

FRESH FENUGREEK LEAF AND CELERY SALAD

The inspiration for this recipe are the many refreshingly light salads I have consumed in Tunisia. Fenugreek leaves are very rarely found, but it is possible to buy them in this country, usually at local farmers' markets, especially in California. This salad has a slightly bitter taste that I think would go well with a rich main course.

1 bunch celery, trimmed and sliced thin at a sharp diagonal (3 to 4 cups sliced)
Leaves from 1 bunch fenugreek, chopped (about ½ cup)
¼ cup extra virgin olive oil
2 teaspoons freshly squeezed lemon juice
1 teaspoon harīsa (page 263)
1 large garlic clove, chopped fine
Salt and freshly ground black pepper to taste

Toss the celery slices and fenugreek leaves together in a serving bowl. Stir the olive oil, lemon juice, *harīsa*, and garlic together and season with salt and pepper. Toss the dressing, celery, and fenugreek together and serve.

Makes 4 servings

FIELD POPPY

Papaver rhoeas L. (Papaveraceae)
ARABIC: *khashkash*; FRENCH: *coquelicot, pavot rouge*; ITALIAN: *rosolaccio, belle bimbe* (Tuscany); TURKISH: *gülotu, gelincik*

PLANT CHARACTERISTICS AND VARIETIES

The field poppy grows to 3 feet. The edible part of this annual is the leaf, which is slightly narcotic. In rural Tuscany, the leaf is used in soups. Field poppies are a popular food in the regions of southern Italy such as Apulia, where it is also called *sckattelòne, sckattarule, paparéine,* and *paparina* and is used in cooked dishes. The garden poppy also belongs to this genus, as does *P. somniferum,* or the opium poppy. *Papaver hortense* is a variety of opium poppy used for its seeds.

PLANT ORIGIN

The field poppy appears to be native to Europe, North Africa, and parts of Asia.

PLANT HISTORY

In the medical formulary of the thirteenth-century Arabic pharmacologist al-Samarqandī, a syrup of sugar and poppies was used for medicinal reasons.

HOW TO GROW AND HARVEST

Harvest field poppies while they are young.

HOW TO BUY, STORE, AND PREPARE FOR COOKING

Field poppy can be cooked like spinach, or it may be used as a soup herb, or in salads.

RECIPE

Rosolacci Stufati
STUFFED FIELD POPPY

To make this recipe from Apulia, take the leaves of 2 pounds of poppies, some turnip tops, cauliflower florets, and wild radishes and put them in a baking dish or heavy saucepan with lots of olive oil and one chopped garlic clove. Add a little water, cover, and cook on the stovetop or in the oven until the liquid is nearly evaporated. Season with salt, add olives, raisins, and walnuts, and cook until all the vegetables are tender. Serve with bread.

FRENCH SCORZONERA
Reichardia picroides L. (syn. *Picridium vulgare* Desf.) (Asteraceae-Compositae)
ITALIAN: *sassello, sassaiolo* (Tuscany)

PLANT CHARACTERISTICS AND VARIETIES

In rural Tuscany this smooth-leaved perennial plant is eaten in vegetable soups and mixed salads. The leaves are mild and slightly sweet. French scorzonera is one of the vegetables used in the herb mixture *preboggion,* which is added to *pansotti,* a large ravioli dish made in Liguria. *Gerbi* is a dish made in the Cinque Terre region of Liguria on the Italian Riviera. It is a mixture of greens, French scorzonera, and herbs eaten with beans and potatoes and dressed with olive oil and vinegar.

FUMITORY
Fumaria officinalis L. (Papaveraceae)
ARABIC: *baqla al-malik, shātiraj;* FRENCH: *fumeterre;* ITALIAN: *fumaria;* SPANISH: *fumaria*

PLANT CHARACTERISTICS AND VARIETIES

Fumitory is a 3-foot-tall climbing annual with lacy leaves and spikelike sprays of white or pinkish tubular flowers. The edible part is the leaf, which is sometimes cooked but is also used in salads. Although its use is not widespread, fumitory is eaten by French, Italians,

Spanish, and some Arabs, usually in rural areas.

PLANT ORIGIN

Fumitory is native to Europe and Asia.

PLANT HISTORY

The *capnos fruticosa* and *capnos trunca* Pliny described as being used medicinally is fumitory. In the ninth-century medical writing of the great Arab doctor and philosopher al-Kindī, fumitory is used medicinally, as it still is today in the Middle East. In 1614 Castelvetro suggested boiling fumitory with hops and other greens to make a kind of healthful concoction.

GALACTITES TOMENTOSA MOENCH. (SYN. *G. PUMILA* PORTA) (ASTERACEAE-COMPOSITAE)

PLANT CHARACTERISTICS AND VARIETIES

This thistle is an annual with a tender flower stem that is covered with densely matted white hairs. The stem is eaten as an herb or vegetable cooked with other vegetables in the region of the Dardanelles, the strait that connects the Sea of Marmara in Turkey to the Aegean Sea.

PLANT HISTORY

Dioscorides described this edible thistle as eaten young, cooked in oil with salt.

GARDEN BURNET

Poterium sanguisorba L. *(syn. Sanguisorba minor)* (Rosaceae)
FRENCH: *pimprenelle;* ITALIAN: *salvastrella, pimpinella* (Tuscany); SPANISH: *sanguisorba, pimpinela*

PLANT CHARACTERISTICS AND VARIETIES

Garden burnet is a rare spring herb and a perennial grass belonging to the rose family. It grows in the wild in grassy places, or among rocks, walls, and ruins. Its aromatic quality makes it a salad herb, although it has a bitter taste. Garden burnet is eaten mostly in Italy, France, and Spain.

PLANT HISTORY

In the seventeenth century Culpeper recommended using garden burnet medicinally.

GARDEN CRESS

Lepidium sativum L. var. *crispum* (Cruciferae-Brassicaceae)
Also called curled cress, broadleaf cress, nasturtium; ARABIC: *karabu, namanām, habb al-rashād;* FRENCH: *cresson alénois;* ITALIAN: *mastruzzo, masturzio d'orto, lepidio, lepidio ortense, crescione inglese;* SPANISH: *mastuerzo, mastuerzo hortense, berro común, lepidio;* TURKISH: *acitere*

Garden cress is a North African annual herb of the mustard family that is cultivated as a salad plant. Its lacy-looking basal leaves have a spicy hot peppery taste. It has narrow reddish brown seeds and three-lobed cotyledons. The quick-growing plant stands about 18 inches high and has small white flowers and seed pods about a ¼ inch long. Garden cress is eaten as a salad green throughout the Mediterranean.

PLANT ORIGIN

Garden cress appears to be native to the eastern Mediterranean, Egypt, and Ethiopia and possibly as far east as Iran. N. Vavilov suggests the area of northwestern India, Tadzhikistan, Uzbekistan, and western Tien Shan Province as the center of origin of garden cress, with the Mediterranean as a secondary center. DeCandolle, in the nineteenth century, suggested Persia as a center of origin.

PLANT HISTORY

In the ancient Egyptian tomb of Kha, seeds of *L. sativum* have been found, but there is no mention of the plant in pharaonic medical texts. Xenophon, writing in about 400 B.C., said that garden cress was eaten by the Persians. In the first century A.D. Pliny describes the garden cress growing in Arabia as being very large. The plant is mentioned by many of the Latin and Arabic authors. There is some confusion about the plant because it is also called nasturtium by the Latin authors,

as well as *cardamum*. Today nasturtium is the name of another related plant (page 238). In the early seventeenth century, Castelvetro mentions garden cress as a salad ingredient.

HOW TO GROW AND HARVEST

Sow seeds thickly in full sun in the early spring. Beds can be seeded every 2 weeks. Stop planting in the hot summer months and begin again in the late summer or early fall. Garden cress can be harvested when it is about a foot high. Pull the entire plant or cut it back halfway and see if the strong shoots will continue growing.

HOW TO BUY, STORE, AND PREPARE FOR COOKING

If a supermarket or farmers' market happens to carry garden cress, look for it to be displayed under cool shade. The leaves should be crisp looking. Store the leaves in the refrigerator and use them within 2 days. Garden cress is usually used in salads or as a garnish.

GARLIC

Allium sativum L. (Liliaceae)
ARABIC: *thūm;* CATALAN: *all;* FRENCH: *ail;*
GREEK: *skordon;* ITALIAN: *aglio;* SERBO-CROATIAN: *češnjak, bijeli luk, beli luk;*
SPANISH: *ajo;* TURKISH: *sarmısak*

PLANT CHARACTERISTICS AND VARIETIES

Garlic is a member of the onion family. The segmented bulbs, covered with a paperlike white skin and located at the base of the plant, are used for adding aromatic flavor in cooking. Garlic is used as a spice, to season foods, and as a vegetable in sauces such as the Greek *skordalia*. It is also eaten roasted. The medicinal claims for garlic have existed for millennia.

Garlic is not known as a wild plant, only as a cultivated plant. Today, and since ancient times, garlic has been propagated vegetatively; it does not set fertile seed. There are hundreds of named varieties of garlic. The two basic types of garlic are hardneck, or "ophio," garlic (*A. sativum* var. *ophioscorodon*) and softneck garlic (*A. sativum* var. *sativum*). Hardneck garlic sends up stiff flower stalks. Softneck does not; it produces bulbs with smaller cloves. Softneck is easier to grow, more productive, and can be grown in a greater variety of soils and climatic conditions. Each of these two divisions has been subdivided further by Ron Engeland, a leading authority on garlic, into five different horicultural types. So-called elephant garlic is of a different species, *A. scorodoprasum*. It is a kind of leek.

PLANT ORIGIN

The wild ancestry of cultivated garlic is not known at this time. Garlic is thought to derive from *A. longicuspis* Regel, a plant that is native to central Asia, the area that N. Vavilov suggests as the primary center of origin of the plant. The Mediterranean is a secondary center of origin.

PLANT HISTORY

Garlic was used extensively by the ancient Egyptians, according to Herodotus, who tells us that inscriptions of Egyptian characters on the pyramids speak of garlic, onions, and radishes as being the food of the workers who constructed the pyramids. The only problem with this interpretation is that the inscriptions on the pyramids do not detail the affairs of mortals. In an Egyptian medical text, referred to by Egyptologists as the *Ebers Codex* (from the Eighteenth Dynasty [1567–1320 B.C.], compiled about 1550 B.C.), garlic is described in a variety of ways as a remedy for some ailments. From this same period, several well-preserved dry remains of garlic have been found in tombs. In ancient Akkadian, an extinct Semitic language spoken in the northern part of Mesopotamia in about 2500 B.C., the word for *garlic* was *šûmu*, a word closely related to the Arabic word for garlic. Garlic has been discovered in the tomb of Tutankhamun and in the sacred animal temple at Saqqara in Egypt. In the Bible (Numbers 11:5) we know that the Israelites complained to Moses after their Exodus from Egypt that they missed the garlic they used to eat. Pliny admired garlic and devoted a lengthy section to its benefits. As with Pliny, the Prophet Muhammad recommended garlic as an antidote to snake and scorpion bites. The Greek writer Aristophanes described athletes eating garlic before exercising to ward off lethargy. The most famous of the Greek writers on natural history—Theophrastus, Aristotle,

Hippocrates, and Dioscorides—all described garlic in a medicinal context. The Romans are said to have been put off by the strong scent of garlic, but they fed it to workers to make them stronger and to soldiers to give them courage.

Garlic has always been thought of as a food of the common people. Charlemagne listed garlic in his *Capitulare de Villis* mentioning that it had an Italian origin (see proviso on page 124). In medieval times, garlic was eaten for dietetic reasons, especially because of the belief that it had a favorable effect on sexual performance. Garlic continued to be thought of medicinally rather than gastronomically throughout the fourteenth, fifteenth, and sixteenth centuries. It was referred to as the peasant's theriaca (a medieval antidote to poison) by the thirteenth-century doctor Arnold of Vilanova when he was a professor of medicine at the University of Montpellier in France. In the Middle Ages, Europeans traded gold and silver for the spices of the East, a fact that displeased kings and finance ministers, who thought the spice trade a poor one. Ferdinand of Spain tried to stop the importing of cinnamon and pepper in exchange for silver by saying, *"Buena especia es el ajo"* (Garlic is a perfectly good spice). But the popular opinion was that garlic *"sempre è cibo rusticano"* (always is a peasant food).

HOW TO GROW AND HARVEST

Garlic is planted in a warm place in the fall in the Mediterranean. Single cloves are set firmly with the scar-side-down about 2 inches deep in sandy, well-drained, fertile soil containing plenty of organic matter. Cut back on watering the plants as harvest time approaches. Once the broken plant tops are brown and dry, usually in mid- to late summer, lift the bulbs up and let them dry in the sun for a few days. Bunch the bulbs you have harvested, about 5 to 10 plants, and hang them up to dry for a few weeks.

HOW TO BUY, STORE, AND PREPARE FOR COOKING

Store both home-grown and store-bought garlic bulbs in a net bag or garlic cellar in a slightly cool room or cabinet, ideally about 60°F. It is not necessary to refrigerate garlic, and you should not freeze it. In supermarkets, avoid garlic in cellophane-wrapped boxes because you will not be able to inspect the heads. Buy loose garlic with large, plump cloves that are firm. The garlic bulb should feel heavy and be well covered with its own outer skin. Garlic will sprout if old, so once you have split the clove, cut out the green sprout if that suits you, although any bitterness in taste that many professional chefs refer to will unlikely be noticeable to the home cook. Older garlic cloves will not be as pungent as younger ones, so you may need to use more garlic than what a recipe calls for.

The quickest way to peel garlic is to line up as many as you need and crush them slightly under the wide blade of a 12-inch chef's knife. You can then peel off the skin easily.

There is also a clever little device called a garlic roller, a tubular piece of semi-hard rubbery plastic. Place the garlic into the roller, roll back and forth with a little pressure from your palms, and the skins will come off easily. Although some people swear by garlic presses, I never use them, preferring to clean the knife I use rather than the garlic press.

RECIPES

Soupe à l'Ail
GARLIC SOUP

In the regions of Languedoc and Provence in southern France, garlic is thought of as a vegetable as well as a spice. It is used as commonly in France as elsewhere in the Mediterranean, for instance, in sauces made of eggs, garlic, and almonds. In the Middle Ages, pepper was expensive, and when it appeared it was usually on the table of a noble family or it was served for special occasions. This heavily peppered soup was traditionally prepared to celebrate the rite of marriage in Languedoc. The wife presents this garlic and pepper soup to her new husband on their first day as a couple. The soup must be a reminder of the lives ahead of them, signifying the hope that their future will be spiritually, if not materially, rich. This opulent-tasting soup (a result of the eggs) needs hard-toasted bread and lots of pepper, so be liberal.

2 quarts water
15 garlic cloves (about 1 head), chopped fine
Bouquet garni, tied in cheesecloth (this herb blend consists of 8 sprigs fresh parsley, 8 sprigs fresh thyme, and 1 bay leaf)
1 cup extra virgin olive oil
Salt to taste
6 large egg yolks
Abundant freshly ground black pepper
8 slices French bread, toasted golden

1. Bring the water with the garlic cloves, bouquet garni, olive oil, and salt to a boil in a 4-quart casserole and boil for 5 minutes. Reduce the heat to low and simmer for 1 hour, uncovered.
2. Beat the egg yolks in a medium bowl. Remove the soup from the heat and pour a ladleful of it slowly into the bowl of egg yolks, beating constantly.
3. When the broth and eggs have cooled for 5 minutes, pour this mixture back into the soup, beating all the time. Pepper the soup generously; I will leave the exact amount up to you, but the soup should be heavily peppered. If it tastes bland after you've added the pepper, it needs more. Leave the soup to thicken a bit over low heat, making sure it does not boil. Divide the bread among individual soup bowls, ladle the soup on top, and serve.

Makes 8 servings

Sauce Rouille
SAFFRON-GARLIC MAYONNAISE

Rouille is the traditional mayonnaise accompaniment to bouillabaisse as it is served in Provence. This mayonnaise contains abundant chile pepper and garlic. Some cooks add tomato paste for coloring only, but I don't find this necessary because the color produced by the saffron and cayenne is assertive enough.

1½ cups diced French bread, white part only
½ cup fish broth (preferably homemade)
4 to 5 garlic cloves, to your taste, peeled
1 teaspoon salt
½ teaspoon ground red chile pepper
Pinch of saffron threads, crumbled
1 large egg yolk
Freshly ground black pepper to taste
1 cup extra virgin olive oil

Soak the diced bread in the fish broth. Squeeze out the broth. Mash the garlic cloves in a mortar with the salt until mushy. Place the bread, mashed garlic, red chile pepper, saffron, egg yolk, and black pepper in a food processor and blend for 30 seconds. Pour in the olive oil through the feed tube in a slow, thin, steady stream while the machine is running. Refrigerate the mayonnaise for 1 hour before serving. You may store whatever you don't use in the refrigerator for up to a week.

Makes 1¼ cups

NOTE: If the *rouille* is separating, add 2 to 3 tablespoons of the fish broth and whisk it in until the mayonnaise is smooth and re-emulsified.

Allioli
GARLIC MAYONNAISE

All-i-oli, meaning, literally, "garlic and oil," is a famous emulsion made in Catalonia, as well as to the south in Valencia and the north in France, in the Roussillon, Languedoc, and Provence. Unlike the *aïoli* of Provence and the *aillade* of Languedoc, the true Catalan *allioli* is made using only garlic, olive oil, and salt—no eggs. The garlic is placed in a mortar with salt and pounded until completely mashed and smooth. Then olive oil is slowly drizzled in, almost drop by drop, as, with continued pounding, the oil is incorporated into an emulsion with the garlic.

This emulsion of garlic and oil is the original foundation of the later invention, mayonnaise. Pliny the Elder (A.D. 23–79), who was a Roman procurator in Tarragona on the Catalan coast, seems to refer to an *allioli* when he writes in his *Natural History* (XIX, 112–13) that when garlic is "beaten up in oil and vinegar it swells up in foam to a surprising size."

In preparing *allioli* many Catalan cooks cheat by using eggs, since a proper *allioli* is a bit hard and tedious to pull off. The recipe here uses eggs. If you like a heavier, distinctively olive oil taste to your mayonnaise, go ahead and use extra virgin olive oil instead of the so-called light olive oil I call for.

Allioli is traditionally served with rice dishes or fish preparations, although many Catalans use it as a kind of ketchup for anything and everything.

5 large garlic cloves, peeled
½ teaspoon salt
1 large egg
1 cup light olive oil or ½ cup each pure or virgin olive oil and vegetable oil combined

1. Mash the garlic and salt together in a mortar until the garlic forms a paste. In a food processor, process the egg for 30 seconds.

2. Add the garlic paste to the food processor and slowly drizzle in the olive oil until it is absorbed. Cover the *allioli* with plastic wrap and refrigerate it for 1 hour before using it. It will keep, refrigerated, for a month or more.

Makes 1½ cups

Skordalia
GARLIC SAUCE

Skordalia is a Greek garlic-and-potato sauce with the consistency of mayonnaise. In Greece it is used in a variety of foods such as beet salad and batter-fried salt cod. Palestinians and Lebanese use a version made with garlic and olive oil, called *thūm bi'l-zayt*, for baked chicken. *Skordalia* is related to the Catalan *allioli* and the *rouille* and *aïoli* of Provence. Cooks in Macedonia and the Greek Adriatic island of Kefallinía (Cephalonia) often add walnuts, and older recipes base the *skordalia* on almonds—lead-

ing me to believe that *skordalia* is the Greek version of the Turkish *tarator* (page 126) and Arab *ṭaraṭūr* sauces, which themselves may owe something to Byzantine food.

1¾ pounds boiling potatoes
½ cup light cream, or more to taste
6 large garlic cloves, peeled
2 cups French or Italian bread, crusts removed, cut into ½-inch dice
½ cup extra virgin olive oil
3 tablespoons white wine vinegar
Salt to taste

1. Place the potatoes in a large pot with cold water to cover them by several inches and turn the heat to medium. Once the water begins to boil, about 20 minutes, boil the potatoes until a skewer will glide easily through the center of each potato, another 25 to 30 minutes. Peel the potatoes once they are cool enough to handle. Pass them through a food mill or colander and place them in a bowl. Slowly whip in the cream.

2. Pound the garlic in a mortar until mushy. Add the mashed garlic to the potatoes, mixing well. Soak the bread cubes in a little water until sodden. Squeeze out the water. Pass the bread through the food mill or colander. Blend the bread, potatoes, and garlic together with a fork.

3. Slowly add the olive oil and vinegar in a steady stream as you continue beating with a fork until the mixture has the consistency of a thick mayonnaise. Do not use a food processor because the potatoes will become over-

processed and gummy. Season the sauce with salt and refrigerate until needed.

Makes 3 cups

VARIATION: Add chopped almonds, walnuts, or pine nuts after mashing the garlic.

Bayḍ bi'l-Thūm wa'l-Kharshūf
ROASTED GARLIC CLOVES WITH ARTICHOKE, GARLIC, AND YOGURT SAUCE

The Arabic name for this Syrian preparation, which is usually served as part of a *mazza* table, is "eggs with garlic and artichokes," yet the most obvious features are the garlic and the artichokes. My guess is that in earlier times eggs were prized and rarer than the other ingredients. When would you eat this dish? Breakfast is not a bad time, or even as a brunch dish, and, of course, for a *mazza*. If you are thinking that the amount of garlic in this dish might be overpowering, remember that the pungency of garlic decreases significantly when it is roasted.

2 large artichokes (about 1½ pounds)
6 heads garlic, separated into cloves and peeled
2 tablespoons extra virgin olive oil
3 cups high-quality full-fat plain yogurt, at room temperature
1 large hard-boiled egg, shelled and chopped fine
¼ teaspoon ground cinnamon
Salt and freshly ground black pepper to taste

1. Boil the artichokes whole in a large saucepan of lightly salted water, uncovered, until a skewer will glide into the base easily or the heavier bracts pull off easily, 50 to 55 minutes.

2. Meanwhile, preheat the oven to 400°F. Place the garlic in a baking pan with the olive oil. Bake until golden and soft when pierced by a skewer, 18 to 20 minutes.

3. Drain the artichokes. Trim and chop the hearts fine. Scrape whatever flesh you can off the lower part of the inside of the bracts. You should have about ¾ cup finely chopped artichoke in all. Stir the artichokes, yogurt, egg, and cinnamon together. Add salt and pepper if necessary or desired.

4. Arrange the garlic cloves on a serving plate, spoon the sauce over them, and serve with warm pita bread.

Makes 6 to 8 servings

VARIATION: Bake the garlic heads in their peel and unpeel them once they are soft.

GENTIAN

Gentiana acaulis L. (syn. *G. excisa* C. Presl; *G. kochiana* Perr. et Songeon) (Gentianaceae)
ARABIC: *janṭiyān;* ITALIAN: *genziana, gnziana* (Tuscany)

PLANT CHARACTERISTICS AND VARIETIES
This perennial herb has leaves shaped like the tip of a lance. The roots are eaten raw as a

snack in rural Tuscany. *Gentiana lutea* is one of the ingredients of Angostura bitters. Gentian was used in medieval Arab pharmacological prescriptions as an antidote to scorpion bites.

GIANT FENNEL
Ferula communis L. (Umbelliferae)
ARABIC: *kalkh*

PLANT CHARACTERISTICS AND VARIETIES
Giant fennel is a member of the same family as bulb fennel. The stems of giant fennel grow to about 10 feet high and are used for tinder as well as eaten boiled by members of some Bedouin tribes. Another variety of giant fennel is *F. sinaica* B.

PLANT ORIGIN
Ferula communis L. originates in the Mediterranean.

PLANT HISTORY
Giant fennel is something of an exotic plant. Pliny described it as such. He likened it to dill and mentioned that there are two types, one called Greek narthex, which grows tall; and the other, *narthecia*, which is low growing. The Romans boiled the stems of the giant fennel and mixed them with brine and honey. The root of the giant fennel was mixed with wine and taken for snakebites.

GLASSWORT
Salicornia europaea L. (Chenopodiaceae)
Also called salicornia, sea asparagus, marsh samphire; FRENCH: *salicorne*; ITALIAN: *salicornia*; SPANISH: *sosa, barilla, matojo, almarjo*

PLANT CHARACTERISTICS AND VARIETIES
Found in muddy salt marshes by the sea in the Mediterranean, glasswort is a succulent herb in the goosefoot family, the same family as spinach. This annual plant has long, twiglike leaves that are edible. In southern Italy's Apulia region a variety known locally as *savezudde (S. fruticosa)* is eaten. Some species can be found in inland areas of the American Midwest and southern Canada.

PLANT HISTORY
Since this plant contains a large amount of potash, from Biblical times through the Middle Ages, and until recently, it has been burnt and used in the manufacture of glass, hence one of its common names, glasswort. A good deal of glasswort was gathered under the name *barilla* on the coasts of Spain in the Middle Ages and shipped north to be used in glassmaking.

HOW TO GROW AND HARVEST
Glasswort is easy to collect and is not cultivated commercially any longer.

You are most likely to find glasswort, or any kind of *salicornia,* as I have, in farmers' markets or whole or natural food stores with high-quality produce departments. Keep glasswort in the refrigerator for up to 2 days. Boil glasswort until it is soft. Eat it with butter or olive oil as you would asparagus. The edible part is the green vegetative matter surrounding a wiry stem inside the twiglike spear. The "meat" can be scraped off with your teeth as you would the flesh on the lower inside of an artichoke bract.

GOAT'S BEARD

Aruncus dioicus (Walter) Fernald
(Rosaceae)

PLANT CHARACTERISTICS AND VARIETIES

This perennial herb has pyramidal flower clusters. The edible parts are the young buds, leaves, and stem, which are eaten as a potherb. In the western part of the province of Friuli, in northern Italy, goat's beard is cooked and eaten in *pistic,* a dish made during the spring with more than fifty wild greens.

GOLDEN THISTLE

Scolymus hispanicus L. (Asteraceae-Compositae)
Also called Spanish oysterplant; ARABIC: *sunarīsh;* FRENCH: *carduille, cardon d'Espagne, scolyme d'Espagne;* ITALIAN: *cardo scòlimo, cardoncello selvatico;* SPANISH: *escolimo, cardillo, almirón de España, tagarnina*

PLANT CHARACTERISTICS AND VARIETIES

The golden thistle is a spiny-stemmed biennial or perennial. It is not much cultivated anymore, but it was once grown for its edible leaf stalks and midribs, which were eaten boiled or baked. The young leaves are added to salads or cooked as a potherb. The roots are eaten, too, usually boiled and mashed. One of the Spanish names for spotted golden thistle comes from the Berber word for artichoke, *taga.*

PLANT ORIGIN

The golden thistle is native from the Mediterranean east to southern Russia.

PLANT HISTORY

The plant called *skolumus* and *leimonia* by Theophrastus and the *scolymus* by Pliny is thought to be the golden thistle, although the plant Pliny mentions may be the cardoon. Clusius saw the plant growing wild in Spain in 1576. Spotted golden thistle *(S. maculatus)* may be the *skolumos* described by Dioscorides.

Molde al Tagarinna — Golden Thistle Mold

THIS DELICIOUS RECIPE, WHICH WAS DESCRIBED TO ME BUT WHICH I'VE NEVER HAD THE OPPORTUNITY OF TASTING, COMES from Antonio Muñoz, the owner of the distinctive Ciro's restaurant in Córdoba.

Beat ten eggs with 1 cup of cream and turn the mixture into a mold with 1¾ pounds cooked golden thistle and 1¾ pounds wild mushrooms cooked in ½ cup extra virgin olive oil, with 2 garlic cloves, and ¼ cup tomato sauce. Place the mold in a *bain-marie* and bake it for 1½ hours. Cool the mold and turn it out. Make a sauce with bread fried in olive oil and garlic, freshly ground cumin seeds, paprika, dried mint, and some chicken stock. Blend the sauce in a food processor. Then heat it in a saucepan and serve it with the golden thistle mold.

HOW TO GROW AND HARVEST

Golden thistle is grown in a manner similar to artichoke and cardoon (see entries).

GOOD KING HENRY

Chenopodium bonus-henricus L.
(Chenopodiaceae)
Also called mercury goosefoot, goosefoot, wild spinach, fat-hen, Lincolnshire spinach, poor man's asparagus; FRENCH: *chénopode bon-Henri, bon-Henri, épinard sauvage, ingri* (Roya Valley, Provence); ITALIAN: *farinello buono-enrico, farinaccio* (Tuscany); SPANISH: *zurrón, anserina, buen henrique*; TURKISH: *sirken otu* (pigweed).

PLANT CHARACTERISTICS AND VARIETIES

The edible parts of this triangular-leaved perennial are the leaves, which are cooked. The young shoots are also excellent eaten with melted butter or olive oil like asparagus. Good King Henry is sometimes used as a substitute for spinach, but because the leaves wilt much more quickly after picking than do spinach leaves, spinach has become more popular among commercial growers.

In farmers' markets in California it is possible to find a related plant called lamb's-quarters, fat-hen, or pigweed (*C. album*), which can be cooked in the same way you would good King Henry—that is, like spinach. In Turkey, pigweed or fat-hen (*C. album* L. ssp. *iranicum* Allen) is gathered as a wild green and used in salads. In rural Tuscany, *C. urbicum* L. is boiled and stewed and used in the stuffing for *tortelli*.

PLANT ORIGIN

Chenopodium album L. is native to the Mediterranean region, and it is thought that *C. bonus-henricus* is, too. Seeds of the plant have been found in prehistoric sites in Europe, and prehistoric man may have collected them intentionally to supplement his diet.

PLANT HISTORY

The plant was known by the name good King Henry in the late sixteenth century, although it is not known whether the name is English or an English translation of the German. The *blitum* described by Pliny in *Natural History* (Book XX, 252) might be good King Henry. This easily grown plant was probably introduced to the European Mediterranean and northern Europe by the Romans. William Woys Weaver mentions a depiction of good King Henry on a large ornamented bowl from the third century A.D. on display at the Roman Open-Air Museum at Schearzenacker near Homburg/Saar in Germany. In the Middle Ages, good King Henry was considered a cure for scurvy. It is said that this plant is called "good Henry" to distinguish it from a weed, *Mercurialis annua,* which is known as "bad Henry." Botanists such as Tragus (1553), Lobel (1570), Camerarius (1586), and Matthioli (1598) speak of it as only a wayside plant; they do not mention it as a cultivated vegetable.

HOW TO GROW AND HARVEST

Good King Henry should be planted in a partly shaded location with well-drained soil. It grows best in moist, rich soil (as suits a king!). Compost should be dug into the beds before planting, with manure added during the growing season. The seed can be sown in furrows in the spring 6 inches apart and thinned to 1½ feet apart. Harvest the leaves by pinching them off at the tips of the stem.

HOW TO BUY, STORE, AND PREPARE FOR COOKING

Good King Henry can occasionally be found at farmers' markets, or you can replace it with lamb's lettuce (see entry), another plant entirely, which also can be found occasionally at farmers' markets. Store the leaves in the refrigerator and use within 2 days.

RECIPE

Omelette bon-Henri
GOOD KING HENRY OMELETTE

Prepared in the Languedoc, this is a really nice omelette and quite a delight as a brunch preparation. This recipe makes two or three omelettes, depending on the size of your omelette pan, so divide all the ingredients accordingly. The leaves of good King Henry must be completely dry before they are cooked. Spin them dry and then blot them with paper towels.

5 to 6 tablespoons unsalted butter, to your taste
1 garlic clove, chopped very fine
½ pound good King Henry, trimmed of heavy
*   stems, washed well, dried well, and chopped*
Salt and freshly ground black pepper to taste
6 large eggs, beaten well with a whisk for at least
*   1 minute*

In a nonstick omelette pan, melt 1½ to 2 tablespoons of the butter for each omelette over medium heat. Cook the garlic and good King Henry, stirring frequently, until the greens are wilted, about 1 minute. Season with salt and pepper, add another ½ to 1 tablespoon butter for each additional omelette, then pour in the beaten eggs, and make an omelette incorporating the good King Henry, about 2 minutes. Serve hot.

Makes 2 or 3 servings

GRAPE HYACINTH
Muscari neglectum Guss. ex Ten. (syn. *M. atlanticum; Leopoldia comosa; Hyacinthus racemosus* L.) (Liliaceae)
Also called tassel hyacinth; FRENCH: *muscari;* GREEK: *muscari, volvi;* ITALIAN: *lambascioni;* SPANISH: *almizclena;* TURKISH: *ıt dirseği*

PLANT CHARACTERISTICS AND VARIETIES
The edible part of this bulbous perennial is the bulb, which has a slightly bitter flavor. Boiled grape hyacinth is popular in Greece and southern Italy; one particular variety (that

some taxonomists classify as the same thing as *M. neglectum*) used in Apulia is *M. recemosum* (or *racemosum*). *Muscari alla griglia* is a dish from southern Italy in which grape hyacinth bulbs are grilled over a hardwood fire with olive oil, salt, and pepper.

PLANT ORIGIN
It seems that the plant is native from the Mediterranean to the Caucausus.

PLANT HISTORY
Hyacinth bulbs have long been popular as food in Greece. In classical times, Chrysippus, in his book *On the Good*, as reported by Athenaeus, tells us of a maxim that these bulbs figure in: "In the winter season, a bulb-and-lentil soup, oh me, oh my! For bulb-and-lentil soup is like ambrosia in the chilly cold."

HOW TO BUY, STORE, AND PREPARE FOR COOKING
Grape hyacinth is usually boiled with a little vinegar.

GRAPE LEAF
Vitis vinifera L. (Vitaceae)
ARABIC: *waraq īnab;* FRENCH: *feuille de raisin;* ITALIAN: *foglia d'uva;* SERBO-CROATIAN: *jagoda (boba) grožđa;* SPANISH: *hoja d'uva;* TURKISH: *asthma yaprağı*

Making an Omelette

THERE ARE TWO WAYS OF MAKING AN OMELETTE, AND I USE EITHER OF THEM, DEPENDING ON MY MOOD. A PERFECT omelette is never burnt; it never has any brown marks on it. It can be either a thin layer of solid egg encasing creamy scrambled eggs, all cooked in the same pan, or it can be one thin layer of egg, like a crepe, that you place, pan and all, under the broiler for 15 seconds to cook the top, and then fold over on itself.

To make the first kind of omelette, melt the butter in an 8-inch omelette pan, usually a nonstick pan. Once the butter is sizzling, pour the beaten eggs in all at once, shaking the pan back and forth vigorously. Pull the edge of the omelette up toward the center and tilt the pan so the liquidy egg runs into the exposed part of the pan. Do this continuously and quickly with a rubber spatula; the whole process should take about 15 to 20 seconds. When the omelette is done, there will be very little liquidy part left. Fold the omelette over onto itself as you shake it out of the pan onto a plate.

To make the second kind of omelette, preheat the broiler. Melt the butter until sizzling in a 10-inch nonstick pan. Pour the eggs in and let them cook for about 1 minute. Place the pan under the broiler until there is no more liquid left and the eggs are puffing up. Remove the pan from the broiler and fold the omelette over onto itself on a plate.

PLANT CHARACTERISTICS AND VARIETIES

The edible parts of the grape plant are the fruit and the leaves. The vegetable part is the leaves, which are used for wrapping foods, most prominently in the cuisines of North Africa, the Middle East, Greece, and parts of the Balkans, but they are also used for that purpose in Provence, especially with grilled fish or small birds. The fruit are eaten as table grapes, dried into raisins, and made into wine. The grapevine is a perennial, woody climbing vine. The plant is much manipulated by growers for specific purposes mostly associated with wine growing. Economically, the plant is most valued for wine growing and the production of table grapes. The use of the leaves in cooking is not even being mentioned by most economic botany and gardening books.

PLANT ORIGIN

There are an estimated 10,000 cultivars of *V. vinifera* in the Old World, all of them derived from the single wild species *V. sylvestris,* which is still found in the area ranging from northeastern Afghanistan to the southern borders of the Black and Caspian Seas, although legend has often identified Armenia as the home of the first grape and wine culture.

PLANT HISTORY

Grapes first began to be domesticated when migratory nomads in Central Asia marked forest trees such as poplar, pear, willow, plum, or fig that supported particularly fruitful vines. The trees were often located near the watering holes of the nomads' herds. Exactly when and where this phenomenon occurred, we do not know. As sedentary agriculture developed, mixed deciduous forests were cleared, although fruit-bearing trees and trees supporting fruit-bearing vines were spared along boundary lines where irrigation ditches developed and where the vines were out of the reach of grazing animals. Actual vineyards probably didn't develop until villages were built with walls high enough to keep out the grazing herds. Grape cultivation for wine existed in the Near East as early as the fourth millennium B.C. The Hittites cultivated the grape probably first for wine and second for table grapes. The plant did not exist west of Greece until the first millennium B.C. By Phoenician times, viticulture spread according to sea trade routes. The spread of wine into Roman areas was associated with the birth of Christianity and the role of wine in the consecration of the Mass. The Roman authors Cato, Pliny, Virgil, Varro, and others wrote much about the grape. Vineyard culture in the Middle Ages was closely associated with Catholic monasteries. In pharaonic Egypt, the best vineyards were in the Delta and the oases. The fruit was eaten or used for making wine, and the leaves were used for wrapping foods.

The use of the leaves of the grape for food developed very early, according to a Danish Egyptologist, Lise Manniche. She claims that grape leaves were used to wrap around rice and meat in pharaonic Egypt. But she must be wrong about rice (*Oryza sativa* L.) because it was not known and certainly not used as a food in Egypt until around the Islamic era.

HOW TO GROW AND HARVEST

Consult standard books on grapevine growing. It is neither sensible nor convenient to grow grape vines merely for their leaves. If you already have a grapevine, the leaves can be removed when they are about 4 inches in diameter. After washing and layering the leaves tightly, preserve them in a mixture of salted water and vinegar.

HOW TO BUY, STORE, AND PREPARE FOR COOKING

Most grape leaves used for cooking purposes are sold brined, in jars. Drain them and remove them from the jar. Unfold and separate them gently so they don't rip. If you're using fresh grape leaves that have never been brined, wash them and boil them gently for 5 minutes before using them.

Waraq Īnab bi'l-Zayt
STUFFED GRAPE LEAVES IN OLIVE OIL

A properly made stuffed grape leaf should be a thoroughly inviting morsel, shiny with olive oil, and plump with a rice filling. Throughout the Middle East, stuffed grape leaves are a popular *mazza*, as they call them in Greece and Turkey, small foods served on small plates as a kind of smorgasbord. They are usually served at room temperature when offered as a *mazza* and are served hot as a more substantial dinner. You will notice that this is a very simple recipe, relying on fresh herbs and vegetables rather than on elaborate spicing. The flavor of this recipe is ever so slightly tart. This is the way stuffed grape leaves are prepared in rural Palestine.

4 tablespoons extra virgin olive oil, divided
1 small onion, chopped fine
4 scallions, chopped
1 cup uncooked medium-grain rice, washed well or soaked in tepid water to cover for 30 minutes, and drained
½ cup finely chopped fresh parsley leaves, divided
½ cup finely chopped fresh mint leaves, divided
2 teaspoons salt
Freshly ground black pepper to taste
2¼ cups water, divided
½ pound ripe tomatoes, peeled, seeded, and chopped fine
60 grape leaves
¼ cup freshly squeezed lemon juice

1. Heat 2 tablespoons of the olive oil in a heavy stovetop casserole or saucepan over medium-high heat and cook the onion and scallions until translucent, about 4 minutes, stirring. Add the drained rice, stir, and cook for 1 minute. Add half of the parsley and mint, the salt, pepper, and water. Stir, and bring to a boil. Reduce the heat to low, cover with a paper towel, place the lid of the casserole or saucepan over the paper towel, and cook until all the liquid is absorbed and the rice is tender, 18 to 20 minutes.

2. Transfer the rice to a platter, let cool completely, and stir in the tomatoes. Taste and correct the seasoning if necessary. Layer the bottom of a medium saucepan with 5 or 6 overlapping grape leaves. (Boil the grape leaves for 5 minutes if they are fresh; drain them if they're from a jar.)

3. Lay a leaf in front of you, stem side up and nearest to you. Each grape leaf has a ¼- to ½-inch-long piece of stem. Cut or snip that off to make wrapping easier. Place about a tablespoon of rice stuffing just above the stem end. Fold the leaf over away from you, tuck in the two side portions of the leaf, and continue rolling tightly. Place the rolled up grape leaves snuggly in the saucepan layered with grape leaves. Pour the remaining 2 tablespoons olive oil, the lemon juice, the remaining mint and parsley, and the remaining ¼ cup water over the grape leaves. (If there is more than one layer of stuffed grape leaves, drizzle each layer with equal parts of the olive oil, lemon juice, mint, and parsley.)

4. Place an inverted plate or the lid of a smaller saucepan on top of the grape leaves and turn the heat to medium. Cook over low heat until you see liquid bubbling on the sides, about 30 minutes. Remove the grape leaves from the heat, let cool completely in the saucepan, transfer to a serving platter, and serve at room temperature.

Makes 50 to 60 grape leaves
(some may rip)

GRASS PEA
Lathyrus sativus L. (Leguminosae-Fabaceae)
Also called chickling vetch, chickling pea, blue vetchling; Arabic: *julubbān;* French: *gesse blanche, gesse cultivée, pois carée;* Italian: *cicerchia, robiglio;* Spanish: *arvejo, almorta, meula, tito, guija;* Turkish: *fiğ* (Aksaray Province)

PLANT CHARACTERISTICS AND VARIETIES
Grass pea is a climbing annual or perennial with tendrils and 1¾-inch legumes. The edible parts are the immature seed and pod, which are cooked. The seeds are toxic when eaten in large quantities. Today the seeds are used in soups in some parts of France, but for the most part grass pea is used for fodder.

PLANT ORIGIN
The origin of grass pea is not known. The nearest wild species that is genetically related to the grass pea is *Lathyrus cicera* L. The grass pea belongs to the vetch family and grows from Greece to Iran and Transcaucasia. N. Vavilov suggests the area of northwestern India, Tadzhikistan, Uzbekistan, and western Tien Shan Province as the grass pea's center of origin.

PLANT HISTORY
The grass pea was a common Mediterranean vegetable in the Middle East of about 7000 B.C. and was cultivated in prehistoric times. It

was used as a fodder crop and as a substitute for peas in times of drought. The plant is mentioned by Columella and Palladius. Pliny describes the plant and tells us that the peas are white, sweetish, and easily shelled. This plant was mostly used medicinally. The peas were eaten with a fish or chicken broth to lessen the perceived reaction to the stomach when the peas were eaten plain. In 1614 Castelvetro described the grass pea as a vegetable that generated wind, bad blood, and considerable melancholy.

GUNDELIA TOURNEFORTII L. (ASTERACEAE-COMPOSITAE)

ARABIC: ꜥakkūb, kardī (colloquial), kankar; TURKISH: kengal

PLANT CHARACTERISTICS AND VARIETIES

This plant is a perennial spiny herb found growing in Israel, Palestine, Lebanon, Syria, and Turkey. The edible parts are the leaves, stems, roots, and the undeveloped flower buds, which taste like a cross between asparagus and artichoke. The plant, especially its young thick stem and undeveloped flower buds, is sold in Jerusalem markets. Several ethnic groups gather these plants for culinary purposes, including Muslim and Christian Palestinians, Druze (the Lebanese, Palestinian, and Syrian heterodox Muslim community), and Sephardic Jews in Israel. It is also seen in the markets of Lebanon and Syria. In Turkey, the plant is gathered in the wild. In the Palestinian Arab villages of northern Israel the most popular preparation for *gundelia* entails cleaning the heads, covering them with a chopped meat mixture, frying them in olive oil, and then simmering the meat and vegetable in a lemony broth.

PLANT ORIGIN

This thistle appears to be native to Syria and Israel/Palestine, where it grows abundantly. Some botanists suggest an Irano-Turanian origin.

PLANT HISTORY

The use of this plant is apparently quite old, for it is mentioned in the Babylonian Talmud and the Bible. *Gundelia* is the plant called *silybum* by Dioscorides. The Shroud of Turin, which is alleged by Roman Catholics to be the burial cloth of Jesus, shows signs of the presence of *gundelia*. A 1999 analysis of the shroud, with its faint image of a crucified man and even fainter images of plants, now places its origin in Jerusalem before the eighth century, refuting a 1988 study that dated the cloth no earlier than the mid-thirteenth century. The analysis, presented at the International Botanical Congress in 1999, identified the presence of a high density of pollen of the tumbleweed *G. tournefortii*. An image of *G. tournefortii* can be seen near the image of the man's shoulder. Some experts have suggested that *gundelia* was used for Jesus's "crown of thorns."

Gundelia grows wild and is usually harvested in the morning to be sold in the afternoon at market. This work is undertaken mostly by groups of women from Palestinian Arab villages in Israel. Before the plant bolts, the infloresecent heads are removed by inserting a knife and clipping the stem base a bit below ground level.

HOW TO BUY, STORE, AND PREPARE FOR COOKING

Gundelia is best eaten, and traditionally eaten, on the day it is harvested. Before they are cooked, the fresh heads and the bases of the rosette leaves are trimmed to remove the short, soft thorns.

HEDGE MUSTARD
Sisymbrium officinale (L.) Scop. (Cruciferae-Brassicaceae)
ITALIAN: *erìsimo, cimamarèdde* (Taranto, Apulia); TURKEY: *elgelen hardalı*

PLANT CHARACTERISTICS AND VARIETIES
This annual or biennial herb grows to 3 feet and has flowers with small petals. The edible parts are the young leaves and shoots, which are usually eaten raw with salads, although they are sometimes cooked as a potherb, mostly in southern Italy, Greece, and Turkey. In Turkey, *S. altissimum* L. is a wild edible herb that grows in the mountainous regions of Aksaray Province in Anatolia.

HEDYPNOIS CRETICA (L.) DUM.-COURSET (SYN. H. GLOBULIFERA VAR. TUBAFORMIS)
ITALIAN: *piscialetto, cicurazza* (Brindisi, Apulia), *mariola* (Taranto, Apulia)

PLANT CHARACTERISTICS AND VARIETIES
This annual plant with many branched stems grows to various sizes and is eaten in the Taranto area of Apulia in southern Italy, as well as in rural Turkey.

HOLLYHOCK
Althaea rosea Cav. (syn. *Alcea rosea*) (Malvaceae)
ARABIC: *hatmy*; FRENCH: *rose trémière*; ITALIAN: *altea*; SERBO-CROATIAN: *trando-vilje; vrtni sljez*; SPANISH: *malva hortense*; TURKISH: *hatmi*

PLANT CHARACTERISTICS AND VARIETIES
The hollyhock is cultivated in Cairo for its leaves, which are edible, and used in Egyptian cookery in soups. The plant is similiar to marshmallow (page 222).

HOP
Humulus lupulus L. (Moraceae)
FRENCH: *houblon;* ITALIAN: *luppolo,*
bruscandoli (Veneto); SPANISH: *lúpulo,*
hombrecillo

PLANT CHARACTERISTICS AND VARIETIES
Hop is a climbing perennial that dies to the
ground every autumn and is most commonly
used in the making of beer. In parts of the
Mediterranean, especially in northern Italy,
the edible shoots of the panicle are picked in
spring and eaten as a vegetable, like asparagus,
and, in fact, this vegetable is sometimes called
wild asparagus. The shoots are cooked with
vinegar in omelettes or used in making green
pasta. Hops are usually boiled in salted water
with a little lemon juice and served with butter or cream or used in omelettes. A typical
plate of *cucina povera* (cooking of the poor) in
the Veneto region of Italy is a *risotto di bruscandoli* made in the spring, using the young shoots
of wild hops.

PLANT HISTORY
Castelvetro wrote about hops in 1614, mentioning that the Italians ate hops shoots as a
cooked salad, never raw, seasoned with olive
oil, vinegar or lemon juice, salt, and freshly
crushed peppercorns. He suggested hops as a
healthful concoction for ailments that were
too minor to consult a doctor about but
major enough to cause discomfort. The
shoots should be boiled with fumitory (see

entry), endive (see entry), and borage (see
entry) and eaten as a salad, and the liquid
should be drunk every morning for the next
seven to nine days, he advises.

**HOW TO BUY, STORE, AND PREPARE
FOR COOKING**
Hops are gathered in the wild, usually by
roadsides. The foot-long thin stems are cut
off, the thicker parts discarded, and the rest is
cut into 1-inch lengths. Hops are usually
boiled, but they are also cooked with onions
and olive oil. Hops are almost never eaten in
the United States as a vegetable; in this country the plant is used almost exclusively for beer
making.

HORN OF PLENTY
Fedia cornucopiae DC. (L.) Geartn. (syn.
F. graciliflora; Valeriana cornucopiae)
(Valerianaceae)
Also called valerian, African valerian;
FRENCH: *fédia, corne d'abondance, doucette
d'Alger, valériane d'Alger;* ITALIAN: *lattughella,
cornucoppia;* SPANISH: *cornucopia, trompetillas*

PLANT CHARACTERISTICS AND VARIETIES
This plant is closely related to other
Valerianella such as lamb's lettuce (see entry)
and Jupiter's beard (see entry). Horn of plenty has large bright purple flowers. It is common in the European Mediterranean and is
found growing in olive groves and other open
places. This plant should not be confused

with a mushroom called horn of plenty (*Craterellus cornucopioides*). The edible part is the leaf, which is cooked or used as a salad green.

PLANT ORIGIN
Horn of plenty appears to be native to the Mediterranean.

HORSERADISH
Armoracia rusticana Gaertn., Mey., Scherb. (syn. *Nasturtium armoracia*; *Armoracia lapathifolia*; *Cochlearia armoracia*) (Cruciferae-Brassicaceae)
ARABIC: *fujl* (*fijil*); FRENCH: *cran, armoracie, raifort*; ITALIAN: *cren, barbafonte, rafano rusticano*; SERBO-CROATIAN: *bren*; SPANISH: *rábano rusticano, rábano piccante, rábano silvestre*

PLANT CHARACTERISTICS AND VARIETIES
Horseradish is a winter-hardy perennial herb with curly leaves and fleshy roots and is a relative of the radish. When mature the plant reaches about 2 feet high. The edible parts are the roots, leaves, and sprouted seeds, which are consumed either raw or cooked.

PLANT ORIGIN
Horseradish is thought to be native to Turkey, southern Russia, and eastern Ukraine.

PLANT HISTORY
Horseradish has been cultivated since classical times, when it was mentioned by Dioscorides.

Most likely it was spread throughout the Mediterranean by the Romans, who used it for medicinal and gastronomic purposes. Horseradish is traditionally associated with the Jewish Passover, when it is used as part of the celebratory meal. Since classical times, horseradish has been called *armoracia*. In the Middle Ages, Joannes Ruellius called it by the same name.

HOW TO GROW AND HARVEST
Horseradish is grown from root cuttings; the plant flowers but does not produce seeds. It is easy to grow and once established it can tolerate a fair amount of neglect; in fact, it can escape and grow in the wild, although it does not do well in shaded areas. Plant horseradish root cuttings 2 feet apart in the spring, pushing thin pieces of pencil-sized roots into the soil at a slight angle. Gardeners recommend removing or pushing aside the soil around the root in midsummer to remove any root branches. By removing the superfluous root branches you prevent forking or branching of the root, encourage the growth of a long, smooth central root for harvest, and ensure that multiple crowns don't grow. Rub off the side roots by hand, and repeat the process after 6 weeks. The root branches you remove can be replanted in moist, sandy soil and will have rooted by the following spring. Harvest horseradish root in the late fall.

Look for firm roots without soft spots. Store horseradish in a plastic bag in the refrigerator. Scrape off the skin before grating the root. Horseradish can be kept in the refrigerator for up to a month.

RECIPES

Salsa al Rafano
HORSERADISH SAUCE

This sauce from northern Italy is also found in French cuisine and the cuisines of Eastern Europe. It is typically served over boiled beef, but I like to use it with boiled sausages, too.

1 cup fresh white breadcrumbs
½ cup milk
¼ cup peeled and freshly grated horseradish
½ teaspoon salt
½ teaspoon sugar
½ cup heavy cream, whipped to peaks
1 teaspoon white wine vinegar

I. Soak the breadcrumbs in the milk in a small bowl. Squeeze the liquid out as if you were making a snowball. Return the bread-crumbs to a clean bowl, stir in the horserad-ish, season with the salt and sugar, and beat in the whipped cream. Pass the mixture through a food mill or fine-mesh strainer. Refrigerate until needed.

2. When you are ready to serve this sauce with boiled meat, put the horseradish sauce in a small skillet or saucepan and heat it gently. Stir in the vinegar just before serving.

Makes 1 ½ cups

Umak od Hren sa Jabukom
HORSERADISH AND APPLE SAUCE

This recipe comes from the part of Serbia called Vojvodina, near Hungary. Typically, the sauce is served over boiled beef or ham. It is also nice to serve with a roast suckling pig or a roast pork shoulder. The horseradish should be fresh and not out of a jar. Make the sauce quickly, so the apples do not discolor after they are grated.

3 apples, peeled and grated down to the core
¼ cup peeled and freshly grated horseradish
½ cup cold chicken bouillon (homemade or from
*   a can)*
Freshly squeezed juice from 1 lemon

In a medium bowl, mix together the apples, horseradish, and bouillon. Quickly add the lemon juice so the apples don't discolor. Refrigerate until needed.

Makes ¾ cup

HORSETAIL

Equisetum arvense L. (Equisetaceae)
ARABIC: *kunbath, zayl al-husam;* FRENCH:
prêle des champs; ITALIAN: *coda cavalina;*
SPANISH: *cola de caballo, equiseto menor*

PLANT CHARACTERISTICS AND VARIETIES

Horsetail is a perennial herb. The edible part
is the young spikelike inflorescence of the
plant, which is cooked or pickled. Arabs,
Andalusians, rural French, and some Italians
cook horsetail.

HYACINTH

Hyacinthus orientalis L. (Liliaceae)
ARABIC: *yāsint;* FRENCH: *jacinthe;* GREEK:
uakinthos; ITALIAN: *giacinto, cipiduzzi,
cipuddrizze, cipollacci col fiocco* (colloquial);
SERBO-CROATIAN: *hijacint;* SPANISH: *jacinto;*
TURKISH: *sümbül*

PLANT CHARACTERISTICS AND VARIETIES

Hyacinth grows among rocks and in fields
and has very fragrant, deep blue flowers.
Hyacinthus orientalis and *H. romanus* are popular
hyacinths whose bulbs are pickled in southern
Italy, but it is the grape hyacinth that is
cooked (page 176).

PLANT ORIGIN

The origin of hyacinth is uncertain, although
it appears to be indigenous to Palestine/Israel
and northward through Lebanon. The center

of origin may be southwest Asia, but the plant
was naturalized in the Mediterranean.

PLANT HISTORY

Hyacinth is a plant that was anthropomor-
phized in Greek mythology. Hyacinthus was a
handsome boy loved by Apollo, god of youth
and beauty, and Zephyrus, god of the winds.
Because Hyacinthus preferred Apollo,
Zephyrus killed the boy in a jealous rage.
Apollo transformed the boy into a blue
hyacinth so the plant's beauty and fragrance
would be an eternal reminder of the boy
Hyacinthus. Athenaeus describes bulbs, which
are probably the bulbs of hyacinth, or maybe
iris, and gives us this proverb: "a bulb will do
you no good unless you have the qualities of a
man." Outside of its use for pickling in
Greece and southern Italy, we don't know
much about the culinary history of the plant.

HYACINTH BEAN

Lablab purpurus (L.) Sweet. (syn. *L. niger*
Medik. and *Dolichos lablab* L.)
(Leguminosae-Fabaceae)
Also called lablab, Egyptian black bean,
India bean; ARABIC: *lablāb, lūbiyā ʿāfan; al-
baqla al-bārda, hurṭumān;* FRENCH: *dolique
d'Egypte, pois Indien;* ITALIAN: *dolicho, fagiolo
lablab;* SPANISH: *frijol del antibo, dólicho
lablab*

This is a very beautiful climbing herbaceous perennial plant. The edible parts are the immature seeds, which are cooked. The seeds may be white, light yellow, black or spotted, while the pod is a flattened deep purple. Today hyacinth bean is used mostly as an ornamental plant in the Americas, but it is still eaten in North Africa. The dried seeds contain cyanogenic glucosides in dangerously toxic amounts, so they must be treated with repeated boilings before they can be eaten. It is best to avoid the beans and the seeds of this plant for culinary purposes, especially if small children are about who might accidentally eat them.

PLANT ORIGIN

The hyacinth bean is thought to originate in India. Although Bianchini, Corbetta, and Pistoia say that the plant originated in tropical Africa, it rather seems to have been introduced there.

PLANT HISTORY

Hyacinth bean is quite popular in India and less so in the Mediterranean, where it is eaten mainly in North Africa. The hyacinth bean was cultivated in thirteenth-century Yemen, as we know from the Rasulid agricultural almanac that was compiled at that time. Given the archaic Arabic name for the hyacinth bean (*lablāb*), it seems likely that the Tunisian breakfast stew (*lablābī*), today made with chickpeas, may have originally been made with the hyacinth bean, although the name of the stew may derive from the Turkish word for roasted chickpea, *leblebi*.

ICE PLANT

Mesembryanthemum crystallinum L. (syn. *Cryophytum crystallinum*) (Aizoaceae)
Also called sea fig, sea marigold; ARABIC: *nabat al-thalgh*; FRENCH: *ficoïde, ficoïde cristalline, ficoïde glaciale, herbe à la glace*; ITALIAN: *erba cristallina*; SPANISH: *escarchada, algazul*

PLANT CHARACTERISTICS AND VARIETIES

In the Mediterranean, ice plant, a low-growing, creeping annual, is usually found growing along the coast, on sand dunes and in salt marshes. It is used as a substitute for spinach. The young shoots and leaves are eaten raw in salads, mostly in North Africa but also in Spain and Italy. The plant's name derives from the structure of the cells on the surface of the leaf, which makes the leaf look as if it's covered with frost.

PLANT ORIGIN

Ice plant is native to South Africa and is also found in the wild in the Mediterranean and Arabian Peninsula.

PLANT HISTORY

In his *Manuel du Jardinier* published in Paris in 1829, Louis Noisette claims that the ice plant entered Europe in 1727. It is now not uncommon to find ice plant growing in California, where it typically forms a carpetlike cover on embankments.

HOW TO GROW AND HARVEST

Sow ice plant in late summer and pick the young shoots and leaves through the winter and spring.

INDIAN PEA

Phaseolus maximus L. (Leguminosae-Fabaceae)
ARABIC: *māsh*

PLANT CHARACTERISTICS AND VARIETIES

The Indian pea is a leguminous plant with edible black grains that are traditionally cooked by the Berber tribes of Morocco and Algeria as a couscous.

JACK BEAN

Canavalia ensiformis (L.) DC.
(Leguminosae-Fabaceae)
Also called horse bean, sword bean;
ARABIC: *fūl*; French: *haricot de Madagascar, haricot sabre*; ITALIAN: *canavalia*; SPANISH: *judia sable, canavalia, judia de puerco, judia de caballo*

PLANT CHARACTERISTICS AND VARIETIES

The jack bean is a woody climbing perennial found in the tropics. The immature pods are about a foot long and are eaten the same way green beans are. In the Mediterranean the jack bean is eaten by Arabs and also by some people in Spain and in some parts of France. The white seed coat of the mature beans is said to be poisonous. The sword bean, *Canavalia gladiata* (Jacq.) DC., is related, and the names are sometimes confused.

PLANT ORIGIN

Canavalia ensiformis is a New World plant found originally in the West Indies, Brazil, Peru, and Mexico. *Canavalia gladiata* (Jacq.) DC. is native to Southeast Asia.

JAPANESE LANTERN

Physalis alkekengii L. (Solanaceae)
Also called Chinese lantern, winter cherry, strawberry tomato; ARABIC: *inab al-dīb, kākinj*; FRENCH: *coqueret du Pérou*; GREEK: *keravoulia*; ITALIAN: *alchechengi peruviano*; SPANISH: *capulí, alquequenge del Perú*; TURKISH: *kenger*

PLANT CHARACTERISTICS AND VARIETIES

The American species is called Cape gooseberry (*P. peruviana* L., syn. *P. edulis*; *P. pruinosa* L.) while the species that grows in the Mediterraean, mostly in Turkey, is *P. alkekengii* L. The tomatillo we are accustomed to seeing in supermarkets in the western United States is a member of this genus. The plant is a tall, branching perennial with sprawling vines that spread 4 feet wide. The flowers are yellowish with a green center, and the fruit are yellowish orange when ripe and are enclosed in a paper-like husk with a purplish tint. The name, lantern, alludes to the showy bladderlike calyx (fused sepals) of the mature fruit. The edible part is the ripe fruit, sometimes called a cherry, which is eaten raw or cooked. This fruit has a slightly acid taste and is smaller and sweeter than a tomatillo. In Arabia the fruit is eaten for dessert.

PLANT ORIGIN

Physalis alkekengii L. is native to Asia, while the cape gooseberry is a native of South America.

PLANT HISTORY

Dioscorides described the plant, calling it *phusalis*. The thirteenth-century Arab pharmacologist, al-Samarqandī, described the use of Japanese lantern in a lozenge used for kidney and bladder wounds. The Spanish and Italian words for the plant derive from the Arabic, *kākinj*, which in turn derives from the Sanskrit through the Persian.

HOW TO GROW AND HARVEST

The Japanese lantern is grown in the same manner as tomatoes. Plants produce the most fruit if grown in well-watered soil in hot, dry climates. Harvest the fruit when it is about to drop off the plant.

JERUSALEM ARTICHOKE
Helianthus tuberosus L. (Asteraceae-Compositae)
Also called sunchoke; ARABIC: *tirfās, ṭarṭūfa, kamāiyya balād al-Āmrīk;* FRENCH: *topinambour;* ITALIAN: *topinambur;* SPANISH: *topinambo, pataca, aguaturma;* TURKISH: *yerelması*

PLANT CHARACTERISTICS AND VARIETIES

The Jerusalem artichoke *(H. tuberosus)* or sunchoke (the two are interchangeable) is a tuber related to the sunflower. The tuberous rhizome, which looks like a knobby potato, is eaten raw or cooked and tastes similar to artichoke heart. The plant can grow to 6 feet in a sunny, dry location.

PLANT ORIGIN

The Jerusalem artichoke is native to Canada and portions of the eastern United States.

PLANT HISTORY

Jerusalem artichoke is a New World food that first entered Italy in 1617 and was grown in the Farnese garden in Rome under the name *girasole articiocco* (sunflower artichoke). The English name "Jerusalem" has long been claimed to be a corruption of the Italian word *girasole,* meaning "sunflower," but the agricultural historian Redcliffe Salaman pointed out that the name "Jerusalem" was used to refer to Jerusalem artichokes before *girasole* came to be used. He argues that "Jerusalem" is a corruption of Terneuzen, the town in Holland from which the sunchoke was first introduced to England.

The sunchoke was first introduced to France from Canada no earlier than 1607 by the lawyer and historian Marc Lescarbot and the explorer Samuel de Champlain (1567–1635). It entered Provence about the same time as it did Italy, and recipes are rarely found for sunchokes anywhere else in the Mediterranean but these two locales. The plant is known in Algeria and Tunisia as *tirfās*, an Arabic word for a North African truffle, a vegetable that the sunchoke resembles in appearance, although North Africans also once called the plant *kamāiyya balād al-Āmrīk*, American truffle. The French name, *topinambour*, comes from the name of a Brazilian tribe, and its application to this tuber has nothing to do with the origin of the plant.

HOW TO GROW AND HARVEST

The Jerusalem artichoke is a completely frost-hardy perennial and can be left in the ground through the winter. Plant the tubers 2 inches deep and 2 feet apart in the spring in fine, sandy soil. The tubers are ready to be harvested once the frost has killed off the tops, about a month after the plant flowers.

HOW TO BUY, STORE, AND PREPARE FOR COOKING

Jerusalem artichokes should be firm with unblemished skin and no spongy spots. Choose the least knobby tubers. Store them in a plastic bag in the refrigerator crisper drawer, where they will keep for up to 2 weeks. Jerusalem artichokes go well with meats and goose. Because the tubers can turn black when they are cooking, do not use an aluminum pan.

RECIPE

Topinambours en Daube
WINE-STEWED SUNCHOKES

The sunchoke, or Jerusalem artichoke, is native to Canada. It looks like a knobby potato and tastes similar to an artichoke heart. It is a good accompaniment to meats and goose. These tubers are not eaten widely in the Mediterranean, but this nice recipe from Provence is a delightful way to cook them.

2 tablespoons extra virgin olive oil
1 small onion, chopped fine
1 pound sunchokes, peeled and diced
3 garlic cloves, peeled and crushed
Bouquet garni, tied in cheesecloth, consisting of 6 sprigs each fresh parsley, thyme, and oregano
Salt and freshly ground black pepper to taste
1 cup dry white wine
1 cup water

I. In a medium nonreactive casserole, such as an enameled cast-iron one, heat the olive oil over medium heat and cook the onion until yellow, about 8 minutes, stirring frequently.

2. Add the sunchokes, garlic, and bouquet garni and season with salt and pepper. Pour in the wine and water, reduce the heat to low, cover, and simmer until tender, 45 to 50 minutes. Remove the sunchokes with a slotted ladle and serve hot.

Makes 2 to 4 servings

JEW'S MALLOW

Corchorus olitorius L. (Tiliaceae)
Also called jute, cultivated mauve
ARABIC: *mulūkhiyya*; FRENCH: *corette, méloukhia*; ITALIAN: *cibo degli ebrei, còrcora*; SPANISH: *yute*

PLANT CHARACTERISTICS AND VARIETIES

This erect annual with small yellow flowers has leaves that are mucilaginous when cut. The edible parts are the leaves and tender shoots, which are eaten cooked or raw. The tough fibrous matter in the mature stems is used for making jute rope. Jew's mallow is most popular in Egypt, but it is also eaten throughout the Levant.

PLANT ORIGIN

N. Vavilov believed that *C. olitorius* had an Indo-Chinese center of origin, which includes Burma and Assam.

PLANT HISTORY

Pliny mentions what appears to be Jew's mallow, very briefly, as a medicinal plant used in Egypt. He also tells us that Jew's mallow is eaten in Alexandria. Even today, Jew's mallow is very popular in Egypt. The ancient and medieval Jewish affinity for vegetables derives in part from Talmudic tradition, and this is recognized in the characterization of this mallow as a Jewish vegetable.

HOW TO BUY, STORE, AND PREPARE FOR COOKING

Occasionally, farmers' markets will sell fresh Jew's mallow, which they might sell under the name "okra leaf" or "meloukia." The leaves should be crisp looking, full, dark green, and fresh. Store these greens in the refrigerator crisper drawer and use them within 2 days. Middle Eastern markets may sell frozen Jew's mallow as well as dried.

RECIPE

Mulūkhiyya
JEW'S MALLOW

Jew's mallow is a green-leaved mucilaginous vegetable. Its viscous texture after cooking will remind you of okra, although the two plants are from different genera. Even though the leaf itself is tasteless, in Egypt it is so popular among farmworkers that it can be thought of as an Egyptian national vegetable.

One may encounter many different transliterations for the Arabic word *mulūkhiyya*, such as *melokheya, milookhiyya,* miloukia, mlukhiyyeh, mlukhiyyi, moulouhiyee, mouloukhia, melohkia, molokhiya, melokhiyya, and melookeya. Generally, Egyptians cook mulūkhiyya as a soup enriched with a broth of duck, goose, chicken, or rabbit and flavored with lots of garlic and spices. The fresh mulūkhiyya is usually chopped until nearly a puree with a mezzaluna or what the Egyptians call a makhrata. When the mulūkhiyya is stirred into the broth, it cooks for only a short period, until it is "suspended" in the broth, before it falls to the bottom of the pot. Do not chop the leaves before the step calling for that to be done, otherwise the viscosity of the leaves will affect the finished dish.

This vegetable is definitely an acquired taste. If you witness two Egyptians waxing poetic about mulūkhiyya, you will feel as if you're outside a shared secret.

One 4-pound rabbit, duck, or chicken, cut into 4 pieces (if using duck, remove as much fat as possible)
10 cups water
¼ teaspoon mastic grains
1 cinnamon stick
Seeds from 4 cardamom pods
1 medium onion, peeled and cut into quarters
1 bay leaf
1 teaspoon black peppercorns
2 teaspoons salt
2 pounds fresh mulūkhiyya (or ¼ pound dried), stems removed, leaves washed well and dried well
3 tablespoons extra virgin olive oil
15 garlic cloves, mashed with 2 teaspoons salt
¼ cup finely chopped fresh coriander leaves
¼ teaspoon cayenne pepper
1 loaf Arabic flatbread, toasted brown and broken into pieces

1. Place the rabbit, duck, or chicken in a stew pot and cover with water. Add the mastic, cinnamon stick, cardamom seeds, onion, bay leaf, and peppercorns. Bring the pot to just below a boil over high heat, 15 to 18 minutes, reduce the heat to very low, cover, and poach the meat or fowl until firm, about 45 minutes. Season with the salt. Remove the meat and reserve it. Strain the broth through cheesecloth and return it to the pot, saving ½ cup for the meat.

2. Bring the broth to a boil, add the mulūkhiyya, and cook, uncovered, until it remains suspended on top of the broth, 8 to 10 minutes

(20 to 30 minutes if you are using dried *mulūkhiyya*).

3. Heat the olive oil in a small skillet over medium-high heat and cook the mashed garlic until light golden, 1 to 2 minutes. Stir the mashed garlic into the broth along with the coriander and cayenne. Serve the soup immediately with the toasted Arabic bread.

Makes 6 servings

N O T E : The meat can be eaten afterward with some rice pilaf. Bake the meat with the reserved ½ cup of broth in a 375°F oven until it is light golden, about 15 minutes.

JUDAS TREE

Cercis siliquastrum L. (Leguminosae-Fabaceae)
Also called love tree; GREEK: *koutsoupia*; SPANISH: *árbol del amor, árbol de Judas, algarrobo loco*

PLANT CHARACTERISTICS AND VARIETIES

This deciduous tree can grow to 30 feet, with 3- to 4-inch-long pods. Greeks and Turks gather the pods and use them with other raw vegetables in salads. The flower buds are pickled in vinegar, and the flowers are made into batter-coated fritters.

PLANT ORIGIN

This plant is native to the Mediterranean.

PLANT HISTORY

According to many legends, and as described in Matthew 27:5, Judas hung himself from the Judas tree.

JUPITER'S BEARD

Centranthus ruber (L.) DC. (Valerianaceae)
Also called red valerian; ARABIC: *luḥiya al-rāʿā*; FRENCH: *lilas d'Espagne, valériane rouge, joubarbe*; ITALIAN: *valeriano rosso*

PLANT CHARACTERISTICS AND VARIETIES

Jupiter's beard, an annual, grows in meadows, by roadsides, and on walls. The stems of the plant can reach 3 feet and have billowing masses of fragrant tiny pink, white, or red blooms. The leaves are used in salads, omelettes and herb soups. Jupiter's beard is eaten in North Africa and southern France.

PLANT ORIGIN

Jupiter's beard is native to the Mediterranean.

KALE OR COLLARD

Brassica oleracea L. Acephala group (syn. *B. acephala*, *B. oleracea* var. *acephala* DC., includes *B. oleracea* var. *palmifolia* and *B. oleracea* var. *selensia*) (Cruciferae-Brassicaceae)
Also called borecole, black cabbage, colewort; FRENCH: *chou cavalier, chou fourrager, chou vert, chou frisé*; GREEK:

laxanou; ITALIAN: *cavolo riccio, cavolo da foraggio, cavolo cavaliera, cavolo a penne;* SERBO-CROATIAN: *kejl;* SPANISH: *berza, berza col, col caballar, col gallega, col forragera;* TURKISH: *kıvırcık lahana*

PLANT CHARACTERISTICS AND VARIETIES

Kale is a general name given to plants of the Cruciferae-Brassicaceae family that do not form heads—that is, nonheading cabbage. These plants are very hardy with tall and thick stems, very similar to the wild forms of *Brassica oleracea;* therefore, they are thought to be the earliest of the cultivated Cruciferae-Brassicaceae. The edible part is the leaf, which is cooked. Black cabbage, *cavolo nero,* is a form of kale that is eaten in Tuscany and in the regions of central Italy.

PLANT ORIGIN

See Cabbage.

PLANT HISTORY

See Cabbage.

HOW TO GROW AND HARVEST

Kale grows best in cool weather and can withstand some frost. The plants can also handle hot, dry weather better than cabbage can. Sow the seeds in May and transplant the plants in July about 2½ feet apart. The seeds can also be planted directly in the garden about ¼ inch deep and 1 inch apart in rows 2 feet apart about 3 months before the first frost date. The soil should not be too rich. In the late

winter, a top dressing of high-nitrogen fertilizer will make for lush young shoots. Once established, kale should be thinned to 2 feet apart. In the Mediterranean, kale is usually planted in the late summer. Cool weather sweetens kale, so kale is harvested in early spring or in the fall after a frost. You can start harvesting about 2 months after sowing. Harvest the larger, lower leaves first. The small leaves are the most tender and the best for cooking. Harvest the plant leaf by leaf so you don't terminate plant growth.

HOW TO BUY, STORE, AND PREPARE FOR COOKING

Kale will sweeten slightly if it is refrigerated for 4 days before you use it.

RECIPE

Zuppa di Cavolo Nero
BLACK KALE SOUP

Black kale, *cavolo nero,* is a kind of kale that is popular in central Italy. It is called *toscano* in Tuscany. In this Tuscan soup, the black kale, and it is not actually black, just very dark green, is a natural accompaniment to the substantial texture of the potatoes and beans and the flavors of the aromatic herbs. For me, this is a very warming wintertime dish, and I'll use canned tomatoes if I have to. The *trito* referred to in Step 1 is the same as the French *mirepoix,* a mix-

ture of very finely chopped vegetables that
are fried in oil or butter to become the foundation of the dish being prepared.

6 tablespoons extra virgin olive oil, plus extra
  for drizzling
1 celery stalk, chopped fine
1 small onion, chopped fine
1 carrot, chopped fine
10 large fresh basil leaves, chopped fine
3 ripe tomatoes (about 1 pound), peeled, seeded,
  and chopped fine
1 tablespoon fresh thyme leaves
2 boiling potatoes (about ¾ pound), peeled and
  cut into pieces
¾ pound black kale (or regular kale), washed
  well and sliced into crosswise strips
⅓ cup dried borlotti or red kidney beans, picked
  over and rinsed
2 quarts warm water
Salt to taste
4 to 6 slices toasted black bread, rubbed with a
  cut garlic clove

1. Heat the olive oil in a casserole or soup pot,
over medium-high heat and cook the *trito* of
celery, onion, carrot, and basil until almost
soft, about 8 minutes. Add the tomatoes and
cook them until they are somewhat dry, about
20 minutes. Add the thyme and potatoes.
Cook the potatoes until they turn color
slightly, 4 to 5 minutes. Add the kale and
beans.

2. Reduce the heat to low and cook the kale
until it has wilted, 8 to 10 minutes. Add the
water and salt, turn the heat to high, and, once

small bubbles begin to form, reduce the heat
to very low or use a heat diffuser. Cook the
soup until the potatoes and beans are tender,
about 3 hours. Serve with toasted black bread.

Makes 6 servings

KOHLRABI
Brassica oleracea L. Gongylodes group
(syn. *B. caulorapa, B. oleracea* var. *gongylodes*)
(Cruciferae-Brassicaceae)
FRENCH: *chou rave;* ITALIAN: *cavolo rapa;*
SERBO-CROATIAN: *koraba;* SPANISH: *col rábano;*
TURKISH: *şalgam gibi köklü lahana*

PLANT CHARACTERISTICS AND VARIETIES
The edible part of this plant is the enlarged
stem or corm, a turniplike part of the stem
that is just about ground level. The corm is
eaten raw or cooked, as are the leaves. There
are two varieties of kohlrabi: one is white or
light green, and the other is purplish. The
plant grows quickly and matures in 40 to 70
days. It can withstand drought better than
other Cruciferae-Brassicaceae. Kohlrabi is not
a common vegetable in the Mediterranean. It
is eaten mostly by northern Italians.

PLANT ORIGIN
Kohlrabi developed from cabbage and is
thought to have originated in northern
Europe in the fifteenth century. K. F.
Thompson, on the other hand, argues that
kohlrabi was possibly known by the Romans.
He implies that the plant originated in the

Mediterranean. By the first century A.D. the Romans did have a loose-headed cabbage grown for its soft stem that might have been a precursor to kohlrabi.

PLANT HISTORY

A vegetable similar to kohlrabi was described by Pliny in A.D. 70 as "a Brassica in which the stem is thin just above the roots, but swells out in the region that bears the leaves, which are few and slender." Some botanists thought this was a reference to kohlrabi, while V. R. Boswell thought Pliny's description applied to the cauliflower. In any case, kohlrabi came late to Italy, in 1554, according to the Italian botanist Matthioli, although the botanist-traveler Leonhardus Rauwolffud records that kohlrabi was being grown in the gardens of Aleppo and Tripoli in the Levant in 1573.

HOW TO GROW AND HARVEST

Like other members of the cabbage family, kohlrabi likes cool weather. The plant grows quickly. Sow kohlrabi seeds about ¼ inch deep about 2 months before the first frost date or after the last frost date. Thin the seedlings to 4 inches apart in rows spaced at least 2 feet apart. The soil should be kept fertile and moist. Harvest by pulling the whole plant when the bulbous corm is about 2 inches in diameter; the corms are sweeter and more tender at this stage. When they get larger, they are woody and fibrous.

HOW TO BUY, STORE, AND PREPARE FOR COOKING

Look for kohlrabi that still has its leaves attached. Inspect the leaves, which are delicious, and choose ones that are fresh and crisp. Store kohlrabi in the refrigerator and use the leaves within 2 days and the kohlrabi corm within a week. Remove the leaves so only the bulb part is left, peel the corm, and cook the two separately.

RECIPE

Cavoli Rapa all Chietina
KOHLRABI CHIETI STYLE

This recipe comes from the town of Chieti in the Abruzzi region of central Italy. If you have never tried kohlrabi, I think you will be pleasantly surprised on two counts. First, it's a very easy vegetable to prepare for cooking. Second, it has a very nice and substantial texture, and a mild taste that is pleasing to the palate.

One 1¾-pound kohlrabi, peeled and cut into ½-inch-thick slices
¼ cup extra virgin olive oil
Freshly squeezed juice from 2 lemons
6 tablespoons fresh parsley leaves, chopped fine
Salt to taste
6 cups olive oil, for frying

FOR THE BATTER:

3 large eggs

2 tablespoons unsalted butter, melted

½ cup all-purpose unbleached flour

½ cup milk

Salt to taste

6 lemon wedges

1. Bring a large saucepan full of lightly salted water to a boil and cook the kohlrabi slices until they are tender but firm, 25 to 30 minutes. Drain and place them in a bowl with the olive oil, lemon juice, parsley, and salt. Marinate for 1 hour at room temperature.

2. Preheat the olive oil to 375°F in a deep fryer or an 8-inch saucepan fitted with a basket insert.

3. Meanwhile, make the batter. Beat the eggs with the butter. Stir in the flour, pour in the milk, and stir until the consistency is like that of a crêpe batter. Season with salt. Remove the kohlrabi from the marinade and discard the marinade. Dip the kohlrabi slices in the batter, letting any excess drip off, and fry until golden brown, about 4 minutes. Serve hot with lemon wedges. Let the frying oil cool completely before straining it and saving for future use.

Makes 6 servings

LAMB'S LETTUCE

Valerianella locusta (L.) Laterrade em. Betcke (syn. *V. olitoria; V. eriocarpa* Desv.) (Valerianaceae)

Also called corn salad, mâche; Arabic: *samma;* French: *doucette, valérianelle potagé, laitue de brebis, mâche;* Italian: *raperonzolo, valerianella, saleggia, agnellino, dolcetta, gallinette, galinella, lattughella;* Spanish: *valeriana, lechuga de campo, hierba de loa canónigos*

PLANT CHARACTERISTICS AND VARIETIES

There are about 30 species of *Valerianella* in Europe and in Turkey. *V. locusta* and *V. eriocarpa* (known as Italian corn salad) are the most common, the latter being grown mostly in Italy. Lamb's lettuce looks like a weed, and the smooth oval leaves form small rosettes. The leaves, which are so delicate they seem to melt in the mouth, are used raw in salads and cooked in omelettes. *Valerianella carinata* is used in rural Tuscany in salads, where it is called *pancagiolo* or *pancagiotto.*

PLANT ORIGIN

One theory suggests Holland or northern France as a center of origin, while another suggests southern Europe.

PLANT HISTORY

Lamb's lettuce was frequently mentioned in older treatises on food plants, but it is not too commonly found today.

Lamb's lettuce should be sown thickly in full sun in July, August, or September in well-fertilized and well-drained soil, and sown again in the spring. Cover the seeds with a thin ¼-inch layer of sand. The plant is harvested in late winter or early spring. Single leaves can be picked off the plant for use in salads.

HOW TO BUY, STORE, AND PREPARE FOR COOKING

Store lamb's lettuce in a plastic bag in the crisper drawer of the refrigerator for up to 3 weeks. Do not wash the leaves until you are ready to use them. Rinse them several times to remove grit and sand.

RECIPE

Insalata di Lattughella
LAMB'S LETTUCE SALAD

This salad is popular in northern Italy, where one finds a wide use of various greens in both salads and soups. Lamb's lettuce is a pleasant-tasting salad green that is very much enhanced by this dressing, which contains anchovies.

6 tablespoons extra virgin olive oil

2 tablespoons white wine vinegar or sherry vinegar

1 tablespoon freshly squeezed lemon juice

2 garlic cloves, chopped very fine

2 salted anchovy fillets, rinsed and chopped very fine

Salt and freshly ground black pepper to taste

1 pound lamb's lettuce, washed well, dried well, and ripped into small pieces

Combine the olive oil, vinegar, lemon juice, garlic, and anchovies and season with salt and pepper. Toss with the lamb's lettuce in a serving bowl and serve.

Makes 4 to 6 servings

LEEK
Allium ampeloprasum L. Porrum group (syn. *A. porrum* L.) (Liliaceae)
ARABIC: *kurrāth, kurrāth rūmy, kurrāt, sallābas*; FRENCH: *poireau, porreau*; GREEK: *prassa, prason*; ITALIAN: *porro, poretta*; SERBO-CROATIAN: *poriluk, praziluk*; SPANISH: *ajo porro, ajo puerro*; TURKISH: *pırasa*

PLANT CHARACTERISTICS AND VARIETIES

The leek was once a wild, weedy, biennial plant that grew from southern Europe and North Africa through the Middle East to the Ukraine. The modern leek is not known in the wild. The flowering stems can reach 6 feet tall, and the flower head, called an umbel, is white, pink, or dark red. The edible parts are the pseudostem and leaves, which are eaten either cooked or raw.

Many varieties of leeks are grown, differing in leaf color, hardiness, and the degree of bulbing at the stem base. Kurrat *(A. kurrat)* is an old variety of leek cultivated in Egypt, grown for its leaves rather than for its stem. Some varieties are unique to particular areas of the Mediterranean. For example, *A. melitense* is native to Malta, and *A. hemisphericum* is typical of the island of Lampedusa off Sicily. In Algeria a kind of leek called onion weed or three-cornered leek *(A. triquetrum)* is eaten. Another variety, *A. paniculatum,* is added to herbal cheeses made in the eastern part of Anatolia. Some Turkish villagers gather *A. atroviolaceum,* which they call *yabani sarmısak,* in the wild. In North America, ramps or wild leeks *(A. tricoccum)* can be used in Mediterranean dishes calling for wild leeks or green onions.

Leeks are common in the Mediterranean and eastward to Iran and Tadzikistan. N. Vavilov suggested the Near East and Mediterranean as the center of origin for the leek. The early Bronze Age deposits at Jericho have yielded the bulbs of leeks along with a variety of grain seeds.

The ancient Egyptians referred to leeks as food and used the plant medicinally during the I Dynasty (3200 B.C.). Leeks are also mentioned in the Bible in the account of the exodus of the Israelites from Egypt in 1500 B.C., although those references may be to fenugreek. The Romans used a perennial form of leek, and Pliny describes the wild leek as being used medicinally. Pliny also described Ariccia in central Italy as being famous for its leeks. The Emperor Nero is said to have eaten leek soup every day to make his voice sonorous for delivering orations. Charlemagne ordered leeks to be cultivated in the gardens of his domain in the ninth century. In the Middle Ages leeks were cultivated, particularly in France, around Arras. In Italy leeks are common in the northern part of the country, but not too much in the south. Throughout the Middle Ages leeks were believed to be an erotic stimulant that increased the sperm count and stimulated desire, especially when they were prepared with honey, sesame, and almonds.

Leeks need a long growing season and grow best in a rich, well-drained soil with lots of nitrogen and organic matter. Leeks are harvested from fall to spring. Seeds can be sown indoors in midwinter and planted outdoors in May in V-shaped trenches. The plants should be well watered. Spacing leeks widely when planting them makes for a thicker stem. As the leeks grow, mound the soil from along the sides of the trench around the stems to blanch them white. The soil should be kept moist. Harvest leeks as needed, before the ground freezes or,

Leek

ALTHOUGH LEEKS ARE POPULARLY USED IN THE COOKING OF THE MEDITERRANEAN, THEY MOSTLY APPEAR AS PART OF SOME PREpared dish—that is, when they're not being used for leek soup, which is found in Spain, Italy, the Balkans, Greece, and Turkey. In the Balkans, as well as Greece and Turkey, a number of recipes combine leeks with rice in dishes that are served at room temperature, as well as au gratin. Turkish Jews are known for their "leek-burgers," or *keftes de prassa y carne*, a burger, literally, made with finely chopped leeks, ground beef or lamb, mashed potatoes, and egg.

for fall-sown leeks, before the ground becomes too hot the following summer.

HOW TO BUY, STORE, AND PREPARE FOR COOKING

Home-grown leeks can be stored in the ground where they are growing. Leeks can also be stored in a root cellar. Supermarket leeks are usually sold in bunches of three. When buying leeks, look for straight stems with a white end that is not very bulbous. Avoid leeks with blemished or ripped greens or split bulbs. Store leeks in the refrigerator, untrimmed, for up to a week.

As leeks grow and push up through the soil, dirt can collect in between the leaves, so you must wash leeks thoroughly. Split the leek in half lengthwise and wash in between each leaf, or cut the white stem end in quarters, leaving the leaves attached, and wash under running water, separating and cleaning the leaves with your fingers.

RECIPES

Tarte aux Poireaux
LEEK TART

This dish is not only found in Provence, but throughout France, where it is sometimes called a *flamiche*. I ate this tart once as a first course and thought it was very nice. Leeks cooked in cream is a favorite of mine, and with those Provençal touches such as olive oil and herbs like thyme, this recipe is all the more delectable.

FOR THE DOUGH

1 cup all-purpose unbleached flour (about 5½ ounces)

6 tablespoons (¾ stick) cold unsalted butter, diced

½ teaspoon salt

1 medium egg

1 tablespoon ice water

FOR THE FILLING:

1 tablespoon extra virgin olive oil

1 tablespoon unsalted butter

2 pounds leeks, white and very light green part only, trimmed, split lengthwise, washed well of grit, and chopped

1 garlic clove, chopped fine

2 tablespoons finely chopped fresh parsley leaves

½ teaspoon dried thyme

Salt and freshly ground black pepper to taste

1 tablespoon freshly grated Parmigiano-Reggiano cheese

3 large eggs, beaten

1 cup heavy cream

Pinch of freshly grated nutmeg

1. Make the dough. In a medium bowl, knead the flour, butter, and salt together with a fork until crumbly, like oatmeal. Alternatively, mix the ingredients in a food processor in bursts. Incorporate the egg, trying to handle it as little as possible. Bind the dough with the ice water, roll it into a ball, wrap it in wax paper, and refrigerate it for 1 to 2 hours.

2. Preheat the oven to 425°F. Roll the dough out on a floured work surface until it is a little larger than a 9-inch tart or cake pan. Add flour occasionally to help with the rolling out. Transfer the sheet of dough to the pan and fit it around the bottom and sides. Any pieces of dough that break off can be used to patch the pastry or form the sides. Prick the pastry all over the bottom with a toothpick. Blind bake the dough by covering it with aluminum foil, placing a cup of dry beans in the center, and baking the dough until crispy golden, about 10 minutes. Take the pastry from the oven, remove the foil and beans, and let the pastry cool. Reduce the oven temperature to 400°F.

3. Heat the olive oil and butter in a large skillet over medium-high heat. Once the butter has melted, cook the leeks, garlic, parsley, thyme, salt, and pepper until the leeks are soft, about 10 minutes, stirring. Stir in the cheese.

4. Transfer the leek mixture to the tart and spread it around evenly. Beat the eggs with the cream and nutmeg. Pour the cream over the leeks and bake the tart until the top is golden with a few black specks on the edges of the protruding pieces of leek, about 20 minutes. Serve hot or warm.

Makes 6 servings

Gateau aux Poireaux
LEEK GRATIN

This quichelike dish is a typical lunch preparation that you might imagine eating outdoors in a small village in Provence. It's quite delightful, if a bit rich. Serve it with a green salad.

2 tablespoons extra virgin olive oil

3 pounds leeks, white part only, trimmed, washed
   well of grit, and chopped

¾ pound smoked bacon, chopped

3 shallots, chopped fine

¼ cup finely chopped fresh parsley leaves

1 tablespoon fresh thyme leaves or 1 teaspoon
   dried thyme

1 bay leaf, crumbled

3 large eggs

¾ cup heavy cream

¾ cup milk

Salt and freshly ground black pepper to taste

1. Heat the olive oil in a large skillet over medium-high heat and cook the leeks until soft, about 8 minutes, stirring frequently.

2. Meanwhile, in another large skillet, cook the bacon over medium-low heat, until almost crispy, about 30 minutes. Drain, saving the fat for another use, and set the bacon aside.

3. Stir the bacon, shallots, parsley, thyme, and bay leaf together in the skillet with the leeks and cook for 1 to 2 minutes. Remove from the heat and let cool. Stir in the eggs, cream, and milk. Season with salt and pepper.

4. Preheat the oven to 425°F. Pour the leek and egg mixture into a lightly greased baking dish and bake until the top is golden and slightly crispy looking, about 35 minutes. Serve hot or warm.

Makes 6 servings

Juha od Poriluka
LEEK AND POTATO SOUP

Leeks, onions, and potatoes are all favorite vegetables in Croatia, and in this recipe they come together in a goose and/or duck-based broth called *juha od poriluka.* After the leeks are cooked, it is probably easier to liquefy them in a blender rather than pass them through a food mill or blend them in a food processor. If you use canned chicken broth instead of home-made for this recipe, pay attention to how salty the soup is and adjust your seasoning accordingly.

¼ cup (½ stick) unsalted butter

1½ pounds leeks, trimmed, split in half lengthwise, washed well of grit, and chopped

2 large onions, chopped

6 cups goose or duck broth (preferably) or chicken
   broth (preferably homemade)

Salt and freshly ground black pepper to taste

¾ pound potatoes, peeled and cut into small dice

½ cup sour cream

1. Melt the butter in a casserole or large skillet over medium heat. Add the leeks and onions, reduce the heat to low, and simmer gently, stirring occasionally, until the onions are translucent, about 45 minutes.

2. Add the broth and cook the leeks until they are very tender, about 1 hour. Strain the leeks, reserving the stock. Put the leeks in a blender in batches with a cup of broth each time so the blender can work properly. Run the

blender until the leeks are liquefied, about 1 minute of blending at the highest speed. Transfer the pureed leeks and broth to a large saucepan, season with salt and pepper, and bring to a boil. Add the potatoes and cook until tender, about 15 minutes. Correct the seasoning, add the sour cream to each individual serving bowl, ladle in some soup, and serve hot.

Makes 6 servings

Terbiyeli Zeytinyağlı Pırasa
LEEKS IN LEMON-AND-EGG SAUCE

This Turkish preparation is one of the so-called olive oil foods typically found in both Turkey and Greece. Usually a vegetable is cooked in lots of olive oil and then served at room temperature. But here there is the added attraction of a lemon-and-egg sauce (*avgolemono,* as the Greeks call it), which makes this leek dish particularly delightful.

1¼ pounds leeks, white and light green part only, trimmed, split lengthwise, washed well of grit, and cut into 4-inch lengths
¼ cup extra virgin olive oil
¼ cup water
1 teaspoon salt
¾ teaspoon sugar
1 large egg, beaten
2½ tablespoons freshly squeezed lemon juice

1. Put the leeks, olive oil, and water into a wide skillet. Turn the heat to medium-low,

sprinkle on the salt and sugar, and cook the leeks until they are tender and soft, 25 to 35 minutes, turning them so they cook evenly.

2. Beat the egg and lemon juice together in a small bowl. Turn the heat off under the skillet containing the leeks and stir in the egg-lemon mixture. Let the contents cool in the skillet, then transfer the leeks to a serving platter and serve at room temperature.

Makes 4 servings

LENTIL
Lens culinaris Medikus (syn*. L. esculenta; Ervum lens;* or *Vicia lens*)
(Fabaceae–Leguminosae)
ARABIC: ʿ*adas;* FRENCH: *lentille;* GREEK: *phake, fakes;* ITALIAN: *lenticchia;* SERBO-CROATIAN: *leča;* SPANISH: *lenteja;* TURKISH: *mercimek*

PLANT CHARACTERISTICS AND VARIETIES
The lentil is an annual vetch with small flowers that are usually white and about ½ inch long but can also be mauve. The edible parts are the immature pods and sprouted seeds, which are eaten raw or cooked. Lentils come in short and flat pealike pods with about one or two seeds. Lentils usually accompany wheat and barley cultivation throughout the Mediterranean.

In the supermarket one will find three or four varieties of lentils. Red lentils (although orange in color) are usually used for soups since they disintegrate easily. Brown lentils are used for side dishes in the Mediterranean, especially those served with duck, goose, sausages, lamb, or mutton. Green lentils are cooked and used in salads served at room temperature. The so-called du Puy and beluga are black lentils used in salads and fancied by restaurant chefs.

PLANT ORIGIN

The lentil is derived from the wild lentil, *L. orientalis* (Boiss.) Hand.-Mazz., found in Greece and to the east toward the southern Caucasus and northern Iraq. It is thought that all four species of the wild lentil are native to the eastern Mediterranean, as is the cultivated lentil. N. Vavilov suggests northwestern India, Tadzhikistan, Uzbekistan, and western Tien Shan Province in China as the center of origin of the lentil, although he recognizes Asia Minor as a secondary center. Bianchini, Corbetta, and Pistoia incorrectly state that the lentil is not known in the wild state. The lentil does exist in the wild state, but the cultivated species differs in having an indehiscent pod, because of a single recessive gene, and nondormant seeds (meaning that the plant can germinate). But, it should be recognized that the question of lentil domestication and cultivation is vigorously debated in the academic community and conclusions have not yet been reached.

PLANT HISTORY

The earliest archeological dating of lentils is from the Paleolithic and Mesolithic layers of Franchthi Cave in Greece (13,000 to 9,500 years ago), from the end of the Mesolithic era at Mureybit and Tell Abu Hureya in Syria, and about 8000 B.C. in the Jericho area of Palestine. Other remains come from Çayönü, Turkey, dated at 6700 B.C., and many other sites in the Middle East and Near East.

The lentil was an important crop in ancient times. The size of its seed has slowly increased since then. The lentil is a plant associated with the Old World agricultural revolution in prehistoric times and was domesticated along with einkorn and emmer wheats, barley, pea, and flax. The plant also spread with Neolithic agriculture to Greece and Bulgaria. Then it spread, with wheat and barley, into the Bronze Age agriculture of the Near East and Mediterranean. The lentil played a role with the Jews, as we know from the story of Esau, who gave up his birthright for a dish of lentils (Genesis 25:30–34). The ancient Greeks very much enjoyed lentils, especially in soups. Aristophanes said, "You, who dare insult lentil soup, sweetest of delicacies." The Greeks also made lentils into bread. Pliny describes the growing of lentils from seed and the varieties of the plant. He mentions its medicinal properties and the numerous ways of boiling or otherwise preparing lentils for use in various remedies. The Roman writers Juvenal and Martial both describe a lentil dish that was eaten by the poor called *conchis*, in which lentils were cooked with their pods. Apicius recorded several recipes for lentils. In the sixth century, Anthimus wrote that lentils should be cooked slowly, and, once they are cooked, a little vinegar should be added for

Lentils

LENTILS ARE ONE OF THOSE FOREVER POPULAR LEGUMES THAT ONE ENCOUNTERS EVERYWHERE IN THE MEDITERRANEAN. IN Italy, lentils are often married to meat and sausage dishes such as the famous preparation from Bologna known as *zampone*, stuffed pig's trotter, which is usually served with lentils. Lentils are also a traditional accompaniment to the thick pork sausage called *cotechino* that is often found in the frozen food section of Italian markets in the United States. In Lombardy, cooks love to make a *minestra di riso e lenticchie*, rice and lentil soup. The French aren't as wild about lentils as the Italians are, but they still have some memorable dishes, such as *lentilles au petit salé*, lentils cooked in water with carrots, a clove-studded onion, and garlic before the lentils are fried with lean salt pork. And French-influenced restaurants everywhere can't resist serving lentil salad dressed with olive oil, preferably made with those little black lentils called beluga, which conjure up the image of caviar. As we pass through the Balkans, we don't encounter many lentils—they're just not eaten there as frequently as other legumes are—but by the time we get to Greece and Turkey, we start to see lots of sumptuous lentil soups made into creamy velouté-like broths laced with olive oil and perhaps sprinkled with a little ground cumin and fresh lemon juice.

flavor, along with Syrian sumac, olive oil, coriander seeds, and some salt.

HOW TO GROW AND HARVEST

One to 2 weeks before the last spring frost, sow lentils about 1 inch deep and 4 inches apart in well-drained soil. The lentil can grow in poor, sandy soil, too. Harvest lentils as you would dry beans. After harvesting the pods, leave the lentils in their pods until you are ready to use them.

HOW TO BUY, STORE, AND PREPARE FOR COOKING

Fresh lentils can occasionally be found at farmers' markets, but most lentils are sold in the dried form. Lentils do not need to be soaked before cooking, although you may want to pick through them for stones and rinse them. Fresh lentils should be cooked soon, while dried lentils can be stored in a jar in the pantry cabinet.

Lentejas de Monasterio
MONASTERY-STYLE LENTILS

This Andalusian lentil preparation is said to be typical of the way the friars at the monastery cook lentils. You must use brown lentils in this recipe. Be careful that you do not overcook them, because they will disintegrate. I assure you that although the recipe looks awfully simple, it's quite delicious and goes well with roast chicken or rabbit.

1 pound dried brown lentils (2 cups), picked
over and rinsed
½ cup extra virgin olive oil
½ cup dry white wine
1 medium onion, coarsely chopped
2 carrots, cut into quarters
Bouquet garni, tied with string, consisting of 2
sprigs each fresh basil, parsley, mint, and rose-
mary
Salt and freshly ground black pepper to taste

I. Place the lentils in a medium saucepan and cover by several inches with lightly salted cold water. Bring the pot to a boil and cook the lentils until tender, 20 to 30 minutes, checking them occasionally. Drain and set them aside.

2. Meanwhile, heat the olive oil in a medium skillet over medium heat and add the wine, onion, carrots, and bouquet garni. Cook until the carrots are tender, about 30 minutes. Mix the carrots and onions with the lentils, season with salt and pepper, and serve hot.

Makes 4 to 5 servings

Olla amb Llentilles
LENTIL STEW

This earthy Catalonian stew made of lentils is given body by the potatoes, color by the Swiss chard, and spice by the saffron. It is particularly nice served with pork, although you can certainly eat it as a main course along with a green salad and some bread. If you would like this dish to be more of a soup, use 5 cups of water. If you would rather all the water were absorbed, then use 4 cups, which will give you a dense stew.

1 pound dried green lentils (2 cups), picked over
and rinsed
¼ cup extra virgin olive oil
½ pound Swiss chard stems, white part only,
chopped (about 1½ cups)
2 teaspoons salt
6 ounces Swiss chard leaves, cut into strips, then
cut again crosswise
8 small new potatoes (about ¾ pound), peeled
½ teaspoon saffron threads, crumbled
5 cups water
¼ cup uncooked medium-grain rice

I. Place the lentils in a strainer and soak them in cold water to cover for 10 minutes. Drain. Heat the olive oil in a large saucepan or casserole over medium heat and add the Swiss chard stems and salt. Cook until the stems are soft, about 10 minutes, stirring occasionally. Add the Swiss chard leaves, potatoes, saffron, and water. Cook over medium heat until the pot reaches a boil, 6 to 7 minutes, reduce the heat to low, and cook until the potatoes are still a bit resistant when pierced by a skewer, about 15 minutes.

2. Transfer the drained lentils to the pot and cook until *al dente,* about 50 minutes. Add the rice, push it down into the liquid, cover, and cook until the rice is tender, about 15 minutes. Serve hot.

Makes 4 to 6 servings

LENTILS WITH SCALLIONS AND CORIANDER LEAVES

This lentil dish is inspired by the cooking one finds in Haute-Provence, France, as well as the Piedmont region of northern Italy, which is across the border from France. These lentils are a magnificent accompaniment to whole boiled *cotechino* sausage or roast duck. The kind of lentil called for here is a deep green or nearly black lentil that is more readily found in a gourmet shop or from a greengrocer.

1 pound (2 cups) dried black lentils (du Puy or beluga), picked over and rinsed
Salt to taste
¼ cup extra virgin olive oil
¼ cup finely diced pancetta (optional)
4 scallions, chopped
3 tablespoons finely chopped fresh coriander leaves
Freshly ground black pepper to taste

1. Place the lentils in a large saucepan and cover them with water by several inches. Turn the heat to high and bring the pot to a boil, adding some salt. Once the water reaches a boil, reduce the heat to medium and cook the lentils until they are between al dente and tender, about 35 minutes. Drain.

2. In a medium skillet over medium-high heat, heat the olive oil and pancetta, if you are using it. Add the scallions and cook them until they are soft, about 5 minutes, stirring occasionally. Pour in the reserved lentils and cook them until flavorful, about 5 minutes. Sprinkle in the coriander and black pepper. Stir to mix well and serve hot.

Makes 6 servings

Ezo Gelin Çorbası
LENTIL AND MINT SOUP

In Turkey, soups are favorite preparations during the winter. One forgets how cold it gets in the Mediterranean. These soul-satisfying soups are quite perfect for warming up, feeling good, and exorcising that piercing chill. Turkish cooks think of red lentils as "soup" lentils because they disintegrate rapidly. This recipe is known as the bride's soup because it is the soup made for the soon-to-be married young maiden. In this recipe the red lentils are balanced by the earthy taste of cracked wheat and the mellow hint of mint.

½ pound (1 cup) dried red lentils, picked over and rinsed
2 quarts vegetable or veal and chicken broth (preferably homemade)
1 medium-large onion, grated
¼ cup coarse or medium bulgur, rinsed
1 tablespoons tomato paste, diluted in ¼ cup water
¼ cup (½ stick) unsalted butter
Salt to taste
1 teaspoon paprika
1 tablespoon dried mint

I. Put the lentils, broth, onion, bulgur, diluted tomato paste, butter, and salt into a large saucepan. Bring to a very gentle boil over high heat, about 5 minutes, then reduce the heat to very low and cook the lentils and bulgur until they are tender and the soup has a creamy consistency, about 1 hour. Stir in the paprika and mint, cook 5 more minutes, and serve.

Makes 4 to 6 servings

LETTUCE
Lactuca sativa L. (including var. *longifolia* Lam. [syn. *L. sativa* var. *acephala*], var. *capitata*, var. *crispa*) (Asteraceae-Compositae)

ARABIC: *khaṣṣ, khaṣṣ wariq, salāṭa*; FRENCH: *laitue pommée, laitue romaine, laitue lombard, laitue à couper, chinchon*; GREEK: *marouli* (romaine); ITALIAN: *lattuga; lattuga di taglio, lattuga romana, lattuga a cappuccio, lattuga a testa*; SERBO-CROATIAN: *salata*; SPANISH: *lechuga; lechuga romana, lechuga par cortar, lechuga de hojas, lechuguino, lechuga acogollada, lechuga arrepollada*; TURKISH: *salata, kıvırcık salata; marul* (Aksaray Province)

Lactuca indica L. (Indian lettuce): ARABIC: *khaṣṣ al-hindī*; FRENCH: *laitue d'Inde*; SPANISH: *lechuga de l'India*

Lactuca inermis Forsk.: ARABIC: *qāt al-ruᶜyān*

Lactuca perennis L. (perennial lettuce): FRENCH: *laitue vivace, laurige* (Haute-Provence), *sandrau* (Roya Valley, Provence)

Lactuca viminea subsp. *viminea* (syn. *Scariola viminea* [L.] F. W. Schmidt): TURKISH: *kedi çıtlığı, çukur çıtlığı* (Aksaray Province)

PLANT CHARACTERISTICS AND VARIETIES
Although there are hundreds of varieties of lettuce, taxonomists recognize three main kinds of lettuce (some taxonomists mention four): head lettuce (var. *capitata*), which

includes crisphead types of lettuce such as iceberg lettuce and tender lettuces such as Boston head, butterhead, or bibb lettuce with their floppy leaves; romaine lettuce (var. *longifolia*), favored in the Mediterranean; and leaf lettuce (var. *crispa*), also called looseleaf or cutting lettuce, which forms a rosette of frilly or curled leaves without a head. The iceberg lettuce sold in supermarkets is not the true iceberg lettuce, which has a crisp heart and light green leaves, although it is a crisphead lettuce. Romaine lettuce is the most upright of the lettuces.

Lettuce is used almost exclusively as a salad plant, although there are Mediterranean recipes calling for lettuce to be added to soup or used as a food wrapper in the manner of a grape leaf. There are many wild lettuce varieties. Modern commercial lettuces are bred for resistance to disease and bolting, as well as for different leaf shapes and colors.

In the Mediterranean four less common varieties of lettuce are eaten; that is, they are eaten to a lesser extent than those lettuces already mentioned. Indian lettuce (*Lactuca indica* L.) is eaten only by the Egyptians, cooked, and a few other eastern Arabs. *Lactuca inermis* Forsk. is also eaten in the Arab world. Perennial lettuce is eaten in salads, soups, omelettes, and tortes in the Roya Valley of Provence. *Lactuca viminea* is gathered in the wild for use in salads in parts of Anatolia.

PLANT ORIGIN

Lactuca sativa is one component of a group of four species within *Lactuca,* the others being *L. serriola, L. virosa,* and *L. saligna.* All of these varieties are native to the Mediterranean. Botanists surmise that cultivated lettuce developed from the wild species *L. serriola* L., which grows in a wide-ranging area, from Asia to North Africa to northern Europe. The origin of cultivated lettuce is still uncertain.

PLANT HISTORY

The Latin name *lactuca* refers to the milky sap that runs from lettuce. The ancient Egyptians are thought to have cultivated lettuce around 4500 B.C. Because of its milky juice that resembles semen, lettuce was sacred to the ancient Egyptian god of fertility Min, and aphrodisiacal powers were attributed to this vegetable. In the *Ebers Codex* (about 1550 B.C.), lettuce is mentioned often in medicinal contexts. Several paintings in Egyptian tombs seem to depict a kind of romaine lettuce. The plant may have first been used for its seed oil rather than as a salad ingredient. Lettuce is mentioned as early as Hippocrates for its so-called soporific properties. Herodotus reports that the Persian kings served lettuce at royal banquets. Theophrastus describes a variety of lettuces, saying that the white variety of lettuce was the sweeter and more tender. He describes three kinds—the flat stalk, the round stalk, and the Laconian, the last having a leaf like that of the cardoon. He reports that lettuce was cooked in a pan. Athenaeus relates how various Greek writers looked down on lettuce because it was perceived as an antiaphrodisiac, although it was considered wholesome and nutritious as food. Lettuce also plays a role in several Greek myths, where it was associated with male impotence.

Later, lettuce was grown by Roman farmers and is mentioned by Pliny, Columella, and other Roman authors. Pliny devotes a long section to the medicinal uses of various lettuces. Roman farmers are said to have popularized romaine lettuce, called *cos* because they found it growing on the Greek island of Kos in the Aegean Sea. The Romans also served lettuce as an appetizer.

In the Middle Ages, fewer forms of lettuce seem to have been known, but lettuce was grown regularly in medieval gardens, as we know from various herbals and cookery books such as the fourteenth-century *Ménagier de Paris.* St. Hildegard of Bingen (1098–1179) mentions lettuce as a medicinal herb in her writings. Romaine lettuce was introduced to Italy and France in the sixteenth century as Roman lettuce, and lettuce was introduced to the New World shortly after it was discovered.

Mediterranean cultivars are mostly butterhead lettuces, while in the United States the predominant lettuces are the crispheads. The first definite evidence of the existence of head lettuce was in 1543.

HOW TO GROW AND HARVEST

Lettuce grows well in cool weather in nitrogen-rich, well-drained soil. Throughout the growing season the soil should be kept continually moist. Seeds germinate in cool conditions and can be planted in early spring and fall. Late spring and summer crops can be planted directly outdoors and thinned as they grow. Romaine lettuce takes longer to mature than leaf or head lettuce does, so it is best to plant it in the late summer or fall when it has time to form a large head. Leaf lettuce is the easiest to grow. Plant the seeds in the early spring and again in the early fall.

Butterhead lettuce seeds should be planted in the early spring and again in the fall. Fall-sown seeds will mature just before the beginning of very cold weather, which lettuce generally tolerates. Thin the plants to about 12 inches apart. Plants sown in the spring benefit from being grown in raised beds, which will warm up faster, encouraging the seeds to germinate. Harvest lettuce as soon as the plants can be thinned and are large enough to eat. Pull the whole plant if you expect to use it, or snap off individual leaves as needed.

HOW TO BUY, STORE, AND PREPARE FOR COOKING

All lettuces and salad greens should be fresh looking and crisp. Avoid heads of lettuce that have wilted or yellowed leaves or slimy spots. Lettuce is a highly perishable vegetable and should be refrigerated in the supermarket or displayed under cool shade or on ice in a farmer's market. Examine the outer leaves first, because if those leaves are fresh, then the whole head is fresh. Although it is best to eat lettuce the day you harvest or buy it, if that is

Lettuce

LETTUCE IS THE QUINTESSENTIAL SALAD GREEN, AND THAT IS HOW IT IS MOST OFTEN USED AROUND THE MEDITERRANEAN, AS we see in the recipes that follow. But there are a few preparations in which lettuce is cooked. In France one can find a lettuce soup, and in Greece, too, where the soup might be served cold with yogurt. Also from Greece is a favorite preparation of mine made with lamb and lettuce braised in an *avgolemono* sauce. I can't wait to try a recipe for stuffed lettuce that I collected at the Ristorante Mario Rivaro in Genoa—*latughe ripiene in salsa rossa*. Lightly boiled lettuce leaves are stuffed with a very fine and delicate chopped veal and Parmigiano mixture with spices. The bundles of lettuce are cooked and served with red kidney beans that have been cooked in a soupy and garlicky tomato sauce.

not possible, keep all lettuces and salad greens in a plastic bag in the refrigerator crisper drawer. Butterhead and other delicate leaf lettuces will keep for about 4 days, romaine lettuce will keep for about 10 days, and iceberg lettuce will keep for about 2 weeks.

Lettuces usually need to be washed before they are eaten. That is unfortunate because it is so hard to dry them adequately. Wet lettuce will dilute any dressing you put on the finished salad. A salad spinner is now an essential piece of kitchen equipment for any cook who is serious about salad; it will remove most of the water from lettuce and salad greens. You may have to blot the lettuce with a paper towel to dry it further. Alternatively, some cooks don't wash lettuce at all, preferring to inspect the leaves for dirt and wipe it away. If you are confronted with limp lettuce, it can be revived somewhat by keeping it in a bowl of ice water in the refrigerator until needed.

When tossing lettuce with a dressing, you should use just enough dressing to make the whole salad look shiny, not wet. There should never be any lettuce swimming in even a little puddle of dressing. Minimalism is the key to dressing a salad. Generally, a quick oil-and-vinegar dressing can be made with a ratio of 4 or 5 parts oil to 1 part vinegar, depending on your taste.

Red Leaf Salad à la Provençale

The inspiration for this dish is a Provençal salad I once had in Aix-en-Provence that was served à la greque. This salad is light, refreshing, and a splendid accompaniment to anything grilled.

FOR THE SALAD:

½ pound red leaf lettuce, washed, dried well, and cut up, including stems

½ pound romaine lettuce, central leaf ribs removed, washed, dried well, and cut up

2 ripe plum tomatoes, cut into quarters

1 hard-boiled egg, shelled and cut into quarters

Salt and freshly ground black pepper to taste

FOR THE VINAIGRETTE:

¼ cup walnut oil

1 tablespoon extra virgin olive oil

1 teaspoon white wine vinegar, or more to taste

1 tablespoon finely chopped fresh dill

1 tablespoon finely chopped fresh basil leaves

1 tablespoon finely chopped fresh tarragon leaves

2 salted anchovy fillets, rinsed and chopped

1 large garlic clove, chopped

1 teaspoon Dijon mustard

1. Arrange the cut-up lettuces, tomatoes, and eggs attractively on a large serving platter. Season with salt and pepper.

2. Mix together the vinaigrette ingredients. Whisk vigorously and correct the balance of vinegar and oil, if necessary. Drizzle the dressing over the salad and serve immediately.

Makes 2 servings

Salade du Berger
SHEPHERD'S SALAD

In the rolling hills of the Languedoc region in southwestern France, perhaps the shepherds really did eat a salad like this one, a restaurant creation from the area around Béziers. In any case, this salad is typically made with Batavian lettuce, which has crunchy leaves and a curled head. Batavian lettuce is more commonly found in farmers' markets than in supermarkets.

FOR THE SALAD:

8 thin slices fresh goat cheese (3 to 4 ounces)

8 thin slices French or Italian country bread

1 pound Batavian lettuce, washed, dried well, and ripped into small pieces

1 pound chicory leaves, washed, dried well, and ripped into small pieces

1 pound radicchio, washed, dried well, and ripped into small pieces

FOR THE VINAIGRETTE:

½ cup walnut oil

7 ½ teaspoons white wine vinegar

¼ teaspoon salt

⅛ teaspoon freshly ground black pepper

½ teaspoon Dijon mustard

1. Preheat the oven to 400°F. Arrange the slices of bread on a baking sheet and place a piece of cheese on each slice of bread. Bake until the edges of the cheese are turning brown, 6 to 8 minutes.

2. Meanwhile, toss the lettuce, chicory, and radicchio together in a large salad bowl. Whisk together the vinaigrette ingredients. Toss the greens again with half of the vinaigrette, coating the greens evenly. Check to see if you want to use more dressing and, if so, toss the salad again. Save the remaining vinaigrette. Divide the greens among 8 individual serving plates, top with the baked bread and cheese, and serve.

Makes 8 servings

Salāṭa al-Khaṣṣ al-ᶜArabī
TUNISIAN-STYLE ROMAINE LETTUCE SALAD

In Tunisia this salad is called Arab lettuce salad. It is delicious and goes very nicely with grilled duck or roast goose, although in Tunisia it is typically served alone as a lunch dish, or before a meal, or as part of a *mazza*. Save the romaine lettuce leaves to make Asparagus and Lettuce in Cream Sauce, on page 34.

3 tablespoons extra virgin olive oil

2 teaspoons white wine vinegar

Salt and freshly ground black pepper to taste

1 teaspoon harīsa *(page 263)*

1 head romaine lettuce (about 2 pounds), stems, heart, and innermost leaves only, chopped

8 imported black olives, pitted

2 large hard-boiled eggs, shelled and cut into wedges

1. Stir together the olive oil and vinegar and season with salt, pepper, and *harīsa*. Toss with the lettuce to coat evenly.

2. Arrange the salad on a serving platter. Garnish with the olives and egg wedges. Serve immediately.

Makes 2 to 4 servings

Salāṭat Khaṣṣ Wāriq
SYRIAN-STYLE ROMAINE LETTUCE SALAD

In Syria, salads of all kinds are quite popular, especially as part of a *mazza* table. This very simple salad, made here with romaine lettuce, is sometimes prepared with any kind of wild greens, called *baqlī*, such as chickweed (see entry), or with greens such as watercress.

¼ cup extra virgin olive oil

1 tablespoon freshly squeezed lemon juice

2 garlic cloves, mashed in a mortar with 1
  teaspoon salt

1 head romaine lettuce, cut crosswise into
  ¼-inch-wide strips, including the stems

4 to 6 tablespoons freshly grated pecorino cheese,
  to your taste

1. Stir the olive oil, lemon juice, and mashed garlic together until well blended.

2. In a salad bowl, toss the lettuce, pecorino cheese, and dressing together and serve immediately.

Makes 4 servings

LIMA BEAN

Phaseolus lunatus L. (syn. *P. limensis*)
(Leguminosae)

**Also called butter bean, sieva bean,
Madagascar bean; FRENCH:** *haricot de Lima,
kissi, pois du Cap;* **GREEK:** *koukia, fasoulia
gigontes;* **ITALIAN:** *fagiolo di Lima;* **SPANISH:**
*judia de Lima, poroto de Lima, poroto
de manteca*

PLANT CHARACTERISTICS AND VARIETIES

There are two varieties of lima bean, the large-seeded and the small-seeded, which can be grown to climb or as a bush. Some botanists consider the butter bean to be a different species than the lima bean (the butter bean is smaller), but so many crosses have been made with the plants that these differences are insignificant. The two main varieties found at the market are Fordhooks (also called butter beans) and baby limas, a smaller variety of lima bean with a milder taste.

PLANT ORIGIN

The large-seeded lima bean originated in Peru, where radiocarbon datings show it was grown as early as 5300 B.P. in Chilca and 4,500 years ago in Huaca Prieta.

PLANT HISTORY

The large-seeded *P. lunatus,* or lima bean, was first domesticated in Peru, while the small-seeded bean, or sieva bean, was first domesticated in Mexico about 1,400 to 1,800 years ago. Europeans first saw the lima bean in Peru. The Spanish adopted the lima bean and brought it back to Europe, possibly by way of trade ships that traversed the Pacific to the Philippines and then to Asia carrying foods and precious metals. But there is also evidence that the Portuguese took both the lima bean and the common bean to Africa with the slave trade, where it traveled north to the Mediterranean via inland trade routes. Even today the lima bean is not that popular in the Mediterranean. It is still found mostly in Spanish and Greek cooking, and almost not at all in Italian cooking.

HOW TO GROW AND HARVEST

The lima bean is grown mostly in the warmer southern United States, where planters can take advantage of the long growing season.

The plant is a perennial that requires more heat to grow than common beans do. Lima beans grow best in warm, well-drained soil. Two weeks after the last spring frost date, sow the seeds of bush varieties about 1 inch deep and 6 inches apart in rows spaced 3 feet apart. Pole varieties need to be supported by sturdy 12-foot-long poles lashed together like a teepee. These poles provide an arbor over the rows so that the gardener can access the pods hanging inside the structure. Harvest the beans when they have filled out the pods and when the pods are a good size. Continue picking the beans throughout the season. The remainder can be left to dry on the vine and be used as dried beans.

HOW TO BUY, STORE, AND PREPARE FOR COOKING

The varieties of lima bean with colored seeds, such as brown, green, or striped, must be soaked and boiled before they are eaten to remove poisonous cyanogenetic glucosides, which are not present in the white-seeded varieties such as the Fordhook. Almost all of the commercially grown lima beans in this country are sold frozen or canned. Occasionally, fresh lima beans, either in their pods or shelled, can be found at farmers' markets.

Because nearly all of the lima beans you are likely to buy are frozen, you will not have an opportunity to inspect them. If you do find fresh limas, they should be plump with unwrinkled skin.

Habas con Jamón
LIMA BEANS WITH JAMÓN DE TRÉVELEZ

The lima bean is a New World bean that only entered *huerta* production in Spain in the post-Columbian era. The *huertas* of the Iberian Peninsula were originally established by the Arabs during the Islamic era as vegetable production gardens. Today these gardens are what we would call truck farms.

This dish is one I ate countless times when I was in Andalusia. The fresh lima beans came from the local *huerta*, and they were cooked with the delicate taste of *jamón de Trévelez*, a cured ham of Andalusia that resembles prosciutto. Because it is difficult to find fresh lima beans, you will need to use frozen ones here. *Jamón de Trévelez* is sometimes sold in gourmet stores, or through mail-order catalogues; otherwise substitute imported *prosciutto di Parma*.

1 pound frozen baby lima beans
1 to 2 tablespoons extra virgin olive oil, to your taste
One ⅛-inch-thick slice jamón de Trévelez or prosciutto di Parma (about 2 ounces), diced
Salt to taste

1. Boil the frozen lima beans briefly according to the package instructions. If you are using fresh baby lima beans, place them in a saucepan with a little water and cook them

gently over medium-low heat until tender. Drain the lima beans and set them aside.

2. Meanwhile, in another saucepan, heat the olive oil over medium heat and add the *jamón* or prosciutto and cook until heated through, about 2 minutes, stirring. Add the cooked lima beans, salt lightly, stir, and heat through, about 2 minutes. Serve immediately.

Makes 2 to 4 servings

Koukia me Yaourti
LIMA BEANS WITH YOGURT

This simple Greek recipe will delight everyone, including those who believe they don't like lima beans.

3 tablespoons extra virgin olive oil
1 small onion, chopped
2½ cups dried or fresh lima beans
¼ cup finely chopped fresh parsley leaves
2 tablespoons chopped fresh dill
½ teaspoon sugar
1 tablespoon salt
Freshly ground black pepper to taste
8 cups water
1 cup high-quality full-fat plain yogurt

1. Heat the olive oil in a casserole over medium-high heat and cook the onion until translucent, 2 to 3 minutes, stirring frequently. Add the lima beans, parsley, dill, sugar, and salt. Season with pepper. Pour in the water to cover the beans. Cover the casserole, reduce the heat to low, and cook until the limas are chewable but still firm, about 2 hours for dried beans and 8 minutes for fresh beans. Uncover the casserole and continue cooking until the limas are soft and tender, about 30 minutes to 1 hour for dried beans and 10 to 12 minutes for fresh. Remove the beans and onions to a serving bowl using a slotted ladle and reserve ½ cup of the cooking liquid.

2. In a small skillet, stir the reserved cooking liquid with the yogurt and heat gently over low heat, making sure the liquid never comes to a boil. Pour the heated yogurt over the beans, mix gently, and serve warm, not hot.

Makes 6 to 8 servings

LONGLEAF
Falcaria vulgaris Bernh. (Umbelliferae)
TURKISH: *kazayağı*

PLANT CHARACTERISTICS AND VARIETIES
Longleaf is an annual, biennial, or perennial herb used as a vegetable in Turkey.

LONICERA CAPRIFOLIUM L. (CAPRIFOLIACEAE)
ITALIAN: *ingannacapre, caprifoglio* (Tuscany)

PLANT CHARACTERISTICS AND VARIETIES
This type of honeysuckle is eaten as a vegetable snack in the mountainous rural areas of Italy.

LOOFAH
Luffa acutangula (L.) Roxb. (smooth
loofah) and *L. aegyptiaca* Miller (syn. *L.
cylindrical*) (angled loofah)
(Cucurbitaceae)
Also called Chinese okra, vegetable
sponge, sponge gourd, dishcloth gourd,
smooth loofah; ARABIC: *bāmya sīny;*
FRENCH: *concombre papengaye, eponge végétale
torcho;* SPANISH: *calabaza de aristas, dringi*

Angled loofah; ARABIC: *luffāḥ;* FRENCH:
loofah, éponge végétale, serviette des pauvres;
ITALIAN: *luffa, spugna vegetale, zucca da
spugne;* SPANISH: *calabaza de aristas, esponja,
servilleta del pobre*

PLANT CHARACTERISTICS AND VARIETIES
The smooth loofah is a fast-growing annual
that is cultivated for its fruits, which are huge.
The edible part of both the smooth loofah
and the angled loofah is the immature fruit,
which is cooked in soups and stews, batter-
fried, pickled, and steamed. The angled loofah
has ridges, while the smooth loofah does not.
Its flowers are large and yellow. The seeds can
be used for extracting oil. The interior netted
fibers of the plant are used as washcloths in
the Middle East. The smooth loofah is used
in Turkish baths for scrubbing. The loofahs
are not eaten to any great extent in the
Mediterranean, although Egyptians seem to
favor the plant as food.

PLANT ORIGIN
The loofah is probably native to India. N.
Vavilov identified the mountains of central
and western China and the adjacent areas as
the loofah's place of origin.

HOW TO BUY, STORE, AND PREPARE FOR COOKING
Loofahs are cooked in the same way you
would zucchini (see entry). They do not need
to be peeled. They are most often found in
farmers' markets in California.

LOTUS GEBELIA VENT. (FABACEAE-LEGUMINOSAE)

PLANT CHARACTERISTICS AND VARIETIES
In Aleppo, Syria, the pods of this annual or
perennial herb are eaten as one would eat
string beans.

LOTUS ROOT
Nelumbo nucifera Gaertn. (syn. *N. nelumbo*)
(Nymphaeaceae)
FRENCH: *lotus sacré, lotus Egyptien, fève
d'Egypte, lis du Nil, rose du Nil, racines de
lotus;* GREEK: *lotos;* ITALIAN: *loto d'Egitto,
giglio de nilo;* SERBO-CROATIAN: *lotos;*
SPANISH: *loto sagrado, haba de Egipto, rosa del
Nilo;* TURKISH: *nilüfer*

PLANT CHARACTERISTICS AND VARIETIES

The lotus root is a beautiful plant with waxy green leaves and huge pink flowers held on long and gently curving stalks. When the rhizomes are cut into sections, they show a chain of oval segments that is very pretty. The edible parts of the plant are primarily the rhizomes and leaves, and, secondarily, the seeds—all of which are cooked. Although lotus root is not common or popular in the Mediterranean, the sliced root is pickled and eaten, especially in the eastern part of the Mediterranean.

PLANT ORIGIN

One claim places the origin of lotus root in the Volga delta, the Caspian coast of Iran, and into China, where it has been cultivated since 12,000 B.C. N. Vavilov identified the mountains of central and western China and its adjacent areas as the place of origin of *N. nucifera*.

PLANT HISTORY

In European languages there is some confusion about the lotus plant. The lotus of the Greeks was *Ziziphus lotus,* a member of the buckthorn family (Rhamnaceae), a bush that is native to southern Europe. In ancient times, this lotus was a food for the poor. In pharaonic Egypt the lotus root was called the Egyptian bean and has been found in tombs. The Romans knew a lotus, which they called the Libyan lotus, but it was probably *Celtis australis,* the nettle tree of southern Europe, a member of the elm family.

The Egyptian lotus is a white water lily, *Nymphaea lotus,* while the blue lotus (*N. caerulea*) was the lotus depicted in ancient Egyptian art. The sacred lotus of the Hindus is an aquatic plant *(Nelumbo nucifera)* with white or pink flowers. Both Herodotus (Book II, 92) and Theophrastus (Book IV, chapter 8, p. 11) observed the making of lotus bread in Egypt. The ripe heads of the lotus were left to decay, and then the fruit, which is about the size of millet, was taken out, dried, pounded into flour, and made into loaves. Pliny adds that the dough was kneaded with milk and water, and that the root was eaten, too.

HOW TO GROW AND HARVEST

Although cultivating the lotus root is easy, the plant needs heat and light. A temperature of between 68° and 86°F should be maintained in order for the plant to grow well. The growing season extends about 5 months. Plant young rhizomes in nitrogen-rich mud in water about 6 inches deep. Harvest the mature rhizomes in the fall after the plant's leaves have wilted.

HOW TO BUY, STORE, AND PREPARE FOR COOKING

Ideally, you would want to buy the whole, uncut, lotus root. It can be stored in a dark frost-free place. Lotus root is usually sliced into sections and pickled in vinegar.

LOVAGE

Levisticum officinale Koch. (Umbelliferae)
ARABIC: *kāsham*; FRENCH: *ache de montagne,
livèche*; ITALIAN: *sedano di montagna*; SPANISH:
ligústico

PLANT CHARACTERISTICS AND VARIETIES

This stout perennial with a strong, musty
smell is used as a vegetable and as an herb. The
leaf stalks and stem bases are blanched and
eaten like celery. The young leaves are also
used in soups, salads, omelettes, and, in
northern Italy, risottos.

PLANT HISTORY

Pliny describes lovage as being native to
Liguria in northern Italy and says that it grew
wild in the mountains but was cultivated
everywhere. He recommends lovage only medicinally, as a curative for upset stomachs, con-
vulsions, or flatulence. In his *Natural History*
(Book XX, chapter LXXIII, 187–89), Pliny
goes into some detail about all the medicinal
uses for lovage that were common in the primitive pharmacological practice of the time. In
the sixteenth century, Ruellius seemed to be
aware that lovage was a food grown in
medieval herb gardens.

HOW TO GROW AND HARVEST

Plant seedlings 2 feet apart in the spring in
humus-rich soil, and water the plants every
day in dry weather. Harvest lovage as you need
it by cutting the plants at ground level.

HOW TO BUY, STORE, AND PREPARE FOR COOKING

Look for bunches of lovage with large and
copious leaves. Store lovage in the refrigerator
for up to 2 to 3 weeks.

RECIPE

Risotto con Sedano di Montagne
RISOTTO WITH LOVAGE

Lovage is usually used as an herb in
Mediterranean cooking, but in this dish
it functions as a vegetable. Leaves of lovage
are tough in the same way Swiss chard leaves
are, so they can handle a bit of cooking
quite well. The taste of the leaves is something akin to celery leaves that have been
packed in hay. If that description doesn't
sound appealing, trust me that lovage has a
beguiling taste that is perfect for risotto.
This recipe is typical of the mountain risottos made in Lombardy. Lovage is not so
common anymore, but it can be found in
farmers' markets. If you can't find lovage,
replace it with celery leaves and a leaf or
two of sage. If you are using beef bouillon
cubes or canned beef broth, be sure to use
low sodium ones. If not, then use only ¼
teaspoon salt.

3 cups beef broth (preferably homemade)
Leaves from 3 large-leaved sprigs fresh lovage
  (about 1 ounce)
1 small onion, chopped fine
2 tablespoons pine nuts
¼ cup walnuts, cut into quarters or coarsely
  crushed
1 tablespoons unsalted butter
1 tablespoon extra virgin olive oil
1 cup uncooked Arborio rice
1 teaspoon salt
2 cups dry white wine
1 cup freshly grated Parmigiano-Reggiano cheese

1. In a small saucepan, bring the broth to a boil. Plunge the lovage into the boiling broth and cook for 4 or 5 minutes. Remove the lovage with a slotted ladle, saving the broth and keeping it hot. Chop the lovage and mix it with the onion, pine nuts, and walnuts.

2. Melt the butter with the olive oil in a heavy saucepan or casserole over medium heat and add the rice, letting it cook for about 2 minutes, stirring to coat all the grains with the hot fat. Add half the beef broth and the salt and cook the rice until it is half cooked, about 15 minutes, adding more beef broth as it evaporates and is absorbed, stirring often. Add the lovage mixture and continue cooking, adding the wine ½ cup at a time until the rice is tender, about another 15 minutes. Stir in the Parmigiano cheese and serve immediately.

Makes 4 servings

LUPINE BEAN
Lupinus sativus (spp., e.g., *L. albus*, *L. mutabilis*, *L. termis*) (Fabaceae-Leguminosae)
Also called lupin, wolf-bean; ARABIC: *turmūs*; FRENCH: *lupin, pois de loup*; GREEK: *loupinon*; ITALIAN: *lupini*; SPANISH: *altramuz, lupino, chocos*; TURKISH: *tırmıs, turmus*

PLANT CHARACTERISTICS AND VARIETIES
Lupine bean is a short, hairy annual that grows to 4 feet. The edible parts are the seeds, which are cooked. Many of the *Lupinus* species have toxic alkaloids that must be removed before the seeds can be cooked and consumed. Today, lupine beans are not eaten much as a vegetable in the Mediterranean, but they are often served as a snack with nuts or roasted pumpkin seeds. They seem to be most favored in Turkey, Lebanon, and southern Italy. Lupine beans are also used as green manure in farming. Lupine beans can be found growing wild in Sicily and elsewhere in the Mediterranean Basin. One variety, *L. hirsutus* Linn., called the blue lupin, was cultivated by the ancient Greeks and was a traditional food of poor people. The yellow lupin *(L. luteus)* is cultivated in Italy. *Lupinus termis* Forsk. is a lupine bean cultivated in Italy and Egypt and eaten after boiling. The peduncles are sometimes pickled without cooking. Two other edible varieties are *L. albus* and *L. mutabilis.*

PLANT ORIGIN

Lupine beans originated in the Mediterranean. Some of the earliest seeds have been found in a cave in Palestine and date from about 10,000 B.C. Since they were found with a few grains of barley, it is thought that they were meant for consumption. But no lupine beans have ever been unearthed from later Neolithic sites, leading one paleobotanist, Maria Hopf, to the conclusion that the plant was not cultivated. N. Vavilov suggests Asia Minor as the center of origin of the lupine bean.

PLANT HISTORY

Lupine beans were a late addition to the first crop plants. Apparently, the thick, tough coat, as well as the alkaloid content of the seed, made the lupine bean unattractive as a food plant. Yet reports that the plant was grown in ancient Egypt about 2000 B.C. and used by Greeks and Romans as human food and as forage lead one to conclude that people must have learned how to remove the beans' bitter component in order to make use of the plant's highly nutritious protein content. Athenaeus, Theophrastus, Cato, Columella, and Pliny all mention the lupine bean. The Romans distributed lupine beans freely to the population on holy days and festivals. In the Middle Ages, lupine beans were often used for green manure. In 1614 Castelvetro describes how women and little children ate lupine beans between meals on hot summer days. Lupine beans are still eaten in the same way today in Italy and the Middle East, as a snack, and almost never as part of a cooked dish.

HOW TO BUY, STORE, AND PREPARE FOR COOKING

Nearly all the lupine beans you are likely to come across will be sold in jars in the supermarket. They can be eaten straight from the jar, but they are more pleasant if soaked in several changes of water over a 24-hour period, to remove some of the saltiness. In the unlikely event you run across fresh lupine beans, you should boil them several times before you use them.

RECIPE

Tırmıs Pilakisi
LUPINE BEANS IN OLIVE OIL AND TOMATO

Lupine beans are eaten throughout the Mediterranean almost always as a tidbit with drinks or, in the eastern Mediterranean, as a *meze*. I first had this delicious little dish in the Meydan restaurant in Bergama, Turkey. It was a cold spring day, and this spicy dish did a lot to take the chill out of our bones.

¼ cup extra virgin olive oil

1 medium onion, chopped fine

3 large garlic cloves, chopped fine

1 large ripe tomato, peeled, seeded, and chopped

2 teaspoons sugar

3 tablespoons finely chopped fresh green chile
pepper

2 cups lupine beans from a jar, drained

Heat the olive oil in a skillet over medium-high heat and cook the onion and garlic until they are translucent, about 4 minutes, stirring so the garlic doesn't burn. Add the tomato, sugar, and chile pepper. Stir, reduce the heat to low, and cook for 5 minutes. Add the beans, cover, and cook until the liquid has evaporated, about 30 minutes. Turn the heat off and let the beans cool in the skillet. Serve at room temperature.

Makes 4 servings

LYCHNIS FLOS-CUCULI L. (*CORONARIA FLOS-CUCULI* [L.] A. BRAUN) (CARYOPHYLLACEAE)

ITALIAN: *manine del signore* (Tuscany)

PLANT CHARACTERISTICS AND VARIETIES

This erect perennial has leaves that grow out of the base and flowers on long-stalked dichasia. The leaves are used in vegetable soups in rural Tuscany. The Italian name means "women's dainty hands."

MALLOW

Malva rotundifolia L. (and other species, e.g., *M. verticillata*, *M. crispa*) (Malvaceae)
ARABIC: *khiṭmiyya* (marshmallow), *hatmy*; FRENCH: *mauve*; GREEK: *molocha*; ITALIAN: *malva comune, malva domestica, malva piccola*; SPANISH: *malva, malva de hoja redonda, malva de flor pequena*; TURKISH: *ebegümeci, hatmi* (marshmallow)

PLANT CHARACTERISTICS AND VARIETIES

This perennial or biennial plant that is grown as an annual has a mucilaginous texture and is sometimes considered an herb. Mallow has small round leaves and pink white flowers and grows to 4 feet. The edible parts are the leaves and young shoots, which are cooked. One variety of mallow, *M. neglecta* Wallr., apparently was grown in Egypt as a potherb and is also collected as a wild edible green in the Aksaray Province of Turkey. There are a great number of different types of mallow. Musk mallow (*M. moschata*) grows to about 3 feet high and has rose or white flowers in the summer. High mallow (*M. sylvestris*) has traditionally been used for medicinal purposes, although in rural Tuscany it is also used in vegetable soups and in salads in the Aksaray Province of Turkey. The marshmallow (*Althea officinalis*) is a perennial mallow that is native to eastern Europe and northern Africa and that grows in marshy areas near the sea. The root was once used in making marshmallow confections; the greens are also gathered in the wild and eaten in Turkey.

PLANT ORIGIN

A number of mallow plants are native to eastern Europe and North Africa.

PLANT HISTORY

In ancient Greece, mallow was cultivated on the island of Delos for the Temple of Apollo as a symbol of the first nourishment of man. Diphilus (third century B.C.) says that the mallow is juicy, and that it softens the bronchial tubes and carries off the bitter humors at the top of the stomach; it is specific for irritations of the kidneys and bladder; it is also nourishing and quite easily digested, though the wild is better than the garden variety. Athenaeus says that mallow is nourishing when cooked with oysters, and that it is also good for the bowels. Pliny devotes a section to mallow, describing two kinds, one cultivated and one wild. He also describes the use of mallow for green manure and as a cure-all for all diseases. For the most part, mallow was a medicinal plant for the ancient Greeks.

Mallow was a common vegetable grown in medieval European gardens. In a piece of sixth-century dietetic advice, Anthimus says that mallow was suitable for both summer and winter. It was often grown in Mediterranean gardens for medicinal reasons, to be used as a demulcent. It is said that Charlemagne encouraged the cultivation of marshmallow in 812. In Egypt today, mallow is found growing along the Nile and is extensively cultivated for use in stews and soups. Marshmallow, also found along the Nile, is not native to Egypt; it was introduced from Syria. In 1614, Castelvetro describes eating mallow tips just as they are about to flower; they were cooked and eaten cold with olive oil, salt, and pepper.

HOW TO GROW AND HARVEST

Sow seeds in the spring and transplant them outside in rows spread about 10 inches apart in full sun and moist soil. The young leaves and shoots can be picked as needed.

HOW TO BUY, STORE, AND PREPARE FOR COOKING

Fresh mallow can sometimes be found at farmers' markets, sold under the name "okra leaf," or by other names from a variety of Asian languages. For instance, in California mallow might be sold under its Japanese name, *fuyu aoi*, or its Chinese name, *yuan ye jin kui*.

RECIPE

Al-Buqūl
MALLOW AND LEGUME STEW

Traditionally this Algerian stew, called *al-buqūl*, which means "greens," or specifically "legumes," would be cooked longer than I do here because the dried legumes would need lots of cooking. But I use the entirely satisfactory substitute of canned chickpeas and fava beans. The dried white beans do have to be cooked until almost tender, about 1½ hours, before they can be added to the stew. The kind of canned fava beans you are looking for are the round ones called "bath fava," or foul medammes, the name most likely to be found on the label.

Leaves from 3 bunches mallow (about ¾ pound), washed well, all stems removed, and coarsely chopped

½ cup extra virgin olive oil

4 large garlic cloves, sliced thin

1 tablespoon tomato paste, diluted in ¼ cup water

1 large whole dried red chile pepper

1 tablespoon cayenne pepper

1½ teaspoons freshly ground black pepper

1½ teaspoons salt

2½ cups cold water

1½ cups cooked chickpeas (about one 10-ounce can), drained

1½ cups cooked small white beans

1½ cups cooked fava beans (about one 10-ounce can), drained

1 stalk cardoon, diced, boiled for 1 hour in water to cover with ¼ cup vinegar, and drained, or 4 large fresh artichoke hearts, diced, or 3 celery stalks, cut into 1-inch lengths

2 medium potatoes, peeled and diced

1 cup fresh fava beans (from about 1¼ pounds of pods), skinned (page 152)

1 cup fresh or frozen peas

½ cup pitted imported green olives

Leaves from 1 bunch fresh coriander, chopped fine

1. Bring a pot of water to a boil and cook the mallow until wilted but floating on top, 10 to 12 minutes. Drain.

2. Heat the olive oil in a casserole over medium-high heat and cook the garlic with the diluted tomato paste, chile pepper, cayenne, black pepper, and salt until the water is nearly evaporated, 6 to 8 minutes, stirring frequently so the garlic doesn't burn. Add the water, chickpeas, white beans, and canned fava beans, reduce the heat to medium, and cook until the beans are almost tender, about 50 minutes. Add the semi-cooked cardoon or the artichokes or celery, potatoes, fresh favas, peas, and olives. Stir and cook until the potatoes are almost tender, 40 to 45 minutes.

3. Add the coriander and reserved mallow, reduce the heat to low, and simmer until the stew is thick and syrupy, about 15 minutes. Remove and discard the chile pepper and serve hot or cold.

Makes 8 servings

MASTERWORT
Peucedanum ostruthium Koch.
(Umbelliferae)
Also called hog's-fennel; ITALIAN:
imperatoria; SPANISH: *imperatoria*

PLANT CHARACTERISTICS AND VARIETIES
This perennial grows to 3 feet and has stout, branched rhizomes. The edible parts of the plant are the leaves and roots. The leaves are boiled and eaten as a potherb or used in making herbal cheeses, and the roots are used in stews. Masterwort is also one of the ingredients in an Italian bitter beverage called Ramazzotti.

MEADOW PARSLEY
Oenanthe pimpinelloides L. (Umbelliferae)

PLANT CHARACTERISTICS AND VARIETIES
This erect perennial grows to 3½ feet and has a solid, grooved stem. The roots are said to taste like hazelnuts. In Tuscany the leaves are eaten in stews.

MIGNONETTE
Reseda odorata L. (RESEDACEAE)
ARABIC: *ṣāmūrfī;* FRENCH: *herbe d'amour, mignonette, réséda odorante;* ITALIAN: *reseda, amorino, amoretti d'Egitto, miglionet;* SPANISH: *réseda, miñoneta*

PLANT CHARACTERISTICS AND VARIETIES
Mignonette is an annual or perennial plant that grows to 2 feet. It has simply shaped leaves that are slightly oval, and its flowers are small and white or yellow green with orange pollen sacks on long spikes. The edible parts are the leaves and flowers. They have a musty taste. Mignonette is mostly used in salads. In Turkey, salt flavored with mignonette is used in veal and lamb dishes. It is also used in the cooking of North Africa.

PLANT ORIGIN
Mignonette is native to Europe, North Africa, and parts of Asia.

MILK THISTLE
Silybum marianum (L.) Gaertner
(Asteraceae-Compositae)

PLANT CHARACTERISTICS AND VARIETIES
The edible parts of this robust annual or biennial herb are the young leaves, stems, roots, and flower receptacles, or hearts, which can be used like artichokes. The plant is usually boiled before it is eaten. It is mostly eaten in North Africa.

MINER'S LETTUCE
Montia perfoliata (Donn. ex Willd.)
Howell (syn. *Clayton perfoliata*)
(Portulacaceae)

Also called Cuban spinach; FRENCH: *pourpier d'hiver, claytone de Cuba*; ITALIAN: *portulaca d'inverno, spinacio de Cuba*; SPANISH: *verdolaga de invierno, verdolaga de Cuba*

PLANT CHARACTERISTICS AND VARIETIES

Miner's lettuce is in the same family as purslane (see entry). The leaves, which are eaten mostly in Spain, Provence, and Italy, are often used in salads or are cooked.

PLANT ORIGIN

Miner's lettuce originates in North America.

MOCK TOMATO

Solanum aethiopicum L. (Solanaceae) Also called African scarlet eggplant, garden egg; ARABIC: *al-tuffāḥ al-dhahabī*; FRENCH: *tomate amère, pomme d'amour*

PLANT CHARACTERISTICS AND VARIETIES

The orange red fruits of this plant are the edible parts, as are the leaves, which are cooked. The fruits are cooked and eaten like eggplant. In the Mediterranean, the only people who eat this plant with any regularity are the Egyptians, who eat the boiled or fried fruit as a vegetable.

PLANT ORIGIN

Mock tomato is native to Asia and tropical Africa.

PLANT HISTORY

This plant was once known as the "tomato of the Jews of Constantinople," a reference to the Ladinos, the Sephardic Jews who were expelled from Spain in the fifteenth century and who immigrated to Turkey and Greece.

MUNG BEAN

Vigna radiata (L.) Wilcz. (syn. *Phaseolus aureus, P. radiatus*) (Leguminoseae) ARABIC: *māsh*; FRENCH: *ambérique, haricot doré*; ITALIAN: *fagiolo aureo, fagiolo mungo*; SPANISH: *judia de mungo, frijol mungo, frijol de oro, poroto mungo*; TURKISH: *maş*

PLANT CHARACTERISTICS AND VARIETIES

The edible parts of this plant are the immature pods, sprouting seeds, and seeds. Most people are familiar with mung beans because the sprouts of these beans are sold as "bean sprouts." The mung bean plant is an annual that grows to about 3 feet high and spreads out. The flowers are a showy yellow and are pealike.

PLANT ORIGIN

The mung bean probably originated in India or south China. N. Vavilov suggests an inner-Asiatic center of origin, an area that consists of northwestern India, Afghanistan, Tadzhikistan, Uzbekistan, and the western Tien Shan Province of China.

Although the mung bean is usually associated with the Far East, especially because of its bean sprouts, mung bean has been a food of the poor in North Africa from the Middle Ages up until today. Among poor Berber tribes of the Sahara, mung beans were used in porridges and for couscous preparations.

HOW TO GROW AND HARVEST

See Black-Eyed Pea. The pods cans be harvested as you would green beans.

HOW TO BUY, STORE, AND PREPARE FOR COOKING

Fresh mung beans are sold at whole food stores and some supermarkets with specialty greengrocer departments. Store the beans and the sprouts in the bag you bought them in, in the refrigerator for up to a week.

RECIPE

Maş Pıyazı
MUNG BEANS AND ONION SALAD

Although mung beans have traditionally been the food of the very poor in the Mediterranean, especially in North Africa, this Turkish salad does not seem so poor. I've adapted the recipe from one by the Turkish cookbook writer Nevin Halıcı. Mung beans are peppercorn-size dark green beans that look like du Puy lentils at a quick glance.

The red Aleppo pepper used in this recipe can be found at Middle Eastern markets. To create an acceptable substitute, you can mix three parts Hungarian sweet paprika to one part ground red chile pepper.

1 ½ cups (about ½ pound) fresh mung beans
4 cups water
Salt to taste
1 small white onion, chopped fine
¼ cup finely chopped fresh dill
¼ teaspoon ground red Aleppo pepper

FOR THE DRESSING:
2 tablespoons pomegranate molasses
Freshly squeezed juice from 1 small lemon

1. In a large saucepan, place the mung beans, water, and a little salt and bring to a boil. Cook the beans until they are tender, 15 to 20 minutes. Drain and let them cool.

2. In a medium bowl, mix together the beans, onion, dill, and red pepper and season with salt. Arrange the salad in a shallow serving bowl. Mix together the pomegranate molasses and lemon juice, drizzle over the beans, and serve.

Makes 4 servings

MUSHROOM

Agaricus bisporus (syn. *Psalliota hortensis; P. campestris; P. arvensis*) and many others
ARABIC: *fuṭr*; CATALAN: *rovelló*; FRENCH: *champignon*; GREEK: *manitari*; ITALIAN: *fungo*;

SERBO-CROATIAN: *jestiva gljiva, glive, vrganj;*
SPANISH: *seta, hongo;* TURKISH: *mantar*

PLANT CHARACTERISTICS AND VARIETIES

Mushrooms are fungi and not true vegetables. Fungi are plants that have no roots or leaves. They do not flower or set seed. There are some 35,000 to 40,000 varieties of mushrooms, not all of which are edible, and many of which are deadly poisonous. The only commercially available mushroom in American markets for many years was *Agaricus bisporus,* the smooth, round-capped mushroom known as field, button, or cultivated mushroom that comes in a number of different colors such as the brown ones known as cremini. The field mushroom is also referred to as *A. campestris.*

All kinds of mushrooms are stewed, fried, pickled, and/or roasted in nearly all Mediterranean cuisines. Although there are many edible varieties of mushrooms, the ones you will likely run across in gourmet greengrocers, supermarkets, and farmers' markets are the following:

- *The porcini mushroom (Boletus edulis), also called cèpe, bolete, or cep, is considered the best-tasting mushroom. But the cep is actually a different mushroom known as Ceps boletus.*
- *The chanterelle or girolle mushroom (Cantharellus tubaeformis) is tuba-shaped and very expensive. It is considered a gourmet mushroom.*

- *The oyster mushroom (Pleurotus ostreatus) is a dense, chewy mushroom that is most often used in stews in Mediterranean cooking.*
- *The portobello mushroom is a large brown mushroom with a large cap.*
- *The parasol mushroom (Lepiota procera), as its name implies, is a large umbrella-like mushroom that can grow a foot tall with a cap diameter of 8 inches; in rural Tuscany, people like to roast these mushrooms.*
- *The horn of plenty mushroom (Craterellus cornucopioides) is a distinctive black mushroom that grows in cool, humid forests.*
- *The wood ear mushroom has a flattened cap and is crunchy; it is most often used in stews.*
- *The Caesar's mushroom (Amanita caesarea) is an expensive mushroom often spoken of in the same breath as truffles or morels. Because the two look similar, this mushroom is often confused with the poisonous A. muscaria.*

In southern Italy there are two popular mushrooms called *crosito (Lactarius deliciosus)* and *vavusi (Boleti viscidi).* In rural Tuscany, hen-of-the-woods (*Grifola frondosa* [Picks ex Fr.]) is a popular and flavorful mushroom called *grifone* in the local dialect. Another favorite is *Ramaria botrytis* Fr. Ricken, called *ditola,* whose whole fruiting body is pickled in olive oil.

Another group of mushrooms favored by northern Italians are *Armillariella mellea* (called *rangagno*), *Clitocybe geotropa* (called *cimballo*), *Thricoloma georgii* (called *prugnolo*), and *Thricoloma terreum* (called *morella* or *cardella*)—all of which are used in stews and frittatas and are sometimes roasted or pickled in oil.

Morels *(Morchella esculenta)* and truffles *(Tuber melanosporum, T. aestivum, T. magnatum)* are fungi, but not true mushrooms. Mushrooms are basidiomycetes, a higher fungi having septate hyphae, bearing spores on a basidium. The so-called mushroom is the "fruit," or basidiocarp. Morels and truffles are ascomycetes, and the edible portion aboveground is called an ascocarp. Both morels and truffles are both rare and expensive. Cooked gently with bland foods such as pasta, rice, potatoes, or eggs, these fungi are much prized by connoisseurs.

PLANT ORIGIN

Mushrooms are found all over the world, and it is not known if they have a center of origin.

PLANT HISTORY

There is no evidence of the use of mushrooms before the Neolithic period. There is some inconclusive evidence that mushrooms were eaten in Egypt, perhaps as early as the Late Predynastic period (3650–3300 B.C.). The ancient Greeks and Romans ate mushrooms, although Pliny said he thought it was rash to eat them, warning "how chancy a matter it is to test these deadly plants." The

ancient people also may have eaten porcini mushrooms. Dioscorides wrote about mushrooms and theorized (incorrectly) about how they generated. Most botanical writers over the centuries have advised taking the greatest caution with mushrooms. Mushroom cultivation began with the Romans and Greeks, who grew the small *Agrocybe aegerita*. The Romans collected truffles as we know from Juvenal, who wrote that fungi were thought to arise when lightning struck. We know that around 1600 mushroom cultivation continued in Europe based on advice on growing mushrooms provided by the French agriculturist Olivier de Serres.

HOW TO GROW AND HARVEST

Although some mushrooms are cultivated, many are gathered. It is best to buy your mushrooms rather than gather them because of the very great danger of eating poisonous mushrooms by mistake. Only experienced and trained mycologists should be foraging for mushrooms.

HOW TO BUY, STORE, AND PREPARE FOR COOKING

Look for plump, clean mushrooms and avoid those that look bruised or slimy. Although mushrooms can be eaten raw, it is best to cook them. Storing mushrooms can be tricky because if they get too much moisture, they will become slimy and soggy, and decay. On the other hand, if the conditions are too dry, the mushrooms will dry out completely. The best

Mushrooms

୬

GET OFF THE MAIN ROADS WHILE DRIVING IN THE MEDITER-
RANEAN AFTER A BRIEF RAIN AND YOU MIGHT ENCOUNTER THE
sight of whole extended families of mushroom foragers. Mushrooms are most popular in a swath that arcs from Catalonia, through Languedoc and Provence, and into and
down the Italian peninsula. But everyone in the Mediterranean loves mushrooms, even
the Bedouin desert dwellers who find their *fuṭr* after an infrequent rain and put them
into a stew or cook them with chicken. In Provence, a cook might prepare mushrooms
with pine nuts or with garlic, olive oil, thyme, and white wine. In Croatia, people are
crazy for mushrooms, too. They cook them with noodles or rice. In Slovenia, mushrooms appear in *zec´sa pec´urkama*, roast hare with dried mushrooms and sour cream. In
Serbia, an absolutely delicious dish is *glive sa jajima i pavlakom*, mushrooms cooked in
butter with scrambled eggs, onion, parsley, cream cheese, and cream. In Catalonia,
mushrooms are grilled and appear in many dishes, while in Andalusia, wild mushrooms are cooked with garlic, chile pepper, and sherry or, in a dish called *setas de Sierra
Morena*, with garlic, eggs, and hazelnuts. Mushrooms are stuffed, too, in Spain in a variety of tapas and in Italy as an antipasto. In Italy, mushrooms are cooked on their own
in dishes like *funghi alla panna*, with cream, or *funghi trifolati*, with garlic and parsley. Or
mushrooms are part of a more elaborate dish such as *pasticcio di lasagne ai funghi*, a
lasagne and mushroom pie. In Lombardy, sautéed mushrooms with polenta is a dish
not to be forgotten. In Naples, every household has its *funghi sott'olio* in a jar, preserved
mushrooms in olive oil. In Turkey, a delightful *börek*, a fried pastry, is stuffed with dill-
flavored mushrooms in a cream sauce made with Turkish *kaşar* cheese, which resembles cheddar. In the Turkish countryside, cooks make *meyaneli mantar yemeği*, mushrooms
braised with butter, onions, green bell peppers, and tomatoes. In Lebanon, *fuṭr ḥarra*
is a spicy mushroom dish seasoned with chile pepper, lots of garlic, parsley, and
lemon juice.

way to keep mushrooms, and only for a day, is in an open brown paper bag in the kitchen or, if in the refrigerator, not in the crisper drawer, which is too humid. Mushrooms absorb lots of water, so brush them rather than wash them before cooking.

Dried mushrooms provide an intense flavor. Many cooks use dried morels or porcini because the expense of fresh ones is prohibitive.

RECIPES

Morilles à la Crème
MORELS IN CREAM SAUCE

Morels are a delicious fungus and very expensive. In this recipe from the Languedoc, the morels transmit their flavor to the common mushrooms. The finished dish works as a natural complement to *magret de canard*, grilled fattened duck breast.

Laborers working outdoors in Languedoc are well known for bringing home wild foods, be they snails, wild leeks, truffles found among the roots of prickly holm oak, or large morels—and, when they have their shotgun, a hare or pigeon.

6 ounces fresh morel mushrooms
2 tablespoons unsalted butter
2 tablespoons walnut oil or extra virgin olive oil
1½ pounds button mushrooms
2 ounces shallots, chopped fine
1 garlic clove, chopped fine
1 cup heavy cream
Salt and freshly ground black pepper, if necessary
1 tablespoon finely chopped fresh tarragon leaves

1. Place the morels in a bowl of cold water and wash them well to remove any grit. Drain and pat them dry with paper towels. Place the morels in a heavy 1-quart saucepan and turn the heat to high. Sweat them for 3 minutes. Their own juices will be enough to cook them in; do not add any water. Drain the mushrooms and discard the liquid (or save it for another use). Set the morels aside.

2. Heat the butter and oil together in a large skillet over high heat and cook the morels and button mushrooms for 3 minutes, stirring. Reduce the heat to low, add the shallots and garlic, and cook until soft, about 20 minutes, stirring. Pour in the cream, bring the pot to a boil, and cook at a gentle bubble, shaking not stirring the skillet, until the sauce is thick and gooey, about 5 minutes. Season with salt and pepper. Sprinkle with the tarragon and serve hot.

Makes 4 servings

Funghi Ripieni
STUFFED MUSHROOMS

This preparation from Liguria, the Riviera province of northwestern Italy, is a delightful appetizer. It would also be very nice followed with a grilled chicken or a roasted rosemary chicken. Normally, Ligurian mushroom hunters would look for forest mushrooms for this dish while on their weekend excursions into the surrounding woody hills. But in this recipe the field mushrooms are perfect for stuffing.

3 ounces stale Italian or French bread (about 3 thick slices), white part only, cubed
1 cup milk
1 pound button or field mushrooms (about 14)
1 large garlic clove, peeled
1 cup freshly grated Parmigiano-Reggiano cheese (about 2 ounces)
1 large egg
1 large egg yolk
½ teaspoon dried oregano
1 to 2 tablespoons finely chopped fresh parsley leaves, to your taste
Salt and freshly ground black pepper to taste
2 tablespoons extra virgin olive oil, divided

1. Preheat the oven to 350°F. Soak the bread in the milk in a medium bowl.
2. Remove the mushroom stems and pound them and the garlic together into a paste in a large mortar or process them in a food processor. Transfer the mashed garlic and stems to the bowl containing the bread. Mix in the Parmigiano, the whole egg and yolk, oregano, and parsley. Season with salt and pepper. Stir in 1 teaspoon of the olive oil.
3. Stuff the mushroom caps with all or nearly all of the stuffing. Arrange on a baking tray or pan with a few drops of olive oil sprinkled over each one. Bake the mushrooms until they are golden brown on top, about 1¼ hours.

Makes 4 servings

Torta di Funghi
MUSHROOM TART

This recipe from the Emilia region of Italy can be made entirely with porcini mushrooms, although the cost might be excessive. My solution is to use a combination of mushrooms, and that way nothing is lost to taste. I've settled on some dried porcini to establish the foundation, some chanterelles to provide a certain taste and color, and to provide the bulk of the mushrooms, a combination of portobello and shiitake, even though these mushrooms are not traditionally used in the Mediterranean.

1 recipe short dough (below)

3 medium potatoes (about 1¼ pounds)

2 tablespoons extra virgin olive oil

3 tablespoons unsalted butter

1 medium onion, sliced thin

1 ounce dried porcini mushrooms, soaked in tepid
  water for 15 minutes and drained

3 ounces fresh chanterelle mushrooms, sliced

½ pound fresh shiitake mushrooms, sliced

½ pound fresh portobello mushrooms, sliced

1 pound fresh porcini mushrooms, sliced

Salt to taste

2 large egg yolks plus 1 large egg, beaten together

1½ cups freshly grated Parmigiano-Reggiano
  cheese

1. Make the short dough and let it rest in the refrigerator while you continue with the rest of the preparation. Place the potatoes in a large saucepan, cover them with cold water by 2 inches, and turn the heat to high. Once the water is boiling, about 10 minutes, reduce the heat to medium and cook the potatoes until a skewer will glide easily to the center of each potato, about 20 minutes. Drain, let cool a bit, and peel. Mash 1 potato with a fork and cut the remaining 2 potatoes into ¼-inch-thick slices. Set the potatoes aside until needed.

2. Heat the olive oil with the butter in a large skillet over medium-high heat. Add the onion and cook until translucent, about 5 minutes, stirring. Add all the mushrooms, season with salt, and cook the mushrooms until they are soft and sticking slightly to the skillet, 7 to 8 minutes. Turn the heat off and mix in the mashed potato. Let the mushrooms cool a bit in the skillet. Stir in the beaten eggs and cheese.

3. Preheat the oven to 350°F. Roll out the short dough to ⅛ inch thick, making sure you keep the work surface floured. Fit the sheet of dough into a 9- or 10-inch tart pan. Fold the overlapping edges over onto themselves and crimp. Prick the dough all over with a toothpick and neatly layer the sliced potato around the bottom of the pan. Arrange the mushrooms, mashed potato, and onion on top, spreading them out evenly over the surface, and bake until the mushrooms are dark brown and the crust is golden brown, 50 minutes to 1 hour. Remove the tart from the oven and let it rest until warm. Serve.

Makes 6 servings

Short Dough

Called *pasta frolla* in Italian or *pâte brisée* in French, short dough is used for savory pies.

1¼ cups unbleached all-purpose flour, sifted

6 tablespoons (¾ stick) cold unsalted butter, cut
  into bits

2 tablespoons cold vegetable shortening or lard

¼ teaspoon salt

2 tablespoons ice water, or more as needed

1. Blend the flour, butter, shortening, and salt together in a large, cold mixing bowl. Add 2 tablespoons of ice water. Mix again until the water is absorbed. Add more ice water if necessary to form the dough.

2. Shape the dough into a ball, dust it with flour, and wrap in wax paper. Refrigerate for at least 1 hour before using, then let rest at room temperature for a few minutes before rolling out according to the recipe.

Makes enough for one double crusted 10-inch pie

Setas con Pan Frito
SPICED MUSHROOMS ON FRIED BREAD

Here's a delectable Andalusian tapas that is spicy and excellent served with sangria or some red wine. It's delicious on top of the fried bread, which absorbs some of the richness of the mushrooms. I like to serve it with drinks before my guests and I sit down for dinner.

3 tablespoons pork lard, divided
1 pound button or field mushrooms, cut in quarters
¼ cup freshly squeezed lemon juice
1 teaspoon freshly ground cumin seeds
1 teaspoon paprika
Salt and freshly ground black pepper to taste
4 to 6 slices round French or Italian country bread, each cut into smaller pieces if you are serving this dish as a tapas

1. Melt 1 tablespoon of the lard in a medium skillet over medium heat. Add the mushrooms and cook with the lemon juice, cumin, paprika, salt, and black pepper until most of the mushroom liquid has evaporated and the mushrooms are soft, about 25 minutes.

2. Meanwhile, in another medium skillet, melt the remaining 2 tablespoons of lard over medium-high heat and cook the bread slices until light golden on both sides. Remove the bread and arrange on a serving platter. Cover with the mushrooms and serve.

Makes 4 first-course servings and 8 tapas servings

MUSKMELON
Cucumis melo L. Reticulatus group (syn. *C. melo* var. *reticulatus*) (Cucurbitaceae) Also called nutmeg melon, netted melon, Persian melon; ARABIC: *faqqūs*; FRENCH: *melon brodé, melon réticulé*; GREEK: *peponi*; ITALIAN: *melone retado*; SERBO-CROATIAN: *dinja*; SPANISH: *melón bordado*; TURKISH: *kavun*

PLANT CHARACTERISTICS AND VARIETIES
This annual has thick stems and globelike fruit. The edible part is the ripe fruit, which can range from 1 to 4 pounds and take a variety of shapes. Muskmelon is eaten mostly as a fruit, but in Egypt and other areas of the Levant it is cooked as a vegetable. Persian melons are a variety of muskmelon. When the fruit is mature the rind can be whitish green, cream colored, yellow, or dark green. The taste also varies, depending on the growing conditions, but typically the fruit is sweet, juicy, and musky-scented. The ancient Egyptians also apparently cultivated the chate melon (*C. melo* var. *chate*), a melon with a cucumber-like fruit.

The Arabic word *faqqūs* also refers to a kind of very long cucumber that is eaten raw, also called snake cucumber or Armenian cucumber (*C. sativus* L. var. *flexuosus*). Muskmelons are popular in the eastern Mediterranean and east into Asia, especially in Persia and Turkmenistan, on the eastern shore of the Caspian.

PLANT ORIGIN

Muskmelon appears to have originated in Africa. The wild forms in India are likely to have once escaped from local gardens. N. Vavilov suggests Asia Minor as a center of origin.

PLANT HISTORY

Some scholars believe that the "melon" mentioned in Numbers 11:5 that the Jews so missed when they left Egypt was the muskmelon. The climate of Turkmenistan in central Asia is apparently ideal for growing muskmelons, and this was noticed by the Chinese traveler Tch'ang Te in 1259, who discovered the fruits growing there. In the thirteenth century Albertus Magnus called melon *pepones*, which might be a description of muskmelons. He writes that the melon had a smooth, green skin, which could also be a description of watermelon. One legend has it that around 1519 after he had conquered India, the Emperor Baber, founder of the Mogul Empire, cut open a muskmelon and cried because the sweet taste reminded him of home.

HOW TO GROW AND HARVEST

Muskmelons grow best in raised beds that slope downward away from the plant to create good drainage. They need a fair amount of watering, which is best accomplished with a drip irrigation system installed under mulch. Start seeds indoors a month before the last frost in the spring. Transplant seedlings to 1 foot apart. Harvest the fruits before they are fully ripe, and let them finish ripening indoors. The fruit is ripe when the skin of the fruit turns a yellowish color, smells sweet, and looks netted.

MUSTARD

Brassica juncea (L.) Czernj. & Coss. var. *rugosa* Bailey (Cruciferae-Brassicaceae): Indian mustard, Chinese mustard, brown mustard, large leaf mustard; ARABIC: *khardal*; FRENCH: *moutarde*; ITALIAN: *senape*; SPANISH: *mostaza*; TURKISH: *hardal*

Sinapis alba L. (syn. *Brassica hirta; B. alba*): white or yellow mustard; ARABIC: *khardal, āsfīnār*; FRENCH: *moutarde blanche*; ITALIAN: *senape bianca*; SPANISH: *mostaza blanca*

Brassica nigra Koch (syn. *Sinapsis nigra*): black mustard; ARABIC: *ḥabb al-baraka*; *khardal*; FRENCH: *moutarde noire*; ITALIAN: *cavolo senape-nera*; SPANISH: *mostaza negra, jenape ajenabo*; TURKISH: *hardal*

Botanically, four species of mustard are recognized in commercial growing: white mustard (*Sinapis alba*), brown mustard (*Brassica juncea*), black mustard (*Brassica nigra*), and Ethiopian mustard (*Brassica carinata*), but these designations are often confused. The plant's cotyledon (the first leaf or whorl of leaves developed by the embryo of a seed plant) is eaten cooked or raw. The young flower stalks and seeds are also eaten. White mustard grows wild in most of Europe. Another variety known locally as *marasciuole* or *senape selvatica (S. erucoides)* is eaten in the region of Apulia in southern Italy. In Cairo the leaves of *qarilla (S. allionii)* are eaten raw like a kind of watercress.

Black mustard is an annual herbaceous plant that grows to 6 feet and was mostly grown in past times for its seeds. Today, brown mustard has replaced black mustard because it is more difficult to grow the latter using modern mechanized agricultural methods.

The leaves of most varieties are eaten cooked. With some varieties, the stems are eaten, too. Varieties include *capitata* Hort. (capitata mustard); *crassicaulis* Chen & Yang (bamboo shoot mustard); *crispifolia* Bailey (cut-leaf or curled mustard); *foliosa* Bailey (small-leaf mustard); *gemmifera* Lee & Lin (gemmiferous mustard); *latipa* Li (wide-petiole mustard); *leucanthus* Chen & Yang (white-flowered mustard); *linearifolia* (line mustard); *longepetiolata* Yang & Chen (long-petiole mustard); *megarrhiza* Tsen & Lee (tuberous-rooted mustard); *multiceps* Tsen & Lee (tillered mustard); *multisec-ta* Bailey (flower-like leaf mustard); *involuta* Yang & Chen (involute mustard); *strumata* Tsen & Lee (strumous mustard); *tumida* Tsen & Lee; and *utilis* Li (peduncled mustard). Mustard leaves, such as mizuna, a form of mustard, are sometimes used as salad greens. Mustard greens have a pungent, stinging taste, which is excellent mixed with blander foods. Mustard spinach (*Brassica rapa* Perviridis group) is known as *tat soi* or *komatsu-na* in many Chinese and farmers' markets in this country. It is not commonly eaten in the Mediterranean, but it works well in the recipe that follows. Mustard greens are not frequently eaten in the Mediterranean.

PLANT ORIGIN

The center of origin of black mustard, which is common in central and southern Europe, is thought to be Asia Minor and Iran. White mustard is thought to originate in the eastern Mediterranean. It is thought that mustard or brown mustard originated in the Central Asia and Himalaya region and then migrated to three secondary centers—India, China, and the Caucasus. N. Vavilov suggests northwestern India, Tadzhikistan, Uzbekistan, and the western Tien Shan Province as the center of origin of brown mustard, with Asia Minor as a secondary center. The wild forms of the plant appear most frequently around the Mediterranean littoral, especially in the Aegean. A bag full of white mustard seeds was found at a prehistoric site at Marmariani in Thessaly, Greece.

In a compilation of Assyrian herbals from the second to the first millennium B.C., a variety of mustards are included and called *hadappâmu*. Dioscorides used the word *lampsaun* for "mustard." The Romans grew white mustard. Mustard is one of the oldest spices. Evidence of its use exists in Sanskrit as well as Sumerian records dating to 3000 B.C. Pythagoras mentioned mustard, and Hippocrates (480 B.C.) used it as medicine. The Romans are said to have brought black mustard to Gaul, and today it is cultivated all over the Mediterranean. Both the Greeks and the Romans used mustard seeds as a spice and the leaves as a vegetable. The Romans added the crushed seeds to grape juice to keep it from spoiling. Later, in the Middle Ages, this kind of drink was known as "must" in England and made from "mustseed," which later transformed into the present-day "mustard." Pliny described mustard as a medicinal plant. The "grain of mustard" spoken of in the Gospels of the New Testament is thought by some scholars to be black mustard, although some argue that it is *Sinapsis alba*. In the thirteenth century Albertus Magnus described black mustard as a garden plant. During the Middle Ages, once mustard cultivation became widespread, mustards were known in the trade by where they came from, for example, Danish mustard, or English mustard, or Sicilian mustard.

Mustard is easy to grow. The plant can survive a wide range of weather conditions. Sow the seed in fertile soil in full sun in the fall or early spring and cover with a ¼-inch layer of topsoil. Thin the seedlings to about 10 inches apart. Harvest the greens by pulling up the entire plant or by cutting off the larger leaves and then cutting away the midrib stems. Harvest seeds by cutting the plant when the seed pods are brown but before they split. Hang the pods over a catch basin to collect the seeds. Separate the seeds from the chaff using a colander.

Whether in a supermarket or farmers' market, look for mustard greens that have long, full, dark green leaves. Buy bunches of mustard greens with crisp, dark green leaves, with no signs of wilting or yellowing. Store the greens in the crisper drawer of the refrigerator, where they may keep for a week.

Horta
GREEK WILD GREENS SALAD

A *horta* is a cold salad Greek cooks make from any number of greens gathered in the wild. Basically, the greens are washed and either steamed or briefly boiled, just until they wilt. Then they are drained well, scattered on a platter, dressed with olive oil and lemon juice, seasoned with some salt and pepper, and served as a side dish.

1 pound radishes, green tops only (roots saved for the salad on page 280)
1 pound mustard greens
1 pound baby turnips, green tops only (roots saved for another preparation)
½ pound mustard spinach
½ pound amaranth or chickweed (see entries)

FOR THE DRESSING:
⅓ cup extra virgin olive oil
Freshly squeezed juice from 1 lemon
½ teaspoon Dijon mustard
Salt and freshly ground black pepper to taste

1. Place the radish tops and mustard greens in a steamer and turn the heat to high. After they wilt, in about 5 minutes, add the turnip tops and cook the greens for another 5 minutes. Add the remaining greens and cook until they are all wilted, about another 5 minutes.
2. Drain well and arrange the greens on a serving platter. Whisk together the dressing ingredients, drizzle the dressing evenly over the greens, and serve once the salad reaches room temperature.

Makes 4 to 6 servings

NASTURTIUM
Tropaeolum majus L. (Tropaeolaceae)
Also called Indian cress, Jesuit's cress;
FRENCH: *capucine*; GREEK: *nastarsphum*;
ITALIAN: *nasturzio*; SERBO-CROATIAN: *potočarka, dragušac*; SPANISH: *capuchina, nasturcia*

PLANT CHARACTERISTICS AND VARIETIES
Nasturtium is a succulent herb that grows as an annual or perennial by climbing via coiling petioles. The plant can grow to 12 feet tall. The leaves have a mustard-oil component, which gives them a slightly sharp taste. Nasturtium is also the name of a group of aquatic herbs in the Cruciferae-Brassicaceae family (see Watercress). The leaves are usually used in salads because of their peppery taste. The brilliant funnel-shaped flowers of yellow, orange, and/or red are also edible and used as garnishes. The flowers are frequently used as a garnish by French and Italian restaurant chefs.

PLANT ORIGIN
The nasturtium is native to Mexico, Central America, and northern South America and was introduced to the Mediterranean as a cultivated garden plant.

The nasturtium is said to have been brought to the Mediterranean by the Jesuits.

HOW TO GROW AND HARVEST

Nasturtium should be planted after the last frost date in warm, well-drained soil in full sun. Soak the seeds in water for 12 hours and dry them before planting. To harvest, cut off the leaves and flowering stems near ground level, and new foliage will grow.

NEPITELLA

Calamintha nepeta (L.) Savi (Lamiaceae)
Also called lesser calamint; ITALIAN: *nipotella, nepitella, nipitella* (Tuscany)

PLANT CHARACTERISTICS AND VARIETIES

Nepitella is a perennial herb that grows to 2 to 3 feet. The leaves are used to aromatize mushrooms, artichokes, and zucchini in rural Tuscany.

NIPPLEWORT

Lapsana communis L. (Asteraceae-Compositae)
ITALIAN: *sportavecchia* (Tuscany)

PLANT CHARACTERISTICS AND VARIETIES

This annual or perennial herb has large terminal and small lateral lobes. The young leaves have a bitter, radishlike taste and are eaten raw in salads, boiled in vegetable soups, and used in frittatas in rural Tuscany.

PLANT ORIGIN

Nipplewort appears to be native to Europe. Seeds have been found at Neolithic villages in Germany.

OKRA

Hibiscus esculentus (syn. *Abelmoschus esculentus* [L.] Moench) (Malvaceae)
ARABIC: *bāmiya (also spelled bāmya, bāmyā), wīka;* FRENCH: *gombo, okra, ketmie comestible;* GREEK: *bamies;* ITALIAN: *ibisco, frutto d'ibisco, gombo, gombro, ocra;* SPANISH: *gombo, ocra, chaucha turca, quimgombó;* TURKISH: *bamya*

PLANT CHARACTERISTICS AND VARIETIES

Cultivated forms of okra seem to be complex polyploid hybrids that fall somewhere between some of the 30 species of *Hibiscus* section *Abelmoschus*. Okra is a hot-weather plant that grows to 8 feet high. A heavy wooden central stem branches into long stems with large and slightly spiny leaves. The blossoms are yellow and grow from the leaf axils; the ribbed and edible pods are attached to these axils. Okra has a mucilaginous texture that results from chemical compounds in the plant, namely, acetylated acidic polysaccharide and galacturonic acid.

PLANT ORIGIN

Although the plant is popularly thought to have originated in tropical Africa, botanists do not know with certainty the place of origin of okra, although along the Nile of Egypt or the Sudan has been suggested. N. Vavilov suggested Ethiopia as a center of origin.

PLANT HISTORY

Okra has been cultivated in West Africa, Ethiopia, and the Sudan for a long time. It moved from West Africa to the southern United States with the slave trade. It is not known when okra moved from Africa to the Mediterranean, but cooked okra is eaten mostly in the eastern Mediterranean and North Africa. Abul-Abbas al-Nabati, a Spanish Arab native of Seville, provided one of the first descriptions of okra. Writing of a voyage to Egypt, he describes okra and says that it was eaten when young and tender.

HOW TO GROW AND HARVEST

Okra is a tropical vegetable that needs a lot of heat in order to grow. The soil should be fertile, a loamy clay soil, slightly moist, with a high concentration of potash. The plant needs to grow in heat for 4 months. Wash the seeds in dishwashing detergent, rinse them, and soak them overnight. Then drain and dry the seeds. Sow the seeds after the last frost in groups of three about 1 foot apart. Harvest okra by picking the pods when they are less than 4 inches long, although in eastern Mediterranean cuisine the pods are picked when they are less than an inch long. Cut off the pods at the stem with a knife but don't remove the caps.

HOW TO BUY, STORE, AND PREPARE FOR COOKING

Do not refrigerate okra because the cold, dry air will cause them to deteriorate quickly. In the Mediterranean, the preferred size of okra is quite small. In fact, in Lebanon, cooks like the pods to be no bigger than the length from the tip of the little finger to the first joint. In this country, okra are sold much larger, and, as a result, they are tougher. Buy the smallest okra you can find. Do not wash okra for too long before cooking it because water will make them slimy. Rinse them as you are about to cook them. Store the okra, without trimming or cutting them, in a plastic bag until needed, preferably not for more than a day. Trim the okra just before cooking by cutting off the stem end that looks like a cap.

Okra

Although okra occasionally appears in some of the cooking of the northern Mediterranean, especially in the old-time cooking of Provence (probably an influence of the pieds noirs, the French settlers of North Africa who returned to France), it is almost exclusively an Arab vegetable nowadays. The recipes from Syria and Lebanon that are featured here are good examples of that. In North Africa, okra is very popular, although it appears mostly in a variety of ragouts and stews or served with couscous. In Tunisia, cooks prepare *qanawiyya al-shā'ḥa*, sun-dried okra that is reconstituted in water.

RECIPES

Bāmyā bi'l-Zayt
OKRA WITH OLIVE OIL

It is interesting that this complex dish with all kinds of enticing flavors is so simply named in Arabic. This recipe comes from George Salloum, who is from Homs, Syria. My former mother-in-law, who is Palestinian, would make the same dish without the pomegranate molasses. The kind of okra that Lebanese cooks use is very small, much smaller than you can find in the market here. Ideally, they should be no bigger than the length from the tip of the little finger to the first joint.

1 cup olive oil

2 pounds fresh okra, washed, dried well with paper towels, and trimmed

1 large onion, sliced very fine

2 heads garlic (about 40 cloves in all), peeled, divided

2 pounds ripe tomatoes, peeled, seeded, and chopped

2 tablespoons pomegranate molasses

½ cup freshly squeezed lemon juice

Salt to taste

1 cup loosely packed, finely chopped fresh coriander leaves (from about 1 bunch)

4 teaspoons salt

½ cup water

1. Heat the olive oil in a large casserole or wide saucepan over high heat until smoking, about 10 minutes. Cook the okra in the hot oil until golden crispy on all sides, 3 to 4 minutes. Do not crowd the pan; fry the okra in

batches if necessary. Remove the okra with a slotted ladle as they finish cooking. Drain and set them aside on paper towels.

2. Reduce the heat to medium. In the same oil that you cooked the okra, cook the onion and about 30 cloves of the garlic until they are soft and a little browned, 8 to 10 minutes, stirring. Add the cooked okra, tomatoes, pomegranate molasses, lemon juice, and a little salt. Stir to mix and continue cooking, covered, until bubbling hard, 8 to 10 minutes.

3. Meanwhile, in a mortar, pound the remaining 10 garlic cloves with the coriander and 4 teaspoons salt until a pesto forms. Stir the garlic and coriander into the okra. Pour in the water, reduce the heat to low, and simmer, without stirring, until the mixture is thick, about 30 minutes. Turn the heat off and let the okra cool in the casserole. Serve at room temperature.

Makes 6 servings

Yakhnat al-Khuḍra
LEBANESE-STYLE MIXED VEGETABLE STEW

This Lebanese vegetable stew is the kind of dish that exemplifies what culinary historians mean when they point to the Arabs' love of vegetables. Arab vegetable preparations made an impact on the people of medieval Europe, whose diet had been carnivorous. The sheer variety of vegetables and the spicing make this preparation a favorite throughout the Levant.

2 cups olive oil

2 zucchini (about 9 ounces), ends trimmed, cut in half lengthwise, and cut into 2-inch-thick slices

2 green bell peppers, seeded and cut into 1½-inch squares

1 cup small okra, washed, patted dry with paper towels, and trimmed

1 cup green beans, ends trimmed, cut into 1-inch pieces

2 medium onions, cut into ⅜-inch-thick slices

1 large eggplant (about 1 pound), peeled and cut into ½-inch-thick slices

2 teaspoons salt, and more to taste, divided

½ teaspoon freshly ground black pepper, divided

½ teaspoon ground cinnamon, divided

4 large garlic cloves, chopped fine

½ cup finely chopped fresh coriander leaves

3 ripe tomatoes (about 1½ pounds), peeled, seeded, and cut into ¾-inch-thick slices

1. Heat the olive oil in a 12-inch skillet over medium-high heat and cook each vegetable individually in turn until lightly golden. Be sure to fry the eggplant last. The zucchini will take 2 to 3 minutes; the bell peppers, 4 to 5 minutes; the okra, 2 to 3 minutes, the green beans, 2 minutes; the onions, 4 to 5 minutes; and the eggplant, about 6 minutes. Drain the cooked vegetables thoroughly using a slotted ladle or skimmer. Set them aside on a platter as you continue cooking.

2. Preheat the oven to 350°F. In an 11- or 12-inch-diameter round casserole, preferably earthenware, with a cover, layer the vegetables,

first the eggplant, then the zucchini, onions, and okra. Season with I teaspoon of the salt, ¼ teaspoon of the pepper, and ¼ teaspoon of the cinnamon. Layer the peppers and beans and season with the remaining I teaspoon of salt, ¼ teaspoon of pepper, and ¼ teaspoon of cinnamon. Sprinkle with the garlic and coriander and cover with the tomato slices. Pour a little water on top. Cover and cook the stew until the tomatoes have collapsed and the liquid is boiling furiously, about I¼ hours.

3. Remove the stew from the oven and let it cool until it reaches room temperature. If you like, you can remove some of the liquid, cover the casserole with a round serving platter, invert the casserole, and serve it. In any case, serve the stew warm or at room temperature.

Makes 6 servings

ONION

Allium cepa L. Cepa group (Liliaceae)
ARABIC: *bassal*; FRENCH: *oignon*; GREEK: *krommoun, kremmudi*; ITALIAN: *cipolla*; SERBO-CROATIAN: *luk*; SPANISH: *cebolla*; TURKISH: *soğan*

PLANT CHARACTERISTICS AND VARIETIES
Onions, shallots, leeks, chives, scallions, and garlic are all closely related, belonging to the *Allium* genus. All of these vegetables possess the characteristic onion smell because of the alkyl sulfides they contain. The alliums are mostly herbaceous plants with underground storage structures in the form of rhizomes, roots, and bulbs. Onions are half-hardy perennials that are grown as annuals. They can have a variety of skin colors and shapes; there are about 450 varieties. Vidalia, Maui, Torpedo, and Walla Walla are sweet onions grown in the United States that can be eaten raw. Similar varieties exist in the Mediterranean. *Cipolline* are small, flat onions that are usually used in sweet-and-sour sauces. Spanish onions are large yellow onions that are sweet tasting and sold everywhere. Yellow onions, with skins ranging in color from golden to brown, have a stronger flavor and are not usually eaten raw. Pearl onions and boiling onions are planted densely on purpose so that they never will become big. These onions are picked very young and do not form a bulb.

Green onions, scallions, and spring onions all refer to *Allium fistulosum,* with their differences being one of cultivars. They are also known as bunching onions and are grown for their stalks. They are hardy plants that can survive cold winters and are best eaten in the springtime. The scallion is a very immature onion, pulled from the ground before a bulb has formed. A so-called green onion is a cross between a scallion and an onion; it is pulled when the bulb is still very small but beginning to form. Spring onions, also called bunching onions (although a bunching onion comes from another plant, *A. fistulosum*), are small specimens of common onion with a long neck and a tiny bulb; their bulb is a little larger than that of a green onion or a scallion. Spring onions are sold in bunches with their green tops.

PLANT ORIGIN

Onions are thought to have originated in Central Asia (Afghanistan, Iran, Baluchistan, Pakistan). There is some thinking that onions may have been indigenous in an area ranging from Palestine to India. The Mediterranean, according the N. Vavilov, is a secondary center of origin for the large types of onion.

PLANT HISTORY

Onions have been cultivated since prehistoric times and are not known as a wild plant. The ancient Egyptians certainly cultivated onions about 3200 B.C. and regarded the onion as a symbol of the universe. The vegetable's name may derive from the Latin *unus,* meaning "one." During the era of the pharaoh Tutankhamen (about 1550 B.C.) onions were mixed with wine to form a paste that was placed in a woman's vagina to stop her from menstruating. Onions were known to the Chaldeans before the Christian era, and they were one of the vegetables mentioned in the Bible that the Jews so missed when they left Egypt. Onions were grown 4,000 years ago in ancient Sumer in Mesopotamia. Garlic and onions have been unearthed at the Minoan royal palace at Knossos on Crete. Herodotus said that onions, radishes, and garlic were a part of the staple diet of the workers who built the Great Pyramid at Giza in the third

millennium B.C. Egyptian onions had an excellent flavor, and people ate them both raw and cooked, except for the priests who were prohibited from eating them. From the time of Hippocrates (430 B.C.) to Theophrastus (322 B.C.) to Pliny (A.D. 79), several onion cultivars were named and described. Columella (A.D. 42) speaks about an onion that the country people called *unionem,* a word that appears to be the origin of our word *onion.* There are a number of onion recipes in the fourth-century A.D. Roman cookery book by Apicius, although onions are used there more as a seasoning. St. Peter Damian (1007–1072) describes a dish of edible root vegetables, mostly onions, leeks, and chickpeas, that was eaten at his Benedictine monastery. About 1380 Chaucer mentions onions, as do many herbals. Old Mediterranean folklore relates that when Satan left the Garden of Eden after the fall of man, onions grew from the spot where his right foot touched the ground, and garlic from where his left foot touched the ground. During the medieval era of Charlemagne (late eighth and ninth century), onions played a role as an item people used to pay feudal tithes. Throughout the Middle Ages, onions played an important role in cooking and in the dietetic theories of good health that were prevalent at the time. By the sixteenth century, onions were no longer considered exotic, and the Portuguese physician Amatus Lusitanus (1511–1568) wrote that they were the most common of vegetables.

Onion

THERE ISN'T A CUISINE IN THE WORLD, I THINK, THAT DOESN'T RELY ON THE ONION FOR BASIC FLAVOR. IN THE MEDITER-ranean, onions are the starting point for all Italian *soffritti*, a very finely chopped mixture of onion and other aromatics, which are the foundation for sauces. In France, a *mirepoix* almost always includes onions. In the Arab world, cooks love to put black and brown crispy fried onions on top of all kinds of dishes, and the Greeks seem to cook everything with onions, and lots of them. In Andalusia, *cebollas en cazuela* is a delicious dish of caramelized onions seasoned with cinnamon. In Provence, cooks make *tarte à l'oignon*, which looks inviting and is often served at room temperature. In Corsica, at Le Chariot restaurant in Algajola on the northern coast facing the Ligurian Sea, I once had a *pizza flamiche* that was incredibly delicious. It was an onion and bacon pizza, made with a variety of local Corsican cheeses, olive oil, crumbled bay leaf, and a little red chile pepper. To this day I think of it as one of the best pizzas I've ever had. In Sicily, *cipolline in agrodolce* are made with pearl onions or cipolline onions cooked in white wine, wine vinegar, and sugar. In Morocco I once ate a couscous dish called *siksū bi'l dajāj wa'l-ḥummuṣ*, which was made with chickpeas, chicken falling off the bone, golden raisins, saffron, cinnamon, and caramelized onions that were so sweet that I thought I was in heaven. Mediterranean Jews are also well known for their onion dishes and use of onions, as we know from the Algerian *ṭabīkha*, a spicy bean, tomato, and onion stew cooked with chile pepper paste and fresh coriander, or the *filete estofar con cebollas* of the Sephardim, a skirt steak topped with a mound of fried onions and a little garlic. In Turkey, a variety of onion, *A. akaka*, is added to herbal cheese.

HOW TO GROW AND HARVEST

Onions grow best in a sunny, open position in well-drained, sandy, limey soil. The soil should not be fertilized with organic manures because they can cause bulb rot. Onion planting beds should be moved every year to avoid the buildup of fungal spores. Inorganic fertilizers such as soot or fertilizers with a lot of potash and nitrogen are good to use as a top dressing around the bulbs. Sow seed in April in a warm seedbed about ½ inch deep. Onions have shallow roots and need 1 inch of water per week. Harvest onions when the tops have begun to wither or fall. Pull the plants and let them cure under cover in some shade for 2 days, then dry them completely on a rack or screen in a cool, dry place.

HOW TO BUY, STORE, AND PREPARE FOR COOKING

Color and size are not reliable guides to how an onion will taste; it depends where and when it was grown. Look for firm onions without dark blemishes or green shoots. Avoid a strong smelling onion, which might indicate the beginning of decay. Keep onions in a cool, dark, dry, and open space such as a drawer dedicated to onions, or in a cellar. Avoid storing onions where there might be moisture, for example, in the refrigerator, under the sink, or near foods such as potatoes that give off moisture. If you do store onions in the refrigerator, store them unwrapped in the crisper drawer.

Some people are bothered by tearing when preparing onions, so they either wear goggles, which I find cumbersome and silly, or they slice them by holding them under water in a sink.

To prepare small boiling or pearl onions for cooking, peel them by trimming off the tops and bottoms and plunging them in boiling water for a few minutes; their skins will pop right off. Some cooks use the skins of yellow onions for coloring purposes in the making of stocks.

Scallions should have crisp tops and unblemished white bottoms. Scallions will perish more quickly than onions will, so keep scallions refrigerated in a plastic bag and use them within 3 days. Scallions need to be trimmed of their root ends before they are eaten.

RECIPES

Stufato di Verdure
SARDINIAN VEGETABLE STEW

The Sardinian language is different from the Italian language, and the same is true of Sardinian and Italian food. The food of Sardinia is influenced by several factors. First, Sardinia is an island, and an isolated island throughout much of its history, never having played the important role as an entrepôt as did Sicily to the south. As a result, the island has had few outside influences. The food is simple and local, and it emphasizes fresh vegetables and, to a lesser extent, fish. Second, the terrain of Sardinia is mountainous and hilly, suitable to the raising of goats and sheep. Small game, such as quail, thrush, and rabbit, is very popular.

This earthy vegetable stew has rich, aromatic flavors and is all you need for a wonderful dinner. The secret behind this stew is the pesto used in the *soffritto*, the gently fried onion that is the foundation of this stew. Peel the potatoes if you'd like.

1 large garlic clove, peeled

Leaves from ½ bunch fresh parsley (1 good-size handful)

½ cup extra virgin olive oil

1 pound small white onions, peeled (page 246)

1 large ripe tomato (about ½ pound), peeled, seeded, and chopped

6 fresh basil leaves

Salt to taste

1 pound small new potatoes

1 pound green beans, ends trimmed

I. Pound the garlic and parsley together in a mortar until a pesto forms.

2. Heat the olive oil in a casserole with high sides over medium-high heat and cook the onions, whole, until yellow, about 4 minutes. Reduce the heat to low. Quickly stir in the garlic and parsley pesto so the garlic doesn't burn in the hot casserole. Let the garlic sizzle for I minute and then stir in the tomato and basil. Cook for 30 minutes, covered.

3. Salt the stew and add the potatoes and green beans. Cover and simmer until the potatoes can be easily pierced with the tip of a skewer, about I hour. Serve hot from the casserole dish.

Makes 3 to 4 main-course servings

Cipolle Ripiene
STUFFED ONIONS

This stuffed onion preparation from the area around the town of Barletta in Apulia uses big red onions. Because the onion is the star of the dish, you will want to pay attention to the onions you use. Make sure they are not old, that is, that their odor is not too strong and that they are not developing green sprouts. Or use a sweet onion such as a Maui or Vidalia.

6 large red onions

1 ¼ cups freshly grated Parmigiano-Reggiano cheese

2 large egg yolks

Salt and freshly ground black pepper to taste

Pinch of freshly grated nutmeg

2 tablespoons extra virgin olive oil, divided

I. Boil the onions whole in a large pot of lightly salted water until they are still slightly resistant when pierced by a fork, I5 to 20 minutes. Drain, let them cool, and cut off the tops. Peel each onion. Make a hollow inside each onion, creating a sort of cup. Remove the pulp and chop it fine.

2. Preheat the oven to 375°F. In a medium bowl, mix together the onion pulp, cheese, egg yolks, salt, pepper, nutmeg, and 2 teaspoons of the olive oil. Blend well.

3. Stuff each onion with this mixture. Moisten each stuffed onion by drizzling some of the remaining olive oil over it. Place the onions in an oiled baking pan and bake until black specks appear on top and the onions look soft, 20 to 25 minutes. Serve hot.

Makes 6 to 8 servings

Trīya bi'l-Bassal

EGYPTIAN-STYLE FETTUCCINE WITH ONIONS

The food of Upper Egypt is quite simple because the people are poor. I spent some time in Medinet Habu, a village near Luxor, when I was researching one of my books. There I became friends with Gamal Mohamed, a young man who worked at a local inn that doubled in the daytime as a furniture making workshop. The village was a relaxing place to be, and my friend and I would lounge around with Gamal, whiling away the day making small talk while Gamal took those interminable and somnambulant Egyptian-style breaks from work. One day my friend and I came back ravenous from hiking over to the Valley of the Kings and asked Gamal if there was any food around. Gamal whipped up this dish for us, and we were very delighted, especially when we saw how simple it was and how few ingredients it contained. *Trīya* is an old Arabic word for a kind of pasta like vermicelli, but Gamal used fettuccine when he made this recipe. Egyptians like their pasta cooked soft, unlike the Italian who prefer it al dente.

6 tablespoons extra virgin olive oil
3 very large sweet onions, sliced ¼ inch thick
¾ to 1 pound fettuccine

I. Heat the olive oil in a large skillet over medium-high heat. Reduce the heat to medium, add the onions, and cook them until they are soft and light brown, with some of them having black edges, about 40 minutes, stirring frequently and lowering the heat if the onions are cooking too fast.

2. Meanwhile, bring a large pot of abundantly salted water to a boil and cook the pasta until soft. Drain it. Toss the pasta with the onions and serve without cheese or any other garnish.

Makes 4 servings

ONONIS SPINOSA L. SSP. *LEIOSPERMA* (BOISS.) SIRJ. (FABACEAE-LEGUMINOSAE)

TURKISH: *siğek dikeni*

PLANT CHARACTERISTICS AND VARIETIES
This plant is an annual or perennial dwarf shrub with flowers borne singly on each node. The whole plant is used and eaten as an edible green, either cooked or raw, in the Aksaray Province of Anatolia.

ORACHE

Atriplex hortensis L. (Chenopodiaceae)
ARABIC: *al-dhahabiyya al-baqla (or al-baqla al-dhahabiyya), al-hijaz, qatf; baqlun; āsfānākh rūmī*; FRENCH: *arroche, arroche épinard, arroche cultivée*; ITALIAN: *atriplice*; SPANISH: *armuelle, armuelle de huerta*

Orache, a frost-hardy annual, is a tall plant with small, pointed leaves. It is often used as a substitute for spinach. There are several varieties of orache, including sea orache *(A. halimus)*, gold orache *(A. hortensis)*, and red orache *(A. hortensis rubra)*. Orache is grown throughout Europe and appears in the Mediterranean, especially in Turkey. Orache, as with some other members of the goosefoot family, grows in damp areas in Egypt. It has a fetid smell, giving rise to the coining of some colorful names by Egyptian farmers.

PLANT ORIGIN

Orache appears to be native to central Asia and Siberia.

PLANT HISTORY

Several species of orache were known in ancient Egypt and still are today. Theophrastus described orache, and Dioscorides mentions that orache is eaten boiled. Pliny discusses orache as a kitchen-garden plant. Orache is recommended in the sixth-century dietetic work by Anthimus, *De observatione ciborum,* as being good for both sick and healthy people. In his twelfth-century agricultural work, the Hispano-Muslim writer Ibn al-ʿAwwām instructs the reader who wants to fatten his pigs to wash the animal with human urine and then anoint the tail with the juice of orache leaves mixed with olive oil and wine. The thirteenth-century medical formulary of the Arab doctor and pharmacologist al-

Samarqandī describes orache, one of whose Arabic names means "the golden vegetable," as a food and as an emetic.

HOW TO GROW AND HARVEST

Orache is grown from seed in the early spring. The plant is capable of seeding itself and will flourish in a well-tended garden. It is a popular plant for home gardeners because it is very ornamental. Plant seeds at 3- to 4-week intervals and water the plants frequently. Harvest by pulling up the entire plant when it is young with only eight leaves. The leaves can be harvested as needed.

OX-TONGUE

Picris echioides L. (syn. *Helmintia echioides* (L.) Gaertn.; *H. spinosa* DC.; *P. spinosa* (DC.) Poir. (Asteraceae-Compositae) ITALIAN: *lattaiolo, colalatte* (Bari-Apulia), *elminzia, sprùscana, spràscene* (Bari-Apulia), *radicchio di campo* (Tuscany); SPANISH: *buglossa*

PLANT CHARACTERISTICS AND VARIETIES

This plant is an annual or biennial herb with rigid hairs and slender spines. It has lancelike wrinkled leaves. Picked young, ox-tongue has been used as a potherb, especially in North Africa. This plant is popular used in salads in the Salento area of Apulia in southern Italy because of its bitter taste. In rural Tuscany, people use this plant and *P. hieracioides* L. in vegetable soups.

PLANT ORIGIN

Ox-tongue is found in Europe and North Africa.

PLANT HISTORY

Ox-tongue is given a brief mention in Pliny, who says that the plant had a foliated stem.

HOW TO BUY, STORE, AND PREPARE FOR COOKING

This potherb is usually boiled in salted water and then cooked with olive oil, salt, and pepper.

PAPER PUMPKINSEED
Fibigia clypeata (L.) Medikus
(Brassicaceae-Cruciferae)

PLANT CHARACTERISTICS AND VARIETIES

Paper pumpkinseed is a perennial herb with starlike hairs and green or grayish green leaves. The edible part is the young leaf. In the eastern Mediterranean the leaves are eaten raw as part of a salad.

PARSLEY
Petroselinum crispum (Mill.) Nym. var. *crispum* (syn. *P. hortense*) (Umbelliferae)
ARABIC: *baqdūnis;* CATALAN: *julivert;* FRENCH: *persil;* GREEK: *maintanos;* ITALIAN: *prezzemolo;* SERBO-CROATIAN: *peršin;* SPANISH: *perejil;* TURKISH: *maydanoz*

PLANT CHARACTERISTICS AND VARIETIES

Parsley is a frost-hardy perennial grown as an annual herb. The edible part is the leaf, which is eaten either raw or cooked. Three varieties of parsley are eaten: curly-leaf, flat-leaf (also known as Italian), and parsley root (*P. crispum* var. *tuberosum*), which has a swollen root. Among Mediterranean peoples, this last variety is used mostly in the cooking of Croatia, Bulgaria, Sardinia, and parts of Italy and France. Parsley root, a variety of parsley grown especially for its roots, looks like parsnip and tastes vaguely like parsley.

PLANT ORIGIN

Parsley is thought to have originated in the Mediterranean region of southern Europe. It is not known as an original wild plant, although it has escaped from cultivated areas and does grow wild.

PLANT HISTORY

The ancient Greeks grew and ate parsley. Theophrastus mentioned two varieties in about 320 B.C. Pliny wrote that parsley always accompanied sauces and table presentation. Both Columella and Pliny described its cultivation and varieties. In medieval times, parsley was thought to belong to the devil, and Good Friday was said to be the only day of the year on which it could be sown successfully, and only if the moon was rising. Albertus Magnus tells us that parsley was grown in thirteenth-century kitchen gardens.

The seeds should be sown in the spring for summer use. Seeds sown in August will survive the winter and can be harvested the following year. Most parsley grown by home gardeners is started from seedlings because the seeds germinate too slowly. Choose a location that gets full sun, and transplant seedlings 2 or 3 weeks before the last frost-free date. Flat-leaf parsley is easier to grow than curly-leaf, and is less bitter and stronger flavored. Parsley root needs a growing season of 3 months in well-tilled soil. The cold makes for a sweeter-tasting root. Harvest parsley for its leaves by cutting the plant about 2 inches above the ground. Parsley will continue to grow after a heavy cutting if it is fertilized and watered. Harvest root parsley in the fall, or let it stay in the ground covered with mulch through the winter.

HOW TO BUY, STORE, AND PREPARE
FOR COOKING

Store harvested parsley root as you would home-grown carrots by layering it in a box with wet sand or sawdust. Parsley root is cooked like parsnip (see entry). When shopping for parsley leaf, look for dark green, crisp, big leaves. Many Mediterranean cooks prefer flat-leaf parsley over curly-leaf parsley because they feel it is less bitter. If you are using the parsley within 3 days, you do not need to refrigerate it. After 3 days store parsley in the refrigerator unwashed. Wash the parsley as needed. Alternatively, wash a bunch of parsley before storing it, but make sure it is completely dry before storing it.

RECIPE

Tabbouleh

In the Arab world, tabbouleh (*tabbūla*) is a salad usually made as part of a *mazza* table (page xx) especially in Syria, Lebanon, and Palestine. The masters of the tabbouleh are the Lebanese, who prefer, as I do, a tabbouleh where the majority of the salad is composed of the green herbs, not overwhelmed by the bulgur. The predominant taste of a true tabbouleh should be of herbs, not wheat. The longer the bulgur sits and absorbs the olive oil, lemon juice, tomato, and onion juices, the more it will swell and dominate the salad, so keep that in mind. Many cooks make tabbouleh with a food processor, pulsing in short bursts, although I still prefer the texture that is achieved by the labor-intensive method of chopping all the ingredients with a large chef's knife. Tabbouleh is properly eaten by scooping up small amounts with pieces of romaine lettuce, not with a fork and knife, nor with Arabic flatbread.

½ cup raw medium or coarse bulgur

Freshly squeezed juice from 4 lemons

6 cups finely chopped fresh Italian parsley leaves
(from about 6 bunches)

1 cup finely chopped fresh mint leaves

1 pound ripe tomatoes, peeled if desired, and
chopped very fine

2 large onions, chopped very fine

Salt and freshly ground black pepper to taste

1¼ to 1⅓ cups extra virgin olive oil, as needed

1 bunch romaine lettuce, leaves separated, washed,
and dried

1 bunch scallions, ends trimmed

1. Cover a strainer with cheesecloth and place the bulgur on top. Place the strainer in a pot filled with cold water and soak the bulgur for 10 minutes. Pull up the sides of the cheesecloth, encasing the bulgur, and squeeze out all the water. Transfer the bulgur to a large bowl. 2. Toss the bulgur with the lemon juice. Toss the bulgur again with the parsley, mint, tomatoes, and onions and season with salt and pepper. Stir in the olive oil and leave to rest at room temperature until the bulgur has absorbed enough liquid to be tender, 4 to 6 hours. Correct the seasoning and olive oil, adding enough for the mixture to look shiny and moist but not gooey and oily. Serve with romaine lettuce leaves and scallions.

Makes 6 servings

PARSNIP

Pastinaca sativa L. subsp. *sativa*
(Umbelliferae)

ARABIC: *jazar abyad;* FRENCH: *pastenaque, panais;* GREEK: *daukion;* ITALIAN: *pastinaca;* SERBO-CROATIAN: *pastrnak;* SPANISH: *pastinaca, chirivía, berraza;* TURKISH: *pastinay*

PLANT CHARACTERISTICS AND VARIETIES

The parsnip, like the carrot, is a biennial that is cultivated for its fat wedge-shaped roots. The leaves can also be eaten cooked. Given the space the plants occupy in the garden, parsnips do not produce that much food.

PLANT ORIGIN

The cultivated parsnip has been developed from the wild parsnip, which is found throughout central and southern Europe and the Mediterranean. N. Vavilov suggests the Mediterranean as a center of origin of parsnip.

PLANT HISTORY

In Greek and Roman writings the authors are not clear as to whether they are referring to the parsnip or the carrot or both. Hippocrates and Dioscorides mention a *daucos*, which refers to an umbellifer grown on Crete for medicinal purposes, while Pliny describes *pastinaca* in the first century A.D., which could refer to either parsnips or carrots, and maybe both. *Elaphoboscon*, a plant described by Pliny, has also been taken to be the wild parsnip. Pliny says it was like giant fennel (see entry), with a jointed stem the thickness of a finger, and that the seed clusters hung down like those of hartwort (an old name for a variety of different plants in the *Seseli* genus and other umbellifers), and that the leaves were like those of alexanders (see entry). The parsnip has been praised as a food, Pliny tells us. In the sixteenth century, parsnips were a valuable root vegetable because they could be stored throughout the winter. Once the potato arrived on the Mediterranean scene in the late sixteenth century, the parsnip's popularity receded. But parsnips were very popular during the Renaissance.

HOW TO GROW AND HARVEST

Parsnips grow best in a very deep, well-dug place with fine, loamy soil that has not been manured. Manuring will make the roots fork. A light application of 5-10-5 fertilizer is sufficient. Sow seeds thickly in April or May in groups about 5 inches apart, and then thin the plants later to 6 inches apart. The plants like full sun. Parsnips are usually harvested from October on into the winter when the root is 4 inches long or longer, after about 4 months of growing. Parsnips can also be left in the ground through the winter and harvested in the spring before the plant begins to grow again.

HOW TO BUY, STORE, AND PREPARE FOR COOKING

Choose parsnips that are relatively smooth skinned and straight (because you end up wasting a lot of the crooked ones when you peel them). Don't be fooled into choosing very large parsnips because you think peeling them will be easier: they will be woodier tasting. But if you do use larger parsnips, remove the woodiest-tasting part by cutting them in half lengthwise and then using a paring knife to cut out the inner section, which is a slightly different color. Also, avoid parsnips that have a lot of hairy-looking rootlets, as well as ones that are limp. Storing parsnips in plastic bags in the crisper drawer of the refrigerator will make the roots sweeter. They will keep for a month stored this way.

RECIPE

Pastinaca Grosse
DEEP-FRIED PARSNIPS

One does not encounter parsnips very much in the cooking of the Mediterranean (usually they're used in stews), but they were once popular, as we can see in this recipe from the Renaissance, which is found in Maestro Martino da Como's *Libro de arte coquinaria*, written about 1450.

You will want to choose large parsnips that are not too thinly tapered.

2 pounds parsnips
All-purpose unbleached flour for dredging
6 cups olive oil or vegetable oil for frying
Salt to taste

1. Peel the parsnips, core them, and cut them into wedges or French fry shapes.

2. Preheat the oil 370°F in a deep fryer or an 8-inch saucepan fitted with a basket insert. Dredge the parsnips in flour, put them in a strainer, and tap or shake off the excess flour. Cook the parsnips in batches in the hot oil until they are a light golden color, about 3 minutes. Don't crowd the fryer. Drain on paper towels, salt immediately, and serve once all the batches are cooked. Let the frying oil cool, strain it, and save it for a future use.

Makes 4 to 6 servings

PEA

Pisum sativum L. ssp. *sativum* var. *hortense* (*P. commune*) (Leguminosae): garden pea, sweet pea, green pea; including edible podded pea, sugar pea, Chinese pea; ARABIC: *bizilla*; FRENCH: *petit pois, pois potager*; GREEK: *pison, pixeli, biselia*; ITALIAN: *pisello*; SERBO-CROATIAN: *grašak*; SPANISH: *guisante, guisante común, pésol, arveja*; TURKISH: *bezelye*

Pisum sativum L. ssp. *sativum* f. *macrocarpon* (syn. *P. macropon*): snow pea; FRENCH: *pois mange tout, pois sucré*; ITALIAN: *pisello mangiatutto, pisello dolce, taccola*; SPANISH: *guisante tirabeque, guisante come-todo, guizante azucarado*

PLANT CHARACTERISTICS AND VARIETIES

The pea plant is an annual that grows up to 7 feet and is cultivated for its seeds. The edible parts are the immature seeds, which are cooked fresh, and the tender shoots, which are eaten cooked or raw. When peas are allowed to ripen they are usually dried and eaten as part of a soup or stew.

Peas are divided into two kinds, shell peas and edible pod peas (*P. sativum* L. var. *macrocarpon*), such as snow pea pods, sugar peas, and *mangetout*. Another botanical division separates the peas into three major types: *P. sativum* var. *sativum*, var. *medullare*, and var. *saccharatum*. Peas are related to the *Viciae* or vetches, such as fava beans, chickpeas, and lentils. Although *Pisum* was once divided into a number of species, recent research has shown that there is no cytogenetic basis for distinguishing two species, *P. sativum* and a second one called *P. fulvum*. The most familiar subspecies, *sativum*, has smooth or wrinkled seeds and pods ½ inch wide. Another pea, known as Egyptian pea (*P. jomardi* Schrank.), is eaten in Egypt, and the wild pea, *P. sativum* var. *elatius*, is eaten by the Arab oasis dwellers of the Sahara Desert.

PLANT ORIGIN

The early history of the pea, as well as the wild ancestor of the garden pea, is not definitively known. But excavations of Neolithic settlements in the Near East and Europe that date from about 7000 B.C. have yielded carbonized pea seeds. N. Vavilov considered Ethiopia, the Mediterranean, and Central Asia to be the primary centers of origin, and the Near East to be the secondary center. But it is not known whether these centers are centers of origin or merely centers of diversity. One line of thinking suggests that the pea might derive from the varieties *arvense* (field pea or gray pea, the pea sometimes used for making split pea soup) and *elatius*. Of the two wild subspecies, *P. elatius* Bieb. and *P. humile* Boiss. et Noë, the latter was the first to be cultivated.

PLANT HISTORY

The earliest peas date from about 7000 B.C., and were found at a site at Jarmo, Iraq. There are other deposits dating from the Neolithic age in Jericho, as well as Anatolia and Greece. The cultivated pea is therefore as old as wheat and barley. Peas can be found growing wild in Italy, either because they are the original plants or because they escaped from cultivated areas. The Greeks and Romans knew of peas, although the ancient Egyptians and Hebrew tribes don't seem to have known of them. Between 400 and 800 A.D., peas, along with fava beans and lentils, were a staple food among people who were predominantly poor. Peas seem to have become uncommon by the Middle Ages in Europe, since we know that they had to be reintroduced in places. Peas did not become popular again until the seventeenth century in Europe. After Ruellius's botany was published in 1536, peas are mentioned more often. In 1614 Castelvetro called peas "the noblest of vegetables," especially those that can be eaten whole, pod and all. Fresh peas were so in vogue in the last quarter of the seventeenth century that in a letter from 1696 Madame de Maintenon ridiculed the mania for peas at the court of Louis XIV. The garden pea was the plant used by Gregor Mendel in the first scientific studies in what became the field of inquiry called genetics in the nineteenth century.

HOW TO GROW AND HARVEST

Peas thrive in rich, moist, but not soggy, soil that is slightly sandy and well drained. Peas do not do well in hot weather, and therefore they do best when grown in the spring or fall. In the Mediterranean, they can, in places, be sown in autumn for harvest in the early spring. Sow seeds in full sun in rows about 2 inches apart and 1 inch deep. Once the tendrils appear, the plant needs to be supported by a pole or stake driven into the ground or with a kind of biodegradable fiber mesh netting sold in garden supply stores. Once flowers appear, the plants should be mulched and watered. Harvest edible pod peas by continually picking the young pods when they are about 2 inches long. Harvest shell peas when they are plump enough that they can be shelled easily. Do not let the peas stay too long on the plant; otherwise they will become tough.

Pea

JUST LIKE FAVA BEANS, ARTICHOKES, AND SPRING ONIONS, GAR-
DEN PEAS ARE A MEDITERRANEAN DELIGHT IN THE SPRING.
There are a million recipes, and the two presented here are just a small representation
of the wealth of pea preparations. In France, peas are cooked alone or served with
other foods such as roast veal, grilled mackerel, or steak. Peas and artichokes is a dish
found in France, Sicily, Italy, and Greece. And in Venice, *risi i bisi* is a famous risotto
made with fresh spring peas. The *huevos a la flamenca* of Andalusia, a complex baked
omelette of asparagus tips, potato, cured ham, red bell pepper, and sherry, always
includes fresh peas. In Croatia, *grašak u gnjezdu* is a preparation of mashed potatoes
formed into nests that are filled with fresh peas, smoked bacon, butter, and sour cream.
In Florence, *piselli al prosciutto* is a simple dish featuring the melt-in-your-mouth *prosciutto di Parma*. In the port of Cádiz in Andalusia, *guisantes a la gaditana* is a recipe of
fresh peas cooked with potatoes, onions, garlic, hazelnuts, and saffron. In Italy alone
there are a gazillion different pea recipes. Peas appear in *minestre* or with pasta or in
the famous *insalata Russa* made with peas, carrots, and mayonnaise. In North Africa,
dried peas are favored, and they are often cooked in ragouts. But in Algeria, a perfect
little dish is called *zurūdiya bi'l-jilbāna*, diced carrots cooked with fresh peas in a sauce
flavored with a bunch of chopped fresh coriander, cinnamon, and salt and pepper. In
the Levant, a Syrian speciality is *ruzz bi'l-bazilla*, rice pilaf made with peas and spices
and sometimes ground lamb.

HOW TO BUY, STORE, AND PREPARE
FOR COOKING

Peas sold at supermarkets or farmers' markets
should be displayed under refrigeration or
cool shading because when kept at room temperature, half the peas' sugar content will turn
to starch in 6 hours. Look for pea pods of
medium size that are plump with a ready-to-
burst look. The pods should be green, not yellow or blemished. Pop open a pod to taste a
few peas. Buying pre-shelled peas will save you
some labor time, but they are more expensive
and may not be sweet enough because of the
rapid conversion of sugar to starch. One
pound of pea pods will yield about 1 cup of
peas. Prepare peas the day you buy them, and
refrigerate them for not more than 1 day.
Frozen peas are a satisfactory replacement for

most cooking purposes if fresh peas are not available. Petit pois are simply peas that have been harvested very young. Dried peas are used in North African cooking mostly and in other parts of the Mediterranean for soups. The "split pea" used in split pea soup or in the Indian *dhal* is the pigeon pea (*Cajanus cajan* [L.] Huth.), not the dried garden pea (but see exception mentioned above).

RECIPES

Maraqat al-Khuḍra
TUNISIAN-STYLE MIXED VEGETABLE STEW

This stew is a winter dish in Tunisia. The flavors are robust and spicy hot, and the resulting ragout is syrupy. My recipe uses canned cooked chickpeas and fava beans and is an adaptation of a preparation I once ate cooked by the Tunisian chef Jaouida Farah. The dried peas are typical fare in the wintertime cooking of Tunisia. If you decide to use dried beans in this recipe, they need to be soaked for no less than 24 hours. The kind of fava bean used in this recipe is a small round type known as *fūl ḥammām*, or "bath fava." The cans of cooked beans sold in markets are likely to be labelled *foul medammes*. The dried *ḥammām* fava most likely can be found sold in Middle Eastern markets or whole or natural food stores.

3 tablespoons extra virgin olive oil

1 medium onion, chopped

2 pounds spinach, trimmed of heavy stems, washed well, and chopped

Leaves from 1 bunch fresh parsley, chopped

1 cup dried split garden peas, picked over and rinsed

4 turnips (about 1 pound), peeled and diced (about 2 cups)

1 carrot, diced

1¾ cups water, divided

2 large artichokes (about 2 pounds), trimmed (page 10), and hearts diced

2 tablespoons harīsa *(page 263)*

1 tablespoon tābil *(page 106)*

1 teaspoon cayenne pepper

1 teaspoon ground red chile or red Aleppo pepper

1 tablespoon salt

2¼ cups canned cooked fava beans, drained, or 1 cup dried fava beans, picked over, soaked in water to cover for 24 hours, and drained

2¼ cups canned cooked chickpeas, drained, or 1 cup dried chickpeas, picked over, soaked in water to cover for 24 hours, and drained

I. Heat the olive oil in a casserole over medium-high heat and cook the onion, spinach, and parsley until the onion is soft and wilted, about 5 minutes, stirring frequently. Add the split peas (and the dried fava beans and dried chickpeas, if you are using them), turnips, carrot, and 1 cup of the water, reduce the heat to low, and cook, covered, for 20 minutes. Add the artichokes and cook until everything is tender, but with a little bite to the root vegetables, about 25 minutes, stirring occasionally.

2. Stir the *harīsa* and *tābil* together in the remaining ¾ cup water. Add to the casserole with the cayenne, red chile pepper, and salt. Stir to blend, cover, and cook for 30 minutes over low heat. Add the fava beans and chickpeas, if you are using canned beans, and stir again to blend. Cook, uncovered, until everything is tender and unctuous, 25 to 35 minutes. Serve immediately.

Makes 6 servings

PEA GREENS AND SPRING ONIONS

This is a delightful springtime dish when both peas and spring onions come popping out of the ground. In this Greek-inspired dish, the delicate pea greens are used. They are sweet to behold because they are delicate and their tendrils are lacelike. They require very little cooking. Pea greens are rarely found in a supermarket, so you will need to scout the farmers' markets. The amount of dill you will want to use will depend on how much you enjoy the fragrance of this herb.

2 tablespoons extra virgin olive oil
5 ounces large-bulbed spring onions, white part and three-quarters of the green part, ends trimmed, chopped
2 to 3 garlic cloves, to your taste, chopped fine
¾ pound pea greens, stems removed
1 to 4 tablespoons chopped fresh dill, to your taste
Salt and freshly ground black pepper to taste

In a large casserole or skillet, heat the olive oil over medium heat with the spring onions and garlic until the spring onions are wilted, about 5 minutes, stirring frequently so the garlic doesn't burn. Reduce the heat to low, add the pea greens and dill, season with salt and pepper, and cook until both are wilted, about 6 minutes. Serve hot.

Makes 4 small servings

PEPPER

Capsicum annuum L. Grossum group (syn. *C. frutescens* var. *grossum*) and *Capsicum annuum* L. Longum group (syn. *C. frutescens* var. *longum*) (Solanaceae)
Also called bell pepper, sweet pepper; including chile pepper, cayenne pepper, or hot pepper, and many other names for cultivars, including the botanical genus name *Capsicum*.

Bell pepper: ARABIC: *filfil, filfil rūmī, shaṭṭa* (var.); FRENCH: *poivre d'Espagne, paprica, poivron, piment doux*; GREEK: *piperies, kokkinopipepo*; ITALIAN: *peperone, peperone dolce, peperoncino*; SERBO-CROATIAN:

paprika (povrće); SPANISH: *pimiento, pimiento dolce, pimiento morron, paprica, chile dulce*; TURKISH: *biber ağaci.*

Chile pepper: ARABIC: *filfil ḥarra*; FRENCH: *poivre de Cayenne, piment fort*; ITALIAN: *pepe di cayenna, peperoncino piccante*; SERBO-CROATIAN: *feferon; paprika u prahu*; SPANISH: *chile, guidnilla, pimentón, pimiento picante*

PLANT CHARACTERISTICS AND VARIETIES

Peppers are annual or perennial herbaceous plants with a woody base and leaves with long petioles. The flowers have five white petals, and the fruit are hollow berries of different shapes. The edible part is the mature fruit, which is eaten raw or cooked. The mild-tasting bell pepper and the hot or chile pepper all derived from the genus *Capsicum*. There is some debate about the taxonomy of the pepper. Some botanists see upward of twenty-four species in the genus *Capsicum*, while others say cultivated peppers fall into two species, *C. annuum* and *C. frutescens*. Another suggestion for classification is based on the shape of the fruit. Today, based on the work of the botanists Charles B. Heiser, Jr., and Barbara Pickersgill, five species are recognized. The first is *C. annuum*, the most widely cultivated and economically important species. This species includes bell and other sweet peppers, as well as the hot peppers that are dried, for example, paprika. The second species is *C. baccatum*. It is cultivated mostly in Bolivia and rarely outside of South America. The third species is *C. frutescens*, which is grown mostly in

lowland tropical America and to a lesser extent in southeastern Asia. Only the Tabasco cultivar is grown outside the tropics. The fourth species is *C. chinese*, which is grown in tropical America and most commonly in the Amazon. The fifth species is *C. pubescens*, a highland species grown in the Andes.

The degree of hotness in a pepper depends on the amount of capsaicin, the vanillyl amide of isodecylanic acid, contained in the placenta (the white ribbing) of the plant, which in turn depends on the dominant gene of the plant and perhaps on the level of climatic heat. It seems that the hotter the climate, the hotter the pepper. The most commonly grown peppers in the Mediterranean are of the species *C. annuum.*

PLANT ORIGIN

The pepper, both taxa with the pungent capsaicin and those without, appears to be native to tropical South America, with the centers of diversity an area from Bolivia to southwestern Brazil for the former and Mesoamerica for the latter. On the other hand, the nature of the genus *Capsicum* is not fully understood, and therefore it is difficult to determine the place of origin. The earliest evidence of cultivated pepper is from the earliest archeological levels at Tamaulipas and Tehuacán in Mexico, which date from before 5000 B.C.

PLANT HISTORY

The first record of the pepper in the Mediterranean is after Columbus's voyages to the New World. Columbus saw peppers growing in the Caribbean. In his journal entry for January 15, 1493, he wrote that the natives called the plant *aji* (ah-hee). He named them *pimiento*, after the spice, black peppercorns (*Piper nigrum*), he had been seeking. This is how the capsicums came to be known as peppers. Also in 1493 Pietro Martire d'Anghiera (Peter Martyr), the Italian cleric and historian at the court in Barcelona, stated in a letter that Columbus did indeed find a pepper more pungent than those from the Caucasus (*P. nigrum*). The hot varieties were dried and powdered and used as a substitute by Spanish cooks for the spice pepper *P. nigrum*, which was expensive and imported from the East. Once it was introduced to the Mediterranean, the pepper was accepted almost immediately, unlike tomatoes and potatoes, which took much longer to gain favor. The initial agents of this diffusion from the New World to the Old World were principally Portuguese mariners and traders; the Spanish played a secondary role. Later the Spanish were principally responsible for the diffusion of peppers, and especially chile peppers, throughout the Mediterranean during the late sixteenth century. Seafaring Greek captains brought pepper to Greece and the Balkans by the mid-fifteenth century, and by 1569 the Hungarians used the word *paprika* and were growing pepper as a spice after having been introduced to peppers by the Turks. Today, paprika refers to a ground product of bright red mild peppers of one or more varieties.

HOW TO GROW AND HARVEST

Peppers do well in dry, warm weather. They should not be planted outdoors until the weather is hot. Sow seeds indoors 2 to 3 months before the spring frost-free date and transplant the seedlings when they are about 5 inches high or about 3 weeks after the average frost-free date. Space the plants 2½ feet apart in rows 3 feet apart. Protect the seedlings from the elements with translucent plastic containers with the bottoms cut out. Harvest peppers as you need them. They are fully ripe when their skin turns red, yellow, orange, or some other color. Bell peppers get sweeter as they ripen, and chile peppers get hotter.

HOW TO BUY, STORE, AND PREPARE FOR COOKING

Look for firm, fleshy, glossy-skinned peppers without blemishes. The skin should not be wrinkled, and the stem should be firm. A pepper should feel relatively heavy. All sweet peppers can be kept in a plastic bag in the crisper drawer of the refrigerator; red peppers will keep for a week, and green peppers, for up to 10 to 12 days. Fresh hot peppers can be kept wrapped in paper towels in the refrigerator for up to 3 weeks. Sweet peppers need to be stemmed and seeded before they are used. Many cooks also like to peel peppers before using them because the skin is tough and not pleasantly digestible when the peppers are cooked, although this phenomenon is not as noticeable when peppers are eaten raw. To roast a pepper, place it in a baking dish in a preheated 425°F oven until it has blackened on all sides, 35 to 40 minutes. Let it cool enough to handle and peel off the skin.

The handling of hot peppers is of a little more concern. Because the capsaisin in hot peppers is so potent, any contact with your skin can be highly irritating. Do not touch your eyes, nose, or mouth when handling hot peppers. As soon as you have finished preparing the hot peppers, immediately wash your hands with soap and water.

RECIPES

Plato Árabe de Pimientos
PEPPERS AND TOMATOES

This Granadan preparation, whose Spanish name means "Arab dish of peppers," is known as a kind of *hortalizas*, a vegetable preparation made with vegetables grown in the *huertas*, the local truck farms that were originally established during Spain's Islamic period (746 to 1492). At that time Arab agronomists revived many of the dormant Roman gardens and established new ones based on new agricultural technology. There are a great many dishes prepared with vegetables grown in the *huertas*, and they are served as stews, as accompaniments to meat, and as tapas. I like to serve this dish at room temperature as a tapas with toasted slices of French bread rubbed with garlic.

8 green bell peppers (about 2¾ pounds)
4 fresh red chile peppers (about ¼ pound)
8 ripe tomatoes (about 3¼ pounds), peeled, seeded, and cut into quarters
6 tablespoons extra virgin olive oil
2 bay leaves
Salt and freshly ground black pepper to taste
1 teaspoon freshly ground cumin seeds

I. Preheat the oven to 425°F and char the skins of the bell peppers and hot peppers, turning them to cook all of their surfaces, until the skins are black, 25 to 30 minutes. Alternatively, if you are grilling, char the peppers on the grill. Remove the stems and seeds and quarter all the peppers.

2. Place the peppers, tomatoes, olive oil, bay leaves, salt, and pepper in an earthenware skillet or casserole, turn the heat to medium, and cover. Turn the heat off after 30 minutes, when there is quite a bit of liquid in the skillet or casserole. Mix in the cumin and leave the peppers and tomatoes in the skillet, covered, for 30 minutes. Remove the peppers and tomatoes with a ladle to a serving bowl and serve.

Makes 6 servings

Peperoni Imbottiti alla Barese

STUFFED YELLOW PEPPERS IN THE STYLE OF BARI

The rustic flavors of Apulian cooking very much appeal to me. This recipe from the city of Bari is very flavorful and aromatic, yet light and perfect for hot summer days, when I usually serve it warm rather than hot. The color, too, is very appetizing, as you will see. Notice, too, that the ingredient list calls for fresh, not dry, breadcrumbs.

6 tablespoons plus 1 teaspoon extra virgin olive oil, divided

About 3 cups (6 ounces) fresh breadcrumbs

8 salted anchovy fillets, rinsed and chopped

About ¼ cup salted capers, rinsed

½ pound imported black olives, pitted and cut in half

About ¼ cup golden raisins, soaked in tepid water for 15 minutes and drained

About ¼ cup pine nuts

2 tablespoons finely chopped fresh parsley leaves

2 tablespoons finely chopped fresh basil leaves

Salt and freshly ground black pepper to taste

Pinch of freshly grated nutmeg

6 yellow bell peppers (about 3¼ pounds), seeded and cut in half lengthwise

2 cups tomato puree (preferably fresh)

1. Preheat the oven to 350°F. Heat 3 tablespoons of the olive oil in a medium skillet over high heat and, once it is smoking, brown the breadcrumbs, tossing or stirring them constantly, 1 to 2 minutes.

2. In a medium bowl, mix the browned breadcrumbs, anchovies, capers, olives, raisins, pine nuts, parsley, basil, and 1 teaspoon of the olive oil together. Season with salt, pepper, and nutmeg.

3. Stuff the peppers with the breadcrumb mixture and arrange them in a baking pan oiled with some of the remaining 3 tablespoons olive oil. Drizzle the rest of the oil on top. Pour the tomato puree in the pan around the peppers and bake until the peppers are soft but firm, 50 to 60 minutes. Add water to the tomato puree if it is getting too thick. Serve the stuffed peppers hot or at room temperature.

Makes 6 servings

Peperonata

BELL PEPPER STEW

This Sardinian version of *peperonata*, a dish that is also popular in southern Italy, is made with only yellow peppers, which are grilled and braised slightly with a light tomato sauce in a rich extra virgin olive oil. This recipe is based on a delightful *peperonata* I enjoyed at the Ristorante La Lepanto in Alghero on the western coast of Sardinia. Bell Pepper Stew can be served as a side dish or an antipasto.

5 yellow bell peppers
1½ cups tomato sauce (page 337)
2 tablespoons extra virgin olive oil
Freshly ground black pepper to taste

1. Preheat a gas grill on high for 20 minutes or prepare a hot charcoal fire. Place the peppers on the grill until the skins blister black, turning them to cook all sides, 35 to 45 minutes. Alternatively, preheat the oven to 450°F, place the peppers in a baking pan, and bake them until their skins blister black all over, about 30 minutes. Remove and, once the peppers are cool enough to handle, remove the skin, seeds, and core and discard. Slice the peppers into lengths. Set aside.

2. Prepare the tomato sauce. Once it is ready, add the peppers and olive oil, season with black pepper, and simmer over medium-low heat for 20 to 30 minutes. Serve hot.

Makes 4 servings

Filfil Ākhḍar Muṣabbar bi'l-Zayt
RED BELL PEPPERS PRESERVED IN OLIVE OIL

This recipe is from an Algerian friend, Necim Zeghlache, from whom I have learned a lot about Algerian cooking. Necim served this very delicious red bell pepper preparation as part of a *qimia* table, before he served a lamb and vegetable couscous. A *qimia* is what the Arabs of the Mashraq (the eastern Arab world as opposed to the Maghrib, the western Arab world) call a *mazza*.

16 red bell peppers
Extra virgin olive oil to taste
White wine vinegar to taste
2 large garlic cloves, chopped fine
Salt to taste
2 tablespoons finely chopped fresh parsley leaves

1. Preheat the oven to 450°F.
2. Roast the bell peppers (page 261) until their skins are blackened, about 30 minutes. Place 2 brown paper bags in a large pot (to reinforce the bottom of the bag), put all the peppers inside, and close the bags so the red peppers will steam.
3. After 10 minutes, remove the peppers and peel them. Remove the seeds and core, cut up all the peppers in strips, and place them in a bowl. Sprinkle them with olive oil and vinegar and stir in the garlic. Sprinkle with salt and the parsley and serve.

Makes 12 to 14 small qimia
(mazza) servings

Harīsa
HOT CHILE PASTE

Harīsa is the most important and essential condiment used in Tunisian cooking. In fact, you'll need to make this recipe and keep it in the refrigerator before attempting any other Tunisian dish. This famous hot chile paste is also found in the cooking of Algeria, Libya, and even western Sicily, where it is used in fish couscous. *Harīsa* is sold in tubes by both Tunisian and French firms. Although the Tunisian one is better, neither can compare to your own, freshly made *harīsa* from this recipe. Be very careful when handling hot chile peppers: Make sure that you do not put your fingers near your eyes, nose, or mouth. Wash your hands well with soap and water after handling chile peppers.

2 ounces dried Guajillo chile peppers
2 ounces dried Anaheim chile peppers
5 large garlic cloves, peeled
2 tablespoons water
2 tablespoons extra virgin olive oil, plus more for
*   topping off the paste*
½ teaspoon freshly ground caraway seeds
¼ teaspoon freshly ground coriander seeds
1½ teaspoons salt

I. Cover the chile peppers with tepid water and soak until soft, 45 minutes to 1 hour. Drain and remove the stems and seeds. Place the chile peppers in a food processor or blender with the garlic, water, and olive oil. Puree the mixture, stopping occasionally to scrape down the sides.

2. Transfer the paste to a medium bowl and stir in the caraway, coriander, and salt. Store in a jar and top off, barely covering the surface of the paste with a layer of olive oil so it is not exposed to the air. The *harīsa* must always be covered with olive oil to prevent spoilage. Whenever you use some, always make sure to top off the paste with a little olive oil. Properly stored, without exposure to air, *harīsa* will keep for a year.

Makes 1 cup

VARIATION: To make a hot *harīsa*, use 4 ounces of dried Guajillo chiles and ½ ounce dried de Arbol chiles.

NOTE: To make *ṣalṣa al-harīsa*, used as an accompaniment to grilled meats, stir together 2 teaspoons *harīsa*, 3 tablespoons olive oil, 2 tablespoons water, and 1 tablespoon finely chopped fresh parsley leaves.

PEPPERWORT

Lepidium campestre (L.) R. Br.
(Cruciferae-Brassicaceae)
Also called bastard cress; ARABIC: *shīṭaraj or sīṭaraj*; ITALIAN: *erbo de'tedeschi* (Tuscany)

PLANT CHARACTERISTICS AND VARIETIES
Pepperwort is an annual or biennial herb that grows to 2 feet. The young leaves and shoots taste a little like watercress and are used in *frittate*, salads, and vegetable soups in Tuscany.

PIGEON PEA

Cajanus cajan (L.) Huth (syn. *C. indicus*)
(Leguminosae)
Also called Cajan pea, Congo pea, red gran, no-eye pea, yellow dhal; ARABIC: *ʿadas asfar, ʿadas sudanī*; FRENCH: *pois*

d'Angola, pois cajan, pois du Congo, ambrévade;
ITALIAN: *caiano, pisello dei tropici, pisello arboreo;* SPANISH: *frijol del monte, guisante de Angola, guando*

PLANT CHARACTERISTICS AND VARIETIES

The pigeon pea is a tall, hardy, perennial leguminous woody herb, and its peas are most often eaten in the Indian style of *dhal,* that is, as a "split pea." There are several varieties, which are best adapted to tropical grassland and arid regions. The two main types of pigeon pea, *tur (Cajanus flavus)* and *arhar (C. bicolor),* have Indian names, suggesting that they were derived from Sanskrit words. India is responsible for 95 percent of the production of pigeon peas in the world. The plant is grown in Africa and the Mediterranean, but it is most popular as a food in North Africa.

PLANT ORIGIN

It is thought that the pigeon pea originates in either India or tropical Africa, but as of this writing the true origin of the plant is not known.

PLANT HISTORY

There is some disputed evidence of seeds being found in ancient Egyptian tombs dating from about 2000 B.C., but, in any case, *cajanus* is referred to in a Sanskrit lexicon and a medical text from about 1400 B.C. The pigeon pea did travel west, though, first from India to East Africa, then up the Nile to the Mediterranean.

PILEWORT
Ranunculus ficaria L. (syn. *Ficaria verna* Hudson) (Ranuncolaceae)
Also called lesser celandine; ITALIAN: *favagello* (Tuscany)

PLANT CHARACTERISTICS AND VARIETIES

This fibrous-rooted perennial grows from 1 inch to 2 feet. The edible flower buds are sometimes used as a replacement for capers. The young leaves are eaten raw in salads, and in rural Tuscany they are used in vegetable soups.

PIMPERNEL
Anagallis arvensis Linn. (Primulaceae)
FRENCH: *mouron;* GREEK: *anagallis;* ITALIAN: *anagallide;* SERBO-CROATIAN: *bedrinac;* SPANISH: *pimpinela, pamplina*

PLANT CHARACTERISTICS AND VARIETIES

In the Levant, pimpernel is an annual or biennial with flowers on the upper axils of the leaves, which are eaten as a wild green or in salads.

PLANTAIN
Musa paradisiaca L. var. *paradisiaca* (Musaceae)
ARABIC: *mawz al-jana, ṭalḥ;* FRENCH: *plantain;* ITALIAN: *banana da cuocere, banana verde,*

piantaggine, banano plantain; SERBO-CROATIAN: *trputac, pisang;* SPANISH: *llantén, plántano de concinar, plántano macho*

PLANT CHARACTERISTICS AND VARIETIES

Plantain is closely related to the common banana, and although it is a fruit and more closely associated with New World cooking such as Cuban cuisine, it is eaten as a vegetable in some areas of North Africa. The fruit is usually larger than that of a banana and is eaten cooked; the flower buds can also be eaten cooked.

PLANT ORIGIN

The plantain is thought to have originated from certain wild Musaceae growing in Southeast Asia, Assam, Burma, Indonesia, the Philippines, and probably India. E. E. Cheesman argued that the plantain was derived from *M. balbisiana* and its relatives, while the banana was descended from a hybrid of *M. balbisiana* and *M. acuminata,* a plant of Malaysian origin. But N. W. Simmonds stated that the edible fruit first appeared in *M. acuminata,* and that *M. balbisiana* made a contribution to the edible varieties only after hybridization with *M. acuminata.*

PLANT HISTORY

The history of the plantain is closely related to that of the banana and is, in many ways, indistinguishable. The plantain (as well as the banana) has been cultivated since remote antiquity and is now, from millennia of hybridization and mutation, sterile and can reproduce only from corms. The two fruits probably first became evident to the Mediterranean by way of the botanists accompanying the Alexandrian expedition to India, who saw the plant in the Indus Valley in 325 B.C. Another route for its entry into the Mediterranean was via East Africa and then north along trade routes to Egypt. After the Islamic conquests in the seventh century, the banana is mentioned frequently. Unfortunately, it is impossible to distinguish the banana from the plantain in Arabic literature, the richest source for the history of Musaceae, because the Arabic word *mawz* denotes both plants. An intriguing word in the Koran, *ṭalḥ,* may mean plantain, as it certainly does today.

The sixteenth-century botanists Rumphius, Clusius, and Orta spoke of one, or maybe both, of these plants in Spain and West Africa, but a reading of the botanists' works does not yield any conclusive idea as to which one. Bananas and plantains appeared in the New World in the sixteenth century, but they did not become terribly popular in Caribbean and Central American cooking until the later nineteenth century, and especially after the 1920s, when breeding began in the Caribbean.

HOW TO BUY, STORE, AND PREPARE FOR COOKING

The plantain contains much more starch than the banana and is not eaten raw. When the fruit is green, it is boiled or fried. It can also be dried and ground into a kind of meal, or refined further into flour.

POTATO

Solanum tuberosum L. subsp. *tuberosum* (Solanaceae)

ARABIC: *baṭāṭa;* FRENCH: *pomme de terre;* GREEK: *patata, geomelon;* ITALIAN: *patata;* SERBO-CROATIAN: *krumpir;* SPANISH: *patata;* TURKISH: *patates*

PLANT CHARACTERISTICS AND VARIETIES

The potato is an annual with underground stolons bearing terminal tubers. The edible part is the tuber, which is cooked. The tuber is not a root, but the swollen end of the underground stem. This underground stem extends into stolons, the ends of which can enlarge to form tubers, sometimes more than 20, that are of different shapes and sizes with weights from half a pound to 3 pounds. The leaves and tomato-like fruit of the potato contain the alkaloid solanin, which is poisonous.

There are hundreds of species of potatoes, at least 235 according to one botanist, seven cultivated and the rest wild, and upward of a thousand cultivars of these species. Another source says that there were at one time 800 cultivars grown in the Andes, the ancestral home of the potato. Commercial varieties of potatoes are usually divided into three kinds. The first are harvested after 100 days; the second after 115 days; and the third after 130 days, or they are left in the ground until the fall.

The potato is one of the world's most important food crops, and the excellent quality of its protein has had historical significance.

PLANT ORIGIN

The record of the potato's exact place of origin and how it came to the Mediterranean is scanty. The latest evidence points to the Chiloé island of Chile as the place of origin; it seems that the first potato to reach Europe must have come from Peru and transshipped through Cartagena in Colombia in the mid-sixteenth century.

PLANT HISTORY

The potato was domesticated in the High Andes as early as seven to ten thousand years ago and was widely cultivated by Inca times. Because wild potato tubers taste bitter and contain toxic amounts of alkaloids, the earliest cultivators of the plant in prehistoric times must have aimed at selecting plants that were less bitter and less toxic. It is not known when this happened, but somewhere between 2000 B.C. and 5000 B.C., concurrent with the domestication of the llama, seems likely. The potatoes originally introduced to Europe were quite knobby and unlike the smooth ovals we see today, a result of cultivators working toward that end. It was also at least a hundred years after its arrival in the Mediterranean before the potato came to be accepted in any way as a food there.

The commonly accepted story of the discovery of the potato by Europeans tells of its being found in 1537 or 1538 by a Spanish soldier, Pedro de Cieza de León, in the Cauca Valley of Colombia and introduced as a curiosity to Europe sometime before 1573. The great French botanist Carolus Clusius went to Spain in 1564 with the express purpose of describing rare plants to be found there. He published his results in 1576 and never mentioned the potato. It seems that so attentive and careful a scholar as Clusius, the greatest botanist of his day, would not have overlooked the potato had it been growing in Spain, although it may have been present only in very localized areas. Clusius does seem to have received two tubers and a fruit in 1588 from Philippe de Sivry of Belgium and is credited with introducing the potato to Germany and France. We have definite proof that the potato was eaten at the Sangre hospital in Seville in 1573, so it must have reached Spain from the New World in 1569–1570. Three tubers, the potato, the sweet potato, and the sunchoke, all entered Europe from the New World about the same time, but it was the potato that became the dominant food. The potato probably won out because it was easier to digest and its taste was bland enough to allow for greater uses in a household economy. Most important, it was the starch in potatoes—its caloric value—that made it so attractive as a food. The potato was grown only in small gardens in Spain in the last part of the sixteenth century, but by the seventeenth century we see the potato more and more in the cuisines of Spain and Naples, which was then a dominion of the Spanish Bourbons. The introduction of the potato and its widespread cultivation helped reduce famines in Europe in the seventeenth and eighteenth centuries. The potato was also accepted in North Africa, apparently introduced there by the Spanish.

HOW TO BUY, STORE, AND PREPARE FOR COOKING

Buy potatoes individually rather than in large bags so you can inspect each potato for quality. Buy smooth and evenly shaped potatoes without any evidence of sprouting. A potato should be firm, not soft. Avoid potatoes with green skin spots, which indicate poor handling and storage conditions. The ideal place to store potatoes is in a root cellar. Store home-grown potatoes unwashed in a cool, dark place. If they start to sprout, rub the sprouts off. Do not eat the sprouts. Do not refrigerate potatoes or keep them cooler than 45°F because their starch will convert to sugar, making them too sweet. Should you refrigerate them accidentally, leave them out at room temperature for a few days; the potatoes will reconvert the sugar back to starch. Older potatoes will be fine for 2 months in a cool storage area. New potatoes should be used within a week of pulling or buying them.

Because the skin of the potato is so nutritious, many nutritionists recommend not doing too much to prepare a potato. But many recipes require the skin to be peeled. Once they are peeled, potatoes will turn color when

Potato

❧

The recipes that follow represent North Africa, Italy, and France, but potatoes are well loved in all Mediterranean countries. In Lebanon, cooks make potato *kibbe* with mashed potatoes, bulgur, spices, and fresh coriander. In Syria, they even stuff potatoes with ground lamb, pomegranate syrup, pine nuts, sumac, and mint. The Greeks stuff potatoes, too, usually with sausage, although the most famous Greek potato-and-garlic recipe must be *skordalia* (page 170). In Turkey, *patates silkmesi,* or "shaken" potatoes, is a dish of thinly sliced potatoes cooked with lamb, onions, and tomatoes seasoned with cumin, red pepper, and black pepper. This dish gets its name because the pan is shaken occasionally so nothing sticks. In Sicily, potatoes cooked with sweet red onions, tomatoes, and oregano are known as *patate allo sfincione,* or by an extremely vulgar expression relating to the public perception of the lack of celibacy among priests and the condition of the genitals of their mistresses. Since the potato first entered the Mediterranean by way of Spain, it is not surprising to find many potato recipes there. *Atascaburras* is a simple, yet wonderful, preparation of salt cod and potatoes cooked with garlic and walnuts, while *patatas en salsa verde* are potatoes cooked with garlic and parsley and often served with grilled fish. *Patatas viudas,* or "widowed" potatoes, is a Lenten dish of potatoes cooked with tomatoes, green bell peppers, garlic, onion, oregano, paprika, cayenne pepper, and parsley. The potatoes are "widowed" because there is no meat with them. But sometimes a cook can't resist throwing a few clams or bits of fish into this dish.

exposed to the air, so peel them at the last minute or peel them earlier but keep them covered with cold water.

The classification of potatoes can sometimes be confusing to the consumer. A "new" potato is not a small potato; it is a freshly harvested one. Different potatoes are suited to different culinary purposes. A russet or Idaho potato, which is a starchy potato, is best for baking because it turns out fluffy. A White Rose is an all-purpose potato. A red potato is a waxy potato that is good for boiling. "Waxy" refers to the low starch and high moisture content of the potato. Red potatoes remain firm once cooked, so they are ideal in preparations where you want the potato to maintain its shape. Specialty potatoes, such as fingerlings, or Yukon Gold, yellow Finn, Peruvian purple, and so on, are sold at farmers' markets and specialty greengrocers.

Gâteau de Pommes de Terre à la Sarladaise
POTATO CAKE FROM SARLAT

This recipe is one of my favorites for potatoes. It is always popular because of its gorgeous color when it's cooked. My dad has a little farmhouse near Sarlat, where he has lived for part of the year for a couple of decades now. I have learned a lot about the cooking of the region from one of his neighbors, Odile Lacarrière. Although she has given me a recipe for this potato cake, I decided to adapt it using Paula Wolfert's classic *The Cooking of Southwest France.*

2 tablespoons vegetable oil
2 pounds baking potatoes, peeled
3 tablespoons rendered duck fat
2 garlic cloves, chopped fine
2 tablespoons finely chopped fresh parsley leaves
Salt and freshly ground black pepper to taste

1. Prepare a 10-inch skillet for cooking by washing and thoroughly drying it. Pour 1 tablespoon of the vegetable oil in the skillet and heat over medium heat for 5 minutes. Turn the heat off, let the skillet cool, then wipe it dry with paper towels and repeat the process using the remaining 1 tablespoon of vegetable oil. This process is necessary to keep the potatoes from sticking.

2. Slice the potatoes into 1/16-inch-thick slices, like potato chips, using a mandoline or the largest opening of a 4- or 6-sided grater. Arrange the slices of potato on paper towels, in layers if necessary, placing paper towels between the layers of potatoes. Damp dry all of the slices with the paper towels. This step is absolutely necessary in order to ensure an appetizing finished dish.

3. In the 10-inch skillet, heat the duck fat over high heat. Arrange the potatoes in the skillet in an attractive overlapping spiral, or in any way you wish, and brown for 3 to 5 minutes. Tilt the skillet, remove any fat with a spoon, and save it. Place the flat lid of a skillet that is smaller than the 10-inch one you're using on top of the potato cake and invert the skillet so the cake rests on the lid. Return any fat to the skillet. Slide the potato cake back into the skillet to cook the other side for about 3 to 5 minutes. Reduce the heat to medium-low and press the potatoes down with the flat lid of the smaller skillet. Cover and cook for 6 to 7 minutes, shaking the skillet to keep the cake from sticking. Uncover, turn the cake over with the lid, as before, and press down again. Cover and cook for 6 to 7 minutes. The potato cake should be golden and crispy.

4. Remove the skillet from the burner and leave it to rest for 1 minute without uncovering it. Remove the cover, making sure none of

the condensation on the lid falls back into the skillet. Transfer the cake to a serving platter. Sprinkle the garlic and parsley over the top, season with salt and pepper, and serve immediately.

Makes 4 servings

N O T E : The best way to get duck fat is to collect it whenever you roast a duck. Take off large pieces of duck fat, place them in a baking pan in a 200°F oven, and cook the fat until it is liquid. After the duck is cooked, let the liquid fat cool in the pan, then transfer it to a container and refrigerate. It can stay in the refrigerator for some months.

Gnocchi de Patate
POTATO GNOCCHI

The potato arrived in Italy from the New World, maybe after passing through Spain. We don't know exactly when this happened, but it seems likely to have occurred sometime in the late 1560s.

Before the introduction of the potato, *gnocchi* referred to little balls of wheat flour or bread or both that were boiled. There is a recipe for such a dish, called *nochi*, in the early fifteenth-century cookbook by the anonymous writer known as the Anonimo Meridianale. But even by 1692, when Antonio Latini published his *Lo scalco alla moderna*, gnocchi were still made of flour and considered a kind of macaroni. In Genoa, gnocchi are today called *tròfie*, but in the Middle Ages gnocchi were originally a form of *pasta secca*, made from hard wheat flour and not potatoes.

Potato gnocchi are often heavy, pasty, and unappetizing. The secrets to making gnocchi like little puffs of clouds, so light they melt in your mouth, are manifold. The potato you use should have a relatively low moisture content. Do not use eggs to bind the dough; eggs will create heavy dumplings. Be very careful with the flour; try not to use any more than I have called for. There should be enough moisture left in the potatoes to help with the binding process but not enough to make a heavy *gnoccho* (singular). Do not handle the dough very much; use a fork to mix the batter at first. Then briefly and quickly knead the dough with your hands. Poach the gnocchi very gently (the water surface should only be shimmering) and remove them with a slotted ladle or spoon about 1 minute after they return to the surface. Try serving the cooked gnocchi with *quattro formaggi*, four cheeses, a modern invention from northern Italy. Melt some gorgonzola, taleggio, fontina Val d'Aosta, and mascarpone or grated Parmigiano-Reggiano together and toss with the gnocchi and a grinding of black pepper.

3 pounds baking potatoes
¾ cup all-purpose unbleached flour
1½ teaspoons salt
4 quarts water

1. Puncture the potatoes in 3 or 4 places with the tip of a paring knife or skewer. Microwave

them in their peel until a skewer will glide easily to the center of each potato. Alternatively, bake the potatoes in their skins at 350°F until a skewer will glide easily to the center of each potato.

2. Peel the potatoes while they are still hot, and pass them through a strainer or food mill into a large bowl. Add the flour and salt and mix the dough together quickly with a fork. Try not to handle the dough too much with your hands. Once the potatoes and flour are homogeneous, roll out the dough into long ropes about ¾- to I inch in diameter. Cut into ¾- to 1-inch segments.

3. Place each piece of dough near the end of a fork and roll the dough across the tines of the fork to the tip, pressing gently, or use the largest cheese grating opening on a grater, pressing down gently, and let the *gnocco* drop to the counter surface. Each *gnocco* will be I inch by ¾ inch and have indentations on it, which are perfect for holding the sauce.

4. Bring the water to a gentle boil in a large pot and add some salt. Reduce the heat so the water is shaking a bit, not bubbling. Drop the gnocchi into the water one at a time, slowly, and, once they have risen and are floating on top of the water, let them sit there for about 60 seconds before removing them, a few at a time. If you cook them for too long, they will become waterlogged and heavy. Drain and serve the gnocchi with the sauce of your choice.

Makes 4 servings

NOTE: First drop one *gnocco* into the boiling water, to test it. If it disintegrates add a bit more flour to the dough and start all over again.

Patate e Funghi al Forno
OVEN-BAKED POTATOES AND MUSHROOMS

This guileless dish from the cookery of Apulia in southern Italy demonstrates the culinary conceptions that result from combining simple, local ingredients and meeting the demands of the population for a certain taste. And, of course, this baked dish is a very logical accompaniment to an earthy roast lamb.

1 ½ pounds potatoes, peeled, washed, sliced ¼ inch thick, and dried with paper towels
1 pound portobello or cremini mushrooms, stems removed or trimmed, sliced
1 ½ cups crumbled stale French or Italian round bread
½ cup finely chopped fresh parsley leaves
Salt and freshly ground black pepper to taste
¾ cup freshly grated pecorino cheese
6 to 8 tablespoons extra virgin olive oil

Preheat the oven to 350°F. Arrange a layer of potato slices in a lightly oiled 12 x 9-inch baking dish. Mix together the mushrooms, crumbled bread, parsley, salt, pepper, and pecorino cheese in a medium bowl. Spread this mixture over the potatoes and then place the remaining potato slices on top. Pour the olive oil over everything and bake until the top potatoes are golden brown, 55 to 60 minutes.

Makes 4 to 6 servings

Salsa di Patate e Carciofi
POTATO AND ARTICHOKE SAUCE

This sauce from northern Italy is delicious with ravioli. The marriage of potatoes and artichokes is ideal. Potatoes are a bland food, so their culinary union with other foods can only enhance their taste. If you like, you can sprinkle walnuts on top of the ravioli and the sauce.

5 tablespoons extra virgin olive oil, divided
1 pound potatoes, peeled, sliced thin, and patted dry with paper towels
4 medium fresh artichoke hearts and peeled stems, sliced the same size as the potatoes
Salt and freshly ground black pepper to taste
1 medium onion, sliced thin
¾ cup milk
2 tablespoons walnut oil

1. Preheat the oven to 350°F. Oil the bottom of a baking pan with 1 tablespoon of the oil and layer with the sliced potatoes and artichokes. Salt and pepper each layer as you use up the ingredients. Arrange the onion slices on top and drizzle with the remaining 4 tablespoons of olive oil and the milk.

2. Bake until the potatoes and artichokes are soft and the edges of the onion are blackening, about 1½ hours. Remove the potatoes, artichokes, and onion from the pan and place in a food processor. Drizzle in the walnut oil while processing the sauce. Check and correct the seasonings.

Makes 2 cups

Makbūba
A POTATO AND BELL PEPPER FRITTATA IN THE STYLE OF THE TUNISIAN JEWS

This recipe is said to be typical of the kind of dishes prepared by the Jews of Tunisia, who were always fond of garlic. It is a kind of *shakhshūka* (page 143). The eggs are stirred in at the end of the cooking and allowed to set. It is a spicy hot dish and excellent preceded by *Ajlūk al-Qaraᶜ*, a pumpkin compote served at room temperature (page 316).

½ pound boiling potatoes, peeled and cut into quarters
½ pound green bell peppers, seeded and cut into rings
½ pound small ripe tomatoes, peeled, seeded, and cut in half
6 garlic cloves, crushed in a mortar until mushy with ½ teaspoon salt
½ teaspoon freshly ground caraway seeds
½ teaspoon freshly ground coriander seeds
1½ teaspoons cayenne pepper
3 tablespoons extra virgin olive oil
3 tablespoons water
Salt to taste
4 large eggs, beaten

1. Mix the potatoes, peppers, tomatoes, mashed garlic, caraway, coriander, and cayenne together in a large bowl.

2. Heat the olive oil in a large nonstick skillet over very low heat and add the vegetables along with the water. Cook, covered, until the potatoes are soft, about 1½ hours, pushing and turning the food occasionally, and seasoning with salt at some point. If there is more than ¼ cup of liquid in the pan, remove some of the liquid with a spoon. Pour the beaten eggs in, shake the skillet to distribute them, cover, and continue to cook the frittata until they have set, about 15 minutes. Serve immediately.

Makes 4 servings

Baṭāṭis bi'l-Bzar
POTATOES WITH SPICES

Libya is the least populated area of the Mediterranean, and almost all its people are Bedouin. There has been some urbanization since the end of the Italian occupation in World War II, but most Libyans still lead rural lives. Libyan cuisine, if it can be called that, is very simple. The people eat lots of macaroni and other wheat products, sorghum, potatoes, dates, and milk. This recipe is adapted from Anne Marie Weiss-Armush's *The Arabian Delights Cookbook: Mediterranean Cuisines from Mecca to Marrakesh.* It is a taste of a rare and rather impressive style of cooking.

5 to 7 tablespoons extra virgin olive oil, divided

1¾ pounds new white potatoes, peeled, cut into ½-inch cubes, and blotted dry with paper towels

¾ cup water

1 teaspoon salt

1 large onion, chopped

1 teaspoon red Aleppo pepper

½ teaspoon turmeric

½ teaspoon freshly ground coriander seeds

¼ teaspoon freshly ground cumin seeds

⅛ teaspoon freshly ground cloves

⅛ teaspoon ground cinnamon

⅛ teaspoon freshly ground black pepper

⅛ teaspoon ground ginger

3 tablespoons freshly squeezed lemon juice

2 tablespoons unsalted butter

1. Heat 3 to 5 tablespoons of the olive oil in a large nonstick skillet over medium heat and cook the potatoes until golden on all sides, about 15 minutes, shaking the skillet to toss the potatoes and brown them evenly. Add the water and salt and bring the pot to a boil. Cover, reduce the heat to low, and simmer until the potatoes are still slightly firm when pierced with a skewer, about 10 minutes.

2. Meanwhile heat the remaining 2 tablespoons of olive oil in a medium skillet over medium-high heat and cook the onion until translucent, about 5 minutes, stirring occasionally. Add the spices and stir to coat the onion, cooking for 1 minute so the flavors blend. Add the onion to the potatoes and toss well. Sprinkle with the lemon juice, add the

butter, cover, and simmer until the potatoes are tender, about 5 minutes. Serve hot.

Makes 4 to 6 servings as a side dish

Baṭāṭā Fliyū
POTATOES WITH WILD MINT

I discovered this recipe by way of an Algerian friend from whom I've learned a lot about Algerian cooking. Usually a wild mint is used, one with a strong odor and flavor that is also favored in North African mint teas, but any mint can be used here. This preparation is very nice, very fragrant, and I think quite nice served with fried fish, although it might be even better with veal or lamb. One cookbook writer tells us that this recipe is from the town of Blida in Algeria. Blida is an agricultural center whose agriculture and irrigation history go back to the sixteenth century when Arab-Andalusi immigrants from Spain settled in the town.

3 tablespoons extra virgin olive oil
6 garlic cloves, chopped fine
Salt and freshly ground black pepper to taste
2 pounds potatoes, peeled and quartered
Leaves from 1 bunch fresh mint, chopped fine
   (about ½ cup loosely packed)
¾ cup water
4 large eggs
1 teaspoon harīsa (page 263) or ½ teaspoon
   cayenne pepper

1. Heat the olive oil in a large skillet over medium-low heat and cook the garlic with salt and pepper until it is fragrant but not sizzling, 4 to 5 minutes. Add the potatoes and then the mint and toss well so all the potatoes are coated with oil. Pour in the water, cover, and bring the pot to a gentle boil over medium-low heat.
2. Once the water is boiling, uncover, reduce the heat to low, and continue cooking until the potatoes can be broken apart easily with a fork, 30 to 40 minutes. The water should be quite reduced, about 3 tablespoons at the most. If it isn't, remove the potatoes with a slotted ladle and reduce the liquid until it is creamy, about a couple of tablespoons, then return the potatoes to the skillet. Add the beaten eggs to the skillet with the *harīsa* or cayenne and season with a little salt. Cover and cook the eggs until they are set. Serve immediately.

Makes 6 servings

PRICKLY PEAR

Opuntia ficus-indica (L.) Mill. (Cactaceae)
**Also called Indian fig, cactus pear, tuna;
ARABIC: ṣubār; FRENCH: chardon d'Inde, figuier d'Inde, figuier de barbarie, opunce, raquette; GREEK: phragkosukon; ITALIAN: fico d'India, pero pungente, opunzia, opuntia; SPANISH: higuera de las Indias, chumbera, tuna**

Prickly Pear

ANOTHER CURIOUS NAME FOR THE PRICKLY PEAR, A CACTUS PLANT THAT IS VERY POPULAR IN MEXICO, TOO, IS *TUNA*. SOME years ago the *Los Angeles Times* reported that a Venezuelan ice cream maker had come up with a tuna-flavored ice cream, leading the *Times* to think that the ice cream was made with the meat of the sea animal. More than likely the name *tuna* referred to the prickly pear. *Tuna* was first used in 1526 by the Spanish commentator of the New World Fz. de Oviedo to describe the prickly pear found growing on Haiti, the word deriving from the local Indian name for the plant. In the Mediterranean, prickly pear is eaten mostly by North Africans.

PLANT CHARACTERISTICS AND VARIETIES
The prickly pear is a bushlike spiny cactus that grows to 18 feet in height and has large yellow flowers and white, yellow, or reddish purple fruit. The edible parts are the fruits and cactus-type pads, which are consumed either raw or cooked. Although the plants are often used as fodder, some North African cuisines use the prickly pear in salads, as do the Sicilians. Prickly pear, sometimes cooked, is often associated with poor people's food.

PLANT ORIGIN
The prickly pear is native to the Western Hemisphere.

PLANT HISTORY
The prickly pear was introduced to the Mediterranean via West Africa. Today, it is popular in Sicily and North Africa.

PRICKLY SOW-THISTLE
Sonchus asper L. (Asteraceae-Compositae)
ITALIAN: *cicerbita, crespino* (Tuscany);
TURKISH: *su kangalı*

PLANT CHARACTERISTICS AND VARIETIES
This annual or biennial plant is a thistle with bracts surrounding the flower head. In rural Tuscany this plant and common sow-thistle (*S. oleraceus* L.) are made into vegetable soups. In the Aksaray Province of Anatolia the wild green is gathered and eaten.

PUMPKIN
See Squash.

PURSLANE

Portulaca oleracea L. (Portulacaceae)
ARABIC: *ārnuba, farfḥīn, bighal, barābrā*
(Maghrib), *rijl, rujīla, al-ḥamqāᶜ al-baqla,*
badālqa; kharqa, murṭa (Portulaca linifolia);
FRENCH: *pourpier potager;* GREEK: *andrakln;*
ITALIAN: *portulaca, porcellana, perchjazza*
(Bari, Apulia); SPANISH: *verdolaga;* TURKISH:
semizotu, temizlik (Aksaray Province)

PLANT CHARACTERISTICS AND VARIETIES

Purslane is an annual succulent with reddish
stems and thick leaves that are about 2 inches
long; both the stems and the leaves are edible.
The plant is a common weed throughout the
warmer parts of Europe, Asia, and eastern
Africa. Purslane, once known as kitchen garden pusley, is grown to some extent as a
potherb, mostly in Europe. In North Africa
and the Middle East, purslane is a popular
vegetable and often used in salads. Cultivated
purslane is larger and more succulent than the
wild plant. In North Africa one variety that is
eaten is called *murṭa (P. linifolia).*

PLANT ORIGIN

N. Vavilov suggests northwestern India,
Tadzhikistan, Uzbekistan, and western Tien
Shan Province of China as the center of ori-
gin of purslane.

PLANT HISTORY

Purslane has been grown and eaten since
ancient times. It is assumed that the description of *andraclen* in Pliny, as well as in the
works of the Greek writers Theophrastus and
Dioscorides, is purslane. Albertus Magnus
does not mention the plant in its cultivated
form, only wild, but by 1586 Ruellis describes
the plant in cultivation.

HOW TO GROW AND HARVEST

Purslane is easily grown even in dry soil
because it is able to retain enough moisture to
bloom and ripen seeds even long after the
seeds have been uprooted. Sow seeds in the
spring and you can harvest the leaves and
stems throughout the summer. Because
purslane is an invasive plant, most gardeners
grow it in a container. Press the seeds into
sandy soil in full sun, and water the plant during dry weather. Harvest the leaves when they
are young, before the plant flowers.

HOW TO BUY, STORE, AND PREPARE
FOR COOKING

Look for purslane with full, almost spongy
looking leaves that are green and fresh looking. Store in the refrigerator until needed.

Yoğurtlu Semizotlu Salatasi
PURSLANE AND YOGURT SALAD

This recipe from Turkey may have a long history. The medieval Muslim doctor and philosopher Avicenna, who lived from 980 to 1037, and who tried to reconcile Aristotelian thought with Islam, recommended the medicinal benefits of eating purslane and yogurt. This salad is very refreshing, and I like to make it in the summer, or as an accompaniment to grilled foods.

3 garlic cloves, peeled
2 teaspoons salt
1½ cups high-quality full-fat plain yogurt
1 tablespoon extra virgin olive oil
1½ pounds purslane, heavy stems removed,
  washed well, and dried

In a mortar, crush the garlic with the salt until mushy. Stir the mashed garlic into the yogurt with the olive oil until well blended. Toss with the purslane. Refrigerate for 1 hour before serving. Serve cold.

Makes 4 servings

RADICCHIO
See Chicory.

RADISH
Raphanus sativus L. Radicula group
(Cruciferae)
ARABIC: *fujl, mishtā;* FRENCH: *radis;* GREEK: *rapani, rapanaki, raphanis;* ITALIAN: *radice, rafano, ravanello, ravastrello;* SERBO-CROATIAN: *rotkvica;* SPANISH: *rabanito, rabanete, rabanillo;* TURKISH: *kırmızı turp*

PLANT CHARACTERISTICS AND VARIETIES
Radish is a cool-weather annual that forms small rosettes of dark green leaves. The leaves can be cooked with turnip or beet greens. Some varieties have small red or red and white roots with a slight spicy taste. In the Mediterranean, radishes are usually eaten pickled or as a salad vegetable. Wild and garden radishes are considered by some botanists to be two varieties of the species *R. raphanistrum*, while others consider the garden radish to be a true species called *R. sativus* or *R. radicula*, and the wild radish (var. *niger*) to be a variety of the latter. The subspecies *rostratus* (DC) Thell. grows in the Aegean near seashores and has lilac-colored flowers. Landra or Italian radish (*R. landra*) was once, and may still be, eaten by the poor in Italy. Today there are four types of cultivated radishes: white or red (*radicula*), black (*niger*), oil-seed (*oleifera*), and Mougri (*mougri*). The Mougri is grown mostly in India for its seed pods. White and red radishes are grown in the Mediterranean and Europe for salads. Black radishes are seldom seen today. There are a

number of beautiful cultivars of radish such as the so-called watermelon radish with its pretty purple and white starburst pattern. The winter radish (*R. sativus* var. *longipinnatus*), such as daikon, is not used that much in the Mediterranean.

PLANT ORIGIN

The origin of the cultivated black radish is not a settled matter, although it is thought to have descended from the wild radish and is known to have been first cultivated in the eastern Mediterranean. The origin of the white radish is unknown, although it may have developed from the black radish. N. Vavilov identified the mountains of central and western China and the adjacent areas as the place of origin of the wild and cultivated radishes.

PLANT HISTORY

Because remains of black radishes have been found in excavations, we know that cultivated black radishes were grown in ancient Egypt during the Second Dynasty (c. 2890–2686 B.C.). The *Assyrian Herbal*, a compilation of vegetable drugs undertaken by R. Campbell Thompson in 1924 based on fragments of cuneiform plant lists and tablets of medical texts dating to the end of the second millennium B.C., identifies radish as *puglu*, a word that should be compared to the modern Egyptian Arabic word for radish, *figl*, because of phonetic and semiotic similarity. The ancient Egyptian hieroglyphic words for radish were *smw* and/or *nwm*. According to certain references in Herodotus, "radishes, onions, and garlic" were fed to the workers building the pyramids. Athenaeus tells us that the radish was a very cheap food item, and he relates the expression that he attributed to the playwright Amphis: "Any man who goes to market to get some delicacy and prefers to buy radishes when he may enjoy real fish must be crazy." Theophrastus lists five varieties of radish, and Pliny describes the radish's medicinal uses in Italy during the first century A.D. and how large and sweet Egyptian radishes were. White radishes are first mentioned in Europe in the late sixteenth century. The Italian botanist Matthioli mentions seeing a radish that weighed 100 pounds. The white and reddish globular forms of radish known today were first developed in the eighteenth century.

HOW TO GROW AND HARVEST

Radishes are very easy to grow. All they need are sunlight and good, moist, sandy loam soil. Sow the seeds in the spring or summer in 1- or 2-week intervals in furrows about 2 inches deep. Cover the seeds with a very thin layer of sand. Radishes mature in about 20 days. Harvest radishes as soon as they are big enough to eat.

HOW TO BUY, STORE, AND PREPARE FOR COOKING

If you are buying radishes in bunches, look for ones with fresh, green, crisp-looking leaves. The radish roots should have a good color and not look dull. They should be firm and unblemished. Remove the leaves once you're home (unless you're going to use them), and store the radish roots in a plastic bag in the refrigerator where they will keep for several weeks.

Ravanelli con Pecorino Pepato Fresco
RED RADISHES WITH FRESH PEPPERED PECORINO

This antipasto is a Sicilian one that is really quite nice standing alone. Sicilians have not traditionally eaten *antipasti*; they are a modern introduction from northern Italy.

Because everything is so simple in this recipe, the quality of your ingredients becomes all important. The pecorino required is called *pecorino pepato* in Italian, and it is not too hard to find in this country. It is a semi-soft 6-month-old pecorino made with whole peppercorns thrown into the curd. Almost all Italian delis, as well as gourmet supermarkets, carry it. It is called "table" or "eating" pecorino and may also be called pecorino Crotonese. When a pecorino is older, it becomes hard and is used for grating onto pasta, for instance.

The best radishes to use in this recipe are the young so-called French breakfast radishes; a good portion of their root skin is white.

Use the best-quality estate-bottled olive oil. Don't cut the radishes and let them sit around; otherwise they will emit too much water and make the whole dish unappetizing.

¼ *pound pecorino pepato, cut into thin slices, at room temperature*
½ *pound French breakfast radishes, tops discarded, sliced, at room temperature*
Extra virgin olive oil to taste

Arrange the cheese and radishes in a serving platter or plate and drizzle with the oil.

Makes 4 servings as an antipasto

Salāṭat al-Fijil
RADISH SALAD

This salad would be served in Tunisia as part of an *ādū* table, the smorgasbord that is called *meze* or *mazza* elsewhere in the Mediterranean. Don't cut the radishes too much in advance, because if they sit out for too long they will release too much water and dilute the dressing. The small amount of *harīsa* in this recipe provides just the right amount of zing.

*6 bunches radishes (about 2¼ pounds), tops
  discarded, sliced into thin rounds using a food
  processor*
¼ cup finely chopped fresh parsley leaves
¼ cup extra virgin olive oil
1 tablespoon white wine vinegar
1 teaspoon harīsa *(page 163)*
Salt and freshly ground black pepper to taste

Toss the radishes with the parsley in a large
serving bowl. Stir the olive oil, vinegar, and
harīsa together and toss with the radishes to
coat evenly. Taste and correct the seasoning
with salt and pepper. Serve.

Makes 6 to 8 servings

RAMPION

Campanula rapunculus L. (Campanulaceae)
FRENCH: *campanule raiponce, rampon, raiponce,
rave sauvage, cheveux d'évèque;* ITALIAN:
raperònzolo, raponzo, rapònzolo; SPANISH:
rapónchigo, rapúnculo, ruiponce, raipóntico;
TURKISH: *yer otu* (see below)

PLANT CHARACTERISTICS AND VARIETIES
Rampion is a biennial European bellflower
with little blue flowers. It is grown for its
turniplike roots and leaves, which have a bit-
ing flavor and are used in salads. Cooked like
spinach, rampion is said to have the flavor of
walnuts. The leaves of *C. trachelium* are used in
vegetable soups in rural Tuscany, where they
are called *pizzicacorno*. In Turkey, the blue flowers of clustered bellflower *(C. glomerata)* are

eaten raw in salads, and the leaves and roots of
C. cymbalaria Sm., known in central Turkey as
yer otu, are also eaten. In Greece, variously colored bellflower *(C. versicolor)* is cooked and
eaten as a vegetable.

PLANT ORIGIN
Rampion is native to fields and meadows of
the Eurasian and North African areas of the
Mediterranean.

PLANT HISTORY
Rampion was cultivated in Italy and France.
In 1552 the botanical artist Hieronymous
Tragus described the cultivation of rampion,
as did Petrus Pena and Mathia Lobel in
Stirpium adversaria nova (1570). Castelvetro in
1614 mentions rampion as a salad plant, the
roots being scraped and the leaves eaten, too.
Some Italians of his day, he tells us, cooked
rampion in meat broth and served it with
grated cheese and pepper.

RAPE

Brassica napus L. var. *napus* Pabularia
group (Cruciferae)
Also called colza; FRENCH: *chou navet;*
ITALIAN: *cavolo navone, colza;* SPANISH:
colinabo, nabicol, colza

PLANT CHARACTERISTICS AND VARIETIES
Rape (also rapa), also and incorrectly called
raab or rabe, is a large annual plant with
bristly leaves and yellow flowers. Rape, or

colza, is a member of the mustard family and is not the same plant as broccoli rape, which is a sprouting broccoli. The edible parts of rape are the leaves and young flower stalks, which are eaten cooked. Although some Italians eat rape greens, the plant's oil-bearing seeds are more commonly used. The pods are beak-shaped and contain seeds, called rapeseeds, that yield the vegetable cooking oil known as canola oil, which, in its crude form, is used in making margarine, soap, and lamp fuel.

PLANT ORIGIN

It is not known if a wild form of rape exists, but if it does, it is thought to be an East European–Mediterranean species.

PLANT HISTORY

Rape has been cultivated as an oil-seed crop in the Mediterranean since the Middle Ages.

HOW TO GROW AND HARVEST

Sow seeds thickly and then rake them over in the late summer. Harvest individual leaves in the winter, snipping them off the stalk.

HOW TO BUY, STORE, AND PREPARE FOR COOKING

Look for leaves that are crisp and fresh looking with no signs of yellowing. Store rape leaves in the refrigerator and use them within a few days.

RAPISTRUM RUGOSUM L. (CRUCIFERAE)

ITALIAN: *marmoraccia, castòdde* (Bari, Apulia)

PLANT CHARACTERISTICS AND VARIETIES

This annual herb grows to 2 feet. The leaves are cooked and eaten in the Bari area of Apulia in southern Italy.

RHUBARB

Rheum rhabarbarum L. (syn. *R. rhaponticum; R. palmatum*) (Polygonaceae)
ARABIC: *rāwand;* FRENCH: *rhubarbe;* GREEK: *raxention;* ITALIAN: *rabarbaro, rapontico;* SERBO-CROATIAN: *rabarbara;* SPANISH: *ruibarbo, rapóntico;* TURKISH: *ravend*

PLANT CHARACTERISTICS AND VARIETIES

Rhubarb is a large herbaceous perennial with a very large and short-branched rhizome. When the plant matures, the leaf blades are poisonous because of their calcium oxalate content. Rhubarb is grown for its large succulent leaf stalks, which are eaten cooked. Because rhubarb is tart, sugar is usually added to it. With one variety that grows in eastern Turkey, *R. ribes,* the leaf stalks are gathered and sold by roadside stands for eating. In today's Mediterranean, rhubarb is eaten mostly by the French.

Rhubarb

In the minds of most North Americans, rhubarb is only associated with rhubarb pie. In the Mediterranean, too, rhubarb is generally associated with dessert or sweet preparations such as the rhubarb sherbet one might find in Lebanon or the *budino di rabarbaro* that one finds in Italian home cooking, a rhubarb pudding made with corn flour, sugar, and water. In France, rhubarb is made into jam, although even the great Auguste Escoffier said that rhubarb jam was "one of the most difficult and tedious to make."

PLANT ORIGIN

Rhubarb is said to be native to Tibet, Siberia, or northern Asia generally, although its precise origin is not known. The name *rhubarb* derives from Rha, the ancient name of the Volga River.

PLANT HISTORY

Rhubarb entered Europe, it is said, in the thirteenth or fourteenth century, although it does not seem to have been used as a food until the seventeenth or eighteenth century, when it was first used in pies. The main use of the plant before that time was as a medicinal herb. Pliny describes rhubarb only medicinally. The root is a powerful laxative and was recognized as such by early pharmacologists. The dried rhubarb root was an item of export, and it is said that Marco Polo brought it to Europe from China. It was imported through markets such as Smyrna (Izmir) and was bought by Venetian merchants in Syria in the sixteenth century because it was thought to be a cure for venereal disease. It is said that rhubarb did not become gastronomically important until the eighteenth century, the French being the first to recognize its culinary possibilities.

HOW TO GROW AND HARVEST

Rhubarb is suited to gardens at higher, cooler elevations and in colder climates such as northern Europe. It will not survive a hot summer. Most horticulturalists insist that the preparation of the soil for growing rhubarb is critical. The soil should be rich and moist and the site open to sunlight, not shaded, except in the afternoon. Rhubarb is usually grown from root divisions, since growing it from seed takes a year longer, and the results are not as good. Harvest rhubarb after the second growing season by snapping off the outer stalks. Once half a plant's new growth has been harvested, leave that plant alone.

Rhubarb is always sold as leaf stalks only. Because the leaves are poisonous both cooked and raw, they should never be eaten. Choose firm, crisp-looking stalks that are red and look like celery stalks. Rhubarb will keep in the refrigerator for a week.

ROMAINE LETTUCE
See Lettuce.

ROMAN PIMPERNEL
Tordylium apulum L. (Umbelliferae)
Also called small hortwort

PLANT CHARACTERISTICS AND VARIETIES
The plant is a stout annual that grows to 8 to 15 inches high. In Greece the aromatic young plants are eaten in vegetable pies and stews.

ROSELLE
Hibisicus sabdariffa L. (Malvaceae)
Also called Indian sorrel, red sorrel, jamaica, Florida cranberry; ARABIC: *zuqūqū*

PLANT CHARACTERISTICS AND VARIETIES
This herb or shrub is often grown for ornamental reasons. The flowers and fleshy calyx are edible, and the thick, juicy sepals that surround the fruit are used to make jellies and infused drinks. In the Sudan, the seeds are fermented and used as a meat substitute in a preparation called *furundu*. In Morocco, people eat the seeds, which resemble the seeds of an apple, by dipping their fingers in honey and then plunging them into the seeds and sucking them off. Today, roselle is grown mostly in Jamaica, India, Burma, and Africa. A small production also occurs in southern Florida.

PLANT ORIGIN
Roselle originates in the tropical areas of Asia.

ROUGH HAWKBIT
Leontodon hispidus L. (Asteraceae-Compositae)
ITALIAN: *radicchio di campo* (Tuscany)

PLANT CHARACTERISTICS AND VARIETIES
This perennial plant has a vertical or oblique truncated stock and large leaves. The young leaves are eaten in vegetable soups and salads in rural Tuscany.

RUTABAGA
Brassica napus L. var. *napobrassica* (L.) Reichb. (syn. *B. napobrassica, B. napus* Napobrassica group) (Cruciferae)
Also called swede; ARABIC: *lift*; FRENCH: *rutabaga, navet de Suède*; GREEK: *mega goggulion*; ITALIAN: *rutabaga, navone*; SPANISH: *rutabaga, nabo sueco, nabo de Suecia*

PLANT CHARACTERISTICS AND VARIETIES

The edible parts are the roots and leaves, which must be cooked. There are two basic types of rutabagas, yellow fleshed and white fleshed. Rutabagas are used in the same culinary way as turnips, although the rutabagas are hardier plants. Rutabagas resemble turnips, but are much larger, their roots growing halfway out of the ground. Rutabagas differ from turnips in several ways: the first foliage leaves are glaucous in color, rather than grass green; rutabaga leaves resemble cabbage leaves; the root has a distinct neck; the flesh is firmer and more nutritious; and the roots keep much better during the winter. Because rutabagas are a cool-season crop and require a long time to grow, they are not all that common in the Mediterranean, although they appear in cuisines associated with colder Mediterranean climates. For this reason they are included here. Outside of higher elevations in the Balkans, one does not find rutabagas in Mediterranean cuisines.

PLANT ORIGIN

Rutabagas originated probably by accident as a natural cross between the turnip (*Brassica napus*) and the cabbage (*B. oleracea*) in medieval gardens. It is not known whether the plant exists in wild form. Although many writers tell us that the rutabaga came from Bohemia, where the first recognizable rutabaga is known from 1620, the eminent early twentieth-century botanist N. Vavilov suggested a Mediterranean center of origin for the rutabaga.

PLANT HISTORY

Crossing turnips and cabbages to form rutabagas is difficult under artificial conditions, and therefore it is thought that rutabagas may have developed in medieval gardens where turnips and kale or cabbage were grown in proximity to each other. The first mention of the rutabaga in European botanical literature is by Caspar Bauhin in 1620, but rutabagas are undoubtedly older than this. They arrived in England from Sweden, where they were growing before 1400, and hence they are also known as swedes in the English-speaking world.

HOW TO GROW AND HARVEST

Rutabagas grow best in open fields with rich soil in cold or cool weather. The seeds are sown in May or June and mature in the autumn. Harvest rutabagas by pulling the whole plant. As with all hardy fall crops, rutabagas taste sweeter and better when harvested after the first fall frost.

HOW TO BUY, STORE, AND PREPARE FOR COOKING

Home-grown rutabagas store well in a cold shed packed in a box of moist sand or sawdust or in a punctured plastic bag in the refrigerator. If you are growing your own, you can leave them in the ground until they are needed. Rutabagas can be stored in the refrigerator for up to 2 weeks.

SALSIFY

Tragopogon porrifolius L. (Asteraceae-Compositae)
Also called oyster plant; ARABIC: *liḥiya al-taīs, qᶜabārūn;* FRENCH: *salsifis;* GREEK: *tragopegon;* ITALIAN: *scorzobianca, anca, barba di becco;* SPANISH: *salsifi blanco*

PLANT CHARACTERISTICS AND VARIETIES

Salsify and scorzonera are related both botanically and horticulturally. They are biennial herbs and members of the daisy family, related to dandelion, chicory, and lettuce. The edible parts are the young leaves and roots, which are eaten either raw or cooked. Salisify has a white root, purple flowers, and narrow grasslike leaves. The roots can grow to more than a foot long. They have a a beige skin and are "hairy" looking, since the side rootlets usually are not trimmed. The roots' taste is reminiscent of oysters, hence one of their common names. Salsify is eaten almost everywhere in the Mediterranean, but not frequently.

PLANT ORIGIN

Salsify is native to the Mediterranean.

PLANT HISTORY

Salsify was probably first cultivated in Italy in the early sixteenth century. In the thirteenth century Albertus Magnus wrote of a wild plant, *oculus porce* or *flos campi,* which some people once took to be salsify. Although salsify is mentioned by Matthioli in 1570, it was not known as a kitchen garden plant.

HOW TO GROW AND HARVEST

See Parsnip.

HOW TO BUY, STORE, AND PREPARE FOR COOKING

Freshness is the key with salsify; it should not be stored for longer than a week. Because the leaves and roots look good for weeks, it's difficult for shoppers to know whether or not the ones at the market are fresh.

SALTWORT

Salsola fruticosa L. (syn. *S. kali*) (Chenopodiaceae)
Also called sea grape, marsh samphire; ARABIC: *qily, qāqullā, usbnān, kākanj;* FRENCH: *kali;* SPANISH: *barilla, sosa*

PLANT CHARACTERISTICS AND VARIETIES

This annual shrub grows to 3½ feet and features large leaves. Saltwort grows in deserts, such as North Africa, and in saline and non-saline coastal areas. It is eaten by the Spanish and some Moroccans and Algerians.

PLANT HISTORY

In Biblical-era Palestine, saltwort, glasswort, and other plants were burned to obtain alkaline salts, which were then mixed with olive oil to make soap. Early botanists thought saltwort could cure dropsy and leprosy. One of

Salsify and Scorzonera

ALTHOUGH THEY ARE RELATED PLANTS, SALSIFY AND SCORZON-
ERA ARE DIFFERENT. YET MEDITERRANEAN COOKS SPEAK OF
the two in the same breath. These vegetables are not commonly used, but they are
enjoyed by segments of the population. Typically they are sautéed or cooked in
soups. People in France, and Spain and Italy too, prepare *salsifis frit*—salsify roots cut
into 3-inch lengths, marinated in lemon juice, olive oil, parsley, salt, and pepper and
then batter-dipped and fried in hot fat (the same method is used for *scorzonère frit or
salsifis noir*). The French also make these greens into a cream sauce. In Italy, cooks prepare salsify as a side dish with meat sauce, grated cheese, and béchamel sauce and finish it with breadcrumbs *au gratin*.

the Arabic names for saltwort, *qily,* gives us the
English word *alkaline.*

HOW TO GROW AND HARVEST

Harvest saltwort while it is young and tender.

HOW TO BUY, STORE, AND PREPARE
FOR COOKING

See Glasswort.

SAND LEEK

Allium scorodoprasum L. (syn. *A. sativum*
var. *ophioscorodon*) (Alliaceae)
Also called Spanish garlic, giant garlic,
rocambole; ARABIC: *thūm al-amlak;* FRENCH:
rocambole, ail d'Espagne; ITALIAN: *aglio
romano;* SPANISH: *ajo ramano*

PLANT CHARACTERISTICS AND VARIETIES

Sand leek, also known as Spanish garlic or
giant garlic, is known as a mild type of red
garlic (although it is not a garlic). The plant is
grown in the south of France as well as in the
Greek islands and elsewhere in the Mediterranean. It is usually eaten raw with olive oil
or grilled. Facciola identifies this plant as *A.
sativum* Ophioscorodon group.

PLANT ORIGIN

Sand leek is thought to originate in the
Mediterranean and east to Syria and the
Caucasus.

PLANT HISTORY

Sand leek does not appear to have been cultivated by the ancients. Two of its first

historical mentions are in 1596 by the herbalist Gerarde, who mentions it as a cultivated vegetable, and by the botanist Clusius in 1601.

SARCOSTEMMA FORSKALIANUS SCHULT. (ASCLEPIADACEAE)

PLANT CHARACTERISTICS AND VARIETIES
The young shoots are eaten in Arabia, as are those of *S. stipitaceum*.

SARSAPARILLA
Smilax aspera L. (syn. *S. mauritania* Poir., *S. nigra* Willd.) (Liliaceae)
Also called red-berried rough-bindweed; ARABIC: *ḥabb al-naʿām* (Maghrib), *fashgh*; ITALIAN: *salsapariglia*; FRENCH: *salsepareille*; SPANISH: *zarzaparilla*

PLANT CHARACTERISTICS AND VARIETIES
Sarsaparilla is related to wild asparagus and is eaten in southern Italy, Greece, and Turkey, where it is collected from the maquis. The edible part is the root. The sarsaparilla plant, from the Spanish *zarza* (bramble) and *parrilla* (little vine), is also used as an aromatic flavoring agent. Americans know this plant best as the flavor behind root beer. The plant is a large perennial climbing or trailing vine with short and thick underground stems that produce prickly aboveground stems. The whole plant is harvested and dried in the sun. The roots are gathered into bundles and exported.

PLANT ORIGIN
Sarsaparilla is native to Mexico and Central America.

SAVOY CABBAGE
See Cabbage.

SCARLET RUNNER BEAN
Phaseolus coccineus L. (syn. *P. multiflorus* Willd.) (Fabaceae-Leguminosae)
Also called runner bean; FRENCH: *haricot d'Espagne, haricot moucheté*; ITALIAN: *fagiolo di Spagna, fagiolo coccineofaglione*; SPANISH: *judia escarlata, judia de España, judia roja, judia pinta, poroto de España*; TURKISH: *çalı fasulya*

PLANT CHARACTERISTICS AND VARIETIES
The scarlet runner bean is a perennial that, unlike other beans, forms starchy tuberous roots that are poisonous. The beans look like snap beans, but their leaves are a darker green and their flowers are scarlet. The edible parts are the immature pods and seeds, which are eaten cooked. The white-seeded variety is the most common today, and this type is most often eaten in the Mediterranean, whereas in the United States the plants are more often grown as an ornamental. Although they are

eaten around the Mediterranean, they are eaten infrequently.

PLANT ORIGIN

The plant is believed to originate in Mexico, southwest of Durango.

PLANT HISTORY

Scarlet runner beans were cultivated in pre-Columbian Mexico and found in deposits in the Tehuacan Valley in the Puebla province. This famous site is also one of the earliest sites for the cultivation of maize, from about 7000 B.C. onward. The bean was introduced to the Mediterranean in the sixteenth century, probably as an ornamental plant. It was first introduced to Spain, and this history is reflected in the name the plant has been given in various languages; Sicilians, French, and Spanish call runner beans Spanish beans. The runner bean also became popular in Turkey, and then it traveled north during Ottoman times to reach central Europe. In fact, in German herbals the runner bean was called *Arabische bohnen,* Arab bean, in recognition of its presumed provenance.

HOW TO GROW AND HARVEST

Scarlet runner beans grow best in partially shaded areas, such as the north-facing sides of valleys. The scarlet runner bean is not self-pollinating, as is the green bean. Both bumblebees and hummingbirds appear to pollinate the plant. In their native mountains, where growing conditions are ideal, the plant's roots are kept cool and damp by the surrounding flora. In the garden, the plants will require watering at the root to encourage flowering and pod formation, and mulching so that the roots will retain moisture. Plant the seeds in late May or June in full sun, in a place sheltered from the wind, and in warm soil. The seeds can be planted 1 inch apart in clusters of four seeds that are spaced 2 feet apart. The plants need to be staked for support on poles at least 6 feet high. Harvest the plant when the pods are about 4 inches long and filled with beans.

SCORZONERA

Scorzonera hispanica L. (Asteraceae-Compositae)
Also called black salsify, viper's grass;
ARABIC: *khaṣṣ al-qalb, tālma* (Maghrib); *dabḥ, qᶜabārūn*; FRENCH: *scorzonère, scorzonère d'Espagne, salsifis noir*; ITALIAN: *scorzonera, barba di becco nera*; SPANISH: *escorzonera, salsifí negro*

PLANT CHARACTERISTICS AND VARIETIES

Scorzonera is a perennial herb with a thin, slimy, foot-long, black-skinned and scaly-skinned root with broad leaves and yellow flowers. The edible parts of the plant are the roots and leaves, which are eaten either cooked or raw. The plant's name, scorzonera, derives from the Catalan name for *viper,* because this plant was supposedly an antidote to snakebite. The suggestion that the name came from the Spanish *corteza negra,* meaning "black bark," is not correct. In southern Italy a variety called *latticrèpolo (S. trachysperma)* is eaten in salads. And in Taranto in Apulia, the plant is known as *péne e féfe* in dialect. In North Africa a kind of scorzonera is known as *tālma*. In the Aksaray Province of Turkey, the leaves of *S. cana* (C. A. Meyer) Hoffm. var. *radicosa* (Boiss.) Chamberlein are sometimes gathered as an edible wild green and known as *tekercik* in the local dialect.

PLANT ORIGIN

Scorzonera is native to southern Europe from Portugal to southern Russia and eastward into Siberia. It may have originated in Spain.

PLANT HISTORY

Scorzonera was grown in Spain in the sixteenth century. Writing in 1554, Matthioli does not mention the plant, but by 1570 scorzonera was described by others as a new plant, although not as a cultivated plant.

HOW TO GROW AND HARVEST

Scorzonera is easy to grow, but it takes time to produce a good-size root. The soil should be fine in texture and not manured so the plant's roots won't fork. Sow the seeds in early spring and thin the plants to 4 to 12 inches apart. The roots can be harvested from October onward, after the cold sweetens the roots. Also see Parsnip.

HOW TO BUY, STORE, AND PREPARE FOR COOKING

Store home-grown scorzonera roots by leaving them in the ground through the winter. Prepare the roots for cooking by scrubbing the dirt off them. Then boil the roots and skim off the black root skin under cold running water.

SEA FENNEL
Crithmum maritimum L. (Umbelliferae)
Also called samphire, rock samphire;
ARABIC: *qarīmin*

PLANT CHARACTERISTICS AND VARIETIES

Sea fennel is a plant found growing wild along the shores of the Mediterranean, but today it is cultivated in limited quantities. The edible part is the leaf. The flavor is vaguely like that of fennel, but more bitter and brackish. It is often used in salads, mostly in North Africa.

PLANT ORIGIN

It seems likely that sea fennel is native to the seacoasts of Europe and the Mediterranean, extending into the Caucasus.

PLANT HISTORY

Pliny tells us that some people called sea fennel Gallic asparagus, but he mentions sea fennel only as a wild plant. The first mention of sea fennel as a cultivated plant is found in Jean de la Quintiyne's *Le parfait jardinier,* published in 1683. In nineteenth-century France, the plant was cultivated for its leaves, which were pickled and used in salads and seasonings.

SEA HOLLY
Eryngium maritimum L. (Umbelliferae)
Also called sea-holm, sea eryngo, eryngo root; GREEK: *erygion*

PLANT CHARACTERISTICS AND VARIETIES
This perennial grows in maritime regions. The edible parts are the young and tender shoots and the roots. The shoots are blanched and eaten like asparagus. When the roots are boiled or roasted, they taste like chestnuts. Some Greeks still eat this plant as a vegetable.

PLANT ORIGIN
The plant seems to be native to Asia Minor and the seashores of the Mediterranean and European Atlantic.

PLANT HISTORY
Pliny in *Natural History* (Book XXII, 19–22) describes sea holly as both an antidote to snakebites and as an aphrodisiac. In William Shakespeare's *The Merry Wives of Windsor,* the candied roots of *E. maritimum* are referred to as eringoes.

SEAKALE
Crambe maritima L. (Cruciferae)
Also spelled sea kale; FRENCH: *chou marin, crambe;* ITALIAN: *cavolo marino;* SPANISH: *col marina, crambe*

PLANT CHARACTERISTICS AND VARIETIES
Seakale is a large perennial cabbagelike herb in the mustard family that is native to seashores and cliffs and grows wild along the European Atlantic and in Eurasia. The edible parts are the petioles and young leaves, which are cooked. The large leaves are a waxy blue green with coarsely toothed leaves. Some Spaniards, French, and Italians who live in coastal areas cook and eat the leaves of this plant.

PLANT ORIGIN
Seakale originates along the seashore and cliffs of Eurasia. N. Vavilov suggests the Mediterranean as a center of origin of seakale.

PLANT HISTORY
Seakale may have been known by the Romans (if we can assume that the *batim marinam* mentioned by Pliny is seakale, which it seems to be). They brought it on longer sea voyages because it is a hardy vegetable that keeps well. According to one author, seakale was first cultivated by Quintiyne, the gardener to King Louis XIV of France, although the plant is not mentioned in Quintiyne's book of 1683.

Seakale grows best in soil near the seashore. The ground, though, must be well drained because the plant will not grow in standing water. Start the plants from seed and transplant them to a raised bed with sand underneath, spacing the plants about 2 feet apart. Adding fish emulsion and sea salt to the soil seems to help the plant grow.

SEA ROCKET
Cakile maritima Scop. (Cruciferae)
ARABIC: *qāqully*

PLANT CHARACTERISTICS AND VARIETIES
Sea rocket is one of a number of subspecies that are members of the same family to which mustard belongs. The plant is found in seashore regions. *Cakile maritima,* the species found in the Mediterranean, has thick leaves and pale lavender flower clusters. The young and tender, fleshy and crisp shoots are edible and are used as a flavoring agent. Some North Africans eat sea rocket.

PLANT ORIGIN
Sea rocket is native to North America, Eurasia, western Asia, Australia, and to central Arabian deserts.

SEDUM ALBUM L. (CRASSULACEAE)
ITALIAN: *pizzagallina, risiono* (Tuscany)

PLANT CHARACTERISTICS AND VARIETIES
This plant is a perennial with creeping, woody stems, which bear short, nonflowering shoots. In rural Tuscany, the leaves are eaten as a snack.

SEMPERVIVIUM ARMENUM BOISS. ET HUET VAR. *ARMENUM* (CRASSULACEAE)
TURKISH: *musluk otu*

PLANT CHARACTERISTICS AND VARIETIES
This perennial reproduces vegetatively via axillary stolons. In the Aksaray Province of Anatolia, this plant, whose name loosely translates from the Turkish as "thieves herb," is gathered as a wild edible green.

SHALLOT
Allium cepa L. Aggregatum group (syn. *A. cepa* var. *aggregatum*; *A. ascalonicum*) (Liliaceae)
ARABIC: *bassal al-shallūt*; FRENCH: *échalote, oignon-patate*; ITALIAN: *scalgno*; SPANISH: *chalote, escaluña, ascalonia*

Shallot

In the Mediterranean, shallots are used almost exclusively as the foundation of a sauce or to enhance sauces. Certainly, the shallot is most famous in French cooking, where shallots are sautéed with tarragon and chervil to make béarnaise sauce. In Italian cooking, for some reason, cooks favor the small flattened *cipolline* onions over shallots, although they do not totally exclude shallots.

SEDUM ALBUM L. (CRASSULACEAE)

ITALIAN: *pizzagallina, risiono* (Tuscany)

PLANT CHARACTERISTICS AND VARIETIES
This plant is a perennial with creeping, woody stems, which bear short, nonflowering shoots. In rural Tuscany, the leaves are eaten as a snack.

SEMPERVIVIUM ARMENUM BOISS. ET HUET VAR. ARMENUM (CRASSULACEAE)

TURKISH: *musluk otu*

PLANT CHARACTERISTICS AND VARIETIES
This perennial reproduces vegetatively via axillary stolons. In the Aksaray Province of Anatolia, this plant, whose name loosely translates from the Turkish as "thieves herb," is gathered as a wild edible green.

SHALLOT

Allium cepa L. Aggregatum group (syn. *A. cepa* var. *aggregatum*; *A. ascalonicum*) (Liliaceae)

ARABIC: *bassal al-shallūt*; FRENCH: *échalote, oignon-patate*; ITALIAN: *scalgno*; SPANISH: *chalote, escaluña, ascalonia*

PLANT CHARACTERISTICS AND VARIETIES
The edible parts are the pseudostems and leaves, which are eaten either raw or cooked. De Candolle and other botanists believe the shallot is derived from the onion. Shallots produce only by bulb division. Shallots are like small onions, which grow as a bunch of bulbs. This vegetable is loved throughout the

Scalogno con Crema e Menta
SHALLOTS WITH CREAM AND MINT

This pleasant recipe from Lombardy in northern Italy uses young shallots just pulled from the ground with their green tops still attached. Unfortunately, the shallots sold in supermarkets are usually just the bulbs, already packaged, so your best bet for finding the roots with their green tops is a farmers' market, if you are not growing shallots yourself. As a substitute you may use scallions, ramps, or baby leeks. I like to serve this dish with lamb.

2 tablespoons unsalted butter
1 pound shallots with tops, bulbs peeled
1 cup light cream
Salt and freshly ground white pepper to taste
1 tablespoon finely chopped fresh mint leaves

1. Melt the butter in a large casserole over high heat and cook the shallots until the dark green parts (of the whole shallot or scallion or baby leeks) are wilted and the white parts are slightly browned, about 5 minutes, stirring and tossing.
2. Reduce the heat to low, pour in the cream, season with salt and white pepper, and cover. Cook until the cream is frothy, about 15 minutes. Uncover and cook until the cream is nearly evaporated, about 15 minutes. Stir in the mint, cook another 5 minutes, and serve hot.

Makes 2 to 4 side dish servings

SHEPHERD'S PURSE
Capsella bursa-pastoris (L.) Medikus
(Cruciferae-Brassicaceae)
FRENCH: *bourse à berger*; ITALIAN: *borsa di pastore comune, borsacchina*; SPANISH: *bolsa de pastor común; pan y quesillo*; TURKISH: *kuşkuş ekmeği*

PLANT CHARACTERISTICS AND VARIETIES

This common annual weed is found everywhere. Shepherd's purse grows wild on road banks, in garbage dumps, and in gardens. The mustard-flavored greens are usually used as an herb in cookery. Two other varieties of shepherd's purse, called Turkish rocket (*Bunias orientalis* L.) and corn rocket (*B. erucago* L.), are yellow-flowered weeds that are native to the Mediterranean. The leaves of Turkish rocket are usually eaten as a salad, and the young shoots are eaten like a sprouting broccoli. With corn rocket, the young stems and roots are eaten. Corn rocket grows wild in untilled and poor soils. It is the only variety of shepherd's purse that is cultivated. It has flat heart-shaped green fruits on long flower stalks that end in clusters of four-petalled white flowers. Shepherd's purse is eaten throughout the Mediterranean.

PLANT ORIGIN

Shepherd's purse is native to the Mediterranean, and seeds have been found at an archaeological site at Çatal Hüyük in Anatolia that date from about 5800 B.C. The plants may have been valued as a food because of the high oil content of the seeds.

PLANT HISTORY

One of the two *thlaspi* mentioned by Pliny in the first century A.D. is thought to be shepherd's purse.

HOW TO GROW AND HARVEST

The easiest way to grow shepherd's purse is to find a wild plant and transplant it in the early fall to a spot that gets full sun.

HOW TO BUY, STORE, AND PREPARE FOR COOKING

You are most likely to run across shepherd's purse in a farmers' market. Store the greens in the refrigerator and use within a few days.

SIEBER'S CROCUS

Crocus sieberi Gay (Iridaceae)
TURKISH: *çiğdem*

PLANT CHARACTERISTICS AND VARIETIES

This plant has a fibrous corm with pale lilac to purple flowers. The edible part is the bulb, which is eaten raw in Greece by mountain shepherds. The flavor is said to be similar to that of hazelnuts. In Turkey the leaves of *C. sieberi* Gay are gathered in the wild and eaten as greens.

SILVER THISTLE

Carlina acaulis L. (Asteraceae-Compositae)
Also called dwarf carline-thistle; ITALIAN: *cardo di San Pellegrino, scarzoni* (Tuscany)

PLANT CHARACTERISTICS AND VARIETIES

The receptacles of this thistle are used in salads and boiled to make jam in rural Tuscany or eaten as you would an artichoke.

SKIRRET

Sium sisarum L. (Umbelliferae)
FRENCH: *berle à sucre, chervis, girole;* ITALIAN: *sedanina coltivata, sisaro, shervola;* SPANISH: *escaravia, chirivía de azúcar, sisaro*

PLANT CHARACTERISTICS AND VARIETIES

Skirret is an old vegetable that is rarely seen anymore. It is a perennial that produces a cluster of knobby roots, which are eaten cooked in a manner similar to parsnips. The roots are eaten occasionally in the Mediterranean.

PLANT ORIGIN

Skirret developed from the wild skirret, *S. lancifolium* (Bieb.) Thell., a plant without tuberous roots. It is not known where the tuberous-rooted skirret originates, but the cultivated variety is native in damp places from the Balkans eastward to Siberia and southward to northern Iraq and Iran. Sturtevant suggested China as a center of origin.

Skirret has been grown since the sixteenth century and possibly was cultivated by the Romans. Pliny is thought to be referring to skirret when he mentions a plant that was requisitioned by the Emperor Tiberius from Germany, although some commentators believe this plant might be parsnip rather than skirret. In any case, in ancient times the plant was boiled and then cooked with wine and honey.

HOW TO GROW AND HARVEST

Skirret is best grown deep in rich, moist soil. Thin seedlings to a foot apart, and each plant will have a cluster of roots that can be divided for propagation the following spring. Harvest the roots in the late fall or early winter before the ground freezes.

HOW TO BUY, STORE, AND PREPARE FOR COOKING

Skirret can sometimes be found in farmers' markets. Skirret can be stored in a cold cellar or the refrigerator.

SMOOTH HAWKSBEARD
Crepis capillaris (L.) Wallr. (Asteraceae-Compositae)
ITALIAN: *tassella, tassellora, cassella, cassellora* (Tuscany); TURKEY: *kohum, koyun otu* (Aksaray Province)

PLANT CHARACTERISTICS AND VARIETIES

This annual or biennial has slender roots and copious stems. The leaves are eaten raw or cooked. In the Friuli region of Italy they are picked and cooked in the spring with other wild greens that are gathered for a dish called *pistic.* In rural Tuscany, the leaves are used in vegetable soups. Some other gathered varieties are *C. leontodontoides* All. and *C. sancta* Babcock, which are used in salads and vegetable soups and are boiled in mixtures with other greens. In the rural areas of Aksaray Province southeast of Ankara in Anatolia, the leaves of *C. foetida* L. subsp. *rhoeadifolia* (Bieb.) Celak. are gathered in the wild and eaten in a salad.

SNOW PEA POD
See Pea.

SOLOMON'S SEAL
Polygonatum multiflorum All. (Liliaceae)

PLANT CHARACTERISTICS AND VARIETIES

This stout perennial has creeping rhizomes. The rhizomes, which are an important source of starch, are eaten in the Balkans and Greece. The young shoots are boiled and eaten like asparagus in Turkey.

SORREL

Rumex acetosa L. (Polygonaceae)

ARABIC: *dīrb, ḥummāḍ*; FRENCH: *grand oseille, oseille*; GREEK: *oxalis*; ITALIAN: *acetosa, erba putta* (Tuscany); *zezzora* (Tuscany); *pane e vino* (Tuscany); SERBO-CROATIAN: *kiselica*; SPANISH: *acedera*; TURKISH: *eşkileme, kuzum oğlaği* (Aksaray Province), *evelek* and *kazan kulpu* (R. crispus)

PLANT CHARACTERISTICS AND VARIETIES

Among Mediterranean cooks, sorrel is most popular as a food in Spain and France, where it is used in soups and salads. The leaves of this frost-hardy perennial have a sharp taste and, when cooked, are slightly viscous. So-called French sorrel (*R. scutatus* L.) has a lemony flavor. A third species, *R. patientia* L., is not grown that much anymore. Gathered young, the leaves are cooked like spinach. A fourth species, *R. crispus*, is cooked in vegetable soups. Several other species are also eaten, including *R. obtusifolius* (called *al-baqla al-khurāsāniyya* in Arabic) in Iraq and Iran, the Arabic name meaning "greens from Khorasan," an Arab-speaking region of western Iran.

PLANT ORIGIN

Rumex patientia L. is native to eastern Europe, Turkey, northern Asia, and North Africa. *Rumex scutatus* L. is a native of the mountains in central and southern Europe, Turkey, and northern Iran. *Rumex acetosa* is native to the Mediterranean. Seeds of sorrel have been found in the stomach of Tollund man, an Iron Age man who lived in Tollund, Denmark.

PLANT HISTORY

Pliny mentions a cultivated sorrel called *rumix* (*R. patientia*), and so do other Roman authors. Sorrel is mentioned in the early botanies and was known to grow in the gardens of England in the early sixteenth century.

HOW TO GROW AND HARVEST

In the spring, plant seeds directly in the soil in full sun about a foot apart. French sorrel (*R. scutatus* L.) thrives in drier, better-drained soil than does *R. acetosa*, and is popular in France. Harvest the leaves by cutting them close to the ground once or twice during the growing season. Feed and water the plant to encourage further growth.

HOW TO BUY, STORE, AND PREPARE FOR COOKING

Young leaves should be eaten raw or after a very brief cooking, while older leaves are tart, so it is best to change the water while cooking them.

Sorrel

THIS SHARP-TASTING LEAFY VEGETABLE SEEMS TO APPEAR MOSTLY IN SOUPS AND PUREES IN THE MEDITERRANEAN. Although I have stumbled across recipes calling for fish to be cooked with sorrel, most recipes that feature sorrel resemble the *purée d'oseille* one finds in France, where sorrel is usually cooked with cream, of course, and sometimes accompanied by other ingredients, such as barley, semolina, tapioca, buckwheat, or rice. The Italians cook sorrel in the same way, as a *zuppa crema d'acetosa*, with cream, egg yolks, grated cheese, and croutons. In Lebanon, many cooks replace the spinach of the baked stuffed turnover called *fatīr bi'l-sabānikh* with sorrel. In Lebanese dialect sorrel is called *ḥummayda*.

RECIPE

Acederas Rehogadas
BRAISED SORREL

Sorrel is often used in soups and salads in Mediterranean cooking, but in this preparation from Spain it is braised and becomes part of a deliciously creamy vegetable dish. If you've never had sorrel, this dish is an excellent introduction.

¼ cup extra virgin olive oil
2 garlic cloves, peeled
2 pounds sorrel
1½ tablespoons white wine vinegar
Salt to taste

Heat the olive oil in a large skillet or saucepan over medium heat and add the garlic. Cook the garlic until it is lightly browned, about 2 minutes. Remove and discard the garlic. Add the sorrel and toss in the oil to coat. Pour in the vinegar, season with salt, and cook until most of the liquid has evaporated and until the sorrel is completely wilted and is smooth and creamy looking, about 10 minutes. Serve immediately.

Makes 4 servings

SOUR-GRASS
Oxalis acetosella L. (Oxalidaceae)
ITALIAN: *asprini* (Tuscany)

PLANT CHARACTERISTICS AND VARIETIES
This creeping perennial has slender aboveground rhizomes. The edible part is the sour-tasting leaf, which is used in salads and is eaten as a snack in rural Tuscany.

SOWBREAD
Convolvulus lineatus L. (Convolvulaceae)
TURKISH: *tavşan kulaği* (Aksaray Province)

PLANT CHARACTERISTICS AND VARIETIES
The leaves of this plant in the primrose family are commonly gathered in the wild in the Melendiz River Basin of Turkey and cooked or eaten raw.

PLANT HISTORY
Sowbread was described in Gerarde's herbal, published in 1597, as having many green and round leaves. The plant was eaten in Sicily through the ages, but we don't know how.

SOW THISTLE
Urospermum picroides (L.) Scop. ex F.W. Schmidt and *Sonchus oleraceus* (also *Sonchus tenerrimus* L.) (Asteraceae-Compositae)
ARABIC: *murār; tifāf;* FRENCH: *chardon;* GREEK: *zochos;* ITALIAN: *radicchione selvatico, cristàutu (Salento); crispigno (Viterbo);* SPANISH: *cerraja, cardo ajonhero, cardo ajonjero*

PLANT CHARACTERISTICS AND VARIETIES
This annual herb has a slender spine that is long and hairy. The edible part is the leaves, which are used mostly in the cooking of southern Italy and Greece. In the Salento region of southern Italy the variety *U. dalechampii* is used in salads, while in rural Tuscany it is boiled and used in mixtures with other greens and called *cento coglioni*. In Greece *U. picroides* is used in *hortopita*, a vegetable pie made with seven different wild greens. *Sonchus tenerrimus* L. is a thistle eaten in Italy as a salad. It is a common weed, widespread in gardens, fallow fields, and roadsides in Palestine and Israel. The soft leaves of *S. tenerrimus* are eaten as a salad by the poor; some people also eat the juicy root.

PLANT ORIGIN
Sonchus is native to the Mediterranean.

PLANT HISTORY
The Book of Numbers mentions *Sonchus oleraceus* as one of the "bitter herbs" that the Jews eat for Passover. The plant is called *maror* in Hebrew and *murār* in Arabic. Chicory, watercress, and nasturtium have also been identified among the "bitter herbs" mentioned in the Bible. Dioscorides mentions this thistle as an esculent. One source claims that Pliny describes how Theseus ate a dish of sow thistles before he met the bull of Marathon, but I have never found this reference, although Pliny does talk about the plant and does mention Theseus. Athenaeus reports that Antiphanes described a "dainty dish of sow thistle."

SPINACH

Spinacia oleracea L. (Chenopodiaceae)
ARABIC: *sabānikh* (or *isabānikh*); CATALAN:
espinac; FRENCH: *épinard*; GREEK: *spanaki*;
ITALIAN: *spinacio*; SERBO-CROATIAN: *španak*,
špinat; SPANISH: *espinaca*; TURKISH: *ıspanak*

PLANT CHARACTERISTICS AND VARIETIES

Spinach is an annual plant with dark green leaves. It enjoys cool weather. There are two kinds of spinach, prickly-seeded and round-seeded. Most spinach on the market is derived from the round-seeded kind. Spinach is also classified by the shape of its leaves. Again, there are two major types, smooth leaf or crinkly leaf. Spinach produces dioecious plants, meaning plants that have either male or female characteristics but not both. Spinach plants are pollinated by the wind. Most of the commercial spinach grown is a hybrid that produces high yields and is disease resistant.

PLANT ORIGIN

Spinach comes from a central and southwestern Asian gene center, and the plant may have originated from *Spinacia tetranda*, which is still gathered as a wild edible green in Anatolia. Spinach was unknown to the ancient Mediterranean world.

PLANT HISTORY

The diffusion of spinach into the Mediterranean was almost certainly the result of Arab horticultural ingenuity. Although spinach does not grow well in hot weather, it was successfully cultivated in the hot and arid Mediterranean climate by Arab agronomists, probably as early as the eighth century, through the use of sophisticated irrigation techniques. The first references to spinach are from Sasanian Persia (about A.D. 226–640), and we know that in A.D. 647 spinach was taken from Nepal to China, where it was, and still is, known as the "Persian green." The first written evidence of spinach in the Mediterranean is in three tenth-century works, the medical work by al-Rāzī (known as Rhazes in the West) and in two agricultural treatises, one by Ibn Waḥshīya and the other by Qusṭūs al-Rūmī. Spinach became a popular vegetable in the Arab Mediterranean and arrived in Spain by the latter part of the twelfth century. It was there that the great Arab agronomist Ibn al-ᶜAwwām described it as the "prince of leafy greens." Spinach was also the subject of a special treatise in the eleventh century by Ibn Hajjāj.

When spinach reached Provence, it also became a popular vegetable, behind cabbage. Spinach is mentioned frequently as part of the fifteenth-century Provençal *ortolagia*, the vegetables produced in the garden. In the seventeenth century the famous English philosopher John Locke reports having had a spinach and herb soup during his travels in southwestern France. In Anatolia, spinach was known by the thirteenth century, if not earlier, and was served with meat and covered in garlic-yogurt sauce. This dish was popular with the Seljuk Turks. The Italians were important for promoting this new vegetable in the Mediterranean diet, since beginning in the thirteenth century they favored spinach in their gardens along with several other new vegetables both from the Old and, later, New World. In Venice, cooks integrated Muslim flavoring techniques of using sugar and certain spices in dishes known as *saur*, which were enriched with pine nuts and sultanas. Fish, meatballs, and rice were also flavored in this way, as were spinach dishes.

The Arab influence in Spain is evident even today. Some time ago a stylish dish in Córdoba was *sajina*, also called *ásida*, a kind of watery soup made with wheat flour cooked with spinach or other leafy vegetables. This soup seemed to be obligatory at family gatherings and holiday feasts, where you would also find stews/soups of lima beans or chickpeas. *Sajina* is a direct descendant of a popular stew from Islamic Spain.

Mediterranean Jews, the Sephardim, were also fond of spinach and prepared dishes such as *shpongous*, a savory baked dish of sheep's cheese and spinach that was customary as a dairy dish served on Shavuot, the holiday fifty days after Passover celebrating the Palestinian harvest and the anniversary of the giving of the Law.

In thirteenth-century Damascus, *būrānī* was a popular dish of Persian origin, made with spinach or Swiss chard and yogurt, garlic, and spices. In 1614 Castelvetro calls for spinach to be used as the stuffing for *tortelli*.

HOW TO GROW AND HARVEST

Spinach grows best in cool weather. In the hot summer, the plants will quickly go to seed. Spinach likes rich, well-limed soil with a neutral pH factor (6.5 to 7.5) and a high nitrogen content. Plant spinach in the early fall, as soon as the last of the very hot weather is over, or in the early spring, as soon as the ground can be turned over. The seeds should be planted ½ inch deep and 1 inch apart in rows spaced about 12 inches apart. If transplanting seedlings from flats, do so carefully in rows spaced 6 inches apart. In warm climates, spinach needs partial shade, cool soil, and lots of water. The best fertilizer is dried manure spread around each plant. In cooler climates, spinach can be planted every 2 weeks until mid-spring.

Begin harvesting the outer leaves from the spinach plant when they are about 6 inches long, 40 to 55 days after planting, although you will be able to thin leaves sooner. Continue to pick leaves as needed until the plants look like they're ready to bolt—when the central stem starts to shoot up over the plant. Then remove the whole plant from the ground and prepare it for eating.

Most spinach sold in supermarkets still comes packaged in 10-ounce bags, although loose spinach and baby spinach are becoming more common. This spinach is usually Savoy spinach, the crinkly-leaf kind. Although it has been washed before packaging, you should still give the spinach a rinse. Most spinach that is sold loose, in farmers' markets or supermarkets, is the flat-leaf variety, sometimes called Italian spinach. Its roots can be slightly reddish, too. Look for crisp-looking leaves that are green without any sign of a lightening of color toward either light green or yellow.

If spinach is bought in a bag, leave it in its bag in a refrigerator until needed. With homegrown spinach, it is best to eat it as it's picked. With farmers' market and other store-bought loose spinach, store it in a bag in the cool crisper drawer of the refrigerator. Spinach also freezes relatively well, although it is far more preferable to eat it fresh.

Although it's not necessary, removing the heavier stems from spinach makes for a more attractive and pleasantly textured dish. For crinkly-leaf spinach, hold the two halves of the leaf together and pull or break the stem off. For flat-leaf spinach, simply hold all the spinach together and cut the root stems off with one slice through all of them. Spinach should be washed and rinsed thoroughly before it is eaten.

Spinach is best cooked with only the water remaining from its last rinsing adhering to its leaves, so that the soluble vitamins that remain in the liquid will be kept; if you use too much water you lose all the nutrients of the plant when you drain the cooked spinach.

RECIPES

Épinards au Beurre de Pignons
SPINACH WITH PINE NUT BUTTER

Spinach and Swiss chard are very popular in everyday Provençal cooking. I would serve this fantastic dish with braised pork chops with grapes and potatoes cooked in goose fat. *Crème fraîche* is easily found in supermarkets these days, but if you can't find it, use heavy cream.

2 pounds spinach, washed well and trimmed of
  heavy stems
3 tablespoons pine nuts
1 garlic clove, peeled
¼ cup (½ stick) unsalted butter, softened
Freshly squeezed juice from ½ lemon
Freshly ground black pepper to taste
1½ tablespoons crème fraîche
Pinch of freshly grated nutmeg

I. Place the spinach in a large pot with only the water adhering to it from its last rinsing. Turn the heat to high and wilt, 3 to 4 minutes. Plunge the spinach into cold water to stop from cooking. Drain it well in a strainer,

Spinach

SPINACH IS ONE OF THE FAVORITE VEGETABLES OF THE MEDI-
TERRANEAN. THE NUMBER OF SPINACH RECIPES IS SO GREAT
that I imagine one could write a cookbook filled with nothing but spinach recipes. In
Andalusia, you could have your spinach in the style of Córdoba, made with garlic,
onion, paprika, olive oil, vinegar, and cinnamon; or in the style of Jaén, made with
breadcrumbs, garlic, and dried peppers. In Almería, cooks like to make an unforget-
table pureed soup of spinach, potatoes, rice, and salt cod. In Anatolia a wonderful
salad is prepared with spinach leaves tossed with olive oil and yogurt, and spinach is
also made into *ıspanak kavurması*, fried with olive oil and onions. Spinach also finds its
way into the ever popular *börek*, a Turkish *meze* item, where spinach is rolled in phyllo
pastry and deep-fried. And the same theme is found in Greece, with its pastry called
spanakopitta, which is as ubiquitous in New York as it is in Athens.

Befitting its entry into the Mediterranean via the Arab lands, spinach is quite popular in the Levant, where it is used in soups, salads, and many finished dishes such as
burghul mufalfal bi'l sabānikh, spinach cooked with bulgur pilaf. Spinach is also popular
in North Africa in dishes such as the hot and spicy *sabānikh shaṭīṭḥa*, or "spinach in the
sauce that dances," made with garlic, eggs, olive oil, tomato paste, red chile pepper,
cumin, black pepper, and lemon juice. Countless other ways of preparing spinach are
found in France and Italy.

pushing out excess water with the back of a
wooden spoon.

2. Pound the pine nuts and garlic together in
a mortar until they resemble a smooth paste.
Whisk them into the softened butter with the
lemon juice. Season with pepper.

3. Melt I tablespoon of the flavored butter in
a large saucepan or skillet over medium heat
and toss the spinach in it until it is well coated and soft, about 5 minutes. Add the *crème
fraîche* and nutmeg and cook for 2 minutes,
stirring and tossing to mix well. Add the
remaining flavored butter and stir to coat all
the spinach, cooking for another 2 minutes.
Serve hot.

Makes 4 servings

Scarpassa

SPINACH TORTE IN BREADCRUMB CRUST

The name for this *torta di spinaci alla Piacentina* (spinach torte from Piacenza) in Emilian dialect is *scarpassa*. This stunning preparation for spinach comes from the town of Piacenza in the Po River valley, a town that played an important role in the development of agricultural enterprises and the evolution of capitalism in the Middle Ages. I would advise doubling this elegant recipe because I never have leftovers when I make it.

2 pounds flat-leaf spinach, washed well and trimmed of heavy stems
3 tablespoons unsalted butter, divided
2 tablespoons finely chopped fresh parsley leaves
1 small garlic clove, chopped fine
Salt and freshly ground black pepper to taste
Pinch of freshly grated nutmeg
¾ ounce dried porcini mushrooms, soaked in tepid water for 30 minutes
6 tablespoons light cream
2 cups fresh breadcrumbs, divided
2 large eggs, lightly beaten
2 tablespoons freshly grated Parmigiano-Reggiano cheese
3 tablespoons extra virgin olive oil

I. In a large pot place the spinach with only the water adhering to it from its last rinsing and barely wilt it over high heat, covered, for about 3 minutes. Drain well, squeezing out as much water as possible, chop, and set aside.

2. Melt 2 tablespoons of the butter in a casserole and cook the parsley and garlic over medium-high heat. Add the drained spinach. Season with salt, pepper, and nutmeg and stir. Drain the soaking mushrooms, chop, and add them to the spinach. Reduce the heat to medium-low, pour in the cream, and cook until the mixture looks soupy and creamy, about 15 minutes, stirring occasionally. Add 3 tablespoons of the breadcrumbs and stir. Remove the casserole from the heat and add the beaten eggs and cheese. Stir to mix well and set aside while you continue the preparation.

3. Preheat the oven to 350°F. Heat the olive oil with the remaining I tablespoon of butter in a skillet over high heat. Cook the remaining breadcrumbs, stirring frequently so they don't burn, until they are golden, about 6 minutes. Spread half of the breadcrumbs over the bottom of a small casserole and spread the spinach mixture on top. Spread the remaining breadcrumbs on top to form a top crust. Bake until the torte is heated through, about 15 minutes. Serve hot.

Makes 4 servings

Spinaci alla Piedmontese
PIEDMONT-STYLE SPINACH

Many vegetable preparations in the area of the old duchy of Savoy—today including portions of the Italian provinces of Liguria and the Piedmont, as well as the French regions of Provence, Haute-Provence, and the Savoy—use the interesting addition of salted anchovy fillets, a condiment that harks back to medieval times when many poor townspeople and country folk had access to only salted fish, because fresh fish were far too expensive. This simple method of cooking spinach gains an enormous amount of flavor from these anchovies. But a word of caution: the best preserved anchovies are salted not brined, so small cans of anchovy fillets packed in oil will not be as good as the salted anchovies that are sold whole in 14-ounce cans or individually at some better Italian delicatessens.

2 pounds spinach, washed well and trimmed of
  heavy stems
2 tablespoons unsalted butter
2 tablespoons extra virgin olive oil
3 garlic cloves, chopped fine
6 salted anchovy fillets, rinsed and chopped
Salt and freshly ground black pepper to taste

I. In a large saucepan or stockpot, place the spinach with only the water adhering to it from its last rinsing. Cover the pot and wilt the spinach over high heat, about 4 minutes, turning once or twice. Remove the spinach to a strainer and drain well, pressing out excess water with the back of a wooden spoon.
2. Melt the butter with the olive oil in a medium skillet and add the garlic and anchovies. Once the butter is melted, add the spinach and heat for 5 minutes, stirring to mix well. Season with salt and pepper and serve hot.

Makes 4 servings

Spinaci alla Genovese
GENOA-STYLE SPINACH

Here's another example of old-style cooking from the region that once was the duchy of Savoy. This recipe from Genoa is quite pleasant because of the assertive flavor of the anchovies, but it also shows a closeness to and has an affinity with some elements of Sicilian cooking, for example, in the use of raisins and pine nuts. In fact, this combination can also be found in the region around Rome, in Apulia, and in Catalonia and Andalusia, too. This simple preparation is best when the spinach has not been cooked for too long.

4 pounds spinach, washed well and trimmed of
  heavy stems
¼ cup extra virgin olive oil
¼ cup chopped fresh parsley leaves
6 salted anchovy fillets, rinsed and chopped
2 tablespoons golden raisins, soaked in tepid
  water for 15 minutes and drained
3 tablespoons pine nuts
Pinch of freshly grated nutmeg
Salt and freshly ground black pepper to taste

I. In a large stockpot, place the spinach with only the water adhering to it from its last rinsing. Cover the pot and wilt the spinach over high heat, turning occasionally, about 5 minutes. Drain in a colander, pressing out excess water with a wooden spoon. Chop coarsely and set aside.

2. Heat the olive oil in large casserole or skillet over low heat and add the parsley and anchovies. Cook the anchovies until they are almost melted into the oil, about 5 minutes. Add the spinach, drained raisins, pine nuts, and nutmeg and season with salt and pepper. Cook until the mixture is fragrant and the spinach is completely soft, about 10 minutes. Serve immediately.

Makes 6 servings

Spanakorizo
SPINACH AND RICE

This Greek preparation is identical to one in Turkey, and both Greeks and Turks like the texture to be somewhat gooey. It's a soul-satisfying dish that marries two favorites of the eastern Mediterranean, spinach and rice. Some cooks like to slide several sunny-side-up eggs on top of the finished dish, and you can do the same if you like. *Kefalotyri* is a Greek cheese that can usually be found in Middle Eastern or Greek markets; replace it with provolone or mild cheddar if you must.

¼ cup extra virgin olive oil
1 medium onion, chopped, or 6 scallions, both greens and whites, chopped
1 cup uncooked short-grain rice
1½ cups water
1 teaspoon salt

Freshly ground black pepper to taste
⅛ teaspoon freshly grated nutmeg
3 tablespoons finely chopped fresh mint leaves, divided
3 tablespoons finely chopped fresh oregano or rigani (wild marjoram) leaves, divided
2 pounds spinach, washed well and trimmed of heavy stems
½ cup freshly grated kefalotyri cheese

1. Heat the olive oil in a large casserole over medium heat and cook the onion until yellow, 10 to 12 minutes, stirring occasionally. Add the rice and cook until coated with oil, about 2 minutes. Add the water and salt and bring to a boil. Reduce the heat to low, cover, and cook until the rice has absorbed most of the water, about 20 minutes.

2. Season with pepper, nutmeg, and half the herbs. Place half the spinach on top of the rice and season with the remaining herbs. Place the remaining spinach into the casserole and cover. Cook until the spinach is slightly wilted, about 15 minutes, and stir to mix together the rice, spinach, and herbs. Cover and continue cooking, checking the casserole frequently, until the water is absorbed, another 30 to 45 minutes. Correct the seasoning, cover with the cheese, allow it to melt, and serve hot.

Makes 6 to 8 servings

Ispanak Kıymalı
SPINACH AND GROUND LAMB

I have been in Turkey during the winter, and in the mountains of western Anatolia the weather can become bitterly cold. I always remember eating this kind of dish at a small inn or town restaurant, huddling around a coal- or wood-burning stove, and enjoying every comforting bite. This spinach preparation is flavored with lots of onion, and small bits of lamb are used almost as a condiment. The spicing of cinnamon and cloves marries well.

2 pounds spinach, washed well and trimmed of
    heavy stems
3 tablespoons unsalted butter
1 large onion, chopped fine
½ pound ground lamb or lamb shoulder, trimmed
    of fat and cut into ¼-inch dice
Salt and freshly ground black pepper
2 cups water
1 ½ tablespoons tomato paste
1 cinnamon stick
2 cloves
2 tablespoons uncooked long-grain rice

1. In a large saucepan or stockpot, place the spinach with only the water adhering to it from its last rinsing. Cover the pot and wilt the spinach over high heat, about 4 minutes, turning once or twice. Remove the spinach to a strainer and drain well, pressing out excess water with the back of a wooden spoon. Chop the spinach.

2. Melt the butter in a large skillet over high heat and, once it stops sizzling, cook the onion and lamb, seasoned with salt and pepper, until the meat turns color and the onions are soft, about 8 minutes, stirring frequently. Pour in the water, tomato paste, cinnamon, cloves, and 1 teaspoon salt and season with more pepper. Reduce the heat to low, cover, and simmer until the meat is very tender, about 1 hour. Add the spinach and rice and cook until the rice is tender, 25 to 30 minutes. Turn the heat off and let the dish sit for 15 minutes before serving.

Makes 6 servings

Būrānī
SPICED SPINACH STEW WITH YOGURT

This preparation is a real culinary treasure not often found today even in Syria, where I collected this recipe. *Būrānī* is the name of a number of dishes that were popular in Damascus in the thirteenth century and were influenced by Persian cuisine. The name of this dish derives from *Būrān*, the wife of the Abbasid caliph al-Ma'mūn (A.D. 786–833), the son of the famous caliph Hārūn al-Rashīd of *1001 Arabian Nights* fame.

2 pounds flat-leaved spinach, washed well and
    trimmed of heavy stems
1 cup high-quality full-fat plain yogurt
2 large garlic cloves, mashed in a mortar with ½
    teaspoon salt
2 tablespoons extra virgin olive oil
⅛ teaspoon freshly ground allspice berries
⅛ teaspoon freshly grated nutmeg
⅛ teaspoon freshly ground cardamom seeds
⅛ teaspoon freshly ground cloves
⅛ teaspoon ground cinnamon
1 teaspoon freshly ground coriander seeds
Salt and freshly ground black pepper to taste
⅓ cup chopped walnuts
Arabic flatbread for serving

1. In a large saucepan or stew pot, place the
spinach with only the water adhering to it
from its last rinsing. Turn the heat to medium-
high, cover, and cook the spinach until it
wilts, about 5 minutes. Drain in a strainer,
pushing out excess water with the back of a
wooden spoon.

2. Stir the yogurt and mashed garlic and salt
together in a small bowl and set aside.

3. Heat the olive oil in a medium skillet or
saucepan and cook the spinach and spices over
medium-high heat until heated through,
about 5 minutes, stirring occasionally.

4. Transfer the spinach to a serving plate or
platter, spoon several dollops of yogurt over
it, and sprinkle with the walnuts. Serve immediately with Arabic flatbread.

Makes 4 small servings

Muba ṭṭ ān Sabānīkh
SPINACH BALLS IN SPICY TOMATO SAUCE

I first tasted this delicious preparation on a
trip to Tunisia, and I was really wild about
it. Spinach and rice are mixed together and
formed into balls that are floured and deep-
fried. Then the balls are finished in a spicy
hot tomato sauce that is cooked until it is
syrupy looking. To keep the spinach balls
from falling apart when they are in the
sauce, the spinach should be well drained,
and the balls should be fried until crisp. The
name of the dish is interesting. *Muba ṭṭ ān*
derives from the verb "to hide." In this dish
the spinach is hidden because it takes an
unusual form (a ball) and then it is further
hidden in the spicy ragout.

FOR THE SPINACH-AND-RICE BALLS:
2 pounds spinach, washed well and trimmed of
    heavy stems
¾ cup cooked short-grain rice (from ¼ cup
    uncooked rice)
¼ cup finely chopped onion
¼ cup finely chopped fresh parsley leaves
2 teaspoons tābil (page 106)
Salt and freshly ground black pepper to taste
6 cups olive or olive pomace oil, or vegetable oil
    for frying
1 to 2 large eggs, beaten
All-purpose unbleached flour for dredging

¼ *cup extra virgin olive oil*

2 *tablespoons tomato paste, diluted in 2 cups*
  water

2 *teaspoons cayenne pepper*

2 *teaspoons* harīsa *(page 263)*

1. In a large saucepan or stockpot, place the spinach with only the water adhering to it from its last rinsing. Cover the pot and wilt the spinach over high heat, about 4 minutes, turning once or twice. Remove and drain well in a strainer, pressing any excess water out with the back of a wooden spoon. Chop the spinach very fine.

2. Cook the rice if you haven't already.

3. In a large bowl, mix together the spinach, rice, onion, parsley, *tābil,* salt, and pepper. Form the mixture into 10 balls the size of little eggs.

4. Preheat the oil to 375°F in a deep fryer or an 8-inch diameter saucepan fitted with a basket insert. Dip the spinach-and-rice balls in the beaten eggs and then dredge in the flour, patting off any excess. Fry until light golden, about 3½ minutes, cooking the balls in two batches if necessary so the frying oil is never crowded. Drain on paper towels.

5. In a casserole, preferably earthenware, heat the olive oil and add the tomato puree diluted in the water. Stir in the cayenne and *harīsa* and cayenne. Season with salt and pepper and bring to a boil. Reduce the heat to low, cover, and cook until the tomato and olive oil are separat-ed, about 10 minutes. Add the spinach balls to the sauce, raise the heat to high, and cook until the oil emulsifies and the sauce is slightly syrupy, 5 to 6 minutes. Serve immediately.

Makes 2 to 4 servings

SPOTTED CAT'S-EARS

Hypochoeris radicata L. (Asteraceae-Compositae)

ITALIAN: *ingrassaporci, grassaporci, piattello* (Tuscany)

PLANT CHARACTERISTICS AND VARIETIES
This perennial with branched stems has oblong leaves. The young leaves are eaten raw in salads, cooked in vegetable soups, and in torte in rural Tuscany. The leaves can also be boiled and eaten like spinach.

SQUASH

Cucurbita maxima Duch. ex Lam., *C. pepo* L., *C. moschata* Duch. ex. Lam., *C. mixta* Pangalo (syn. *C. argyrosperma* Huber) (Cucurbitaceae)

Also called winter squash, summer squash, pumpkin, zucchini, and many other names; also see Zucchini; ARABIC: *qarac, qarac sūdānī, yaqṭīn* (var.) *qabuwya, fatr*; FRENCH: *potiron, courge muscarde, grosse courge, giraumon*; GREEK: *kolokunthe*; ITALIAN: *zucca moschata, zucca gigante, zucca torta*; SERBO-CROATIAN: *bundeva, buča, tikva*; SPANISH: *calabaza grande, calabaza gigante, calabaza de Castilla, calabaza moscada, calabaza almisclada, calabaza almiscarada, calabaza amelonada zapallo*; TURKISH: *balkabağı*

PLANT CHARACTERISTICS AND VARIETIES

The edible parts are the mature fruit and seeds. There are many plants called squashes or pumpkins, and they belong to any of the four species of *Cucurbita*: *C. pepo* L., *C. maxima* Duch. ex. Lam., *C. moschata* Duch. ex. Lam., and *C. mixta* Pangalo. Some taxonomists identify a fifth cultivated species, *C. ficifolia*. *Cucurbita maxima* is distinguished from *C. pepo* by having a peduncle that is cylindrical, while *pepo* has a short and many-sided one. Pumpkins or squash are easily hybridized, so that the range of colors and shapes is quite varied, and it is difficult to tell one variety from another. Remember when reading the cataloguing below that not all taxonomists accept this categorization, and it can change with the latest research.

Cucurbita pepo L. is a vigorous annual with trailing stems and long tendrils that includes both summer and winter squash. The flowers are yellow. Cultivars of *C. pepo* L. are divided into three groups in one scheme and six horticultural groups in another scheme:

1. var. *pepo*: pumpkins (the pumpkins are rounded or flattened with ribbed fruits); also included are pattypan, scallop, custard squashes, as well as various so-called acorn squash. In the United States, these pumpkins are sometimes used for jack-o'-lanterns.
2. var. *medullosa* Alef.: zucchini (see entry), also called courgette or marrow, which have long, rounded fruit of various colors.
3. var. *melopepo* Alef.: summer squash, which are subdivided into custard squash (also a name used for var. *pepo*), straightneck squash, crookneck squash (not to be confused with below), and spaghetti squash. There are many varieties of summer squash.

In the second scheme, the six horticultural groups are

1. Acorn squashes with small fruits of varying shapes and colors and always grooved,
2. Crookneck squashes with long fruits with curved necks and very hard yellow or orange rinds with warts around the rind,

3. Marrow squash with long fruits with green patterns on the rind,
4. Ornamental gourds, which are not eaten,
5. Pumpkins, large fruit with hard rinds used for jack-o'-lanterns and pie making,
6. Scallop squashes with flattened fruits, such as pattypan squash.

Cucurbita maxima Duch. ex. Lam. is a vigorous annual with trailing stems, long tendrils, and large leaves. The flowers are yellow. The fruit stalk is quite distinct from *C. pepo,* in that it is cylindrical, soft, and corklike. Cultivars of *C. maxima* are divided in two groups in one scheme and six horticultural groups in another. In the first there are

1. var. *turbaniformis* Alef: turban squashes, with large protruding ovaries off the receptacle.
2. var. *maxima:* winter squash, including acorn (a name used for summer squash, too), buttercup, mammoth, Chioggia, and Hubbard squash. The fruit ripens in the fall and can be stored for long periods. These are thought of as the "true" pumpkins; the largest of all vegetables, some grow to weigh many hundreds of pounds under certain conditions. It is this "pumpkin" that is the familiar pumpkin used for Halloween and the pumpkin-growing contests in the United States. The seeds can be roasted and eaten, and they store well.

In the second scheme are the following divisions:

1. Banana squashes with long fruit pointed at both ends such as the cultivars Banana or Plymouth Rock,
2. Delicious squashes with turbanlike fruit and hard rinds such as Delicious or Faxon,
3. Hubbard squashes with oval fruits and very hard rinds such as Hubbard or Brighton squashes,
4. Marrows with oval fruits such as Boston Marrow or Ohio squash,
5. Show pumpkins with large orange fruits and soft rinds such as Mammoth or Atlantic Giant,
6. Turban squashes with turban-shaped fruit such as acorn, buttercup, and turban squashes.

Cucurbita mixta Pangalo is the species cultivated mostly in the southern United States. It has large curved fruit and is striped dark green. It is similar to *C. moschata* but has a hard, swollen corklike stalk. There are three domesticated varieties of *C. mixta;* var. *argyrosperma* such as Silverseed Gourd, var. *callicarpa,* and var. *stenosperma* grown mostly for its seeds. Some cultivars are

1. Tennessee Sweet Potato, with a large, pear-shaped fruit and pale yellow skin with green stripes,
2. Green Striped Cushaw, with a bottle-shaped fruit and curved neck and beige skin with green stripes.

Cucurbita moschata Duch. ex. Lam. is the earliest of the species to have been cultivated. These are winter squash, predominantly long trailing or climbing plants, with some bush varieties. The fruit is usually smooth skinned with orange flesh. There are three horticultural groups:

1. Cheese pumpkins with cultivars such as Kentucky Field (a flattened sphere) or Quaker Pie,
2. Crooknecks (with a smooth skin) with cultivars such as Winter Crookneck or Golden Cushaw,
3. Bell squashes with cultivars such as Butternut (a straight-necked bottle-shaped squash) or African Bell.

Another cultivar is the Naples squash, which is popular in southern Italy.

Cucurbita ficifolia is a perennial grown only in the tropical highland regions of Mexico, Central America, and northern South America.

The cytogenetic background of the *Cucurbita* is not well known and contributes to some of the confusion about taxonomy. Furthermore, more confusion is added because of the distinction between cytotaxonomy and folk taxonomy, which does not always recognize species, and which attributes common names indiscriminately to different cultigen species. In fact, most of the distinctions between squashes are based on culinary terms, not botanical ones. For example, "summer squash" refers to the immature fruits of *C. pepo*. "Winter squash" refers to the mature fruits of *C. pepo, C. maxima, C. moschata,* and *C. mixta* that are used as storable vegetables and in jams and pies and for baking. The flesh of these winter squash is fine grained and mildly flavored. "Pumpkin" refers to the mature fruits of *C. pepo, C. maxima, C. moschata,* and *C. mixta* that have coarse flesh and are strongly flavored; these squash are not usually served as a table vegetable. "Cushaw" refers to the mature fruits of *C. mixta,* which are used mostly for baking. "Zucchini" or "vegetable marrow" or "courgette" refers to the fruits of *C. pepo;* the immature fruits are used as vegetables and the mature fruits for jams and storage.

The main difference between summer and winter squashes is that summer squash are soft skinned and the flesh tender because the fruit is harvested while immature. Winter squashes are thick skinned, their flesh hard, as the fruit is not harvested until maturity.

PLANT ORIGIN

There is a group of wild species of small, bitter *Cucurbita* in Mexico and Guatemala that are closely related to cultivated species, and it is thought that this area is one of the centers of origin. The seeds of these species are not bitter, though, and they are tasty and nutritious. Over time it is likely that these species were chosen by primitive farmers and, via selection, the plants evolved into the plants we know today. Although it is not conclusive, there is evidence that the five cultivated species are derived from these small, bitter gourds. *Cucurbita pepo* L. is native to North America from 10000 B.C. in Florida, 8000 B.C. in Mexico and 5000 B.C. in Illinois. *Cucurbita maxima* Duch. ex. Lam. is native to coastal Peru, where there is evidence of domestication from 2500 B.C., and in Chile, Argentina, Bolivia, and Uruguay, while *C. moschata* Duch. ex. Lam. appears to have been used in Tehuacán, south of Mexico City, around 3400 or 5000 B.C. and in Peru about the same time. *Cucurbita mixta*'s (specifically *C. argyrosperma* var. *argyrosperma*) origins appear to be in the southwestern United States and northeastern Mexico, but quite recently, the earliest evidence being from only A.D. 1200.

PLANT HISTORY

Wild species of squash are usually small and very bitter, while cultivated squashes are large and flavorful. This must be a result of a long period of cultivation. It is likely that squash were first used as musical instruments (rattles) and bowls, and only later were the plants cultivated as food. The *Cucurbita* are associated with humankind in the Americas for at least 10,000 years. The five cultivated species were cultivated by Native Americans in the pre-Columbian era and were staples in their diet. *Cucurbita* did not reach the Mediterranean until after Columbus's discovery of America. The word *squash* derives from a Native American Indian language, while the word *pumpkin* comes from the Greek word *pepon*, meaning "ripened." The word *pepo* was adopted in Latin to mean "large fruit," and this is the way the word is used by Pliny. The so-called Old World squashes were various kinds of cucumbers, melons, and gourds and maybe the loofah (see entry). The members of the Cucurbitaceae are a much studied vegetable. Two important, but different, books have been written that anyone interested in learning more must be familiar with, Thomas W. Whitaker and Glen N. Davis's *Cucurbits* (1962) and Davis M. Bates, Richard W. Robinson, and Charles Jeffrey's, eds., *Biology and the Utilization of the Cucurbitaceae* (1990).

The introduction of both winter and summer squashes began very early. By 1550, European herbalists were familiar with both. Many cultivars are depicted in Flemish and Dutch paintings of the late sixteenth century. From Europe, squash spread to North Africa and the Near East. Squash is eaten throughout the Mediterranean.

HOW TO GROW AND HARVEST

All the squashes require soil that is well fertilized with manure. The plants grow quite large, so ample space is needed between each plant, at least 3 feet. The plants should be watered regularly. Seeds can be planted indoors and transplanted outdoors after the last frost in late May or early June. Harvest pumpkins before the fall frost, leaving about 3 inches of stem on the fruit. Harvest zucchini and summer squash when the fruit is immature, not more than 6 inches long, during the late summer.

Squash

SQUASH, THAT IS, WINTER SQUASH SUCH AS PUMPKINS, ARE FOUND IN ALL MEDITERRANEAN CUISINES. SOME OF MY FAVORite recipes, which I have published elsewhere, are Sicilian, such as *cucuzzu al'agrodolce,* a sweet-and-sour dish made with a kind of marrow squash called *zucca gialla,* that is found only in Sicily. It somewhat resembles a butternut squash in appearance. The squash is sliced very thin and cooked with golden raisins, onions, garlic, red wine vinegar, olive oil, and pine nuts. There is another recipe that includes a piece of vanilla bean and cinnamon. Although Sicilian folklore attributes Arab overtones to this squash dish, some commentators see a Spanish introduction, as testified by the saying *a cucuzza vinni cauda d'a Spagna* (pumpkin came warm from Spain), an expression that is used also to make fun of people who resemble ignorant Spanish aristocrats, meaning that their head is empty inside like a pumpkin.

One of the more unusual Sicilian squash dishes is called *fegato di sette cannoli,* which translates to a totally incomprehensible English phrase, "liver of the seven spouts." The story of the origination of this dish of pumpkin fried with mint and pepper revolves around the Garrafello fountain and its seven waterspouts, located near the Vucciria market in Palermo. Apparently, there was once a street vendor who stood near the Garrafello fountain. He sold sweet-and-sour pumpkins with veal liver, but when veal became too expensive, he dropped the costly ingredient but kept the fountain's name.

HOW TO BUY, STORE, AND PREPARE FOR COOKING

For all winter squashes such as pumpkins, banana, buttercup, butternut, calabaza, Delicata, Hubbard, spaghetti, turban, and so forth, look for undamaged, dry skins without soft spots. Check the stem to make sure it is attached and sturdy; if it collapses, pass that squash by. The skin should be dull looking; if it is shiny, it means the squash was pulled too early. The longer the squash grows, the sweeter it will be. The squash should feel heavy, given its size. Some supermarket squash are so big that to market them, the store will cut them up into sections, with or without their skin. With these squash, examine the flesh to see if it is hard and of a good color. Store pumpkins in a cool place such as a cellar, where they will keep for more than a month. But, if you refrigerate squash, they will deteriorate faster and will keep for only about 2 weeks at the most.

To prepare winter squash, first rinse off any dirt. Then cut the squash in half with a heavy chef's knife. To make sure the blade doesn't slip, make an insertion with the knife before pushing down to cut the squash. Scoop out the seeds with a spoon, and cut the squash into smaller, more manageable chunks. Finally, slice off any skin with a vegetable peeler.

Summer squashes can grow very large, but the best tasting ones will be small; for instance, zucchini should not be more than 6 inches long. Look for small summer squash that are firm all over. Farmers' markets and some greengrocers sell very immature squash, about an inch or two long. These are sweet. Store summer squash in the crisper drawer of the refrigerator for up to a week. Summer squash doesn't need to be seeded unless it is bigger than the size suggested here.

RECIPES

Zucca Gialla con Ricotta Forte

PUMPKIN WITH RICOTTA SALATA

In the region of Apulia in southern Italy, pumpkin is prepared using a strongly flavored dried ricotta cheese called *ricotta salata*. This fragrant dish is seasoned with anchovy, capers, garlic, onion, and olives. It is served as a vegetable side dish, almost always served at room temperature, which allows the flavors to mellow nicely.

6 tablespoons extra virgin olive oil
1 medium onion, thinly sliced
1 celery stalk, chopped
1 large garlic clove, peeled and lightly crushed
4 salted anchovy fillets, rinsed and chopped
2 tablespoons capers, chopped if large
2 pounds pumpkin flesh, cut into pieces
1½ cups pitted imported black olives (about ½ pound)
1 tablespoon freshly grated hard ricotta salata
Salt and freshly ground black pepper to taste

1. Heat the olive oil in a large casserole over medium-high heat and cook the onion, celery, garlic, anchovies, and capers until the onion is translucent, about 5 minutes, stirring so the garlic doesn't burn. Remove and discard the garlic.

2. Add the pumpkin, cover, reduce the heat to medium-low, and cook until tender, about 25 minutes. Add the olives and cook until they are heated through, about 8 minutes. Transfer the contents of the casserole to a serving dish, sprinkle with the *ricotta salata*, season with salt and pepper, and serve at room temperature, on toasted bread if desired.

Makes 4 to 6 servings

Ajlūk al-Qara^c
PUMPKIN COMPOTE

Winter squash from the New World entered the Mediterranean from Spain, and from there it traveled to North Africa, Italy, and Turkey more or less simultaneously in the sixteenth century. In Tunisia, squash became a popular vegetable in everything from couscous to this *ajlūk*, a colloquial word from northern Tunisia meaning a kind of compote that is served as part of a Tunisian *ādū*, another colloquial word meaning a *mazza*. This recipe is said to be typical of Tunisian Jews and is adapted from Edmond Zeitun, the author of a Tunisian cookbook.

1 pound pumpkin or winter squash, seeded, peeled, and cut up

3 tablespoons freshly squeezed lemon juice, divided

3 tablespoons extra virgin olive oil, divided

2 garlic cloves, mashed with ½ teaspoon salt in a mortar until mushy

½ teaspoon harīsa *(page 263)*

1 teaspoon freshly ground caraway seeds

1 teaspoon freshly ground coriander seeds

12 imported black olives

4 small loaves Arabic flatbread

1. Bring a large saucepan of lightly salted water to a boil and cook the pumpkin or squash flesh until soft, about 12 minutes. Pass the cooked squash through a food mill or process in a food processor until it resembles a puree. Return the squash to the saucepan. Heat it for 1 or 2 minutes to evaporate a bit of the remaining liquid.

2. Beat the puree with a fork and stir in 2 tablespoons of the lemon juice, 2 tablespoons of the olive oil, the mashed garlic, *harīsa*, caraway, and coriander. Beat again, check the seasoning and correct, and transfer the squash to a small serving platter. Garnish the top with the remaining 1 tablespoon olive oil, 1 tablespoon lemon juice, and the black olives. Serve and eat with heated Arab flatbread.

Makes 4 servings

Qara^c *bi'l-Ṭaḥīna*
PUMPKIN WITH SESAME SEED PASTE

This recipe is popular among Lebanese, Syrians, and Palestinians, who make it as a *mazza*. This is the pumpkin version of a recipe that is usually made with chickpeas (hummus). I think you will find it lighter and more intriguing. Tahini is sesame seed paste that can usually be found in supermarkets, natural food stores, and certainly in Middle Eastern markets.

5 pounds pumpkin flesh, cubed

½ cup tahini

4 large garlic cloves, mashed in a mortar with 2
teaspoons salt until mushy

½ cup freshly squeezed lemon juice

1 to 2 tablespoons finely chopped fresh parsley
leaves, to your taste

Extra virgin olive oil for drizzling

½ teaspoon freshly ground cumin seeds

Seeds from ½ pomegranate

Several loaves Arabic flatbread

1. Place the pumpkin cubes in a large pot and cover them with water. Turn the heat on, bring the pot to a gentle boil, and cook the pumpkin until soft, about 40 minutes. Drain well and pass through a food mill. Return the pumpkin to the pot and cook over medium-high heat until all the liquid is nearly evaporated, about 25 minutes. Transfer the pumpkin to a food processor and process until creamy. Transfer to a large bowl.

2. Stir the tahini paste into the pumpkin and mix well. Add the mashed garlic and lemon juice. Mix well and transfer to a serving platter. Garnish with the parsley, some olive oil, and the cumin. Decorate the outside edges of the platter with the pomegranate seeds and serve with Arab flatbread to scoop up the dip.

Makes 6 servings

STAR THISTLE
Centaurea calcitrapa L. (Asteraceae-Compositae)
ARABIC: *qanṭūriyūn*

PLANT CHARACTERISTICS AND VARIETIES
This biennial whose stems can grow to 3½ feet has gray leaves when young. The edible parts of the plant are the stems and leaves, which are typically eaten raw in Egypt.

PLANT ORIGIN
Star thistle is native to the Mediterranean, North Africa, and temperate regions of Asia.

STINGING NETTLE
Urtica dioica L. (Urticaceae)
ARABIC: *qurrāṣ*; FRENCH: *ortie*; ITALIAN: *ortiga maggiore*; SPANISH: *ortiga, hierba del ciego*; TURKISH: *cızlagan*

PLANT CHARACTERISTICS AND VARIETIES
The edible part of the plant is the leaf, which is served cooked. Stinging nettle is a wild perennial that grows to a height of about 2½ feet. Handling the plants will result in skin irritations, even if you just brush against them, so it is important to wear gloves when touching them. In rural Tuscany, the leaves are used in frittatas, vegetable soups, and *tortelli* stuffing.

PLANT ORIGIN

Stinging nettles are native to northern temperate regions.

PLANT HISTORY

Stinging nettle was once called Roman nettle because it was thought to have been introduced to Great Britain from the Mediterranean by the Romans. Pliny describes a variety of nettles, asking "What can be more hateful than the nettle?" He describes the plant in terms of its medicinal value.

HOW TO GROW AND HARVEST

Stinging nettles can be planted, although they are usually collected in the wild. They are not a kitchen garden plant and, as they are invasive, they are best planted in an out-of-the-way corner of the garden in moist soil about 6 inches apart in the spring after the last frost. Wear long sleeves and gloves when harvesting the plant. Clip the tips of the stems, taking just the small leaves.

SWEET CICELY

Myrrhis odorata (L.) Scop. (Umbelliferae)
Also called cicely or garden myrrh;
ARABIC: *summāq al-bustān;* FRENCH: *cerfeuil musqué;* ITALIAN: *mirride delle Alpi, mirride odorata;* SPANISH: *perifollo oloroso, perifollo almizclado*

PLANT CHARACTERISTICS AND VARIETIES

Sweet cicely is a perennial with fernlike leaves and white flowers. The leaves, roots, and seed are usually eaten raw. The plant smells and tastes like anise. In northern Italy it is used in salads and is added to cooked salt cod preparations.

PLANT ORIGIN

Sweet cicely is native to central and southern Europe and Asia Minor.

PLANT HISTORY

Sweet cicely was once grown as a potherb and used medicinally for its stimulant properties. It is mentioned in many of the early botanies.

SWEET POTATO

Ipomoea batatas (L.) Lam. (Convolvulacae)
ARABIC: *baṭāṭa ḥulwa;* FRENCH: *patate douce;* ITALIAN: *patata americana, patata dolce, batata;* SPANISH: *batata, boniato, camote, papa dulce, moniato*

PLANT CHARACTERISTICS AND VARIETIES

The sweet potato is a tender perennial that grows quickly. The edible parts are the cooked roots and leaves. It is infrequently eaten in the Mediterranean.

PLANT ORIGIN

The sweet potato originated in America, and Mexico has been suggested as the center of genetic diversity, although the oldest archaeological remains of the sweet potato are from Peru.

PLANT HISTORY

The story of the sweet potato (*Ipomoea batatas*) is quite different from that of the potato. The sweet potato was discovered by Columbus in 1492 and brought to Spain from Haiti a year later. The plant was being grown in Spain within a few years. By 1556, Hieronymous Cardanus mentions sweet potatoes in his *De rerum varietate*. When one encounters references to the "common potato" in early-seventeenth-century writers, it is the sweet potato to which they refer.

HOW TO GROW AND HARVEST

Sweet potatoes can be grown from root cuttings. They grow best in sandy loam. Fertilize the plants lightly at first and then in midseason again to help the roots set. Mulch the area around the plant to keep the soil warm. Harvest sweet potatoes by probing the soil beneath the vines to feel what the size of the roots are, and, if they are a good size, pull them out, making sure you don't puncture them.

HOW TO BUY, STORE, AND PREPARE FOR COOKING

After sweet potatoes are pulled, they are usually cured for a week or so at 85°F in a heated room. Afterward they are stored in a cool, dry, airy place. In stores, look for firm, heavy tubers with no bruises or decayed spots. Do not refrigerate sweet potatoes, because if you do they will develop a hard core and a slightly unpleasant taste. Sweet potatoes will keep for a month or more if the temperature of a cellar can be kept at 55°F, but they should be used within a week if kept at room temperature.

SWEET VIOLA
Viola odorata L. (Violaceae)
ITALIAN: *viola* (Tuscany)

PLANT CHARACTERISTICS AND VARIETIES

Sweet viola is a perennial with leaf rosettes and rooting stolons. In rural Tuscany, the leaves are used in vegetable soups. Elsewhere in Italy, the leaves are dipped in batter, fried, and served as an antipasto.

SWINE'S CRESS
Polygonum arenastrom Boreau (syn.
P. aviculare) (Polygonaceae)
Also called knotgrass, buckshorn, iron grass; SPANISH: *centinodia, grama;* TURKISH: *at mercimekeği*

PLANT CHARACTERISTICS AND VARIETIES

Swine's cress is an annual whose 2-foot-tall stems are freely branched, forming a mat. The edible parts are the flowers and leaves. In the Aksaray Province of Turkey, *P. bellardii* All. and *P. cognatum* Meissn. are gathered in the wild and used in salads. The Turkish name for swine's cress means "horse cress lentil."

Swine's cress may be native to Asia Minor.

Carbonized seeds dating from the tenth century A.D. have been found at a Byzantine site, Beycesultan, in Turkey. The first written mention of swine's cress is in a thirteenth-century herbal. In the seventeenth century, swine's cress is mentioned by Castelvetro as an ingredient added to a mixed salad.

SWISS CHARD

Beta vulgaris L. Cicla group (syn. *B. vulgaris* subsp. *cicla*) (Chenopodiaceae)
Also called chard, silverbeet, seakale beet, leaf beet, perpetual spinach, rhubarb chard, spinach beet; ARABIC: *silq;* FRENCH: *bette, blette, poirée à couper;* ITALIAN: *bieta (bietola) a foglia, bietole (biete) da costa;* SERBO-CROATIAN: *blitva;* SPANISH: *bleda, acelga;* TURKISH: *pazı*

PLANT CHARACTERISTICS AND VARIETIES
Swiss chard is a biennial grown as an annual for its thick, broad white or red stalks and broad, dark green leaves. Swiss chard is a rugged plant that regenerates leaves even with heavy harvesting. Technically, in Italian, *bietole da costa* is Swiss chard, so named because the plant originally was grown and thrived in the saline soil that is found along the coasts. *Biete da orta* are beet greens, so named because beet greens were always a cultivated vegetable gar-

den plant (*orta* meaning garden). To complicate matters, in Italian *costa* also refers to the thick central stem ribs of the Swiss chard leaf, which are usually used to make soups, but the word sometimes refers to the whole plant. The French *blettes* or *bettes* comes from the Latin *blitum* (a tasteless herb used in salad), deriving from the Greek, while the Spanish word for Swiss chard, *acelgas,* comes from the Arabic word *al-silq,* meaning Swiss chard or beet greens.

PLANT ORIGIN
The origin of Swiss chard is linked to the development of the beet (see entry) to which it is intimately related; beet greens, too, were originally a seashore plant that is native to the northern Mediterranean.

PLANT HISTORY
Swiss chard, with its broad stalks, is first mentioned in Caspar Bauhin's *ΦΥΤΟΠΙΝΑΞ : seu enumeratio plantarum ab Herbariis nostro seculo descriptarum, cum earum differntiis* published in Basel, Switzerland, in 1596. All earlier references to *beta* refer to beets. Schery says that Swiss chard may have developed from the wild beet 2,000 years ago. Aristotle mentions a red-stalked beet chard around 350 B.C.

HOW TO GROW AND HARVEST
Swiss chard is easy to grow as long as the plant has water and nitrogen. The soil should be moist with lots of manure. Plant seeds in April and later thin the plants to about a foot

Swiss Chard

SWISS CHARD IS USUALLY COOKED QUITE SIMPLY, BOILED AND THEN DRIZZLED WITH SOME OLIVE OIL AND LEMON JUICE, OR maybe given a gratin finish. In North Africa, Swiss chard is popular in ragouts because, as a leafy green vegetable, it is rather hardy and can take a fair amount of cooking without disintegrating. In Lebanon and Syria, people stuff Swiss chard as one would stuff grape leaves. In Liguria, Swiss chard is commonly used as a stuffing with Parmigiano cheese for tortellini and ravioli.

apart. A second crop may be sown in August to be harvested the following summer. Working potash into the soil is also recommended by growers. Harvest Swiss chard as needed, clipping off leaves at ground level when desired. After harvesting leaves, feed and water the remaining plant.

HOW TO BUY, STORE, AND PREPARE FOR COOKING

Swiss chard keeps better than spinach, but it should be treated the same way. Look for crisp, dark green leaves with no signs of wilting or blemishes. Store Swiss chard in the crisper drawer of the refrigerator and use it within 2 days. Usually cooks separate the leaves from the stems and cook them separately for different preparations. Typically, in the Mediterranean, the stems are used in soups and the leaves are eaten as cooked greens or used for stuffing.

RECIPES

Biete al Foglia alla Genovese
SWISS CHARD, MUSHROOMS, AND ONIONS AU GRATIN

This recipe comes from Genoa and is popular throughout the Italian and French Rivieras. Many of the mushrooms used in Genoese cooking are forest mushrooms, not the field mushrooms that are so common in this country. Very often the cooks themselves will do the foraging, even in this hectic day and age when people allegedly don't have time. This dish can be served at room temperature, although I prefer it hot.

1 bunch Swiss chard (about 1¼ pounds), leaves trimmed of heavy stems, washed well, and sliced into strips
Salt to taste
½ cup extra virgin olive oil
¾ pound red onions, sliced
2 tablespoons finely chopped fresh parsley leaves
2 garlic cloves, chopped fine
½ pound mushrooms of your choice, sliced
2 large eggs, lightly beaten
Freshly ground black pepper to taste
2 tablespoons freshly grated Parmigiano-Reggiano cheese
½ cup dry breadcrumbs, divided

1. Preheat the oven to 375°F. Place the Swiss chard in a large saucepan or skillet with only the water adhering to it from its last rinsing. Add some salt, cover, and turn the heat to medium. Cook until the Swiss chard has wilted, about 8 minutes, stirring occasionally. Remove the Swiss chard to a strainer and press the excess liquid out with the back of a wooden spoon.

2. In the same saucepan or skillet, heat the olive oil over medium heat and cook the onions until soft, about 10 minutes, stirring frequently. Add the parsley, garlic, mushrooms, and Swiss chard and cook until the mushrooms are soft and brown, about 8 minutes. Remove the contents from the pan and let cool in a bowl.

3. Add the eggs, pepper, and Parmigiano to the bowl and season with salt. Mix well. Lightly oil a casserole and sprinkle with some

of the breadcrumbs, shaking the casserole so the surface is evenly coated. Pour the Swiss chard mixture in and top it with the remaining breadcrumbs.

4. Bake the casserole until the top is glistening and golden, 25 to 30 minutes. Serve hot or at room temperature.

Makes 4 servings

Acelgas a la Málagueña
MÁLAGA-STYLE SWISS CHARD

The Andalusian coastal port of Málaga is known for its seafood, but the local cooking is also favored with some appetizing vegetable preparations, such as this one for Swiss chard that might have a provenance from faraway lands. Although the taste is typical of Andalusia, because of the use of the raisins and vinegar (typical Sicilian culinary traits), the dish may have a connection with medieval Sicily, which was once under the rule of the Spaniards. This dish is really quite nice with grilled duck.

2 pounds Swiss chard, heavy central stem ribs removed, washed well, and drained
6 tablespoons extra virgin olive oil
3 large garlic cloves, chopped fine
¼ cup golden raisins
1 tablespoon paprika
Salt and freshly ground black pepper to taste
1 teaspoon white wine vinegar

1. Place the Swiss chard in a large steamer and wilt, covered, over high heat with only the water adhering to it from its last rinsing, 4 to 5 minutes. Drain well, pressing out the excess water in a strainer with the back of a wooden spoon. Chop coarsely.

2. In a large skillet, put the Swiss chard, olive oil, garlic, raisins, paprika, salt, pepper, and vinegar and turn the heat to medium-high. Cook until the Swiss chard begins to sizzle, about 3 minutes, reduce the heat to low, and cook until the Swiss chard is well coated and the ingredients are blended, about 15 minutes. Serve immediately.

Makes 4 servings

Blette Bouillie
BOILED SWISS CHARD LEAVES

The leaves of Swiss chard can become quite big. The stems are thick and white and are normally removed in Mediterranean cooking to be used in other dishes such as soups or the gratin in the following recipe. In this recipe, which is typical of Nice, where the plant is a great favorite, the leaves are prepared quite simply. This dish is an excellent accompaniment to grilled sausages, roast chicken, or pork chops.

4½ pounds Swiss chard, leaves trimmed of stems and washed well
Salt to taste
Extra virgin olive oil

1. In a large saucepan, place several large handfuls of Swiss chard leaves with only the water remaining on them from their last rinsing. Wilt the Swiss chard over high heat, adding more handfuls of leaves into the saucepan as room is made available by the wilting, until all the chard is wilted, 5 to 6 minutes. Drain the cooked leaves in a large colander for 2 hours without pressing any of the liquid out.

2. Arrange several leaves of wilted chard on a serving platter and season with salt and a drizzle of olive oil. Continue layering in this manner until the chard is used up. Serve warm or at room temperature.

Makes 8 servings

Côte de Blette au Gratin
GRATIN OF SWISS CHARD STEMS

This Provençal preparation is ideal for using all those large white stems that are reserved from other recipes. They are blanched in a light court bouillon and then run under the oven for an au gratin finish. This preparation is excellent with roast chicken or rabbit.

2 large garlic cloves, peeled and crushed

1 large onion, cut in half and layers separated

12 sprigs fresh parsley

8 sprigs fresh thyme

2 bay leaves

2 dried red chile peppers

3 quarts water

FOR THE SWISS CHARD:

2½ pounds Swiss chard stems (save the green
   leaves for another preparation), sliced into
   1-inch pieces

Salt and freshly ground black pepper to taste

2 salted anchovy fillets, rinsed

2 or 3 large garlic cloves, to your taste, peeled

2 tablespoons extra virgin olive oil

3 tablespoons all-purpose unbleached flour

1 tablespoon finely chopped fresh parsley leaves

1. Combine all the court bouillon ingredients in a large saucepan or casserole and bring to a boil. Reduce the heat to medium-low and simmer, covered, for 1 hour.

2. Blanch the Swiss chard stalks in the court bouillon for 10 minutes. Drain the stems, saving 3 cups of the court bouillon. Arrange the stems in a buttered gratin or baking dish. Season with salt and pepper.

3. Preheat the oven to 450°F. In a mortar, pound the anchovy and garlic cloves together to form a paste. In a small saucepan, make a roux with the olive oil and flour by blending them together with a small whisk or a fork. Turn the heat to medium and cook until the roux is fragrant from the smell of the olive oil,

about 4 minutes. Add the garlic and anchovy mixture and the parsley. Slowly whisk in the reserved court bouillon 1 cup at a time as the sauce becomes thickened. Simmer the sauce over low heat until it is quite syrupy, 30 to 35 minutes. Check the seasoning.

4. Pour the sauce over the Swiss chard and bake it in the oven until the top is lightly browned, 15 to 20 minutes. Serve hot.

Makes 6 servings

Kıymalı Pazı Dolması
STUFFED SWISS CHARD LEAVES

In Turkey, stuffed grape leaves are a very popular *meze*. But Turkish cooks also like to stuff other vegetables, including peppers, zucchini, cabbage leaves, and, in this incredibly delicious dish, Swiss chard leaves, which will remain a beautiful dark green after cooking.

1 bunch red Swiss chard (about 2 pounds),
   leaves trimmed of heavy stalks and washed
   well

4 tablespoons extra virgin olive oil, divided

1 large onion, chopped fine

¼ cup plus 2 tablespoons water, divided

½ cup uncooked medium-grain rice, soaked in water
   for 30 minutes and drained or rinsed well

10 ounces ground lamb

Leaves from 1 bunch fresh parsley, chopped fine

½ teaspoon freshly ground allspice berries

Salt and freshly ground black pepper to taste

1 cup high-quality full-fat plain yogurt, whisked
   until smooth

1. Place the Swiss chard leaves in a large stew pot with only the water adhering to them from their last rinsing. Turn the heat to high, cover, and wilt completely, about 5 minutes. Remove and plunge in cold water.

2. Heat 2 tablespoons of the olive oil in a medium skillet over medium-high heat and cook the onion until translucent, 4 to 5 minutes, stirring. Add ½ cup of the water, the drained rice, meat, parsley, allspice, salt, and pepper, reduce the heat to low, and cook until the rice is al dente, 12 to 15 minutes. Stir and fluff the rice and meat.

3. Arrange the Swiss chard leaves in front of you on a plate. Take one of the leaves and lay it down with the stalk end pointing toward you and the inside of the leaf facing up. Place a walnut-size piece of stuffing on the end of each leaf and press the stuffing into a cylindrical shape. Carefully fold the stalk over and away from you over the stuffing, being careful not to rip the leaf. The stalk should be a little stiff but soft enough to bend. Fold the sides in and roll up the leaf like a cigar. Stack the rolled Swiss chard leaves tightly in a small saucepan and cover with the remaining 2 tablespoons of olive oil and 2 tablespoons of water. Cover with a small inverted plate, then place the saucepan lid on and cook the stuffed leaves over medium heat until the water is bubbling and they are cooked through, 35 to 40 minutes. Check doneness by cutting open a roll and tasting it. Serve with the yogurt on the side.

Makes 4 servings

Silq bi'l-Ṭaḥīna
SWISS CHARD STALK AND TAHINI DIP

In the cooking of Lebanon and Syria there is such a variety of vegetable preparations served as part of a *mazza* that the ingenuity of the cook never fails to amaze me. Here is an ingenious idea for using those thick Swiss chard stalks that many people discard. Besides using them in soups and stocks, you can process them into a hummus-like dip as in this recipe.

1 pound Swiss chard stalks (save the leaves for another preparation)
1 teaspoon salt
6 garlic cloves, peeled
½ cup tahini, stirred if oil and sesame seed paste have separated
½ cup freshly squeezed lemon juice
Extra virgin olive oil
2 tablespoons pine nuts fried for 1 minute in 1 teaspoon hot olive oil
1 teaspoon dried mint
6 loaves Arabic flatbread

1. Place the Swiss chard in a pot of boiling water to cover and steam until soft, about 20 minutes. Drain well and chop. In a mortar, mash the salt and garlic together until they form a paste.

2. Place the Swiss chard stems in a food processor and run continuously until the consistency is smooth. Add the tahini paste and mashed garlic and run the food processor

until they have been incorporated. Pour the lemon juice into the feed tube as the processor is running and process the mixture until the juice has been absorbed. Remove the dip from the food processor and correct the seasoning if necessary.

3. Transfer to a serving bowl or platter, spreading it out with the back of a spoon and making fan-shaped furrows with the flat of a knife. Drizzle with a little olive oil and garnish with the fried pine nuts and mint. Serve with pieces of Arabic bread.

Makes 6 servings

TARO

Colocasia esculenta (L.) Schott (Araceae)
Also known as colocasia; ARABIC: *qulqās*; FRENCH: *taro, aronille*; ITALIAN: *colocasia, aro di Egitto*; SPANISH: *colocasia, malanga, yame de Canarias, alcocaz*; TURKISH: *kulkas*

PLANT CHARACTERISTICS AND VARIETIES

Taro is a member of the edible aroids, any of the genus of Old World plants with flowers in a fleshy spathe subtended by a leafy bract. In the Arab world, a variety of taro (*qulqās*) is known as elephant's ear (*C. antiquorum*). The corm and immature leaves are eaten cooked. Taro leaves and tubers are poisonous if eaten raw. They must be cooked to destroy their acrid calcium oxalate. Taro is not known to grow in the wild. It requires the same conditions to grow that rice does, partially submerged and very warm in the summer. All the varieties of taro known today were selected and propagated by subsistence farmers, and modern science has played virtually no role in developing or improving cultivars. Taro is eaten mostly by Arabs in the Mediterranean, especially Egyptians.

PLANT ORIGIN

Ethnobotanical evidence suggests that taro probably originated about 4,000 to 7,000 years ago in the wetter parts of India or Indo-Malaya that now grow rice. N. Vavilov identified the mountains of central and western China and its adjacent areas, as well as India and the Sunda islands, as possible centers of origin.

PLANT HISTORY

Taro is an ancient crop that owes its development to vegetative mutation or chance seeding and selection by prehistoric man. Some anthropologists argue that taro was humankind's first irrigated crop, and that the ancient rice terraces of Asia were originally constructed for taro. Although many authors have claimed that the ancients in the West knew of taro, the ancients probably only heard of it and had never seen it. The ancients confused it with the lotus, the water lily, the arum lily, the beet, the turnip, and the Egyptian bean. These authors were misled by the use of the word *colocasia* to refer to many other plants, leading them to falsely believe that taro was a plant grown in pre-Islamic times in the Levant, Egypt, and Mesopotamia. Some authors claim that Pliny describes taro, but his description could be of any number of plants (*Natural History*, Book XXIV, 91). The *colocaseum* described by Palladius is probably *Faba Aegyptica*. By the tenth century, taro seems to have been known in Mesopotamia, the Levant, and Egypt. Ibn Waḥshīya mentions it without much detail. In Spain, Ibn ᶜAwwām discusses the cultivation of taro in the twelfth century. A thirteenth-century Baghdad cookery book gives five ways of preparing it. Taro seems to have been an important crop in Egypt in the Middle Ages, as many writers remark upon this fact. In Morocco, taro is not mentioned until the fourteenth century, when it is described growing only as an ornamental plant. Taro seems to have moved directly from Egypt to Sicily, and been called *kulkas*, about the same time.

HOW TO GROW AND HARVEST

If the climate is very warm and wet and the soil is rich, taro can be grown. Taro can be harvested 7 months after planting.

HOW TO BUY, STORE, AND PREPARE FOR COOKING

The leaves are commonly used in soups in Egypt, only after they have been cooked first. The corms of taro are similar to potatoes but slimier. The tuber and leaves contain calcium oxalate crystals, which must be destroyed through thorough cooking. Taro can be found in supermarkets, especially ones that serve Americans of West Indian, Pacific island, or Southeast Asian heritage.

RECIPE

Qulqās bi'l-Ṭaḥīna
TARO WITH TAHINI SAUCE

Taro is a favorite root vegetable among Egyptians. They typically cook it with lamb in a stew. In this recipe, the slightly sweet, yet starchy and bland taro is smothered in tahini sauce. This dish is best eaten with some spicy grilled mutton or lamb.

¼ cup extra virgin olive oil
1 pound onions, sliced thin
1 pound taro, peeled and cut into 1-inch chunks
2¼ cups water, divided
Salt and freshly ground black pepper to taste
1 cup tahini
Freshly squeezed juice from 5 lemons (about 1 cup)

1. Heat the olive oil in a casserole over medium heat and brown the onions, 14 to 15 minutes. Add the taro and 2 cups of the water and bring to a boil. Cook the taro until tender, 17 to 20 minutes. Season with salt and pepper.
2. Meanwhile, in a small saucepan, heat the tahini with the lemon juice and the remaining ¼ cup water and season with salt and pepper. Once the taro is cooked and there is no water remaining in the casserole, pour the tahini sauce over the taro. Mix gently, but well, and cook the sauce over low heat until it thickens, about 8 minutes. Serve immediately.

Makes 4 to 6 servings.

TELEPHIUM IMPERATI L. (CARYOPHYLLACEAE)

ARABIC: *tāsarghant*; BERBER: *tasserint*

PLANT CHARACTERISTICS AND VARIETY

The plant, a member of the pink family, has a cylindrical many-veined calyx with bracts at its base. It grows mostly in western Algeria and Morocco. The root is something like that of the horseradish.

PLANT HISTORY

I have no idea if the practice still continues, but traditionally Arab women in Morocco would add the root of this plant to their couscous in the belief that the root would contribute to the development of Rubenesque figures. In their culture both the women and their menfolk measured physical beauty by plumpness.

TOMATO

Lycopersicon lycopersicum (L.) Karsten (syn. *L. esculentum*) (Solanaceae)

ARABIC: *ṭamāṭim, qūṭa, tumāṭa, banādūra*; FRENCH: *tomate, pomme d'amour*; GREEK: *dolmades* (also *dolmates, dolmathes*); ITALIAN: *pomodoro*; SERBO-CROATIAN: *rajčica, paradajz*; SPANISH: *tomate*; TURKISH: *domates*

PLANT CHARACTERISTICS AND VARIETIES

There are many varieties of tomatoes that are grown both commercially and as heirlooms.

The tomato is a perennial plant grown usually as an annual. The only edible part is the fruit. Commercial tomato breeders who supply the supermarkets have developed tomatoes that are disease resistant and are easily handled by machines. They have also developed varieties with determinate growth. That way the plant stops growing after a certain number of nodes have developed, and all the tomatoes can be harvested at once, an ideal situation for commercial growers. Unfortunately, the home grower will have difficulty finding tomato seeds or plants that are meant to be grown for flavor rather than for convenience in harvesting. The tomato is probably the most practical plant for someone who is interested in Mediterranean cookery to grow. Given ideal conditions, a tomato plant can produce as much as 50 pounds of fruit, which can be used for pastes and sauces in Italian recipes, for salads, for stuffing, and for a wide variety of cooking traditions.

There is an enormous variety of tomatoes one can buy or grow. For culinary purposes, I divide tomatoes into sauce tomatoes, such as plum tomatoes, and eating tomatoes, such as Big Boy tomatoes. But one can use any tomato for any purpose.

PLANT ORIGIN

When the Spanish arrived in the New World, they found the tomato to be already a well-developed cultigen. The plant was taken to Europe in the sixteenth century and later disseminated to many parts of the world. But the origin and early history of the cultivated tomato in the Americas are not definitive. It has long been thought that the tomato originates in western South America. The publication of the research of J. A. Jenkins in 1948, which has been supported by subsequent research, shows that the bulk of historical, linguistic, archaeological, and ethnobotanical evidence points to the area of Vera Cruz-Puebla in Mexico as the source where the first cultivated tomatoes were transported to the Old World. But for a variety of reasons, the debate continues about the center of origin of the cultivated tomato. The reason for believing Mexico was the center of domestication in spite of the undisputed distribution of the genus in South America is based on fragmentary or negative evidence. Archaeological data does not favor any particular region. The dearth of tomato representations on Peruvian pottery artifacts is considered significant, since pre-Columbian cultures were known for depicting cultigens on their pottery. Genetic evidence is also not much more conclusive either way. There is a great morphological variability in the cultivated tomatoes of Mexico. Such information is often used as evidence to support theories of centers of origin. But a similar level of variation also exists in Central American and coastal Peru. More important for determining centers of origin than genetic variability is genetic distance, which is determined by the degree of genetic differentiation between modern cultivated tomatoes and the tomatoes in the supposed areas of origin. Still, research is not conclusive in this area either. All we know is that the tomatoes introduced by Spanish explorers, which are the basis for all modern cultivars, were only a tiny portion of the germ plasm available in the same species. One of the world's foremost researchers on the origin of the tomato, Professor Charles M. Rick of the University of California at Davis, says that the geography of domestication of the tomato suggests that the immediate ancestor was probably var. *cerasiforme*, the common, weedy, wild counterpart of the same species, which bears more genetic resemblance to the cultivated tomato plant than does *L. pimpinellifolium*, which was the ancestor suggested by Sophie Coe, in her book *America's First Cuisines* (University of Texas Press, 1994). *L. pimpinellifolium* is probably a by-product rather than a member of the stem-line of the crop.

PLANT HISTORY

Once the conquest of Mexico was completed by Hernando Cortés by 1523, the tomato was brought to Europe. Seville, which dominated the American trade, was probably the first place in Europe where tomatoes were grown. Although it is sometimes claimed that the tomato originated in Peru, and its wild ancestor did, it was in Mexico that the tomato was first domesticated. Spanish herbals published in the mid-sixteenth century do not mention the tomato, although Spanish chroniclers of the New World do mention the tomato. In his *The General History of the Things of New Spain,*

Bernardino de Sahagún mentions all kinds and colors of tomatoes being sold at the Tlateloco market in Tenochtitlán in 1519. There are many other descriptions by other chroniclers. The first description of the tomato in the Mediterranean was in 1544 by the Italian botanist Pierandrea Mattioli. He described a yellow-fruited variety, and it has been suggested that this variety is responsible for the Italian name for tomato, *pomodoro* (apple of gold). It is not clear how this word was transformed into the apple of love *(poumo d'amour)*, as the tomato was known in Provence, although the fruit may have taken on aphrodisiac properties in the minds of some people. Another theory of the origin of *pomme d'amour* that is not generally accepted is that it is a corruption of *pomme des mours*, apple of the Moors, in recognition perhaps that the two important Solanaceae, the eggplant and tomato, were favorite Arab vegetables. At first the tomato was only an ornamental plant in Mediterranean gardens, because growers recognized it as a member of the nightshade family, which included plants such as mandrake that were known only as poisonous plants.

The tomato arrived in Italy before 1550, in either Naples or Palermo, then under Spanish rule. Tomatoes required extra watering and therefore it seems likely that the first use of the tomato plant in Italy was as an ornamental in gardens, as it was in Spain, perhaps at the Neapolitan or Palermitan villas of the Spanish viceroys. In any case, although the tomato arrived in Italy shortly after the dis-covery of America, it did not become generally accepted into Italian cuisine until the late nineteenth and early twentieth centuries. At the time of the tomato's arrival in Italy, pasta was still being made in Naples in the centuries'-old Arab-influenced style of using lots of sugar and cinnamon, as late as the publication of Antonio Latini's *Lo scalco alla moderna* (The modern carver) in 1692. Latini has the first recipe I am familiar with that uses the tomato (a tomato sauce that he calls *salsa di pomadoro, all spagnuola*), although Matthioli observed in 1544 that tomatoes were fried in oil with salt and pepper, like the eggplant and Costanzo Felici provides a culinary description of the tomato as early as 1572 in his *Del'insalata e piante che in qualunque modo vengono per cibo dell'homo* (Of salads and plants that are foods for man), describing it as looking better than it tasted. Not until a century after Latini, in 1790, with the publication by the Neapolitan chef Francesco Leonardi's *L'Apicio moderno (The Modern Apicius)* does the spaghetti and tomato sauce of today begin to emerge.

The history of the arrival of the tomato in other Mediterranean countries is not known at this time, but it seems likely that the tomato had dispersed everywhere by 1600. One botanist, Edgar Anderson, credits the Turks with the diffusion of the tomato in the eastern Mediterranean. They brought the chile pepper to Hungary possibly as early as 1526, and therefore this seems likely.

The tomato, a fruit, was officially declared a vegetable in the United States by the

Supreme Court in a decision made in 1893 because of a tariff dispute.

HOW TO GROW AND HARVEST

Tomatoes should be planted outdoors well after the last possible frost, usually late May or early June. Seeds can be started in pots indoors 6 to 8 weeks before that time; they will germinate at temperatures between 75°F and 85° F. The soil should be fertile with good drainage. Tomatoes do best in hot summers with nights that range between 60°F and 65°F. They need lots of water after their planting, but not in the early stages of growth. Once the fruit begins to ripen, the soil can be drier. Once the plants reach a certain height, they can be staked so the fruits do not touch the ground. Side shoots should be pinched off as they form in order to encourage the plant to produce more fruit. Maintain a soil pH of 6.0 to 7.0. Harvest tomatoes when they are completely ripe on the vine and can almost fall off with a good tap. Tomatoes can also be harvested as they begin to turn red and will ripen when kept in a paper bag.

HOW TO BUY, STORE, AND PREPARE
FOR COOKING

Tomatoes should never be bought from a refrigerated case or be stored in a refrigerator. Exposure to lower temperatures prevents a tomato from ripening well. Refrigeration makes tomatoes tasteless and sometimes mealy. When shopping for tomatoes in a supermarket, remember that if the tomato is not locally in season, meaning if it is not between June and October in most states, not including warm weather states such as Florida or California, then it is likely that the tomato has been shipped from a great distance or has been imported. This means that the tomato probably was picked while still green and has been refrigerated. If you are unable to get fresh in-season tomatoes, either from your garden or at a local farmers' market, it is best, for most recipes in this book, to use canned tomatoes. It is not always possible to do without fresh tomatoes, of course. But it is better to pass a recipe by than to make it with inferior ingredients. Overripe tomatoes, on the other hand, are perfect for making sauces. Once tomatoes have been cooked, such as in tomato sauce, they can be frozen.

When shopping for in-season ripe tomatoes of whatever variety and color, look for firmness. At farmers' markets, don't worry about misshapen or cracked tomatoes—these are perfectly fine. You will not see these tomatoes at supermarkets because supermarket managers buy for uniformity. Remove the stem end before cooking. Many recipes call for peeling the tomato before cooking. You can do this easily by plunging the tomato into boiling water for about a minute or two, then draining and peeling it, or by cutting the tomato in half, squeezing the seeds out, and grating it against the largest holes of a four- or six-sided grater, keeping your hand flat and using the peel to protect your palm.

Tomate Confite aux Douze Saveurs
Twelve Tastes Stuffed Tomatoes

∽

THE TOMATO IS AN AMAZING THING. THE SUBLIME SUBTLETY OF SINKING ONE'S TEETH INTO A JUICY FIRE-ENGINE RED PLUM of a tomato picked off the vine as opposed to the complex multilayered tastes that one experiences with the latest creation shows that the tomato is mighty versatile. One of the most intriguing creations for the tomato is *tomate confite aux douze saveurs* (twelve tastes stuffed tomatoes), an artistic and inspired creation of the French chef Alain Passard of Arpège in Paris, who turns the tomato back from its role as a vegetable to what it actually is, a fruit. This recipe was published in the magazine *Gambero Rosso*, no. 11, 1997.

5 tablespoons firmly packed brown sugar, divided
1 large apple, peeled, cored, and chopped
1 large pear, peeled, cored, and chopped
1 slice fresh pineapple, peeled, cored and chopped
½ teaspoon grated orange zest
½ teaspoon grated lemon zest
½ teaspoon peeled and grated fresh ginger
4 cloves
½ teaspoon aniseed
¼ teaspoon ground cinnamon
1 tablespoon raisins
4 fresh mint leaves
1 tablespoon chopped walnuts
1 tablespoon chopped almonds
1 tablespoon chopped pistachios
1 teaspoon pure vanilla extract
4 small ripe tomatoes, tops sliced off and insides scooped out
Freshly squeezed juice from 1 orange
1 vanilla bean
4 scoops vanilla ice cream

1. Caramelize 4 tablespoons of the brown sugar in a frying pan. Add the apple, pear, and pineapple. Cook over high heat until the fruit is almost soft. Add the 12 tastes: orange zest, lemon zest, grated ginger, cloves, aniseed, cinnamon, raisins, mint, walnuts, almonds, pistachios, and vanilla.

2. Stuff the tomatoes with the 12 tastes mixture. Sprinkle the remaining 1 tablespoon brown sugar into a small frying pan and caramelize it over low heat. Moisten brown sugar with the orange juice and add the vanilla bean.

3. Preheat the oven to 400°F. Place the tomatoes and caramelized orange juice in an oven-proof pan and bake for 5 to 7 minutes, or more. Spoon the juice over the tomatoes and serve them with the ice cream.

Makes 4 servings

I and other food writers advise that you seed tomatoes. This is merely a habitual and general remark. The seeds of the tomato are bitter, and you would not want that to affect your final dish. You need not get every last seed out. I usually seed tomatoes by giving each one a quick swipe to get a few of the seeds out.

RECIPES

Ensalada de Tomates
TOMATO SALAD

As most people know, Andalusia is the home of gazpacho, but it is also the home of other tomato dishes that are just as satisfying, such as this pretty salad, which can be served as a tapas, too. If you can find a variety of different tomatoes, such as orange cherry tomatoes and teardrop tomatoes to throw in, the salad will be all the more attractive. Make the salad about 30 minutes before serving at the earliest, and do not refrigerate it.

*1½ pounds ripe tomatoes of different varieties
  and colors*
1 ripe avocado, pitted, peeled, and diced or sliced
1 small garlic clove, chopped fine
1 tablespoon finely chopped fresh basil leaves
Salt and freshly ground black pepper to taste
½ teaspoon sugar
Extra virgin olive oil to taste
Very good quality Spanish sherry vinegar to taste

Trim the tomatoes and cut the larger ones and cherry tomatoes in half. Squeeze out the seeds. Toss the tomatoes with the avocado and garlic. Sprinkle on the basil, salt, pepper, and sugar. Drizzle on the olive oil and vinegar and toss gently again. Serve.

Makes 4 servings

GAZPACHO

Gazpacho is a liquid salad or cold soup from the southern Spanish region of Andalusia, made of ripe tomatoes, bell peppers, cucumbers, garlic, and bread moistened with water that is blended with olive oil, vinegar, and ice water. It is Andalusia's best-known dish and probably originated as a soup during the time when Spain was part of the Islamic world in the Middle Ages, a soup the Spanish call an *ajo blanco.* It contained garlic, almonds, bread, olive oil, vinegar, and salt. Today *ajo blanco* is associated with Málaga and is made with fresh grapes. Gazpacho comes in a variety of different intraregional versions, some of which contain almonds and no tomatoes and peppers (tomatoes and peppers came to gazpacho after Columbus). There is *gazpacho de antequera*, made with homemade mayonnaise blended with lemon juice and egg whites and pounded garlic and almonds; *gazpacho de Granada* is made with pounded garlic, cumin, salt, bell peppers, and tomatoes, with olive oil blended in until the soup is creamy. Then water and bread are added on top. *Gazpacho de la serrania de Huelva,* from the mountainous country around Huelva, is a puree of garlic, paprika, onions, tomatoes, and bell peppers with sherry vinegar and olive oil stirred in

until the soup is creamy. It is then served with cucumber and croutons. *Salmorejo Córdobés* (also translated as rabbit sauce) is made with garlic, bell peppers, tomatoes, and moistened bread pounded into a paste, with olive oil stirred in until the mixture has the consistency of a puree. It is served with eggs, oranges, and toasted bread. *Sopa de almendras* is an almond soup; *gazpacho caliente* uses hot peppers. There are also gazpachos that include green beans or pine nuts. Some food writers believe that a dish that contains vinegar points to Roman provenance, since the Roman culinary culture popularized vinegar. This seems a little too much of a generalization, though.

The growth in the popularity of gazpacho out of Andalusia into the rest of Spain is attributed by Alicia Rios and Lourdes March, authors of Spanish cookbooks, to the work of Eugenia de Montijo, the wife of the French Emperor Napoleon III in the nineteenth century. Gazpacho was unknown, or little known, in the north of Spain before about 1930. According to Juan de la Mata in his *Arte de reposteria,* published in 1747, the most common gazpacho was known as *capon de galera.* It consisted of a pound of bread crust soaked and softened in water and put in a sauce of anchovy bones, garlic, and vinegar, sugar, salt and olive oil. Then one added "some of the ingredients and vegetables of the Royal Salad [a salad composed of various fruits and vegetables]." Interestingly, *capon de galera* is thought to be a historical predecessor to the Sicilian caponata.

An American cookbook published in 1963 tells us that "gazpacho, the soup-salad of Spain, has become an American food fashion." The author Betty Wason goes on to tell us that in Mary Randolph's *The Virginia Housewife*, published in 1824, there is a recipe for gazpacho. The French poet and critic Théophile Gautier (1811–1872), wrote about gazpacho, too.

The origin of the word *gazpacho* is uncertain, but etymologists believe it might be derived from the Mozarab word *caspa*, meaning "residue" or "fragments," an allusion to the small pieces of bread and vegetables in a gazpacho soup. On the other hand, *gazpacho* may be a pre-Roman Iberian word that was modified by the Arabic. One hears a lot about Mozarab when speaking of historic Andalusia. *Mozarab* is a corruption of the Arabic *must'arab*, "would-be Arab." Mozarabs were those Hispano-Romans who were allowed to practice their religion on condition of pledging their allegiance to the Arab caliph. The *muwalladun* were Hispano-Romans who converted to Islam.

José Briz, who wrote a book on gazpacho, also suggests that the word derives from the Hebrew *gazaz*, meaning "to break into pieces," referring to the bread base. Gazpacho was traditionally eaten by workers in the fields, whether vineyards, olive plantations, citrus groves, wheat fields, or cork farms. Originally gazpacho was nothing but bread, water, and olive oil, all pounded in a large wooden bowl called a *dornillo*. It was poor people's food.

Gazpacho is traditionally made in a mortar, and the ideal bread to use is about a week old. The bread-and-vegetable mixture is pounded to a paste, and then you begin to add the tomatoes, then the olive oil, and finally the vinegar, tasting the mixture all the time to make sure you've got the flavorings right. The tomatoes should always go through a sieve so there are no seeds in the finished dish.

The secret to gazpacho is not to allow any of the ingredients to stand out over the others. The result should be completely harmonic, an orchestra of flavors. And above all, the tomatoes must be of the sweetest, vine-ripened, height-of-the-season type. Of the two best gazpachos I've ever had, and the ones I have synthesized to create this recipe, one I had at a country fair held at the Guillen family estate, the Hacienda Guzman, in rural Andalusia, about an hour's drive from Seville. The other was from the El Tablon restaurant, Cardenal Gonzalez, 75, in Córdoba. In both cases, the gazpacho was nearly a creamy pink and orange soup, very smooth, and full of fresh vegetable flavor that was bursting with sweetness. The list of garnishes below is not meant to be used in its entirety; choose four or five, and they should be at room temperature when they are served.

4 large garlic cloves, peeled

2 teaspoons salt

1 red or green bell pepper, roasted (page 261),
peeled, and seeded

2 slices week-old French bread with or without
crust

2½ pounds very ripe tomatoes (such as Carmello
tomatoes), peeled, chopped, and passed through
a sieve to remove all seeds (save some of the
juice to soak the bread in)

6 tablespoons extra virgin olive oil

1 small cucumber, peeled, seeded, and chopped

¼ cup good quality Spanish sherry vinegar

Yolk of 1 hard-boiled egg

Salt and freshly ground black pepper to taste

Freshly ground cumin seeds to taste

12 ice cubes

GARNISHES (CHOOSE 4 OR 5):

Ripe, firm tomato, peeled, seeded, and chopped
fine

Green bell pepper, seeded and chopped fine

Hard-boiled egg, shelled and chopped fine

Cucumber, peeled, seeded, and chopped fine

Scallions, both white and green parts, chopped fine

Sweet onion, finely chopped

Finely chopped fresh parsley leaves

Freshly ground cumin seeds

Croutons, cut small

Paprika

Jamón Serrano, chopped small

Homemade mayonnaise

Canned tuna in olive oil, flaked

Chopped imported black olives

Chopped imported green olives

A few drops of red wine

Finely chopped fresh tarragon leaves

Pine nuts

1. In a mortar, pound the garlic and salt together until mushy. Transfer the mashed garlic to a food processor and pulse until mushy. Add the green bell pepper and process.

2. Soak the bread in the juice from the tomatoes and a little water. Squeeze out the bread as if you were making a snowball. Add the bread to the food processor and pulse a couple of times with the garlic and pepper until the ingredients are well blended. Add the tomatoes and process for 5 seconds. Pour in the olive oil while running the food processor continuously. Add the cucumber and process some more. Drizzle in the vinegar and add the egg yolk while continuing to process. Season with salt, pepper, and cumin, if desired.

3. Transfer the soup to a large serving bowl and add the ice cubes. Leave in the refrigerator for several hours before serving, stirring occasionally, and serve with a selection of the garnishes once the ice cubes have melted.

Makes 4 servings

La Bohémienne
Tomato and Eggplant Ratatouille

*L*a Bohémienne (or *bóumiano* in Provençal and also called *guincho-clau* in the Provençal dialect), is a kind of ratatouille from Avignon, but it is quite different from the famous dish from Nice. It is cooked with only tomatoes and eggplant. Some cooks make a liaison of melted anchovies, flour, and milk to thicken the ratatouille, but I don't think that improves the dish at all.

½ cup extra virgin olive oil
2 pounds eggplant, peeled, sliced, cut in half, salted, and left to drain on paper towels for 30 minutes, then patted dry
2¾ pounds ripe tomatoes, peeled, seeded, and sliced
6 large garlic cloves, peeled and crushed
¼ cup finely chopped fresh parsley leaves
Salt to taste
2 tablespoons fresh breadcrumbs
¼ cup freshly grated Gruyère cheese

1. Put the olive oil, eggplant, tomatoes, garlic, parsley, and salt in a large oven-proof skillet, preferably earthenware. Turn the heat to high and, once everything is sizzling, reduce the heat to low, and cook the eggplant until it is tender, about 1¾ hours, mashing it occasionally with a wooden spoon.
2. Preheat the oven to broil. Transfer everything to a gratin dish if the skillet is not oven-proof, sprinkle with the breadcrumbs, and place under the broiler until browned on top. Remove the skillet from the oven, sprinkle with the Gruyère cheese, and serve.

Makes 4 servings

Salsa di Pomodoro
Tomato Sauce

The tomato did not reach Italy until the first half of the sixteenth century, and, in fact, it did not become ubiquitous in Italian cooking until the early twentieth century. In the Mediterranean, the tomato spent all those centuries as an ornamental plant for gardens.

This is a basic tomato sauce that can be used whenever a recipe calls for tomato sauce. Italian families don't freeze sauce as much as Americans do. Italian cooks are more likely to preserve their tomato sauce in jars or bottles and use it throughout the winter to dress spaghetti or make more complex ragouts. Normally, I make three times the amount called for in this recipe. Although fresh, vine-ripened tomatoes are best, canned whole or crushed tomatoes, tomato paste, and tomato puree are fine to use when tomatoes are not in season—just not the canned "tomato sauce" because manufacturers usually flavor sauces in their own way.

¼ cup extra virgin olive oil

2 garlic cloves, peeled and slightly crushed

1 medium onion, chopped fine

2 pounds ripe plum tomatoes, peeled, seeded, and chopped

6 large fresh basil leaves

Salt and freshly ground black pepper to taste

1 tablespoon dried oregano (optional)

1. Heat the olive oil in a casserole or deep saucepan over medium-high heat and cook the garlic until it begins to turn light brown, about 1 minute. Remove and discard the garlic and add the onion. Cook the onion until translucent, 5 to 6 minutes, stirring frequently. Add the tomatoes and basil and season with salt and pepper. Cook, uncovered, until the sauce is dense, 15 to 25 minutes, reducing the heat if the sauce is sputtering too much. Stir occasionally with a long wooden spoon so the bottom doesn't burn. Add small amounts of water if necessary to prevent scorching.

2. When the sauce is finished, turn the heat off, add the oregano, if you are using it, and let the sauce steep for 10 minutes before using it or storing it.

Makes 3 cups

Dolmates Plaki

BAKED TOMATOES AND ONIONS

Onions are a very well liked vegetable in Greece, and not just as the start to something else. One finds stuffed onions, onion salads, and a nice preparation such as this one—nice for a summer day because it is served at room temperature. Because this tomato dish is very oniony, make sure your onions are good-quality sweet onions. The tomatoes and onions are baked and then left to cool in the pan.

4 tablespoons extra virgin olive oil, divided

2 pounds ripe but firm tomatoes, peeled and sliced

2 large sweet onions (about 2 pounds), sliced very thin

Leaves from 2 bunches fresh parsley, chopped fine

Leaves from 1 bunch fresh dill, chopped fine

2 teaspoons dried oregano

Salt and freshly ground black pepper to taste

1 teaspoon sugar

Freshly squeezed juice from 1 lemon

1. Preheat the oven to 400°F.

2. Pour 1 tablespoon of the olive oil in a 12-by-9-inch baking casserole. Layer the bottom with sliced tomatoes, overlapping them slightly. Cover with a layer of onion slices and sprinkle with a third of the parsley and dill. Sprinkle with half of the oregano, salt and pepper to taste, and the sugar. Drizzle with 1 tablespoon of the olive oil. Continue layering until the ingredients are used up. Pour the remaining olive oil and all the lemon juice over the top. Cover and bake until the onions are soft, 35 to 40 minutes. Let cool completely in the baking pan and serve the tomatoes and onions at room temperature.

Makes 6 servings

Zeytinyağlı Domates Dolması
TOMATOES STUFFED WITH RICE AND CURRANTS

The Turks are wild about stuffed vegetables, and this recipe for stuffing tomatoes is so delicious you'll want to make it every day. I find that tomatoes stuffed with rice are perfect for a summer meal. This dish should be served at room temperature so the flavors have a chance to mellow and perfume the entire tomato.

FOR THE STUFFING:

3 tablespoons extra virgin olive oil

1 tablespoon pine nuts

1 medium onion, chopped fine

½ cup uncooked short- or medium-grain rice, rinsed well or soaked in water for 30 minutes and drained

1 tablespoon dried currants, soaked in tepid water for 15 minutes and drained

½ teaspoon ground cinnamon

½ teaspoon freshly ground allspice berries

½ teaspoon freshly ground white pepper

½ teaspoon salt

½ teaspoon sugar

1 cup water

¼ cup finely chopped fresh mint leaves

Leaves from ½ bunch fresh dill, chopped

FOR THE TOMATOES:

4 large, ripe but firm tomatoes (about 2 pounds), top stem piece sliced but left attached to act as a lid, the tomato hollowed out with a spoon, drained for 1 hour

1 tablespoon extra virgin olive oil

Pinch of salt

Pinch of sugar

1. Heat the olive oil in a medium skillet over medium heat and brown the pine nuts, about 2 minutes, tossing or stirring constantly. Add the onion and cook until it turns color, about 4 minutes. Add the rice and cook until some grains turn crusty, about 6 minutes, stirring. Add the currants, cinnamon, allspice, white pepper, salt, and sugar, stir. Pour in the water. Reduce the heat to low, cover, and cook until the water is absorbed, about 20 minutes. Once the rice mixture is cool, stir in the mint and dill.

2. Meanwhile, preheat the oven to 475°F. Arrange the tomatoes in a greased baking dish and sprinkle them with the olive oil, salt, and sugar. Bake them until they are nearly collapsing, about 10 minutes. Remove them from the oven and let them cool.

3. Stuff the tomatoes with the rice and serve them at room temperature.

Makes 4 servings

TRAGACANTH

Astragalus creticus Lam. and *A. gummifer*
Lab.; *kurdicus; leioclados; hamosus; christianus*
L. (Fabaceae-Leguminosae)
ARABIC: *kathīrā*; GREEK: *dragante*; SPANISH:
tragacanto, adraganto; TURKISH: *keven*

PLANT CHARACTERISTICS AND VARIETIES
Tragacanth is a leguminous plant that produces a gum that is used in some Greek sweet
making on the island of Kythera. Another
variety, yellow milk-vetch (*A. christianus* L.) is
eaten in the Taurus mountains in southern
Turkey. The edible part is the root.

PLANT ORIGIN
Most of the varieties of tragacanth are native
to Greece, Asia Minor, Syria, or Iran.

PLANT HISTORY
In the thirteenth-century medical formulary
of al-Samarqandī, tragacanth is described as a
purgative.

TRAGOPOGON PRATENSIS L. (ASTERACEAE-COMPOSITAE)

ITALIAN: *barba di becco* (Tuscany);
TURKISH: *yemlik*

PLANT CHARACTERISTICS AND VARIETIES
This annual or perennial plant has a cylindrical rootstock and linear lancelike leaves. In
rural Tuscany, the leaves and young buds are

boiled. In the Aksaray Province of Turkey, *T.
buhthalmoides* (DC.) Boiss. is gathered in the
wild and eaten as a green.

TRIGONELLA ARABICA L. (LEGUMINOSAE)

ARABIC: *nafal*

PLANT CHARACTERISTICS AND VARIETIES
The plant, a legume, is an annual with leaves
that are usually toothed. The Bedouin of the
Sinai and Negev flavor their *samna* (clarified
butter) with the leaves of *Trigonella arabica*, a
kind of clover.

TUBEROUS COMFREY

Symphytum tuberosum L. (Boraginaceae)
ITALIAN: *salosso* (Tuscany)

PLANT CHARACTERISTICS AND VARIETIES
The leaves of this plant, which is related to
borage, are used in vegetable soups in rural
Tuscany. The ground, roasted roots were once
used as an ersatz coffee.

TURNIP

Brassica rapa L. var. *rapa* (DC.) Metzg.
syn. *B. campestris* L. (including *B. rapa* var.
utilis and *B. rapa* var. *septiceps*)
(Cruciferae-Brassicaceae)
ARABIC: *lift, saljam*; FRENCH: *navet, navet*

potager; GREEK: *goggulion;* ITALIAN: *rapa da foglia, rapa senza testa;* SERBO-CROATIAN: *nabo;* SPANISH: *nabo, nabo de brotes;* TURKISH: *šalgam, turp*

PLANT CHARACTERISTICS AND VARIETIES

The turnip is a frost-hardy biennial plant whose enlarged roots, leaves, and inflorescence are eaten, usually cooked. *Brassica rapa* is the plant related to ordinary cabbage from which turnips, varieties of Chinese cabbage such as bok choy, *mizuna, tat soi, gai choi,* Napa, and many others were developed. The turnip has been combined with ordinary cabbage to form the rutabaga or swede (page 284). *Brassica rapa* subsp. *sylvestris* is the wild form found growing throughout Europe usually as a weed in open ground or by streams. *Brassica rapa* subsp. *rapa* is the cultivated turnip with its white and yellow flesh and yellow, white, or purple skins. There are a great many varieties of turnips; the differences are usually in the plants' roots. Turnip greens are cooked in Italian cuisine, especially in the region of Campania, where *friarelli,* a dialect word for "young turnip tops" (but sometimes used to refer to a kind of broccoli), are cooked in olive oil and garlic and served at room temperature.

PLANT ORIGIN

Two main centers of origination have been suggested. The European forms of the plant are thought to originate in the Mediterranean, while eastern Afghanistan and part of Pakistan is another primary center of origina-tion. A secondary center of origin is Asia Minor, Transcaucasia, and Iran. According to Don and Patricia Brothwell, authors of *Food in Antiquity: A Survey of the Diet of Early Peoples* (1969), the turnip is indigenous to the region between the Baltic Sea and the Caucasus, suggested by the fact the turnips still grow wild in eastern Europe and Siberia.

PLANT HISTORY

The time and place of domestication of the turnip are not known. Because there are old Arabic and Hebrew names for the plant, somewhere in southwestern Asia in pre-classical times has been suggested as one place the turnip was first cultivated. Theophrastus described the growing of turnips in Greece in the fourth century B.C. Both Pliny and Columella in the first century A.D. spoke of *napus,* which is believed to be the turnip. Pliny tells us that turnips are the third most important crop after wine and an unspecified corn in the country north of the Po River. Columella provided a recipe for pickling turnips in a mustard and vinegar liquid. The Greek historian Plutarch tells the story of the Roman general Manius Curius, who retired to his modest home in the country after a long and successful career. One day some Samnite ambassadors came and found him boiling turnips. They offered him some gold and he responded, "Why would a person satisfied with such a supper need gold?" Apicius offers a pickled turnip recipe using myrtle berries in vinegar and honey. In the sixth century,

Anthimus suggests turnips cooked with bacon and vinegar for flavor. The eleventh-century Arab physician Ibn Buṭlān in his *Taqwīm al–ṣiḥḥa,* which was translated into Latin and illustrated in the fourteenth century, spoke about the health benefits of turnips and radishes. Only after the introduction of the potato did turnip use decline. Turnips have long been considered a simple peasant food. The cultivation of turnips for the seed oil is thought to have started in Europe in the thirteenth century.

HOW TO GROW AND HARVEST

Turnips are not difficult to grow, as long as they are well watered. They mature about 70 days after the seeds are sown. Turnips for winter storage are usually sown 4 to 6 inches apart in July and August, while an early summer crop is sown in March or April. Turnips are best when harvested small. Harvest the greens leaving about 3 inches of stem above the root. The roots can be left in the ground through the winter and pulled when needed. Keep the plant mulched against frost damage.

HOW TO BUY, STORE, AND PREPARE FOR COOKING

Turnip tops are edible, but they should not be stored as the roots are. Look for fresh, crisp-looking leaves without any signs of yellowing. Clip off the leaves and keep them in a plastic bag in the crisper drawer of the refrigerator, for up to a week. A turnip root should be firm and feel heavy, with smooth skin that is not shriveled. Smaller turnips are preferred because they are sweeter. Turnips will keep for a week in the refrigerator. The roots do not store well in a root cellar.

RECIPES

Yoğurtlu Şalgam
FRIED TURNIPS WITH YOGURT

In the mountains of Anatolia in the thirteenth century, turnips were a common food. The combination of certain vegetables with yogurt, the vegetables usually cooked and the yogurt cool, was a typical Turkish preparation even then. The Persian mystic Jalal al-Din Muhammad Din al-Rumi, who lived in the thirteenth century and whose followers founded the Whirling Dervishes that had branches in Turkey, makes many references to food in his literary works. For example, he categorized meats stewed with vegetables and foods served with yogurt.

This recipe of turnips and yogurt is adapted from a much later date, from Turabi Effendi, the author of one of the first Turkish cookery books translated into English in the mid-nineteenth century.

1 pound small turnips

All-purpose unbleached flour for dredging

4 tablespoons (½ stick) unsalted butter,
  divided

Salt

⅔ cup beef broth (preferably homemade)

1 to 2 cups high-quality full-fat plain yogurt, to
  your taste

Freshly ground black pepper to taste

1. Boil the turnips whole in a large saucepan with water to cover until they can be easily pierced to the center with a skewer, about 25 minutes. Drain, peel the turnips when they are cool enough to handle, and cut them into ¼-inch-thick slices.

2. Preheat the oven to 350°F. Dredge the turnip slices in flour, tapping off any excess. Melt 3 tablespoons of the butter in a large skillet over medium-high heat and fry the turnips, salting to taste, until golden on both sides, 8 to 10 minutes. Remove to a baking pan.

3. Pour the beef broth over the turnips and bake them until tender, about 15 minutes. Remove from the oven and coat with the remaining 1 tablespoon butter. Cover the turnips with the yogurt and a grinding of pepper and serve.

Makes 4 servings

Turshy
PICKLED TURNIPS

Turshy is a word used for any kind of pickled vegetable dish, usually combining carrots, cucumbers, beets, turnips, onions, and maybe eggplant too. Pickled turnips are strictly called *lift mukhalil*, but when I had this dish in Egypt, it was called *turshy.* The beetroot is included in the pickling to tint the turnips an attractive pink color.

2 pounds medium turnips, scrubbed and cut into
  ¼-inch-thick slices

1 medium beetroot, scrubbed and cut into
  ⅛-inch-thick slices

2 cups water

3 tablespoons salt

1 cup white wine vinegar

In a 2-quart canning jar, layer the turnips, interspersed with layers of beet. Bring the water and salt to a boil, then set aside to cool. Add the vinegar to the water and pour the liquid over the turnips to completely cover them. The turnips and beets should not be exposed to the air. Close the jar and set it aside for 10 days before using. Once you have opened the jar, refrigerate it and the turnips will keep for a month. After 10 days, the turnips will become pink in color from the beets.

Makes 2 quarts

Broccoli Rapa a Crudo
BROCCOLI RAPA WITH SWEET VINEGAR SAUCE

Broccoli rapa is like a sprouting broccoli, but it is actually a relation of the turnip. It is also called turnip broccoli, rapini, *sparachetti*, and *cima di rapa*. It is popular throughout southern Italy, where it is often prepared with garlic and olive oil. This dish from Naples is usually served at room temperature. It is also a great accompaniment to grilled or roasted meats. Try to keep the broccoli rapa as green as possible, by not overcooking it. That way your presentation will look very delectable.

1 quart water
1½ pounds broccoli rapa
2 teaspoons sugar
2 tablespoons red wine vinegar
2 tablespoons extra virgin olive oil
3 large garlic cloves, chopped fine
Salt and freshly ground black pepper to taste

1. Bring the water to a boil in a medium saucepan and cook the broccoli rapa until the leaves are wilted and the stems are soft, about 12 minutes. Drain well. Dissolve the sugar in the vinegar in a small bowl.
2. Heat the olive oil in a medium skillet and cook the garlic over medium heat. Add the broccoli rapa, stirring in the sugared vinegar and seasoning with salt and pepper. Cook the broccoli rapa until it is soft and the vinegar is mostly evaporated, 5 to 7 minutes. Serve immediately.

Makes 4 servings

UPLAND CRESS
Barbarea verna (Mill.) Asch. (syn. *Campe verna* [Mill.] A. Heller) (also *plantaginea* DC) (Cruciferae-Brassicaceae)
Also called American cress; FRENCH: *cresson alénois*; ITALIAN: *crescione d'orto*, *crescione inglese*; SERBO-CROATIAN: *dragušac*, *potočarka*; SPANISH: *lepidio*; TURKISH: *götlez götü*

PLANT CHARACTERISTICS AND VARIETIES
Upland cress is a cool weather biennial that grows quickly into a weedy plant like dandelion. The dark green leaves, which are eaten raw in salad, have a piquant taste. They are eaten throughout the Mediterranean, but are especially popular in Provence.

PLANT ORIGIN
Upland cress is native to Europe.

HOW TO GROW AND HARVEST
Sow seeds in late summer and harvest the leaves in the fall or early spring. In hot climates the plants need afternoon shade. Harvest by pulling the whole plant or pick the leaves as needed through the winter, if the plant is protected from frost.

Look for fresh, crisp leaves without any sign of yellowing. Store the greens in the refrigerator and use them quickly. Upland cress is usually found in farmers' markets.

RECIPE

Potage de Cresson Alénois
SOUP OF UPLAND CRESS

In the more rural areas of Provence, away from the touristy coast, in the small valleys and foothills, one finds cooks who are more willing to use wild salad greens in their preparations than are the bourgeois housewives of the cities. These greens, such as cress, are rarely cultivated, although some are. They appear for the most part in soups, salads, and omelettes. Upland cress is usually sold by gourmet greengrocers and at farmers' markets.

5 tablespoons unsalted butter, divided
¾ pound upland cress (garden cress), heavy stems
    removed, washed well, chopped
1 quart vegetable or chicken broth
10 ounces boiling potatoes, peeled and sliced
Salt and freshly ground black pepper to taste
¼ cup heavy cream
Croutons for garnish

Melt 4 tablespoons of the butter in a medium saucepan over medium heat. Cook the cress, covered, until it wilts, 2 to 3 minutes. Add the broth and potatoes and cook over medium-low heat until the potatoes are tender, 20 to 25 minutes. Pass the cooked vegetables and broth through a sieve or food mill and return to the saucepan. Season with salt and pepper, add the cream and remaining 1 tablespoon butter, and heat thoroughly. Serve with croutons.

Makes 4 servings

VENUS' COMB
Scandix pecten-veneris L. (Umbelliferae)
Also called shepherd's needle, scandix;
GREEK: *kafkalithra*; SPANISH: *peine de pastor*

PLANT CHARACTERISTICS AND VARIETIES
This umbellifer has feather-shaped leaves with narrow lobes. The edible parts are the young leaves and stem tops. In Greece, the greens are used in vegetable pies.

PLANT HISTORY
Scandix is mentioned as a potherb by Theophrastus and Pliny, and Dioscorides describes the greens as being eaten raw or cooked.

WALL ROCKET
Diplotaxis muralis (L.) DC. (syn. *D. tenuifolia*) (Cruciferae-Brassicaceae)
ITALIAN: *rucoletta*

This annual or perennial plant is many-stemmed, and its leaves are confined to a basal rosette. Wall rocket is often used as a salad green in Italy. Because of its sharp and piquant taste, it is never used alone; it is usually mixed with arugula. It is also boiled in mixtures of other greens as a side dish.

WATERCRESS
Nasturtium officinale R. Br. (syn. *Rorippa nasturtium-aquaticum*) (Cruciferae-Brassicaceae)

ARABIC: *ʿuqiriyūn, qariyūn, karsūn mahi, thuffāʾ, ḥurf*; FRENCH: *cresson d'eau, cresson de fontaine*; GREEK: *kardamo*; ITALIAN: *nasturzio acquatico, crescione d'acqua*; SERBO-CROATIAN: *potočarka*; SPANISH: *berro, berro de água, mastuerzo acuático*; TURKISH: *acitere, su teresi*

PLANT CHARACTERISTICS AND VARIETIES
Watercress is an aquatic plant that grows in ponds and brooks by forming mats of stems and leaves that float on the surface of the water. The plant requires a plentiful supply of high alkaline spring or artesian water with a certain level of nitrates. Watercress is a hardy perennial that can also be grown as a soil-based plant. The edible part is the leaf, which is eaten raw or cooked. Watercress's pungent flavor is derived from the presence of chemical compounds known as isosulfocyanic glucosides.

PLANT ORIGIN
According to Joe Carcione and Bob Lucas, authors of *The Greengrocer: The Consumer's Guide to Fruit and Vegetables* (1972), watercress is native to Turkey and the Mediterranean. Watercress is widespread throughout Europe and Asia.

PLANT HISTORY
There is evidence from Dioscorides's *Materia medica* from the first century A.D. that points to the use of watercress as a medicinal plant. Watercress appears to have been one of the tributes entitled by the Kings of Erin by royal prerogative. Xenophon recommended watercress to the Persians, and the Romans ate it with vinegar as a remedy for a deranged mind. Watercress was a wild plant, and it was first cultivated on a large scale in south Germany around 1750. The plant is said to have been cultivated in France as early as the twelfth century, although H. W. Howard says it was not cultivated there until the nineteenth century.

HOW TO GROW AND HARVEST
Watercress requires special growing conditions, and for this reason it is rarely grown by home gardeners. The plant should not be grown in garden pools. An ideal site would be a natural stream or spring- or stream-fed pond. Gardens that contain a chalk or limestone spring or pure stream water are best suited to produce a safe, unpolluted crop. Gardeners can simulate such an environment with shaded and very moist soil. The soil pH should be around 7.0 with moderate to high

amounts of fertilizer added. The plant can be started from seeds, which need to be soaked for a day before planting, or from cuttings of watercress sprigs rooted in water. Harvest watercress by cutting off the tips of the leaf stalks where they set roots.

HOW TO BUY, STORE, AND PREPARE FOR COOKING

Among Mediterranean countries, watercress is most popular in France. Look for bunches of watercress whose stems are sitting in water basins or are kept wet and cool. Store watercress in the crisper drawer of the refrigerator for up to 3 days. Some people remove the stems, but I prefer them for their crunchy texture when used raw in salads.

RECIPE

Potage au Cresson
WATERCRESS SOUP

This beautifully colored soup, found everywhere in France, was adapted from a recipe in my friend Alexandra Leaf's *The Impressionists' Table: Recipes and Gastronomy from Nineteenth-Century France*. The soup is delicate without being creamy or heavy, and it's perfect served before roast veal or chicken.

1 medium potato

2 tablespoons unsalted butter

1 small onion, chopped fine

Leaves from 2 bunches watercress (about 1 pound)

4 cups vegetable or chicken broth

½ cup heavy cream

2 large egg yolks

Salt and freshly ground black pepper to taste

1. Place the potato in a medium saucepan and cover with water by several inches. Turn the heat to medium-high, and, once the water comes to a boil, about 15 minutes, reduce the heat to medium and cook until the potato can be pierced easily with a skewer, about another 20 minutes. Drain, peel, crumble, and set aside.

2. Melt the butter in a medium casserole or saucepan over low heat and cook the onion until it is translucent, about 10 minutes, stirring a few times. Add the watercress and cook it until it has wilted. Add the broth and cook for 10 minutes. Transfer the soup to a blender with the crumbled potato and puree for 3 minutes.

3. Blend the cream and egg yolks in the saucepan or casserole and return the soup from the blender to the pot. Cook the soup over low heat, seasoning with salt and pepper, until hot, about 10 minutes, without ever letting it come even near to a boil. Serve hot.

Makes 4 servings

WATER SPEEDWELL
Veronica anagallis-aquatica L.
(Scrophulariaceae)
Also called cress; TURKISH: *camak*

PLANT CHARACTERISTICS AND VARIETIES
Water speedwell is not the true cress (upland cress, page 344) and is not commonly found anymore. It is a water plant with about six small leaves on its top and is used in salads. In the Aksaray Province of Turkey it is gathered in the wild as an edible green.

WATER SPINACH
Ipomoea aquatica Forsk. (syn. *I. reptans*)
(Convolvulacaea)
Also called *kangkong* or swamp morning glory; FRENCH: *liseron d'eau, patate aquatique*; ITALIAN: *patate acquatica, villucchio d'acqua*; SPANISH: *batatilla acuatica, boniato de agua, camotillo*

PLANT CHARACTERISTICS AND VARIETIES
The tender shoots and leaves of this plant are eaten raw or cooked. The leaves are long and slender and look like tarragon leaves, although they taste much more like a weedy salad green. This plant is actually a form of turnip developed for its leaves and leaf stalks. Water spinach is found all over the tropics with its stems running over the surface of water. In the Mediterranean, it is eaten in Spain, Italy, and France.

PLANT ORIGIN
N. Vavilov identified the mountains of central and western China and the adjacent areas as the place of origin of water spinach.

RECIPE
See the recipe under Amaranthus.

WHITE DEAD-NETTLE
Lamium album L. (Lamiaceae)
FRENCH: *ortie blanche*; ITALIAN: *ortica bianco, ortica dolce* (Tuscany); SPANISH: *lamio blanco, ortiga muerta*

PLANT CHARACTERISTICS AND VARIETIES
This perennial plant is densely hairy, and its leaves can irritate the skin. The edible parts are the young leaves and stems. In France the leaves and stems are boiled and then used in omelettes and soups. White dead-nettle is the plant that is used in the French eel and sorrel preparation known as *anguille au vert à la flamande*, eel braised in wine, stirred with eggs and lemon juice, and served cool. The plant is not eaten much further south than a Provençal latitude.

WILD LEEK

Allium ampeloprasum L. Ampeloprasum
group (Liliaceae)
Also called ramps; ARABIC: *thūm al-raᶜs;*
FRENCH: *ail d'orient, ail gros, poireau d'été;*
ITALIAN: *porrandello, porraccio, porro selvatico;*
SPANISH: *puerro agreste, puerro salvage, puerro
silvestre, ajipuerro*

PLANT CHARACTERISTICS AND VARIETIES

The edible parts are the bulbs and leaves,
which are eaten either cooked or raw in Spain,
France, and Italy.

WILD RADISH

Raphanus raphanistrum L. (Cruciferae-
Brassicaceae)
Also called jointed charlock; ITALIAN:
ravastello; TURKISH: *terme*

PLANT CHARACTERISTICS AND VARIETIES

Wild radish is a widespread annual weed of
the mustard family. The plant has a hardy tap-
root and a rosette of unevenly divided leaves
with a bristly flowering stalk that grows to 2
feet. The leaves are eaten in Italy and Turkey.
The plant's energy goes into leaf growth
rather than root growth. Wild radish is popular in various cooked vegetable dishes in
Apulia in southern Italy.

PLANT ORIGIN

Wild radish is native to Eurasia and is
thought to be the ancestor of the domestic
radish *(R. sativus).* N. Vavilov identified the
mountains of central and western China and
the adjacent areas as the place of origin of the
wild radish.

PLANT HISTORY

Both the ancient Chinese and the Egyptians
knew of the wild radish. Pliny describes a
wild radish that he tells us the Greeks called
cerain and the Romans called *armoraciam.*

RECIPE

See the recipe under Field Poppy.

WINGED PEA

Tetragonolobos purpureus Moench (syn.
*Lotus tetragonolobus; Psophocarpus
tetragonolobus*) (Leguminosae)
Also called asparagus pea, winged lotus,
Goa bean; FRENCH: *pois asperge, lotier rouge,
lotier cultivé;* ITALIAN: *veccia pisello, lotto
rosso, pisello asparagio;* SPANISH: *bocha
cultivada, guisantillo rojo*

PLANT CHARACTERISTICS AND VARIETIES

The winged pea is a creeping small annual
plant with red flowers and winged pods, hence
its name. The pods can be eaten when very
young, at about 1 inch long, or when they are
mature at about 3 inches long, although the
pods can grow to 9 inches and have 4 fluted

wings along their length. There are other sub-species with flowers of different colors or other differences. The winged pea is eaten today mostly by North Africans.

PLANT ORIGIN

One suggestion for the center of origin of the winged pea is the Mediterranean, in Sicily it is thought, while another theory suggests the Maghrib, and yet another (the least likely) tropical Asia.

PLANT HISTORY

The pods of the winged pea have traditionally been a food for the poor of Sicily and Spain, especially in the Middle Ages. The winged pea is mentioned in a number of herbals from the Renaissance, and Clusius first saw the plant in a druggist's garden in 1579 and called it *pisum rubrum.*

HOW TO GROW AND HARVEST

Winged peas need to grow in a warm and open spot in light, rich soil. Sow seeds in April and May about 1 inch deep in rows, and space plants about a foot apart or in groups of three around poles. They should be well watered through the growing season. Harvesting begins about 12 weeks after sowing. Once the pods reach about an inch, they can be picked regularly, although they will be 4 inches when they are half-grown. The harvesting can last between June and August, although typically the plant will not bear fruit until the early fall.

HOW TO BUY, STORE, AND PREPARE FOR COOKING

The pods can be steamed, and the ripe or dried seeds can be roasted to make them more digestible. The tubers can also grow quite large and can be peeled, sliced, and eaten raw or cooked.

WORMWOOD

Artemisia absinthum L. (Asteraceae-Compositae)
Also called absinthe; FRENCH: *armoise;* SPANISH: *ajenjo*

PLANT CHARACTERISTICS AND VARIETIES

Wormwood is a silky, aromatic perennial herb. There are many species of wormwood. The plant was long used as a medicinal herb in France. Today it is used among the Bedouin of North Africa and occasionally finds its way into sauces. In central Europe, the flowering tops were used to counteract the greasiness of goose and duck. Another related plant, spiked wormwood (*A. spicata,* syn. *A. genipi*), is the one used in the long-banned French alcoholic liqueur known as *eau d'absinthe.*

YELLOW VELVETLEAF
Limnocharis flava (L.) Buchenau
(Limnocharitaceae)
ARABIC: *makmaliyya*; SPANISH: *hoja de buitre*

PLANT CHARACTERISTICS AND VARIETIES
This plant is a kind of water plantain and is cultivated in ponds. The young leaves, petioles, and floral shoots are eaten cooked in North Africa.

PLANT ORIGIN
Yellow velvetleaf is native to tropical America.

ZEDOARY
Curcuma zedoary Roscoe (syn. *C. pallida*)
(Scitaminae)
ARABIC: *zarunbād*; FRENCH: *zédoaire, curcuma*;
ITALIAN: *zedoaria*; SPANISH: *cedoaria, curcuma redonda*

PLANT CHARACTERISTICS AND VARIETIES
Zedoary, a plant related to ginger, has large green leaves, red or green bracts, and yellow flowers. In the Mediterranean today, zedoary is mostly used in spice mixes in North Africa, but the rhizomes are eaten cooked. Turmeric is the usual substitution for zedoary.

PLANT ORIGIN
N. Vavilov identified India, Burma, and Assam as the area of the center of the origin of zedoary.

PLANT HISTORY
Zedoary was used in the Middle Ages mostly medicinally and was considered a digestive aid.

ZUCCHINI
Cucurbita pepo L. (Cucurbitacae)
Also called summer squash, yellow squash, marrow, courgette; also see Squash; ARABIC: *kūsā, biṭīkh, ẓarf al-qaraᶜ* (dried zucchini); FRENCH: *courgette*; GREEK: *kolokothaki*; ITALIAN: *zucchini, zucca, zuccheta*; SPANISH: *calabacin, zapallito*; TURKISH: *dolmalık kabak*

PLANT CHARACTERISTICS AND VARIETIES
Also see Squash. The edible part is the young and mature fruit. Zucchini is one kind of summer squash, a squash with a soft skin. Others include yellow crooknecks, smooth yellow straightnecks, yellow squash (summer squash), and pattypan squash. A very long zucchini is grown in Sicily known as *tenerume* or *cucuzza*. It grows to about 3 feet long at a maximum and is used in soups. Zucchini are popular in all Mediterranean cuisines.

Zucchini

⟡

WHAT IS IT ABOUT ZUCCHINI THAT IT BEGS TO BE STUFFED? EVERYWHERE IN THE MEDITERRANEAN, COOKS HOLLOW OUT zucchini and stuff them. Arab cooks have invented for themselves a useful tool for hollowing out zucchini called a *naqqāra*, a wooden-handled device with a metal cylinder. In Lebanon, cooks stuff zucchini with rice, onion, garlic, spices, mint, and parsley; while in Tunisia cooks stuff it with ground beef, rice, tomato, and *barīsa*; and in Algeria the stuffing might be ground lamb, rice, parsley, egg, and cinnamon. In Greece, the pulp of the zucchini is chopped and stuffed back into the cavity with a mixture of garlic, cumin, raisins, mint, and dill. In Turkey, cooks also like to use rice mixed with dill and mint or beef mixed with rice, currants, and dill. In Italy, one might find zucchini stuffed with grated cheese, tomato, and tuna. In northern Italy, cooks in Genoa stuff these marrow squash with Parmigiano cheese, porcini mushrooms, and prosciutto, and, in neighboring Lombardy and Emilia, a stuffing of breadcrumbs, egg yolks, and béchamel sauce is enjoyed.

PLANT ORIGIN
See Squash.

PLANT HISTORY
See Squash.

HOW TO GROW AND HARVEST
See Squash.

HOW TO BUY, STORE, AND PREPARE FOR COOKING
See Squash.

RECIPES

Zucchette alla Poverella
POOR PEOPLE'S SUMMER SQUASH

This simple recipe from the region of Apulia in southern Italy is excellent in the summer when you don't want to serve steaming hot food and when delicious baby zucchini are being harvested. In Apulia cooks serve the dish as part of a *tavola calda*, a buffet table with many different dishes served at room temperature. This recipe can be made with any kind of marrow squash.

1½ pounds zucchini or summer squash, ends
  trimmed, cut into ¼-inch-thick slices
Salt
6 tablespoons extra virgin olive oil
3 tablespoons white wine vinegar

1. Cover a wooden board with paper towels. Arrange the squash on the paper towels and sprinkle with salt. Leave the squash in direct sunlight until they dry, blotting them occasionally with paper towels.

2. Heat the olive oil in a large skillet over medium-high heat until the oil begins to smoke. Cook the squash in one layer, if possible, until golden on at least one side, 8 to 10 minutes, tossing a few times. Remove the squash from the skillet with a slotted ladle, letting excess oil drip back into the skillet, and transfer the squash to a serving platter or bowl.

3. Add the vinegar to the skillet with the oil and boil until the liquid is reduced by half, 1 to 2 minutes. Pour 1½ to 2 tablespoons of this liquid over the squash and leave the squash, covered with plastic wrap, at room temperature for 24 hours before serving. Discard the remaining liquid.

Makes 4 small servings

Verdure al Forno
VEGETABLES IN THE OVEN

This is a preparation for which there are many variations, depending on the season. In Campania, it is generally known as *gianfottere*. The secret to this dish is absolutely fresh vegetables, and if you can also use young heirloom-type vegetables, all the better. Although I provide some examples in the list of ingredients, make do with whatever is available locally. The baking process slowly softens and sweetens the vegetables, and the resulting dish is quite heavenly. It is best served with a golden roasted chicken.

½ cup extra virgin olive oil, or to taste, divided
½ pound baby carrots (about 8), peeled and
  trimmed slightly, leaving on a bit of their stem
¾ pound new Russian Banana (fingerling)
  potatoes (about 4) or new Yukon Gold
  potatoes about the size of a golf ball, halved
3 small red onions (about 1 pound), cut in half
  lengthwise
5 young summer (yellow) squash or zucchini
  (about 1 pound), split in half lengthwise
Salt and freshly ground black pepper to taste
2 large garlic cloves, peeled and crushed
3 tablespoons finely chopped fresh basil leaves
2 tablespoons finely chopped fresh oregano leaves
Pinch of saffron crumbled in a mortar with
  ½ teaspoon salt
½ teaspoon sugar
2 sprigs fresh rosemary
One ¾-pound ripe Big Boy tomato, sliced

1. Preheat the oven to 350°F. Lightly oil a 12-by-9-inch baking pan. Arrange the carrots, potatoes, onions, and squash in the pan. Season with the salt and pepper and the garlic, basil, oregano, salt and saffron mixture, and sugar. Stuff the rosemary sprigs in between the vegetables. Lay the tomato slices on top and

season again with salt and pepper. Pour the remaining olive oil over the vegetables.

2. Bake until the tomatoes look like they have melted and the potatoes and carrots can be pierced easily by a skewer but are not breaking apart, 1¼ to 1½ hours. Serve hot or at room temperature.

Makes 4 servings

Zucchini Bianchi Lessati con Salsa di Menta
WHITE ZUCCHINI WITH MINT SAUCE

This is a delightful dish prepared all over Italy and served for a *tavola calda* during the summer. White zucchini is simply a cultivar that produces a light green zucchini. If you can't find it, use zucchini or another summer squash. The zucchini is boiled and then dressed with a vinegary mint sauce that is slightly sweet. The dish is served at room temperature, not hot.

2 pounds white zucchini, ends trimmed and cut into ¾-inch-thick slices
4 teaspoons sugar
7 tablespoons good-quality white wine vinegar
6 tablespoons very finely chopped fresh mint leaves
Salt to taste
Extra virgin olive oil to taste
Fresh mint sprigs for garnish

1. Bring a large pot of lightly salted water to a boil and cook the zucchini slices until soft, about 15 minutes. Drain well and place in a large bowl.

2. Dissolve the sugar in the vinegar and stir in the mint. Season the zucchini with salt and pour the vinegar and mint sauce over it. Dress lightly with olive oil and let the zucchini come to room temperature before serving. Garnish with fresh mint sprigs.

Makes 4 to 6 servings

Zucchine Trifolate
ZUCCHINI WITH GARLIC AND OREGANO

Sardinians have some intriguing vegetable preparations. Many of them are served at room temperature, and they always seem to have a perfect balance of flavors. The recipe for this attractive *contorno*, or side dish, comes from the Ristorante La Lepanto in Alghero, Sardinia. A dish that is cooked *trifolato* is a dish cooked with garlic and parsley or oregano.

4 zucchini, ends trimmed
1 garlic clove, finely chopped
2 tablespoons extra virgin olive oil
½ teaspoon dried oregano
Salt and freshly ground black pepper to taste

Preheat a gas grill on high for 20 minutes or prepare a hot charcoal fire or preheat the oven to 450°F. Place the zucchini on the grill or on a rack in a roasting pan in the oven. Grill or bake the zucchini until the skins loosen from the flesh, 35 to 45 minutes. Slice the zucchini ⅜ inch thick.

2. Transfer the sliced zucchini to a medium skillet with the garlic, olive oil, and oregano. Season with salt and pepper and cook over medium heat, stirring, until the zucchini are slightly golden, about 15 minutes. Serve at room temperature.

Makes 2 to 4 servings

ZUCCHINI AND CHICKPEAS

This recipe is inspired by the many wonderful chickpea dishes I have enjoyed in Turkey. In this recipe, meant to be made at the end of summer when you can harvest young zucchini from what I presume will be the plant you are growing, the two main vegetables are very simply flavored, the balance being important to the final taste and texture. If the zucchini are store-bought, buy the smallest ones possible.

2 tablespoons extra virgin olive oil
1 pound baby zucchini, trimmed and sliced about ¼ inch thick
16-ounce can cooked chickpeas, drained
2 large garlic cloves, chopped fine
Salt and freshly ground black pepper to taste
2 tablespoons finely chopped fresh parsley leaves

Heat the olive oil in a large skillet over medium heat and cook the zucchini, chickpeas, garlic, salt, and pepper until the zucchini are slightly soft, about 20 minutes. Toss with the parsley and serve hot or at room temperature.

Makes 4 servings

Kūsā bi'l-Dibs Rummān
ZUCCHINI WITH BREAD AND POMEGRANATES

This preparation is typical of the cooking of Aleppo, Syria. Many Aleppine cooks like to add a spicy hot element to the preparation by using chile pepper, but I prefer this mellow version. Pomegranate molasses can usually be found at Middle Eastern markets, but check your local supermarket first, since you might find it there. The use of pomegranate molasses is typical of the cooking of northern Syria and southeastern Turkey. The dish is ideally served at room temperature or slightly warm.

1 ½ pounds zucchini, ends trimmed, peeled, and
  sliced ¼ inch thick
3 tablespoons water, plus more as needed
1 loaf stale Arabic flatbread, broken into small
  pieces
4 large garlic cloves, chopped or lightly crushed
1 medium onion, chopped
½ cup extra virgin olive oil, plus extra for
  drizzling
2 tablespoons pomegranate molasses
½ teaspoon dried mint leaves
Salt and freshly ground black pepper to taste
½ cup pomegranate seeds
4 scallions, cut into 2-inch lengths

I. Place the zucchini in a medium to large skillet with the water and turn the heat to medium-high. Cook the zucchini until tender, about 20 minutes, adding 2 to 3 tablespoons of water whenever you hear the zucchini sizzling and sticking to the skillet. Do not add too much water; the zucchini should never be soaking, just moist enough not to stick.

2. Add the bread and cook until soft, 6 to 7 minutes, stirring. Add the garlic, onion, olive oil, pomegranate molasses, and mint and season with salt and pepper. Cook until the mixture looks dense, 8 to 10 minutes, adjusting the heat so the food is never boiling. Transfer to a serving platter, garnish with pomegranate seeds and scallions, and drizzle with more olive oil, if desired.

Makes 4 servings

Jazar wa Kūsā
CARROTS AND ZUCCHINI

This Egyptian recipe almost seems too simple, but the flavors are perfectly melded. It is excellent as an accompaniment to grilled meats. Incidentally, the Egyptians pronounce the Arabic *j* as a hard g, so carrots are called *gazar*.

2 large, fat, carrots, sliced diagonally about
  ¼ inch thick
2 zucchini, ends trimmed, sliced diagonally about
  ¼ inch thick
1 teaspoon freshly ground cumin seeds
Salt and freshly ground black pepper to taste
3 tablespoons extra virgin olive oil

I. In a large bowl, toss the carrots and zucchini together with the cumin and season with salt and pepper.

2. Heat the olive oil in a large skillet over medium-low heat and cook the carrots and zucchini until crispy and tender, 25 to 30 minutes, tossing frequently. Serve hot.

Makes 4 servings

Al-Madarbal al-Qara^ca
Zucchini and Lamb Casserole

This Tunisian preparation is a delicious fall dish that is cooked in an earthenware casserole that looks like a tambourine. A Spanish earthenware *cazuela*, sold by Williams-Sonoma or the West Coast chain Sur la Table, would be perfect for cooking this dish. Even though the zucchini-to-lamb ratio is 2 to 1, you can make it 3 to 1 and the results will still be delicious.

3 pounds zucchini, ends trimmed, peeled, and cut into ¼-inch-thick slices

6 large garlic cloves, chopped

1 teaspoon freshly ground black pepper

1 teaspoon freshly ground caraway seeds

1 teaspoon ground cinnamon

1 teaspoon salt

¼ teaspoon ground ginger

1 teaspoon turmeric

4 teaspoons harīsa (page 263)

1 cup water

1½ pounds boneless lamb or mutton shoulder or leg, trimmed well of fat and cut into ½-inch cubes

¼ cup extra virgin olive oil

1½ cups canned chickpeas (about ¾ pound), drained

6 cups olive oil for frying

¼ cup white wine vinegar

1. Place the zucchini slices in a large bowl covered with salted water and let them soak for 30 minutes. Drain and dry with paper towels. Stir the garlic, spices, and *harīsa* together in a measuring cup with the water.

2. Place the meat and olive oil in a large earthenware (preferably) or cast-iron casserole. Turn the heat to medium-low and cook, tossing occasionally, until the meat turns color on all sides, about 10 minutes. Add the chickpeas and spiced water, reduce the heat to low, and cook until the liquid is almost completely evaporated and the sauce is thick and syrupy, 35 to 40 minutes.

3. Meanwhile, preheat the frying oil to 375°F in a deep fryer or an 8-inch saucepan fitted with a basket insert. Cook the zucchini in batches until light brown, 1 to 2 minutes. Don't crowd the fryer. Drain and set aside on paper towels.

4. Add the zucchini to the meat casserole, toss well, moisten with the vinegar, and cook until it is dense and looks like a syrupy stew, about 10 minutes. Serve immediately.

Makes 4 servings

RECIPE LIST

SEED SUPPLIERS

For an extensive listing of seed sources in the United States and Canada, visit http://csf.colorado.edu/perma/stse/seed_src.htm.

The Cook's Garden
P.O. Box 535
Londonderry, VT 05148
(800) 457-9703
www.cooksgarden.com

Gurney's Seed and Nursery
110 Capital Street
Yankton, SD 57079
(800) 806-1972
www.gurneys.com

J. L. Hudson, Seedsman
Star Route 2, Box 337
La Honda, CA 94020
www.jlhudsonseeds.com

Johnny's Selected Seeds
Foss Hill Road
Albion, ME 04910
(207) 437-4301
www.johnnyseeds.com

Native Seeds/SEARCH
2509 North Campbell Avenue
Suite 325
Tucson, AZ 85719
(520) 327-9123
www.nativeseeds.org

Nichols Garden Nursery
1190 North Pacific Highway
Albany, OR 97321
(541) 928-9280
www.nicholsgardennursery.com

The Pepper Gal
P.O. Box 23006
Fort Lauderdale, FL 33307
(954) 537-5540
http://www.inter-linked.com
/dir/t-19545375540.html

Pine Tree Garden Seeds
P.O. Box 300
New Gloucester, ME 04260
(207) 926-3400
www.superseeds.com

Ronninger's Seed Potatoes
Star Route
Moyie Springs, ID 83845
(208) 267-7938

Seed Savers Exchange
3076 North Winn Rd
Decorah, IA 52101
(319) 382-5990
www.seedsavers.org

Shepherd's Garden Seeds
30 Irene Street
Torrington, CT 06790
(860) 482-3638
www.shepherdseeds.com

ABBREVIATIONS

A. D.: anno domini

Alg.: Algeria

Apul.: Apulia

B.C.: before Christ

B.P.: before the present

coll.: colloquial

c.: about

d.: died

Eg: Egypt

Eg. Ar.: Egyptian Arabic

fl.: flourished

Leb.: Lebanon

Magh.: Maghrib

Prov.: Provençal, Provence

Sic.: Sicilian, Sicily

sp.: spelling

Syr.: Syrian

Syr.-obs: obsolete Syrian Arabic

Tus.: Tuscan, Tuscany

var.: variation

Ven.: Venetian, Venice

wr.: wrote

BIOGRAPHIES

ABŪḤANĪFA AL-DĪNAWARĪ (D. 895):
Muslim (Persian) historian, lexicographer, and botanist who wrote in Arabic. His Kitab al-nabat (Book of plants) is of very great importance in the history of botany.

ABŪ AL-KHAYR (FL. ELEVENTH CENTURY?): Arab agronomist and author of *Kitāb al-filāḥa* (Book of farming).

ALBERTUS MAGNUS (1193?–1280):
A Dominican friar also known as Albert the Great and one of the most important medieval philosophers. He was one of the first to recognize the true value of the newly translated Greco-Arabic scientific and philosophical works. He also wrote a book on vegetables.

ANDRÉ, JACQUES: Director of Studies at the École Pratique des Hautes Études, Paris, and author of numerous works on plants and botany, including *L'alimentation et la cuisine à Rome.*

ANTHIMUS (SIXTH CENTURY A.D.): A Byzantine refugee who wrote a codex, called *De observatione ciborum,* on dietary matters for the French Merovingian king, Theodric I (511–534), son of Clovis.

APICIUS (FL. IN FIRST CENTURY A.D.):
Roman gourmet and author of what is called the first cookbook, although this work was not compiled until the fourth century A.D.

ARISTOTLE (382 B.C.–322 B.C.): Greek philosopher and natural scientist.

ATHENAEUS (A.D. C. 170–C. 230):
Greek antiquarian of Naucratis in Egypt who lived in Rome and wrote a fifteen-book work called the *Deipnosophists,* which is mostly concerned with food and dining.

ERMOLAO BARBARO (HERMOLAUS BARBARUS) (1454–1493): Italian scholar whose study *In Dioscoridem corollariorum libri quinque* covers various plants.

FRANCESCO BIANCHINI, FRANCESCO CORBETTA, AND MARILENA PISTOIA: The authors of *The Complete Book of Fruits and Vegetables* are the curator of the Botanical Section of the Civic Museum of Natural History in Verona, Italy; a lecturer in botany at the University of Bologna, Italy; and an illustrator, respectively.

V. R. BOSWELL: Contemporary English botanist and author of scholarly articles on vegetables.

HENRI BRESC: Contemporary French historian and author of numerous works on medieval Sicily, especially the gardens and agriculture.

RICHARD BURTON (1821–1890): English explorer, writer, and linguist. Burton translated the Arabic *1001 Arabian Nights* into English.

JOACHIMUS CAMERERIUS (WROTE C. 1586): Botanist and author of books on plants, including *De plantis epitome utilissima*.

HIERONYMOUS CARDANUS (WROTE C. 1581): Author of *De rerum varietate*, published in Basel in 1581.

GIACOMO CASTELVETRO (1546–1616): Professor of Italian at Cambridge University and author of *Brieve racconto di tutte le radici, di tutte l'herbe et di tutti i frutti, che crudi o cotto in Italia si mangiano*, translated into English as *A Brief Account of the Fruit, Herbs and Vegetables of Italy*, an attempt to encourage the English to eat more vegetables.

GEOFFREY CHAUCER (C. 1340–1400): English poet and author of the *Canterbury Tales*.

CATO (234 B.C.–149 B.C.): Roman statesman who wrote an important treatise on farming.

E. E. CHEESMAN (MID-TWENTIETH CENTURY): Botanist and author of studies on cacao and plantain.

CICERO (106 B.C.–43 B.C.): Roman orator, politician, and philosopher. A republican opponent of Caesar, he was a man of letters who wrote philosophical and rhetorical works and revealed facets of Roman life.

CAROLUS CLUSIUS (SEVENTEENTH CENTURY): The preeminent botanist of his day and author of *Rariorum plantarum historia*.

COLUMELLA (FIRST CENTURY A.D.): Roman agricultural writer whose *De re rustica* (On agriculture) is the most comprehensive, systematic, and detailed of the Roman agricultural works.

Nicolas Culpeper (1616–1654):
English writer on astrology and medicine and author of *Culpeper's Complete Herbal.*

Alphonse de Candolle (nineteenth century): Famous French botanist and author of *Origin of Cultivated Plants.*

Pedanius Dioscorides (first century a.d.): Greek physician and author of a standard work on the substances used in medicine.

Ron Engeland: Contemporary American horticulturalist and leading expert on garlic.

Erasmus (1469?–1536): Dutch humanist, Catholic priest, and teacher who wrote satires and edited Greek and Latin works.

Stephen Facciola: Contemporary author and compiler of *Cornucopia II: A Source Book of Edible Plants.*

Galen (c. 130–c. 200): Greek physician who systematized medical learning. Vastly influential, Galen's authority was undisputed into the sixteenth century. Eighty-three of his medical works are extant.

John Gerarde (1545–1612): English herbalist and surgeon; author of *The Herball or generall historie of plantes,* published in 1597.

Jack R. Harlan: Late professor of plant genetics at the Crop Evolution Laboratory of the Department of Agronomy at the University of Illinois and author of *Crops and Man.*

Herodotus (484? b.c.–425? b.c.): Greek historian, called the father of history.

Hippocrates (c. 460 b.c.–370 b.c.): Greek physician recognized as the father of medicine and the first person to attempt to establish medicine on a scientific basis through observation of disease.

Horace (65 b.c.–8 b.c.): Roman lyric poet and author of *Satires, Odes, Epistles* among other works.

H. W. Howard: Contemporary researcher at the Plant Breeding Institute in Cambridge, England.

Ibn al-ᶜAwwām (fl. twelfth century): Spanish Arab agronome and one of the preeminent agriculturalists of his day. Author of the *Kitāb al-filāḥa* (Book of farming).

Ibn al-Baytār (1197–1228): Foremost medieval Islamic botanist and systematizer of pharmacological knowledge. Author of *The Independent Treatise concerning Simple Drugs,* listing 1,400 drugs.

Ibn Riḍwān (d. 1068): Renowned medieval Islamic doctor and author of *On the Prevention of Bodily Ills in Egypt.*

JOSEPHUS (A.D. 35–A.D. 95?): Jewish historian and soldier who wrote *The Jewish War*.

JUVENAL (FIRST AND SECOND CENTURIES A.D.): Roman satirical poet whose works denouncing the immorality and tyranny of the Romans gave a vivid picture of that society.

LINNAEUS (1707–1778): Swedish botanist and founder of modern systematic botany. He established the binomial method of designating plants and animals.

MATTHIAS LOBEL (SIXTEENTH CENTURY): French botanist and physician to English King James I. Author of *Icones Stirpium*, published in 1591, and other works on plants.

FRANÇOISE D'AUBIGNÉ MAINTENON, MARQUISE DE (1635–1719): Second wife of Louis XIV of France and a well-known writer of essays and letters on education.

MARTIAL (A.D. c. 40–c. 104): Roman writer whose witty verse became a model for the modern epigram.

MAESTRO MARTINO (FL. 1450–1475): A native of Como in northern Italy, Martino was the chef to Ludovico Trevisan, Patriarch of Aquilea, and the author of one of the most important Renaissance cookery books, *Libro de arte coquinaria*.

PIERANDREA MATTIOLI (SIXTEENTH CENTURY): Italian botanist and author of *Discorsi di pedacio Discoride Anazarbeo della materia medicinale*, published in Venice in 1559. He provided the first description of the tomato in the Mediterranean in 1544.

GREGOR MENDEL (1822–1884): Austrian scientist who conducted some of the first experiments in genetics and heredity.

PHILIP MILLER (EIGHTEENTH CENTURY): Author of *The Gardener's Dictionary*, published in 1724.

LOUIS NOISETTE (NINETEENTH CENTURY): French author of *Manuel du Jardinier*, published in 1829.

OVID (43 B.C.–A.D. 18): Latin poet whose poems reflect the ideal of poetry as the ministry of pleasure.

PALLADIUS (FOURTH CENTURY A.D.): Roman author who wrote a poem on agriculture (*De re rustica*), although the material was mostly derived from Columella and other authors.

PENA, PETRUS AND MATTHIAS LOBEL (SIXTEENTH CENTURY): Authors of *Stirpium adversaria nova*, published in 1570.

PETRONIUS DIODOTUS (D. A.D. 66): Roman satirist whose *Trimalchio's Dinner* and *Satriycon* are vivid studies of the life and manners of Rome in his age.

ROGER PHILIPS AND MARTYN RIX: Contemporary authors of *The Random House Book of Vegetables*.

PLATINA (1421–1481): The name used by Bartolomeo Sacchi, the Vatican librarian and author of one of the most important cookery books of the Renaissance, *De honesta voluptate et valetudine*, published in 1474.

PLINY (A.D. C. 23–79): Roman naturalist whose surviving *Natural History* in thirty-seven books is a prodigious collection of information on the natural world, mostly secondhand.

PYTHAGORAS (C. 582 B.C.–C. 507 B.C.): Greek philosopher who believed that the essence of all things was number, and that all relationships could be expressed numerically.

AL-QAZWĪNĪ (C. 1203–1283): Arab historian and geographer who wrote an important botanical encyclopedia.

JOHANNES (OR JEAN) DE LA QUINTIYNE (OR QUINTYNE, QUINTINIE) (1626–1688): French author of a book on gardening, and gardener to King Louis XIV of France.

LEONHARDUS RAUWOLFFUD (SIXTEENTH CENTURY): Botanist and traveler who noted plants grown in Middle Eastern gardens.

JOANNES REULLIS (SIXTEENTH CENTURY): Botanist who wrote *De natura stirpium libri tres*, published in Paris in 1536.

ST. HILDEGARD OF BINGEN (1098–1179): First great female theologian and a keen observer of the natural world.

REDCLIFFE SALAMAN (TWENTIETH CENTURY): Trained as a medical doctor, Salaman is the author of the classic *History and Social Influence of the Potato*.

AL-SAMARQANDĪ (D. 1222): Muslim physician and author of the pharmacological work calld the *Aqrābādhin* or "Medical Formulary."

R. W. SCHERY: Contemporary author of *Plants for Man*, published in 1954.

N. W. SIMMONDS: Contemporary botanist at the Edinburgh School of Agriculture and author of important works on the evolution of crop plants.

P. M. SMITH: Contemporary botanist at the University of Edinburgh in Scotland.

EDWARD LEWIS STURTEVANT (1842–1898): American botanist, doctor, and agriculturalist whose *Edible Plants of the World*, although outdated, remains a standard.

TAILLEVENT (C. 1312–1395): Chef to King Philip VI, and, by 1381, to King Charles VI. His real name was Guillaume

Tirel. He was the first of the famous French chefs and author of *Le viandier.*

ANTONIO TARGIONI-TOZZETTI (NINETEENTH CENTURY): Italian botanist and author of *Cenni storici sulla introduzione de varie piante nell'agricoltura ed orticoltura toscana.*

THEOPHRASTUS (C. 372 B.C.–C. 287 B.C.): Greek philosopher and naturalist who wrote the important *Enquiry into Plants.*

K. F. THOMPSON: Contemporary botanist at the Plant Breeding Institute, Cambridge, England, and author of studies on crucifera vegetables.

L. TRABUT: Twentieth-century French botanist and author of numerous studies on the plants of North Africa.

HIERONYMOUS TRAGUS (SIXTEENTH CENTURY): Artist who, along with botanist Leonhard Fuchs (1501–1566), first illustrated the common bean from the New World in 1542.

NICOLAY I. VAVILOV (1887–1943): Russian botanist and geneticist and a giant of twentieth-century science. His *Origin and Geography of Cultivated Plants* is a classic. He died of starvation in Stalin's prison.

VIRGIL (70 B.C.–19 B.C.): Roman poet, author of the *Aeneid,* an epic masterpiece; he idealized the rural life.

ANDREW WATSON: Contemporary professor emeritus of economic history at the University of Toronto and author of *Agricultural Innovation in the Early Islamic World.*

WILLIAM WOYS WEAVER: Contemporary American author of food and gardening works, including *Heirloom Vegetable Gardening.*

XENOPHON (C. 430 B.C.–C. 355 B.C.): Greek historian and soldier who wrote *Anabasis,* the story of his retreat from a disastrous military adventure.

GLOSSARY

ascocarp: the mature fruiting body of an ascomycete fungus.

ascomycetes: any of a class of higher fungi with septate hyphae.

basidiomycetes: a higher fungi having septate hyphae, bearing spores on a basidium.

basidium: a structure on the fruiting body of a higher fungi.

bract: a leaf born on a floral axis; it subtends the flower head of a composite plant.

calyx: the outer whorl of a flower consisting of sepals.

capitulum: a simple inflorescence with the axis shortened and dilated to form a rounded or flattened cluster of sessile flowers.

chromatography: a process in which a chemical mixture carried by a liquid or gas is separated into components as a result of differential distribution of the solutes as they flow around or over a stationary liquid or solid phase.

corm: a rounded, thick modified underground stem base bearing membranous or scaly leaves and buds and acting as a vegetative reproductive structure.

cotyledon: the first leaf or whorl of leaves developed by the embryo of a seed plant.

cyme: an inflorescence that ends in a single flower.

diachasia: a cymose inflorescence that produces two main axes.

diploid: having the basic chromosome number doubled.

electrophoresis: the movement of suspended particles through a fluid or gel under the action of an electromotive force applied to electrodes in contact with the suspension.

Elysian fields: in ancient Greece, the happy place in the otherworld where heroes favored by the gods go.

exocarp: the outermost layer of the pericarp of a fruit.

flavanoid: any of a group of aromatic compounds that includes many common pigments.

hyphae: one of the threads that make up the mycelium of a fungus.

hypocotyl: the part of the axis of a plant embryo or seedling below the cotyledon.

inflorescence: the unfolding bud of blossoms.

isozyme: any of two or more chemically distinct but functionally similar enzymes.

Mishna: the canonical collection of Jewish law that constitutes part of the Talmud (see entry).

monoecious: having pistillate and staminate flowers on the same plant.

mycelium: the mass of interwoven filamentous hyphae that forms the vegetative portion of the thallus of a fungi.

Old Kingdom: an Egyptian dynastic period lasting from about 2686 B.C. to 2181 B.C., comprising the third, fourth, fifth, and sixth dynasties. It was during this period that the great pyramids of Egypt were built.

panicle: a compound inflorescence.

pericarp: the ripened and variously modified walls of a plant ovary.

petiole: a slender stem that supports the blade of a foliage leaf.

rhizome: a somewhat elongated and usually horizontal subterranean plant stem that is often thickened by deposits of reserve food material, produces shoots above and roots below, and is distinguished from a true root by having buds, nodes, and usually scalelike leaves.

septate: having a septum, a dividing wall or membrane.

sessile: attached directly at the base, that is, not raised on a stalk or peduncle.

spathe: a sheathing bract partly enclosing an inflorescence.

stobili: a spike with persistent overlapping bracts that resemble a cone; it is the pistillate inflorescence.

stolon: a horizontal branch from the base of a plant that produces new plants from buds at its tips or nodes.

Talmud: the codified collection of the Jewish oral tradition over many centuries, which contains the Mishna (see entry) and the commentary upon it.

A SHORT BIBLIOGRAPHY

The works consulted in writing this book are identical to the full bibliography listed in my *A Mediterranean Feast: The Story of the Birth of the Celebrated Cuisines of the Mediterranean from the Merchants of Venice to the Barbary Corsairs* (New York: William Morrow, 1999). This short bibliography is weighted toward botanical works that I found particularly important in the writing of the present book. Not listed here are the enormous resources I used that are available through AGRICOLA, the National Agriculture Library's bibliographic database, online or on CD-ROM.

André, Jacques. *Lexique des termes de botanique en Latin.* Paris: C. Klincksieck, 1956.

———. *L'Alimentation et la cuisine à Rome.* Paris: Les Belles Lettres, 1981.

Athenaeus. *The Deipnosophists.* Translated by Charles Burton Gulick. Loeb Classical Library. Cambridge, Mass.: Harvard University Press, 1969–1993, 7 vols.

Barbari, Hermolai. *In Dioscoridem corollariorum libri quinque.* Cologne: Ioan. Soterem, 1530.

Bianchini, F., and F. Corbetta. *The Complete Book of Fruits and Vegetables.* Translated by Italia and Alberto Mancinelli. New York: Crown, 1976.

Bois, D. *Les plantes alimentaires chez tous les peuples et à travers les âges.* 4 vols. Paris: Paul Lechevalier, 1927–1937.

Bresc, Henri. "Les jardins de Palerme (1290–1460)." *Mélanges de l'École Française de Rome: Moyen Âge-Temps Modernes* 84, no. 1 (1972): 55–127.

Brookes, John. *Gardens of Paradise: The History and Design of the Great Islamic Gardens.* London: Weidenfeld and Nicolson, 1987.

Brothwell, Don and Patricia. *Food in Antiquity: A Survey of the Diet of Early Peoples.* Expanded ed. Baltimore: Johns Hopkins University Press, 1998.

Brouk, B. *Plants Consumed by Man.* London: Academic Press, 1975.

De Candolle, Alphonse. *Origin of Cultivated Plants.* New York: Hafner, 1959.

Castelvetro, Giacomo. *The Fruits, Herbs and Vegetables of Italy.* Translated by Gillian Riley. London: Viking Penguin, 1989.

Cato. *On Argiculture.* Translated by William Davis Hooper. Loeb Classical Library. Cambridge, Mass.: Harvard University Press, 1993.

Chevalier, Aug. "Les production végétales du Sahara." *Revue de botanique appliquée et d'agriculture tropicale* 12, nos. 133–34 (September–October 1932): 742–43.

———. "Les origines et l'évolution de l'agriculture Méditerranéenne." *Revue de botanique appliquée et d'agriculture tropicale* 19, nos. 217–218 (September–October 1939): 613–62.

Crescentiis, Petrus de [1233?–1321]. *Liber ruralium commodorum.* Venice: Matteo Codeca', 1495.

Dalby, Andrew. *Siren Feasts: A History of Food and Gastronomy in Greece.* London and New York: Routledge, 1996.

De Biberstein, Kazimirski, A. *Dictionnaire Arabe-Français.* 2 vols. Paris: G.-P. Maisonneuve, 1860.

De Herrera, Gabriel Alonso. *Obra de agricultura.* 1539. Reprint, Madrid: Atlas, 1970.

Dozy, R. *Supplément aux dictionnaires arabes.* 2 vols. Leyden: Brill, 1881; Beirut: Librarie du Liban, 1991.

Estienne, Charles. *De re hortensi libellus, vulgaria herbarum, florum, ac fruticum, qui in hortis conseri solent nomina Latinis vocibus efferre docens ex probatis autoribus.* Paris: Roberti Stephani, 1536.

Facciola, Stephen. *Cornucopia II: A Source Book of Edible Plants.* Vista, Calif.: Kampong, 1998.

Gast, Marceau. *Alimentation des populations de L'Ahaggar: Étude ethnographique.* Mémoires du Centre de Recherches Anthropologiques Préhistoriques et Ethnographiques, Conseil de la Recherche Scientifique en Algérie. VIII. Paris: Art et Métiers, 1968.

Gibault, Georges. *Le cardon et l'artichaut.* Paris: Gibault, 1907.

———. *Histoire des légumes.* Paris: Librarie Horticole, 1912.

Harlan, J. R. "Plant Domestication: Diffuse Origins and Diffusions." In *The Origin and Domestication of Cultivated Plants,* edited by C. Barigozzi. Developments in Agricultural and Managed-Forest Ecology, vol. 16. Amsterdam: Elsevier, 1986, pp. 21–34.

———. *Crops and Man.* 2d ed. Madison, Wisc.: American Society of Agronomy and Crop Science Society of America, 1992.

Hawkes, J. G. *The Diversity of Crop Plants.* Cambridge, Mass.: Harvard University Press, 1983.

Hehn, Victor. *Cultivated Plants and Domesticated Animals in Their Migration from Asia to Europe.* Amsterdam: John Benjamins, 1976.

Heiser, Charles B., Jr. *Seed to Civilization: The Story of Food.* New ed. Cambridge, Mass.: Harvard University Press, 1990.

Helbaek, Hans. "Palaeo-ethnobotony." In *Science in Archeology: A Survey of Progress and Research,* rev. ed., edited by Don Brothwell and Eric Higgs, New York: Praeger, 1969, pp. 206-14.

Herodotus. *Herodotus.* 4 vols. Rev. ed. Translated by A. D. Godley. Loeb Classical Library. Cambridge, Mass.: Harvard University Press, 1922–1981.

Hessayon, D. G. *The New Vegetable and Herb Expert.* London: Expert Books, 1997.

Horace. *Satires, Epistles and Ars Poetica.* H. Rushton Fairclough, trans. Loeb Classical Library. Cambridge: Harvard University Press, 1966.

Ibn al-ᶜAwwām, *Kitāb al-filāḥa. Le livre de l'agriculture.* 2d ed. J.-J. Clément-Mullet, trans. Tunis: Editions Bouslama, 1977. 2 vols.

Ibn-al-Baiṭār. *Traité des simples.* 3 vols. Translated by L. Leclerc. Notices et extrits des manuscrits de la Bibliothèque Nationale, vols. xxii, xxv, xxvi, Paris, 1877–1883.

————. *The Cilician Dioscorides' Plant* Materia Media *as Appeared in Ibn al-Baitar, the Arab Herbalist of the 13th Century.* Mohamed Nazir Sankary, ed. Aleppo: Institute for the History of Arab Science, University of Aleppo Publications, 1991.

Ibn Riḍwān [998–1068]. *On the Prevention of Bodily Ills in Egypt. Medieval Islamic Medicine.* Michael W. Dols, trans. Berkeley: University of California Press, 1984.

Kiple, Kenneth, and Kriemhild Coneè Ornelas, eds. *The Cambridge World History of Food.* 2 vols. Cambridge, England: Cambridge University Press, 2000.

Levey, Martin, and Noury al-Khaledy, trans. and eds. *The Medical Formulary of Al-Samarqandi and the Relation of Early Arabic Simples to Those Found in the Indigenous Medicine of the Near East and India.* Philadelphia: Unviersity of Pennsylvania Press, 1967.

Lewicki, Tadeusz. *West African Food in the Middle Ages.* Cambridge, England: Cambridge University Press, 1974.

Manniche, Lise. *An Ancient Egyptian Herbal.* Austin, Tex.: University of Texas Press with British Museum Publications, 1989.

Margen, Sheldon, and the Editors of the University of California at Berkeley Wellness Letter, eds. *The Wellness Encyclopedia of Food and Nutrition: How to Buy, Store, and Prepare Every Variety of Fresh Food.* New York: Rebus, 1992.

Moldenke, Harold N., and Alma L. Moldenke. *Plants of the Bible.* New York: Dover, 1952.

Phillips, Roger, and Martyn Rix. *Vegetables.* New York: Random House, 1993.

Pliny. *Natural History.* H. Rackham, W. H. S. Jones, D. E. Eichholz, trans. Loeb Classical Library Cambridge, Mass.: Harvard University Press, 1938–1962.

Renfrew, Jane M. *Paleoethnobotany: The Prehistoric Food Plants of the Near East and Europe.* New York: Columbia University Press, 1973.

Salaman, Redcliffe N. *The History and Social Influence of the Potato.* Cambridge, England: Cambridge University Press, 1949.

Sarton, George. *From Homer to Omar Khayyam.* Vol. 1 of *Introduction to the History of Science.* Baltimore: William and Wilkins for the Carnegie Institution of Washington, 1927.

Sauer, Carl O. *Agricultural Origins and Dispersals.* New York: American Geographical Society, 1952.

Sauer, Jonathan D. *Historical Geography of Crop Plants: A Select Roster.* Boca Raton, Fla.: CRC Press, 1993.

Schnell, R. *Plantes alimentaires et vie agricole de l'Afrique noire: essai de phytogéographie alimentaire.* Paris: Larose, 1957.

Schwanitz, Franz. *The Origin of Cultivated Plants.* Cambridge, Mass.: Harvard University Press, 1967.

Serres, Olivier de. *Le Théâtre d'agriculture et mesnage des champs.* 1605. Reprint, Paris: Huzard, 1804–5.

Simmonds, N. W. *Evolution of Crop Plants.* London: Longman, 1979.

Sizer, Frances Sienkiewicz, and Eleanor Noss Whitney. *Nutrition: Concepts and Controversies.* 7th ed. Belmont, Calif.: West/Wadsworth, 1997.

Spencer, Colin. *The Vegetable Book.* New York: Rizzoli, 1996.

Sturtevant, E. Lewis. *Sturtevant's Notes on Edible Plants*, edited by U. P. Hedrick. Albany: State of New York, Department of Agriculture, 1919.

Taylor's Guide to Vegetables & Herbs. Boston: Houghton Mifflin, 1961.

Tutin, T. G. et. al., eds. *Flora Europaea*. 5 vols. Cambridge, England: Cambridge University Press, 1976.

Ucko, Peter J., and G. W. Dimbleby, eds. *The Domestication and Exploitation of Plants and Animals*. Chicago: Aldine, 1969.

Varro. *On Agriculture*. William Davis Hooper, trans. Loeb Classical Library. Cambridge, Mass.: Harvard University Press, 1993.

Vavilov, N. I. *Origin and Geography of Cultivated Plants*. Doris Löve, trans. Cambridge, England: Cambridge University Press, 1992.

Watson, Andrew M. *Agricultural Innovation in the Early Islamic World: The Diffusion of Crops and Farming Techniques, 700–1100*. Cambridge, England: Cambridge Unviersity Press, 1983.

Wehr, Hans. *A Dictionary of Modern Written Arabic*. 3rd ed. Ithaca, N.Y.: Spoken Language Services, 1976.

Zohary, Daniel, and Marcia Hopf. *Domestication of Plants in the Old World: The Origin and Spread of Cultivated Plants in West Asia, Europe, and the Nile Valley*. Oxford, England: Clarendon Press, 1988.

INDEX